Recreation: Programming and Leadership

FOURTH EDITION

H. Dan Corbin
Purdue University

Ellen Williams
Kean College and New York University

Prentice-Hall, Inc. Englewood Cliffs, New Jersey 07632

Library of Congress Cataloging-in-Publication Data

Corbin, H. Dan. (date)
   Recreation: programming and leadership.

    Rev. ed. of: Recreation leadership / H. Dan Corbin.
3rd ed. 1970.
    Includes bibliographies and index.
    1. Recreation leadership. I. Williams, Ellen.
II. Corbin, H. Dan. Recreation leadership. III. Title.
GV14.5.C65 1987   790'.023   86-15142
ISBN 0-13-767963-7

Editorial/production supervision and
  interior design: **Jane Bonnell, Natalie Brenner and Patrick Walsh**
Cover design: **Wanda Lubelska**
Manufacturing buyer: **Harry P. Baisley**

Printed in the United States of America

10 9 8 7 6 5 4 3 2 1

ISBN 0-13-767963-7 01

Prentice-Hall International (UK) Limited, *London*
Prentice-Hall of Australia Pty. Limited, *Sydney*
Prentice-Hall Canada Inc., *Toronto*
Prentice-Hall Hispanoamericana, S.A., *Mexico*
Prentice-Hall of India Private Limited, *New Delhi*
Prentice-Hall of Japan, Inc., *Tokyo*
Prentice-Hall of Southeast Asia Pte. Ltd., *Singapore*
Editora Prentice-Hall do Brasil, Ltda., *Rio de Janeiro*

To the Recreation Profession:

Our kudos for not yielding in its steady progress throughout the years we have been privileged to share its bounty.

One of the occupational hazards in professional preparation is despair. Whatever pitfalls we succumb to, we should remain steadfast keepers of vision, hope, and determination: vision that is based on principles, high standards, and research; hope that springs from having witnessed the "impossible" take place through concerted effort; and enlightened determination that is the catalyst, the priceless ingredient, in our advancement as a profession.

HDC
EW

Contents

Contents

Preface

In this fourth edition, chapters have been updated and expanded and significant consolidations made. In addition, the following chapters have been added: Career Options, Program Planning—Principles and Practices, Leisure Education in Program Planning, and The Present is Prologue: A Challenge to the Leisure Services Profession. Focus has been given to the practical as well as the theoretical so that students and practitioners have a balanced coverage of the field. The "How" and "Why" are emphasized as are principles, practices and techniques essential to the recreation professional. Part One concerns the leadership and programming of recreation programs, an appropriate prelude to Part Two which discusses the program activity areas, the essentials of programming. The chapter The Present Is Prologue is actually the book's epilog, giving the reader the societal context within which to apply the principles and practices gleaned from the text. The appendices include resources helpful to the recreation professional, including a list of media helpful in the leadership of the program activity areas.

Our debt to the pioneers in this field is gratefully acknowledged. Without their groundwork, books of this nature would not have been possible. Incentive for undertaking this work is traceable to the many students the writers were privileged to teach. Acknowledgement is extended to Jane

L. Kelly and Royalen F. Maynez of Purdue University for writing the Dance chapter. We also wish to acknowledge those who have contributed to chapters: The late Edna Bottorf, Professor Emeritus, Lock Haven University (Arts and Crafts), Spencer G. Shaw, Professor of Communications, University of Washington, Seattle (Mental/Linguistic/Literary), Dorothy W. Lynds, Professor of Speech and Dramatics, State University of New York, Geneseo (Drama), Dr. Gerald O'Morrow (Career Options), Stephen Waltz of Cummins Diesel (Career Options), Gordon Jones (Social Recreation) and Carleton A. Robertson (Nature Lore section of Outdoor Recreation). The cooperation of Dr. Jerry G. Dickason, Professor of Recreation and Leisure Studies at Montclair State College is also acknowledged. The encouragement of Susan D. Hanlon of Florida State University is gratefully appreciated. Special acknowledgment is extended to Catherine, David, Larry and Michael Williams as well as Patricia Cohrs and Madelyn Abruzzo for their typing and printing assistance.

H. Dan Corbin

Ellen Williams

I would like to dedicate my efforts on this book
to the memory of my late father, Earl Williams,
who died during my revision of this text.
With his unfailing love and assistance,
my father supported every endeavor I pursued.
My work on this book is a reflection
of the education and exploration he encouraged within me.
For his spirit and support,
which I feel with me still,
all my love and thanks forever.

EW

1

Professional Development
of Recreation Leaders

Recreation professionals are involved in a daily dynamic exchange of services with the public. In performing these services, recreation professionals come into contact with diverse populations and varied individual needs; they stimulate, educate, and motivate the public to achieve full leisure satisfaction. Since social interaction is a basis of the profession, recreation professionals must enjoy working with people. It is highly important, then, that the personnel of this "people profession" possess the characteristics and skills to help participants bring out the best in themselves and their leisure. Leadership ability is basic to being an effective recreation professional. This chapter will outline the importance of leadership in professional training.

Leadership is the skill of facilitating goal achievement in the individual or group with whom one is working. Whether the recreation professional guides an individual staff member in program development or guides a biking group up a mountain, the quality of leadership will greatly affect whether or not those aims are achieved.

LEADERSHIP ROLES

The term *recreation leader* is used widely without full recognition of the diversity and scope represented by the title. Recreation leaders are not solely instructors of activities such as music, athletics, and dance. Activity leadership is only one career option within the leisure services profession.

In terms of scope, the title *recreation leader* can be used to describe both line and staff employees in a recreation agency. A *line employee* is an individual responsible for direct service to and instruction of participants. Included within this category would be the activity leader just described—such as the outreach worker or the recreation specialist skilled in a specific activity (for example, a drama specialist). Line employees can be referred to as the direct providers "on the line"; they provide face-to-face leadership, engaged in "hands on" service.

The *staff employee*, however, does not work directly with participants but instead provides line personnel with the resources they need to carry out their direct service. A staff employee's responsibilities include program development, staff supervision, maintenance, budgeting, program promotion; in summary, the staff employee is the conceptualizer of the agency's goals and purpose. Staff employee positions consist of a managerial/administrative function and include such titles as manager, supervisor, director, planner, developer, policymaker, administrator, general area supervisor, and supervisor of activity leaders.

Martin Ibrahim in *Leisure—An Introduction* defines leadership positions in leisure services according to the following classification:

> At the administrative level the objectives that are sought are concerned with: setting appropriate goals for the organization; writing policies which provide guidelines for the operation of the organization within the parameters determined by the operating authority; obtaining necessary resources; and operationalizing policies.
>
> At the supervisory level the objectives that are sought are concerned with: setting guidelines for reasonable and appropriate behavior for personnel performance; providing feedback to personnel; distributing resources in relation to needs; evaluating the performance of personnel; and determining appropriate tasks for personnel.
>
> At the program level the objectives sought are in the area of: developing activity programs; providing instruction and supervision for activity programs; developing promotional and public information materials related to activity programs; and determining resource needs for the various activity programs offered.
>
> At the technical level the objectives sought are in the area of: preparation of facilities in accordance with stated specifications; the maintenance of resources in accordance with specifications; carrying out the policies of the organization as they relate to personnel; and the operation of facilities and physical resources in accordance with specifications.
>
> At the aide level the objectives sought are in relation to providing assistance to other personnel as directed.[1]

1. Martin Ibrahim, *Leisure—An Introduction* (Los Alamidas, CA: Hwong Publishers, 1982) pp. 134–135.

A recreation leader need not be thought of as solely responsible to a single agency or program; rather, a recreation leader can choose to be a facilitator who provides service in terms of a total community view. In this manner, the recreation leader would engage in such functions as: providing technical assistance to individuals and community groups on recreational activities; forming joint agreements with other agencies for shared facilities, programs, and personnel; and offering publicity to community programs.

The skill requirements for a recreation leader will vary depending on the particular job responsibilities. For instance, the leadership approach necessary for an activity leader of a preschool rhythm class differs widely from that needed by a staff supervisor.

For instance, Maryhelen Vannier advises the following leadership approach for the activity leader or line employee:

1. Briefly explain what is being taught.
2. Demonstrate how the skill is done.
3. Have the group practice by imitating the demonstration given and gaining an understanding of the verbal explanation given of it.
4. Have each evaluate his/her progress.[2]

The staff supervisor or staff employee, on the other hand, is not responsible for leading an individual or group in a recreation activity, but is responsible for leading the line employees in the performance of their functions. In that capacity, then, the staff employee must be skilled in such areas as interpersonal communication, personnel management, fiscal administration, and the maintenance and supervision of facilities.

ACADEMIC PREPARATION FOR RECREATION LEADERSHIP

To prepare future recreation leaders for line or staff employee leadership positions, academic courses have been outlined to equip individuals with the competencies necessary for each role. For instance, the future activity leader or line employee is advised to select courses in sociology, psychology, and education because the knowledge of learning and motivational theories, human behavior, and educational psychology are essential in responding to the needs and abilities of recreation participants. In addition, classes in the humanities and recreation skills areas are necessary so that the recreation leader can respond to participants' needs and abilities with the knowledge of a broad spectrum of recreational options. The future supervisor or staff employee would take the same behavioral sciences as those we have listed in order to relate more effectively with staff; however, the need for course work in activity areas is not imperative since supervisors

2. Maryhelen Vannier, *Methods and Materials in Recreation Leadership* (Philadelphia: Lea and Febiger, 1972), p. 57.

and staff employees are not involved in direct activity leadership. In lieu of these activity classes, the student would enroll in course work in business administration to develop the necessary managerial skills.

Professional laboratory experiences should begin as early as possible in the student's education. Usually field experiences are initiated in the freshman year with field work introduced on the sophomore/junior levels and internship at the junior/senior levels. Field experiences refer to any contacts with the field for the purpose of observation, leadership, or programming. A field experience need not require any actual direct service but can consist solely of visitation and observation. Wherever possible, field experiences should be required in core and elective courses. For instance, in a correctional recreation class, each student may be assigned as a companion to a probationer for the purpose of recreation guidance and companionship. While a field experience may consist of only a field trip to an agency, field work and internship require that the student perform some function in the agency. While both field work and internships are referred to as *practicums*, they are distinct in that field work is usually taken in conjunction with other academic requirements while the internship can be the sole academic requirement for the semester, for it approximates a 40-hour workweek.

While it is important to distinguish between the requirements of administrative or activity leadership, the aim of this chapter is to present the universal theory and skills that one must bring to any recreation leadership situation. The text will include programmatic examples of how leadership principles may be reflected differently in the unique functions of the administrative or activity leader; however, the student is ultimately expected to make these correlations independently.

This chapter discusses the many characteristics and functions that comprise the recreation leader's role. Prior to further discussion, it must be stressed that an essential requirement of recreation leaders is that they develop a conscious philosophy of recreation and understand how its application in their daily leadership duties may have positive or less positive effects. For instance, if an individual recreation leader comes from a philosophical orientation that stresses competition against self and others as a central value of recreation, this will be reflected in the leadership style in numerous ways. For example, an activity leader or line employee with a competitive philosophy might project the message that the recreational activity, be it soccer or short story writing, derives its recreative value not from one's sheer involvement, but one's level of excellence. An administrative leader or staff employee with such a philosophy might establish a competitive work environment that may divide rather than unify staff. As another example, a recreation leader's philosophy that recreation is any activity that "re-creates" the individual will be reflected in that leader's willingness to consider limitless programmatic possibilities. In summary then, basic to any study of leadership, there must be the individual's willingness to examine her or his own attitudes and beliefs regarding recreation, to understand how these conceptions are reflected in a personal leadership style, and to be open to making modifications in this philosophy and leadership style where their impact on staff and participants is found to be unproductive.

TOWARD PROFESSIONALIZATION—A HISTORICAL PERSPECTIVE

Development of the professional preparation of recreation leaders pursued a path similar to the growth of the recreation movement itself. The usual informal approach, used by perhaps most professions in the early stages of their development, was followed by training institutes and eventually college and university specialization.

Professionalization was spurred on by such developments as the People's Institute of New York in 1916 and the Playground and Recreation Association's training institutes. These training institutes were first offered in 1918 when the Playground and Recreation Association was commissioned by the U.S. Department of War to conduct recreation leadership training in localities adjacent to military quarters. The Playground and Recreation Association also operated community recreation schools where basic leadership essentials were taught in 6-week training institutes. It was in the 1920s that the first graduate institute was sponsored by the Playground and Recreation Association.

State institutions of higher learning have also contributed to the professionalization of recreation leadership training. This work has been conducted largely through their extension divisions by field recreation consultants. For example, the Agricultural Extension Service (which is administered by state agricultural colleges and universities), and the 4-H program have offered training. In the 1930s, American colleges began developing recreation curricula. In 1962, curriculum guidelines were established by AAHPER (American Alliance for Health, Physical Education, and Recreation). In 1963, interest in accreditation developed and by 1977 some colleges had submitted credentials for accreditation review. The late 1960s and early 1970s saw a rising interest in 2-year A.A. (associate of arts) recreation degrees at community colleges.
These A.A. degrees attracted individuals interested in direct leadership positions, often in their own immediate neighborhoods; as a result, grassroots leadership and minority representation were encouraged.

The expanded content within college recreation curricula reflects growing recognition of the scope of leisure services. Previously, a career in recreation was viewed with limited perception of its possibilities; people felt that someone became a recreation leader for any number of stereotypical reasons ("Recreation's a good career for him. He likes athletics." "Good career choice. She always loved the outdoors.") People's limited view of the recreation profession is reflective of their limited view of what recreation itself offers. Someone who thinks of recreation solely as physical activity is going to think that a recreation leader must be athletically inclined. Because people are unfamiliar with the terminology, they are often ignorant of the fact that certain services are being offered under the auspices of recreation departments, rather than education or occupational therapy divisions, for example. As illustration:

> In many hospitals, recreation professionals are known as activity therapists, in school systems, recreation programs may be described as community education, in the armed forces they are part of Special Services and in industry recreation is connected to personnel management.[3]

However, more and more the public is realizing the breadth of services available under the auspices of recreation agencies, whether they are commercial, industrial, municipal, therapeutic, private, or voluntary. College recreation curricula have helped promote professionalism and creative leadership in the field. Curricula now include specializations in therapeutic recreation, park management, college union management, industrial recreation, commercial recreation, recreation administration, outdoor recreation and education, and youth-serving organization management.

Recreation agencies themselves provide frequent in-service training programs for staff to keep them abreast of professional developments which, in turn, maximize job performance. Professional organizations such as the National Therapeutic Recreation Society provide conferences and literature to encourage professional development.

In recent years, the NRPA (National Recreation and Park Association) has joined with universities in sponsoring professional development institutes in a variety of topics of interest to practitioners (for example, arts management, therapeutic recreation programming, revenue sources management). The NRPA has also been in the vanguard in the promotion of the *accreditation, registration,* and *certification* processes that are so critical to the assurance of quality leadership in the profession. NRPA accreditation is given to college recreation curricula that meet standard competency requirements. Registration and certification apply to standards of professional qualifications for personnel. Registration is the process of reviewing the job background of a professional to see job standards are met. Certification involves licensing, which is designated by state legislation. Qualifications are determined on the basis of education, tests, experience, and recommendations. The recreation profession as well as the general public benefit from the quality assurance inherent in these processes.

EFFECTIVE LEADERSHIP

Qualities of the Effective Leader

The qualities that have been attributed to an effective leader include the following:

3. Richard Kraus, *Recreation and Leisure in Modern Society* (Glenview, IL: Scott, Foresman and Company, 1978), p. 283.

Dependable	Sociable
Fair/ethical/just	Emotionally mature
Sensitive	Tolerant
Skillful	Sense of humor
Broadminded	Hard-working
Creative/innovative/experimental/	Wide range of interests/well-rounded
ingenious	Calm/composed/poised
Respects individuality	Perceptive
Flexible	Candid/frank
Possesses sound philosophy of leisure	Thoughtful
on which to base leadership style	Courageous
Enthusiastic	Patient
Intelligent	Courteous
Good judgment	Takes initiative
Self-confident	Takes risks
Consistent	Persistent/determined

In *Managerial Effectiveness,* William J. Reddin defines the effective leader as one who possesses

> sensitivity to the situation, which involves the manager's ability to accurately perceive a given situation
>
>   leadership flexibility which involves the leader's ability to change his style based on a given situation
>
>   and situational management skill which is his ability to overcome resistance to change.[4]

Functions and Responsibilities of the Effective Leader

While leadership roles are varied, the following can be summarized as general functions and responsibilities of an effective leader:

> Presents positive image of agency goals and activities
> Develops indigenous leadership
> Sets goals
> Communicates well with staff and participants
> Inspires/motivates
> Capitalizes on individual skills and interests in the group
> Educates
> Adjusts to group members' individual capacities
> Coordinates
> Guides
> Unifies
> Anticipates needs and problems
> Sees and develops linkages between programs and agencies
> Establishes guidelines and structures
> Involves staff and participants in decision making
> Establishes climate for productivity

---

4. William J. Reddin, *Managerial Effectiveness* (New York: McGraw Hill, 1970), p. 135.

Imparts sense of security
Acknowledges staff and participant achievement
Provides resources and information
Makes decisions on policies, procedures, and approaches
Summarizes and restates individual and group goals
Guides the evaluation process.

Evaluation as a Safeguard of Leader Effectiveness

As Chapter 3 on program planning explains, an evaluation process is necessary to insure the quality of a program. The evaluation of the program leader's ability and performance is a critical part of that review process. Evaluation can include any number of approaches such as the following:

1. *Achievement and ability tests.* These ascertain a person's ability to lead an activity (e.g., a tennis ability test for a prospective tennis coach). The results help the individual see areas that require improvement.
2. *Personality tests.* Since certain personality traits are more appropriate to certain leadership situations, using personality tests to reveal these traits may assist in determining an individual's suitable leadership placement.
3. *Attitude or value inventories.* Since an individual's attitudes and values are projected to the people being led, determination of an applicant's views is significant for the employer. For instance, someone with negative views on religion may not function appropriately within a recreation agency with strong denominational sponsorship.
4. *Stress tests.* Job candidates may be intentionally exposed to stress situations to see how they respond to pressure. Candidates' reactions may reveal positive or questionable behavior under stressful leadership responsibility.
5. *Sociometric instrument.* This records the levels of social acceptance within a group and indicates if the candidate is accepted as a leader.

Evaluation can and should be done on many levels. It should be done by individuals themselves, perhaps in the form of self-rating scales or journals of program objectives and results. Oftentimes a leader's effectiveness is measured according to how well the participants demonstrate acquisition of the skill or information being taught. For instance, a basketball coach might be evaluated in terms of an individual team member's performance level before and after the playing season. Superiors and fellow staff members can make observations of the individual's effectiveness as a leader in diverse leadership situations. Professional outside evaluators can be called in to assess the entire program, including the professional's leadership abilities.

The evaluation process is discussed more thoroughly in Chapter 3, which also includes sample evaluation forms. Figure 1–1 is a sample of a leadership self-evaluation form.

FIGURE 1–1 Self-Evaluation Report

Name_____ Job title_____
Summary of job description

Instructions: In each of the following sections indicate what you consider to be your strengths and weaknesses in relation to the questions in each section. Then give yourself a rating on the eight-step scale with eight as the highest rating. Your supervisor will use the same form and rate you in the same way. Your final rating will be the outcome of a conference between you and your supervisor.

Section 1—*Professional approach to my job*

   1. How have I improved my professional capacity?
   2. What have I contributed to the profession?
   3. To what extent have I interpreted the meaning of leisure to the groups that I lead and to the public in general?

Rating

1	2	3	4	5	6	7	8

Section 2—*Personal*

   1. What are my personal leadership strengths and weaknesses?
   2. What personal fulfillment am I receiving from being a leader in leisure services? Is it the right job for me?
   3. Do I fully uphold the policies of the department?
   4. Do I present a good image for the department through my behavior, dress, efforts?
   5. Do I bring sufficient energy to the job for maximum performance, or do I permit off-the-job activities to dissipate my energies?
   6. Am I professionally mature enough to be able to ask for help with problems without creating extensive personal anxiety for myself?

Rating

1	2	3	4	5	6	7	8

Section 3—*Program*

   1. In developing programs do I plan with groups rather than for them?
   2. Do I determine the needs and interests of the people with whom I work?
   3. Do I plan my day-to-day program to ensure maximum involvements by participants?
   4. Do I ensure that all facilities, equipment, and supplies are available and in working order for use by participants?
   5. Do I prepare for each program? How effective is the preparation, and what changes should be made to make it potentially more effective?
   6. Do I assess my capability for leadership of a specified group and try to increase that capacity?

Rating

1	2	3	4	5	6	7	8

Section 4—*Relations with people*

   1. To what extent am I able to accept all people for what they are, as human beings with worth and dignity?

Professional Development of Recreation Leaders   **9**

2. Do I honestly like people, or would I prefer to work with things?
3. How much do I understand about the interaction of people in groups, and what understandings do I find most important in leading groups?
4. What do I do in my groups to help people to function together as a harmonious group? Is what I do effective? Why?
5. How do I ensure that each person in the group has maximum opportunity for participation?

Rating

1	2	3	4	5	6	7	8

Section 5—*Administration*

1. Do I know what the policies of the department are?
2. What department policies do I always follow and which ones do I tend to overlook?
3. Am I always prompt in filing reports and records?
4. What democratic practices do I follow in my groups, and when am I authoritative? Do I regularly interpret correctly when to be democratic and when to be authoritative?
5. What practices do I follow to ensure the safety of the participants?
6. What public relations practices do I use to inform the public about the program?
7. Do leaders and others under my supervision know their duties and responsibilities and have the delegated authority to carry them out?
8. How do I supervise my subordinates?
9. Do all persons under my supervision have regular means of communication with me and other staff members?
10. How do I accept people for programs?
11. How do I evaluate the extent to which the participants are achieving their goals?
12. Is recognition given to people who make outstanding contributions to a program? How is this done?
13. How do I develop awareness in participants that all facilities are to be maintained so that everyone can use them to full capacity?
14. When vandalism occurs, what steps do I take to correct it at present and prevent it in the future?
15. How do I relate my programs in the department and in the community?

Rating

1	2	3	4	5	6	7	8

Rating Total_____ Rating score_____ (total divided by 5)

Signed_____

Summary of Evaluation Conference

Final Rating_____

Unsatisfactory score	2
Poor	4
Average	5.5–6.5
Good	6.5–7.9
Excellent	8

Source: Edith L. Ball and Robert E. Cipriano, *Leisure Services Preparation: A Competency Based Approach* (Englewood Cliffs, NJ: Prentice-Hall, 1978), pp. 198–200. Reprinted by permission.

THEORIES OF LEADERSHIP

The subject of leadership has received much attention in an effort to determine if there are any characteristics universal to effective leaders. Results have generally revealed that the intangibles of human interaction do not lend themselves to scientific study and that leadership is very much a dynamic, nonconcrete process that is unique to a given time, place, needs, and personalities. The following is an overview of the observations and theories proposed in the course of leadership research.

In their research, Kurt Lewin, Ronald Lippitt, and Ralph K. White identified three leadership styles and studied their effects on participants.[5] In the autocratic style, the leader assumes an authoritarian stance, delegating no responsibility and permitting no input in decision making. The democratic style, on the other hand, invites staff and participant involvement in goal setting. Unlike the authoritarian leader who tends to squelch initiative, the democratic leader is inclined to bring out the best in others. In the laissez-faire style, the individual exercises no active leadership, but plays a permissive, passive role, serving solely as a resource if approached. Interpreters of this research generally regard the democratic leadership style as a preferable leadership style. Others have taken the view that each of these styles can be appropriate depending on the leadership requirements of the situation. For instance, the same leader may exercise a laissez-faire attitude with a self-directed group at a drop-in center, but exercise democratic leadership with a newly emerging youth social group.

Another approach, trait theory, attempts to classify those qualities inherent to leadership, viewing these as hereditary characteristics that comprise the "born leader." Trait theory seeks to determine the charismatic elements that cause people to be drawn to follow a particular individual.

The situational theory of leadership stresses that leadership is not dependent on the individual's personality but on the components of the situation at hand. A leader's emergence in a group will be dependent on (1) what the group seeks to accomplish, (2) what the existing organizational structure is, and, (3) how the individual's characteristics and skills complement these group goals and organizational structure. For instance, if a performance troupe's immediate concern is fundraising for their touring show and the organizational structure of their sponsoring agency encourages individual initiative, the individual with public relations/profit-making ideas will likely become the leader. That same individual, however, will not necessarily remain a leader when the needs of the troupe turn more to theater production skills. The term *emergent leadership* has been used to define this turnover in leaders, as each emerges in response to a particular situation for which her or his skills are suitable.

Fiedler's contingency model of leadership effectiveness is also similar to the situational theory in that it defines leadership as being "contingent" on the situation itself.[6] These contingencies include:

5. Kurt Lewin, Ronald Lippitt, and Ralph K. White, "Patterns of Aggressive Behavior in Experimentally Created Social Climates." *Journal of Social Psychology*, Vol. 10 (1939) p. 271.
6. Fred E. Fiedler, *A Theory of Leadership Effectiveness* (New York: McGraw-Hill Book Company, 1967) p. 14.

1. The leader-member relationship
2. The type of goal to be achieved (degree of task structure)
3. Power position (leader's place in the organization).

Fiedler divides leadership into task-oriented and relationship-oriented styles; task-oriented are those styles primarily concerned with the quality of the work produced, whereas relationship-oriented styles emphasize the quality of the group interaction process leading up to the task achievement. For example, in leading a hiking expedition, the recreation leader who stresses the acquisition of information and the completion of given assignments would be considered a task-oriented leader. A recreation leader who would be primarily concerned with the establishment of group rapport among the hikers and the effects of the hiking experience on their social/emotional maturity would be viewed as a relationship-oriented leader. Thus, the success of recreation leaders will be dependent on whether their task-oriented or relationship-oriented style is appropriate to the type of leader-member relationship, task structure, and power position existing in their specific situation. Critics of this view would take issue with the dichotomy between the task-oriented and relationship-oriented styles on the basis that an effective leader should have a blend of both approaches.

According to the situational theory of leadership and Fiedler's contingency model of leadership, the group's collective aims and its members' individual aims must complement those of the leader. The followers need to feel that the leader embodies their goals and aspirations. This mutual understanding is necessary to successful leadership; the alternative is a cognitive dissonance that occurs when a group's interpretation of group goals conflicts with that of the leader's. For instance, if participants in an arts and crafts program are interested in the class solely for self-enrichment while the leader is operating from the belief that the participants are working towards display and sale of their work, there will be cognitive dissonance which detracts from the group's effectiveness.

In any leadership situation, the fact that the group endorses—and ideally selects—their leader is of critical importance to the achievement of group goals. Appointed leadership in which leaders are assigned by outside authorities to lead a particular group often result in program failure because the group and leader have not mutually decided to make an investment in each other. An example of elected leadership would be a group of recreation agency volunteers selecting their own volunteer coordinator.

The group function theory of leadership as defined by Jay Shivers states that "leadership is not vested in individuals but is derived from group structure. Any member of the group may undertake leadership functions as group needs and goals change."[7]

7. Jay Shivers, *Essentials of Recreation Service* (Philadelphia: Lea and Febiger, 1978), p. 252.

To illustrate, within every group, be it recreation staff or activity group, there are different functions that must be carried out in order to move the group towards accomplishment of its goals. At various stages within the group's development, certain functions will assume more importance, and therefore require the individual with that needed skill to emerge and in effect become the leader. According to this group function theory of leadership, these leadership roles blend and overlap as the group's work evolves. For instance, as the recreation staff designs a promotional event, the conceptualizer emerges as the leader. Consequently, the staff member with the technical expertise to carry out the concepts assumes leadership as does the staff member skilled in publicity/public relations. Other staff members share in this group function theory of leadership as their particular skills are called into play. The group function theory of leadership applies not only to staff, but to recreation participants as well. For instance, among the participants in a pageant will come leaders in the areas of costume making, song selection, volunteer recruitment, and so forth, as various individuals apply their skills to the tasks at hand. But it is not only individual skills that determine emergence as a leader; it is also the interplay of an individual's personal qualities within the group. For instance, in the pageant preparation, the individual with a strong sense of discipline and perseverance becomes the leader when the group's commitment wavers. In turn, the peacemaking individual assumes leadership when artistic and/or personality differences threaten the effectiveness of the group.

The group function theory of leadership gives focus to the process of group dynamics, which is defined as the "functions of any group and the behavioral reactions of the membership in response to group functioning."[8]

GROUP DYNAMICS AND THE RECREATION LEADER

Recreation leaders, whether they are line or staff employees, should view understanding the principles of group dynamics as being essential to their leadership effectiveness. Recreation leaders have a responsibility to assure the well-being of the group(s) they are leading as well as to enhance the group's ability to achieve its goals. Through an understanding of group dynamics, recreation leaders are sensitized to those conditions that have an impact on various well-being and productivity factors. These conditions include the following:

•What is the nature of the relationship among the group?
  (For example, a fundraising group may be less likely to set high achievement standards for itself if the group is composed of lifetime friends who have settled into an informal pattern of relating to each other.)

8. Ibid., p. 252.

•Who makes major decisions? plans? empowers the group? decides? solves problems?

> (It is hoped that these responsibilities are shared and not absorbed by more aggressive individuals in the group. If the recreation staff feels that most of the issues under review are already predetermined and predecided by select staff members, there will be less motivation to perform to capacity.)

•How did the group form?

> (For example, a folklore group that formed spontaneously out of mutual interest in the subject will have a different dynamic than one that is formed through mail registration.)

•How do different types of leadership affect the group process?

> (For example, a fragmented basketball team may respond positively to an authoritarian type of leadership because team members are, in essence, craving some guidance; a self-determined team, however, may resent the authoritarianism as thwarting their enthusiasm.)

•What is the status and interrelationship of members?

> (For example, it may come to light in a recreation staff meeting that a staff member resents one of the volunteers because she feels the individual is somehow moving towards acquisition of her job. The status of the relationship between these two individuals will affect group morale and productivity.)

•How does the group work together?

> (For example, a camping group that, by the nature of its activity, must be interdependent, will be impeded in its tasks if dominated by highly independent, competitive individuals.)

•How do different types of group structures affect the attitudes and productivity of members?

> (For example, in planning a special event, would the recreation staff prefer a rotating chairpersonship so that all share the leadership responsibility or would more be accomplished by the natural division of labor according to talents?)

•How does the group influence larger social institutions?

> (For example, perhaps the after-school recreation program has had such a positive impact on delinquency reduction that the recreation staff is invited to become part of a larger number of related groups such as probation, Police Athletic League, etc.)

As this last point illustrates, recreation leaders' understanding of group dynamics is essential, not only to their direct contact with staff or participants, but also to other professional associations pertaining to the job.

A knowledge of group dynamics presupposes the recreation leader's familiarity with key terms in the process. These terms are defined in the following paragraphs.

In group dynamics, *potency* is "the degree to which a group has primary meaning for its members insofar as personal needs are satisfied through group association."[9] For example, a performing folk dance group sponsored by a recreation department will have potency for the individual members if their personal needs revolve around performance and social

---

9. Ibid., p. 256.

recognition. However, this folk dance group will not have potency for group members if their aims are not towards preparation for performance. In summary then, it is critical that leaders know the needs of their group members so that leaders can create a climate and structure that has potency for the group.

Another group dynamics term is *reference group*. If a group becomes a reference group for individual, we mean that the "individual identifies with the standards and beliefs of a specific group and uses these as criteria against which s/he defines and identifies him/herself."[10] For instance, there is a natural sense of affiliation within a recreation staff if the members feel they are in consensus with the group's mission; the staff then becomes a reference group for each individual and the basis from which the individual works with motivation and pride.

A group should be examined for its *permeability*, which is defined as the degree to which a group permits ready access to new members. As an example, a choral group that becomes so insular and self-protective as to discourage new members becomes stagnant and inhibits the growth that could come from the influx of new people. Since the essence of leisure is freedom, the recreation leader should assure that the public has free access to all activities and experiences the permeability of the group.

The *stability* of the group is also an important factor as it pertains to the degree to which the group will persist over time with essentially the same dynamic and purpose. For instance, it is well understood that excessive turnover in a recreation staff can weaken the staff's understanding of their collective purpose and can hamper program effectiveness. Therefore, the staff's stability should be of concern to the leader.

The degree of *group cohesiveness* or togetherness will contribute to the level of accomplishment in the group. Each member must feel that he or she shares the same objectives as the others and is responsible for a fairly distributed amount of the group's work. No one group member should feel pressured to assume major responsibility for a project. If the leader's expectations of an individual are unrealistic, then morale is weakened, thus resulting in poor motivation and lack of commitment. For example, if plans for an orientation night for campers' parents fall primarily on an individual staff member, the group cohesiveness of the staff is lacking. But if the program planning process is shared equally among staff in terms of publicity, program content preparation, technical arrangements, and so forth, the orientation night would materialize at an encouraging level of progress and boost the morale of the staff. However, if the individual staff member feels burdened with the primary responsibility, the resultant resentment and frustration will minimize the success of the orientation night. Since it is essential to the success of a program that individuals have a high degree of self-identification with its purpose, the orientation night will fall far short of its intent since the coordinator has had the responsibility imposed from without instead of developing the motivation from within.

10. Ibid., p. 257.

A poorly planned orientation night will also be likely if the coordinator does not have available the necessary resources to carry out the project successfully. For instance, while the coordinator may see the necessity for distributing promotional material to campers' parents, she will be frustrated in this goal if no funds have been allocated for graphic personnel and/or materials.

In studying group dynamics, the recreation leader should note that groups, both staff and participants, develop to satisfy a variety of purposes and motivations. A group may form to work on a mutual task such as the planning of a carnival special event or the creation of a newsletter to publicize the recreation program. A group may also originate to explore a topic such as the feasibility of a new park or methods of expanding recreation services to the homebound. Finally, a group can be developed to meet participants' needs by offering activities of interest to its members such as choral group, soccer team, dance class, and the like.

Motivational Theory

To understand why such groups form and why individuals join them, the recreation leader should be familiar with motivational theory. According to Maslow's hierarchy of needs, people are motivated in their daily behavior by a variety of needs that range in ascending levels of aspiration from the most basic physiological needs (that is, food, shelter, and clothing) and security needs (for example, job security) on up to needs for socialization, esteem, and self-actualization (see Figure 1–2). Socialization, esteem, and self-actualization needs are primary motivators in the individual's choice of job or activity. Therefore, the administrative leader should be concerned with how attractive a recreation staff position is in terms of meeting the employee's desire for challenging, creative, self-fulfilling work. Similarly, the recreation activity leader should examine whether the participants' involvement in a recreation program is actually meeting their self-actualization needs.

In building on Maslow's theory, Frederick Herzberg confirmed the priority of self-fulfilling activity as being the primary motivator of participation. In his study, Herzberg distinguished between hygiene factors and motivators as they affect motivation to participate. Herzberg's motivation-hygiene theory is illustrated in Table 1–1. Hygiene factors, or what might otherwise be called the basic maintenance factors surrounding the group, include such items as work policies, types of supervision, working conditions, interpersonal relationships, salary, status, and job security. These items correspond to the physiological, security, and belonging needs of Maslow's hierarchy. Herzberg's motivators, on the other hand, correspond to Maslow's self-actualization and esteem needs and include such items as work content, achievement, recognition, mutually shared goals, equal consideration of all members, clearly defined job descriptions and group goals, consistent policy of rewards, and adequate level of supervision. Herzberg

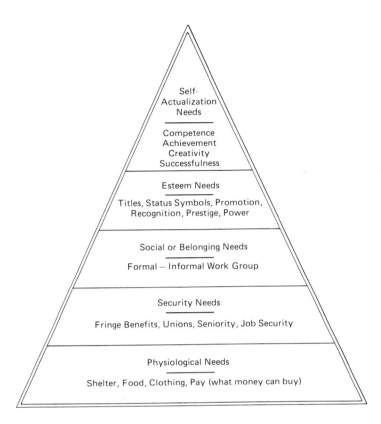

```
                    /\
                   /  \
                  / Self-\
                 /Actualization\
                / Needs  \
               /----------\
              / Competence \
             / Achievement  \
            / Creativity     \
           / Successfulness   \
          /--------------------\
         /    Esteem Needs      \
        / Titles, Status Symbols, Promotion,\
       /   Recognition, Prestige, Power      \
      /----------------------------------------\
     /                                          \
    /        Social or Belonging Needs           \
   /                                              \
  /         Formal — Informal Work Group           \
 /--------------------------------------------------\
```

FIGURE 1–2 Maslow's Hierarchy of Needs.

Source: From Christopher E. Edginton and John G. Williams, *Productive Management of Leisure Services Organizations: A Behavioral Approach* (New York: John Wiley and Sons, 1978), p. 57.

concludes that while hygiene factors are reinforcers to motivate participation, it is principally the motivators or self-actualizing factors that must exist to assure commitment and involvement.

For example, in a newly formed drama program, the participants may not be confident of the hygiene factor of security since the program has no history of progress. However, this lack of security will not inhibit motivation if the program appeals to their higher needs of challenge, self-esteem, and personal development. If the drama program is appropriate to their skill level and encourages growth and self-expression, these are the primary motivators beyond any basic hygiene factors such as long-term security or duration of the program.

Similarly, if a recreation staff member directing the drama program feels that the program provides him the climate in which to pursue the work that has meaning to him, motivation to remain on staff will continue. If his work is encouraged and recognized and an effort is made to communicate its importance to other staff and the public, a high degree of self-

TABLE 1–1 Motivation-Hygiene Theory of Frederick Herzberg

I. Hygiene factors	Motivators
Job dissatisfaction	Job satisfaction
II. Provide for job dissatisfaction when not maintained	Motivate employees

III. 1. Supervision
2. Company policy and administration
3. Working conditions
4. Interpersonal relationships with
   (a) Peers
   (b) Subordinates
   (c) Superiors
5. Status
6. Job security
7. Salary
8. Personal life
	1. Achievement
	2. Recognition for achievement
	3. Work itself
	4. Responsibility
	5. Advancement
	6. Possibility of growth

Source: Christopher E. Edginton and John G. Williams, *Productive Management of Leisure Services Organizations: A Behavioral Approach*, (New York: John Wiley and Sons, 1978), p. 91.

actualization will exist. In light of this, the absence of an auditorium or other good working conditions will not have a major impact on motivation since such hygiene factors as environmental conditions do not determine motivation but merely reinforce the self-actualizing activity that must already exist.

In summary then, recreation leaders have the responsibility to assure that motivators exist within the activity engaged in by the group—whether staff or participants.

Using Group Dynamics Techniques for Staff Development

In helping to provide this self-actualizing environment that motivates staff, recreation leaders should be concerned with the provision of staff development opportunities. These would include such approaches as direct counseling, rotation and transfer of employment, guest speakers, supervised readings, audiovisual presentations, staff meetings, panel discussions with key professionals, and the opportunity to observe the leadership style of fellow workers. Special workshops ranging from single afternoon sessions to several days' duration can be targeted to such topics as new program ideas, professional skill development, personal health and maintenance, organizational training, and so forth. For instance, a knowledge of time management, brainstorming, and problem-solving techniques would enhance the recreation leader's leadership style and would serve as valuable content for in-service training sessions. Each will be discussed in the following sections.

Time Management

The effectiveness of recreation leaders is minimized by scattered and unproductive allocation of time resources. To eliminate this tendency, leaders should monitor their time arrangement. You, as leader, may accomplish this by observing the following points:

1. List things that must be done according to priorities so that the most imperative are accomplished first. Keep track of time deadlines.
2. Learn to say "no" to requests that will take you beyond your scope of duties. If you are unclear about the scope of your job description, you are likely to be distracted from your central purpose. Learning to delegate responsibility goes hand in hand with learning how to say "no".
3. Know the method by which you best absorb and retain information. If you rely primarily on aural recall, then you may prefer to request oral reports from staff. If your visual retention is superior, then written staff reports would be preferable. A combination of both aural and visual information may even be more advantageous.
4. To maximize the use of your time, it is wise to know the times of the day or night when you are generally at peak work performance. For instance, it would be unwise to schedule a critically important meeting of city-wide representatives at the end of the day when your energy and concentration levels—and theirs—are flagging.

Problem Solving

Problem solving refers to those steps that recreation leaders and staff or participants must consider in working towards the achievement of a given group goal. For the purpose of illustration, we will select our goal to be the coordination of a city-wide festival of recreation opportunities for older adults. Since the development of this festival will require the input and cooperation of a wide number of city agencies serving older adults, a sophisticated level of organization is required of the recreation leader.

In problem solving the planning of the festival, you, as recreation leader, will be concerned with the following factors:

1. The clarity or lack of clarity of leadership. In reviewing the level of clarity of your leadership style, you may find that your verbal or written directions to staff are often perceived as being incomplete. Staff are thus frustrated in the sense that they are moving ahead on program planning without knowledge of critical factors affecting the programming. For instance, in asking the health/fitness staff to coordinate an exercise component for the festival, you neglected to mention that this aspect of the program was designed as a demonstration to be videotaped and would therefore be restricted to only ten participants. Such knowledge of group size limitation is essential to the successful planning of a program. Having noted the tendency towards incomplete communication in your leadership style, you would do well to schedule more staff meetings surrounding the planning of the festival in order to give staff the opportunity to ask questions regarding possible incomplete details.

2. Capabilities and interests of the group matched to the nature of the task to be done.   In your meeting with the other city-wide coordinators of the festival, you may have found the others interested in dividing up the labor by assigning single tasks to each agency (such as, the senior citizen center would be responsible for transportation, the municipal recreation department for programming, the retirement village for publicity). However, the senior citizen center leader, knowing the capabilities and interests of her staff, may feel that their talents will be wasted if they are restricted to the scheduling of transport busses. On the basis of that knowledge, this recreation leader is likely to reject this directive method of planning the festival and instead devise a mechanism by which her staff can have more creative input into the design of their contribution to the festival.

3. Deadline factors.   Since the festival planning involves a series of tasks, the deadline for each task must be known so that you and the other organizations' leaders can prioritize usage of staff resources. Since the festival is an additional program beyond your staff's normal day-to-day duties, it is particularly imperative that the festival deadlines are clear so that the staff can integrate them into their existing responsibilities.

4. Physical resources.   In planning the festival, you and your staff will depend on such physical resources as facilities for scheduling events, equipment and supplies for scheduled activities, access to printing materials, material and work space to design decorations. In making available to staff all of the physical resources necessary to complete their tasks, you will facilitate the group's progress.

5. Group size.   The larger the group, the wider the range of personalities and the greater the need for high levels of cooperation. In planning the festival, your staff not only must relate to each other in the planning process, but must also work with a group of a larger size, that being the representatives from other participating agencies. In response to this, you may announce a flexible meeting schedule in which staff members are permitted to arrange their own planning sessions with the agency representatives with whom they plan to work on particular aspects of the festival. Your endorsement of staff members' determination of necessary meetings outside the office is an example of a leader's response to the large number of outside agency people involved in the project.

6. Climate in the general community and in the group itself.   The evolution of the festival will be affected by the general climate of the group as well as the overall community itself. For instance, if there is tension and strain among the staff due to the demands of their normal jobs, they will be less likely to approach the additional responsibility of a festival with enthusiasm. Similarly, if the participating community agencies are currently divided by competitive bids for limited city funds, this dynamic may interfere with the interagency cooperation necessary to the success of the festival.

Brainstorming

As discussed throughout this chapter, it is important for staff and participants to be involved in the decision-making process with the recreation leader. To insure that staff and participants do have input, the recreation leader would do well to conduct brainstorming sessions as issues arise. Brainstorming is defined as group problem solving that encourages the contribution of any and all ideas without recourse to judgement or censorship. As suggestions are tossed out for consideration, they are recorded on poster or blackboard. Following the session, the leader reviews the suggestions and places them in categories according to their benefits and strengths (such as minimal cost to program, high public exposure, time-saving approach, attractive challenge to staff, highly reflective of the philosophy of the agency). This information is then circulated to those who participated in the brainstorming session so that they can fill in any additional ideas that they would like considered at a follow-up session. Various brainstorming sessions can be called until all alternatives have been fully explored to the satisfaction of the group. Ultimately, the group decides which of the categories is the most important at present and uses this as a guideline for the decision that is made. To use the festival of recreation opportunities for older adults as an example, it may have come to the attention of the organizers that the festival has been geared solely to the active older adult who is an independent community resident and neglects the population living in nursing and convalescent homes. In a brainstorming session, suggestions might include such ideas as:

1. Organization of a separate festival for institutionalized older adults later in the year;
2. Arrangement for activity leaders to conduct programs during the festival at both community and institutional sites;
3. Provision of transportation for any institutionalized older adult to attend the festival in the community;
4. Conscious decision not to incorporate the needs of the institutionalized elderly in order to highlight the lifestyles of the well-aged.

In the process of categorization, then, each response would fall under one or more categories. For instance, the fourth response would certainly fall under such categories as minimal cost and time-saving approaches. However, if the staff has agreed that the decision of who to include must be highly reflective of the philosophy of the agency, a philosophy which includes equal provision of activity for disabled and nondisabled individuals, then the fourth response would be unacceptable. If committed to the philosophy of mainstreaming or blending special populations into the mainstream, the agency would be inclined to focus on the second and third responses as tangible ways of carrying out that philosophy programmatically. To help determine the viability of carrying out either or both responses, the staff would initiate another brainstorming session in which the consequences of each response are discussed and further categorized in such terms as impact on staff resources, physical resources, budgetary guidelines, and so forth. If there have been similar program requests in the agency's history, it would be advisable to review past responses to brainstorming sessions.

Role Playing

Role playing can be used as an effective adjunct to brainstorming. In role playing, the staff or participants assume the roles of the individuals involved in the subject at hand, in this case the roles of festival coordinator, nursing home director, recreation staff leader, and so forth. By acting out the various responses they have brainstormed, the group can visibly identify strengths and weaknesses of each approach. Role-reversal or the exchanging of roles permits the players to become more sensitized to the positions and views of conflicting parties. The techniques and values of this process, also referred to as sociodrama, are discussed more thoroughly in the drama chapter.

Obviously, the recreation leader will not employ such techniques as brainstorming in situations over which staff or participants can have no decision-making impact—such as prior budgetary decisions—at this would only be cause for frustration. However, it should be a golden rule of any recreation leader to keep the staff or participants abreast of developments as they affect the recreation program. People do not want to be perceived as mere cogs in a wheel; they want to be respected for their contribution to the overall progress of the recreation program. Many recreation programs fall short of their full potential because the morale of those involved has been reduced by their feeling of being left out of the mainstream of communication.

Balance of Communication

To insure that the necessary communication channels are established and maintained, the recreation leader should insure a balance of downward, upward, and lateral communication. In downward communication, the recreation leader informs the staff or participants of information they need to know to carry out their activities. This communication includes such details as policies and procedures, scheduling information, program ideas, instructional resources, and so forth. In upward communication, recreation leaders seek the input of their staff or participants. Upward communication would take such forms as a consistent open door policy, frequent meetings with staff/participants and observations of their activities, suggestion boxes, staff and participant questionnaires, and grievance committees. In lateral communication, recreation leaders facilitate the communication between peers, whether staff members or program participants. Recreation leaders can promote lateral communication through the establishment of such structures as department head meetings, committee formats, and other cohesive group arrangements.

VOLUNTEER LEADERSHIP

Leadership development is not restricted to the professional staff of a recreation agency but also applies to the volunteer sector. Individuals who select volunteerism as a leisure choice should be assisted in developing their leadership capacities. Volunteers can enhance the leadership capacity of the professional staff who find that the labor of volunteers frees them to devote more time to program leadership.

In recruiting volunteers, the recreation agency should be interested in helping each volunteer engage in an activity that is of interest to that individual. In the initial interview between staff person and prospective volunteer, care should be taken to insure that agency and applicant goals coincide. For instance, while the agency may be desperately seeking a volunteer typist, a retired secretary may not be interested in volunteering to do something he has done all his life. The agency needs to respect this and work to mutually explore other possibilities. At no time should individuals feel that they are being pigeonholed to fit an existing need at the agency; rather the interview should be conducted with the philosophy that new volunteer roles can be created to satisfy individual needs and interests. The volunteer can assume any number of roles including researcher, administrator, advocate, program leader, and so forth. Some volunteers may want to use their work skills, others may want to do something completely different. Since volunteerism is often associated with service agencies, people often mistakenly view volunteerism as being limited to municipal or therapeutic settings. This is far from true; profit-making commercial establishments can also benefit from volunteer service and the volunteer in turn benefits from the learning experience.

Motivations to Volunteer

People choose to volunteer for a variety of reasons and it is only the individual who can determine the volunteer placement conducive to meeting his or her needs. Motivations for volunteering include (1) to make job contacts; (2) use skills; (3) support a cause; (4) feel needed; (5) receive recognition; (6) socialize; (7) learn information.

Recruitment of Volunteers

The recruitment of volunteers should be an organized effort. In all community contacts, the public should be apprised of the agency's philosophy, policies, goals, objectives, and programs. Projected volunteer needs should be publicized, with any necessary qualifications indicated. If the budget allows, it is preferable to hire a volunteer coordinator who would (1) initiate the volunteer program, (2) identify needs and opportunities for volunteers, (3) write job descriptions for volunteers, (4) work with supervisors and boards, (5) develop policies and written materials, (6) conduct interviews and arrange orientation workshops, and (7) schedule periodic meetings with staff and volunteers.

Volunteers should not be recruited unless one has clear ideas as to how they might function and be supervised. A weakness of many program leaders is that they enthusiastically advertise for volunteers without really asking themselves what duties these volunteers can perform.

A year round recruitment plan should be designed that outlines the peak times for approaching individuals and groups. For instance, college recreation departments should be contacted in the early part of each semester when students are selecting their field placement sites. The recruitment coordinator should find out the priorities of local service agencies and when they select their charity project. For instance, if a local Kiwanis Club has chosen visual disabilities as its concern, the recreation agency should be aware of the proper time of the calendar year for approaching them with an appropriate volunteer service project (for example, purchase of braille recreational materials such as cards and table games, or the provision of one-on-one companionship to visually disabled community center members). High school guidance classes should be approached with the idea that volunteerism is a means of career exploration. Many young volunteer camp counselors are attracted to the recreation profession as a result of their volunteer experiences. In some cases, academic credit can be given on the high school level for community volunteer work as it is for college field work/internship.

Industry is becoming more supportive in encouraging its employees to volunteer. As an aspect of industrial recreation, it is felt that volunteerism improves employee morale, which in turn enhances work performance. As an example, Chase Manhattan Bank sponsors Chase Community volunteers, and IBM gives vacation time and full and partial leaves of absence for volunteerism. While these programs obviously benefit the community, they are also very positive public relations efforts that enhance industry's image in the community. Industrial newsletters can, like community newspapers, carry a volunteer opportunities column that lists volunteer openings, volunteer jobs wanted, and profiles on volunteers. Industry's encouragement of volunteerism demonstrates a concern that employees develop potential leisure interests for the postretirement years. Preretirees and retirees constitute a vast potential for volunteerism.

The volunteer coordinator should scan the town paper for articles on interesting hobbyists who might be contacted to serve as volunteer instructors of their hobbies. Participants engaged in recreation activities can be observed for potential teaching ability. A volunteer fair is an ideal way of drawing all resource information on volunteer opportunities together for public access. The fair should include speakers and films on volunteerism as well as on-site volunteer placement interviews. Certain placements in particular can run consecutively throughout the day. It is important that the volunteer recruiter not fall into the pattern of recruiting the stereotyped volunteer pool (housewives, students, and retirees). Effort should be made to recruit handicapped, institutionalized, and minority persons. If money is a factor restricting volunteerism (for example, the cost of transportation or babysitting fees), efforts should be made to provide this funding. Volunteerism should be the right of anyone interested in engaging in it and no physical or attitudinal obstacles should prevent this.

Placing the Volunteer

In the initial interview between staff person and volunteer applicant, questions should be asked that allow the applicant to reveal attitudes and interests pertinent to determining a successful volunteer placement. Directive questions that elicit only cursory factual data should be kept to a minimum (for example, Do you have a means of transportation? Are you currently employed? If so, where?). Instead, nondirective questions should be asked that permit the subject to elaborate. Examples include:

> What have you enjoyed most in previous volunteer positions? What have you enjoyed least?
> What kind of people do you work best with?
> What kind of supervision do you prefer?
> What clients would you prefer to serve?
> What would you consider to be your ideal volunteer job?
> What do you like to do in leisure?
> What are your motives for seeking volunteer work? Socialization? Recognition? Challenge? Responsibility? Career guidance? Leadership?

The applicant's response to this last question should be of particular importance to the volunteer coordinator for a volunteer placement is more likely to be successful if the coordinator is aware of why the individual is volunteering. In this way, the coordinator can try to match the position to the individual's needs. For instance, a person seeking socialization would be unhappy in a volunteer position involving solitary mental activity. Someone seeking leadership responsibility would be dissatisfied to join a pool of volunteers in an annual fundraiser. The agency should consider volunteerism as an opportunity for growth. Volunteers should have the flexibility to try out different roles should they be dissatisfied with an assignment. In turn, administrators should feel free to inform volunteers if they are dissatisfied with the way the work is being done. As with paid staff, there are performance standards that must be adhered to if the recreation agency is to deliver services effectively. The fact that an individual is a volunteer and is not paid does not mean that mediocre work should be accepted. In the case where a volunteer is more of a hindrance than a help, reassignment or dismissal is considered.

Orientation and Supervision

Following the placement of a volunteer, the success of the experience is largely affected by the following four steps: (1) volunteer orientation, (2) volunteer supervision, (3) volunteer evaluation, and (4) volunteer recognition. The orientation should include a welcome and tour of the facility including introduction to staff. An orientation manual should be distributed including (1) philosophy, purposes, and history of the facility; (2) organizational structure; and (3) volunteers' roles in relation to the program. A written job description should include job title, line of command, time commitment, qualifications, duties, requirements, attire, and confidentiality code. The volunteer should be given some form of identification such as a pin or badge. In the course of the volunteer assignment, the volunteer should be observed and assisted by other staff people. In-service workshops should be held to increase volunteers' understanding of the agency and their role in it. Each volunteer should be periodically reviewed by a supervisor and should be evaluated as to achievement of goals and objectives stated in the original volunteer job description. Some form of recognition is in order and can take the form of written thank you letters, certificates, pins, or recognition programs, teas, or parties.

Challenges

In working with volunteers there are some factors that deserve mention. Power plays between volunteers must be eliminated. Since volunteerism is not obligatory, but a matter of free choice, the turnover of departing volunteers may reduce the effectiveness of programs. In light of this potential for turnover, the recreation leader must be aware of not giving volunteers so much responsibility that they become indispensable to the success of a program.

The coordinator should be aware that unless the staff is informed of the purpose of the volunteers and is involved in the interviewing, orientation, and supervision processes, they may feel insecure. They may falsely assume that the new volunteers are being primed to assume their jobs. Staff persons may resent the fact that the volunteer has the luxury to assume the "fun" parts of the work while they must work on unglamorous details to keep the program itself going. Since most agencies are understaffed, some staff may feel too overburdened to assume the responsibility of supervising a volunteer. Further, the staff should understand whether the volunteer is being asked to enrich and maintain existing programs or to develop new ones. With this knowledge, the staff can then help to channel appropriate information and resources to the volunteer.

LEADERSHIP IN CLUB ORGANIZATIONS

There is need for creative leadership that can uncover interests and develop them in group situations. The leader's role in this phase of recreation leadership calls for a working understanding of both individual and group behavior problems. The vast majority of recreational activities lend themselves admirably to the group work approach.

Group work concerns itself with all recreational activities, with the group providing the nucleus for recreational expression. These experiences offer admirable opportunities for learning to associate with others, for social recognition, self-expression, and self-development. Dependability, cooperativeness, initiative, leadership, and skill acquisition often develop through an acceptance of the responsibilities that go with group endeavours. The club offers a splendid means for the organization of a group wherein common interests can find expression and be strengthened—with the individual's welfare a prime concern.

Clubs Defined

Clubs are a grouping of individuals possessing a common interest. Since interests play so prominent a part in the organization of a club, a recreation leader must be able to unearth these interests and capitalize on these discoveries by channeling them into appropriate clubs.

There are two types of clubs: general interest and special interest. A general interest club is comprised of members who join out of a commonality in social needs. Examples would be age affiliated clubs (for example, Teen Club, Retiree Club), ethnic clubs (for example, Friendly Sons of the Shillelagh, Sons of Italy), corecreational clubs (such as Parents Without Partners, Singles Club), and religious clubs (such as Catholic Alumni Club, Jewish Federation). The special interest club, on the other hand, is comprised of members who join out of a commonality in subject interest. Examples would be drama club, hiking club, writing club, and so forth. Special interest club members are not concerned with the fact that the club is composed of people of different social needs or backgrounds from them. In summary, then, the general interest club member is concerned with meeting people; the special interest club member is concerned with exploring a subject of interest.

Club titles are endless as there is no limit to the interests to be explored. The following are typical of possible special interest clubs:

Archery	Radio	Dramatics
Square dancing	Ornithology	Book review
Spelunking	Model train	Painting
Newspaper	Art	Tap dancing
Folk dancing	Knitting	Winter sports

Choral	Sewing	Photography
Hiking	Naturalist	Cooking
Camping	Boating	Stamp collecting
Crafts	Social dancing	Cycling

How to Organize

At the start, an informal meeting might be held with those who are interested. While the possession of a common interest bond is usually in evidence, it need not be. The leader may find that the group is predominantly concerned with playing together without any specific activity interest. The spark for a club based on a more specific interest may come in time. With the leader serving as advisor, the group may decide on a meeting time, place, officers, constitution, and bylaws. Or if it is not ready to do so, it may decide to remain on an informal basis for the time being. The wishes of the group should be respected. Other symbols in a club's growth are the decision by the group on an appropriate name to give it identity, or the possible use of a uniform to bolster the members' sense of belonging.

Objectives of Clubs

Basically, the club should be concerned with pleasurable activities and outcomes. There is nothing inconsistent with coupling fun with desirable goals. The following are sample goals for a club:

1. To explore and develop interests
2. To create and nurture social values
3. To strengthen the ability to initiate and lead
4. To foster desirable character traits
5. To foster socialization skills.

Appreciation of other cultures is increasing in this country and exploration of other cultures can be undertaken as part of a club's program. For example, a music club can study the music of other lands and come to an appreciation of the composers' backgrounds and the cultural factors that influenced their compositions. In a similar vein, the folk dancing club can acquaint itself with the background that accounts for the pageantry and dances of other lands. An art club can explore the customs, mores, and cultural lives of the artists whose paintings are under consideration.

The Committee

A committee is a group charged with the responsibility of fulfilling a task, preparing recommendations, or arriving at a solution to a problem for the club. Some clubs are structured as clusters of committees with various functions. Some clubs are governed by a single committee. After an appraisal of a committee's function, the recreation leader as advisor could select prospective members who are interested and equipped to do the work. Since the committee chairperson is the one who sets the pace for the committee, it is essential that he or she be capable of inspiring the committee to operate as a unit.

The chairperson should elicit responses from all members and not superimpose personal ideas on the committee. Appreciation of the interests and contributions of each member should be expressed by the chairperson. Receptivity to the ideas expressed by others on the committee can do much toward making the committee a functioning unit. Through efficient committees, the recreation leader as advisor can extend the scope of the club's activities and further its accomplishments.

For those clubs wishing a more formalized operating structure, some procedures are outlined in the following section.

Preparing a Constitution

The preparation of a club constitution should be delegated to a committee by the leader or temporary chairperson of the group; this committee should consist of a minimum of three members. The constitution committee will need the advice of the leader in this task. As soon as the constitution is completed, it should be presented to the group at its next regularly scheduled meeting. At that time, the constitution should be read before the group, section by section. Each section should be read, discussed, and approved or disapproved before passing on to the next.

Not until each section is accepted should the constitution be considered for approval. The constitution can then be adopted in toto. This measure comprises a very important part of a club's life and deserves careful and thorough consideration. The leader should be alert to the fact that the democratic process is to be respected with regard to new membership as well as in adopting each section of the constitution.

Duties of Officers

There should be a clear-cut understanding of the duties of each officer. This can prevent confusion and lead toward a better and smoother functioning club. The duties of each officer are as follows:

President. The President (1) presides as chairperson of the meeting; (2) calls the meeting to order; (3) follows the order of business and enforces the bylaws; (4) repeats clearly all motions under consideration after a member has seconded them; (5) preserves order; (6) appoints the necessary committees; (7) does not express personal opinions while presiding (hands over the gavel when he or she desires to speak on a question); and (8) calls special meetings.

Vice-President. The Vice-President (1) serves in place of the President during his/her absence; (2) assists the President in executing various tasks; (3) helps to administer and serve on committees; (4) acts as presiding officer when the President decides to speak on a motion; and (5) assumes the Presidency when the office of President becomes vacant until it is filled by an election.

*Sample Constitution and By-Laws
for an Athletic Club*

CONSTITUTION AND BY-LAWS

of the _____ A.C.

of the _____ Community Center

Articles

ARTICLE 1—*Name*

This organization shall be known as the _____
Athletic Club of the _____ Community
Center.

ARTICLE 2—*Purpose*

To awaken and promote a thorough and sane interest in healthful physical
activities, fellowship, wholesome living, and to live up to the ideals of the
_____ Community Center.

ARTICLE 3—*Membership*

All members in good standing in the Community Center shall be eligible for
membership. (Election at a regular meeting by a two-thirds vote may be included if desired.) (A stipulation as to age may also be stated at this point.)

ARTICLE 4—*Officers*

There shall be a President, Vice-President, Secretary, and Treasurer, to be
elected as hereinafter provided. The club adviser shall be _____
of the _____ staff.

(play area)

ARTICLE 5—*Amendments*

This Constitution may be amended by a two-thirds vote of the membership.
All amendments are to be submitted in writing and signed by three members
and to be read at a regular meeting.

Bylaws

ARTICLE 1—*Officers*

Section 1. All officers shall be elected annually (or semiannually) by a
majority of the members on a ballot.

Section 2. Election of officers are to be held in the month(s) of _____

ARTICLE 2—*Executive Committee*

Section 1. The officers of the club and the club adviser shall comprise the
Executive Committee.

Section 2. The Executive Committee shall meet whenever circumstances
warrant or on the advice of any Executive Committee member, including the
adviser.

Section 3. The adviser shall serve as chairman of the Executive Committee.

Section 4. The club Secretary shall also be secretary of the Executive Committee.

ARTICLE 3—*Meetings*

Regularly scheduled meetings shall be held every _____ at

(day)

_____ in the club room of the _____
(time)   (play area)

ARTICLE 4—*Dues* (if deemed necessary)

Section 1. Membership dues shall be _____ for each _____
                                    (amount)   (period)
(A majority of the membership may change the dues.)

Section 2. Failure to pay the dues for _____ periods shall cause the
                                        (number)
matter to be brought before the Executive Committee. After due consideration
of hardship factors, the Executive Committee may recommend suspension.
(Note: For hardship cases, some clubs provide added duties so that these
members may work for their dues.)

Section 3. The Secretary shall inform the suspended member of the Executive Committee's action. Voting privileges shall be denied the suspended member until the account is paid.

ARTICLE 5—*Expulsion of Members*

The repeated failure of a member to support the club's objectives and activities may call for Executive Committee action. The member shall be permitted to defend himself before the membership. Only after a warning to mend his ways has failed shall expulsion be considered. A four-fifths vote of the membership shall be required to expel a member.

ARTICLE 6—*Amendments and Quorum*

Section 1. An amendment to the Constitution shall be possible when a two-thirds vote of the membership favors it.

Section 2. A quorum of _____ members shall be necessary
                        (number)
before a meeting is held. (A quorum usually is considered a majority of those on the club's rolls.)

Order of Business

The President is charged with the duty of following the accepted order of business:

1. Call the meeting to order
2. Secretary reads the minutes
3. Reading of letters and other communications
4. Committee reports
5. Unfinished business
6. New business
7. Adjournment

Secretary. The Secretary (1) keeps the minutes of each meeting; (2) records a statement of every motion made; (3) notifies the members of each meeting (this may not be necessary where the group meets more often than once per month); (4) keeps a record of all committee members; and (5) records the resolutions passed, along with the number for and against them.

Treasurer. The Treasurer (1) collects dues; (2) pays all bills (checks should be countersigned by one other officer); (3) presents a periodic financial report; and (4) keeps the group informed as to money taken in, money expended and for what, and the balance as of a given date.

Definition of Terms

The following extracts from parliamentary law and terminology are intended to assist in club management:

The Chair. The President or one serving momentarily in his/her stead.

Addressing the Chair. Making a statement directed at the President.

Obtaining the Floor. Securing the right to speak from the President.

The Motion. In presenting a motion, the member is to stand. After receiving recognition from the Chair the member is to state the motion. It is to be a single proposal. Upon being seconded by another member, the President then presents it for group action. Discussion for or against the proposal may ensue or an amendment to it may be proposed. The member who presents the motion is permitted to speak first and last on that motion.

Amendments. The modifying or changing of a *motion's* wording while adhering to the form and intent of the original motion. No more than two amendments to a motion may pend at any time. Should there be an amendment under consideration, then the amendment to the amendment is taken up first. Once it is rejected, the President restates the motion as originally stated; if the amendment is accepted, the motion should be restated in the amended form. A vote on the motion in its final wording follows.

Question. Matter or business under consideration. After adequate discussion, the President may ask, "Are you ready for the Question?" Should no one ask for the floor, then the President takes a vote on the motion (puts the motion). Those who are for it are requested to say "Aye" and the opposed to say "Nay." The outcome is then announced.

Calling for the previous question. A request that the motion pending be voted on after due consideration.

Tabling the motion. Postponing action on a motion to a later meeting so that added consideration may take place.

Question of privilege. Securing attention from the Chair immediately for the purpose of asking a question, and making a point of order (a question growing out of a previous question or motion). It does not call for a second and is not debatable. It takes priority over a member on the floor.

Two-thirds vote. A two-thirds vote is required for: (1) suspension of rules; (2) amendment to bylaws; (3) discharging a committee; (4) considering business out of order; (5) stopping or restricting debate (calling for the previous question); (6) unwillingness to consider a business matter; and (7) special order of business.

Suspension of rules. Rules may be suspended: (1) when there is no question on the floor; (2) while a question is on the floor, providing the purpose of the suspension is related to the question. Privileged motions take priority when a motion to suspend the rules is presented; a motion for suspension is not to be amended and cannot be debated.

Special orders. A question under consideration may be put off for a future meeting. It can be debated, amended, and passed by a two-thirds vote.

Viva voce vote. This is a voice vote with "Ayes" designating those for and "Nays" indicating those against the business under consideration.

Ballot vote. Voting for election of officers and on controversial issues usually are by a closed ballot.

Pro and con. A "pro" vote is a vote for a position; a "con" vote is one against a position.

Unfinished business. The inability to complete business at one meeting calls for its transference to the next session for consideration. Unfinished business also may be referred to as old business.

Agenda. An agenda is a list of matters to be considered at the meeting.

Time limit. A time limit is a limit placed on the amount of time and the number of pros and cons that can be imposed on a motion.

Refer to committee. The President may refer a question to a committee for further study.

Recommitted. A question may be referred to the committee for a second time after it has been reported to the group.

SUGGESTED READINGS

AUSTIN, MICHAEL. *Supervisory Management for the Human Services.* Englewood Cliffs, NJ: Prentice-Hall, 1981.

BALL, EDITH L. AND CIPRIANO, ROBERT E. *Leisure Service Preparation—A Competency Based Approach.* Englewood Cliffs, NJ: Prentice-Hall, 1978.

BANNON, JOSEPH J. *Problem Solving in Recreation and Parks.* Englewood Cliffs, NJ: Prentice-Hall, 1972.

DANFORD, HOWARD. *Creative Leadership in Recreation.* Boston: Allyn and Bacon, 1964.

EDGINTON, CHRISTOPHER E. AND WILLIAMS, JOHN G. *Productive Management of Leisure Services Organizations—A Behavioral Approach.* New York: John Wiley and Sons, 1978.

HERSEY, P. AND BLANCHARD, K. H. *Management of Organizational Behavior: Utilizing Human Resources* (4th ed.). Englewood Cliffs, NJ: Prentice-Hall, 1982.

KRAUS, RICHARD G. AND BATES, BARBARA J. *Recreation Leadership and Supervision: Guidelines for Professional Development.* Philadelphia: W. B. Saunders, 1981.

SHAW, MARVIN. *Group Dynamics: The Psychology of Small Group Behavior.* New York: McGraw-Hill Book Company, 1971.

SHIVERS, JAY S. *Recreational Leadership—Group Dynamics and Interpersonal Behavior.* Princeton, NJ: Princeton Book Company, 1980.

STRAUSS, G. AND SAYLES, L. *Behavioral Strategies for Managers.* Englewood Cliffs, NJ: Prentice-Hall, 1980.

2

Career Options

Career opportunities in the leisure services field are numerous and varied. This chapter is intended to acquaint the reader with many of these career options, providing a sound base for further career exploration.

Leisure services careers fall within two major categories—recreation program services and park management/natural resources. Recreation program services are concerned with the delivery of recreation programs to people. Examples of positions in this area include: community center director, music specialist, recreation therapist, armed forces special services director, and the like. Park management/natural resources positions, on the other hand, deal with the design and maintenance of facilities and landscapes conducive to the recreation programs. Examples of positions in this area include: park manager, outdoor recreation planner, park landscape designer, facilities maintenance coordinator. While recreation majors in both areas share some core course requirements, there is also a divergence in curricula for each specialization.

JOB DESCRIPTIONS

Job titles are often referred to rather freely with little attention paid to their respective requirements or levels of responsibility. To avoid that lack of clarity, the following outlines the responsibilities of some leadership jobs:

Administrator Manager Director Superintendent	Recruits and supervises staff Oversees area planning and maintenance Budgets Supervises public relations
Supervisor	In charge of all facilities and/or activities within a geographical area (general supervisor) or a specialized area of the program, such as crafts or sports (special supervisor) Carries out administrative duties in respect to his/her own area of supervision
Director of Centers or Facilities	Responsible for staff and facilities Usually responsible to area supervisor
Direct Leader	Provides actual leadership of programs (e.g., drama coach, tennis instructor)
Educator in College Leisure Services Department	Instructs future professionals in the concepts and practices of the field Screens unqualified applicants for the profession Develops curricula in response to the profession's needs and trends

In terms of qualifications, it is becoming increasingly necessary for educators to have a doctorate in recreation. A master's degree is sometimes accepted at the community college level. The positions of administrator, manager, superintendent, director, and supervisor usually require a master's degree in recreation, though a bachelor's degree with considerable experience is sometimes substituted on an individual basis. It is preferred that the direct leader have at least a bachelor's degree in recreation with appropriate training in the area of specialization. In the event that an individual possesses a high degree of expertise in that specialty and has the teaching and leadership skills to project that knowledge to others, the lack of academic experience in recreation is usually not a stumbling block in hiring.

Types of Positions

The following illustrates how various staff positions within a municipal recreation department interrelate. With modifications—such as the elimination of references to the Recreation and Parks department, this leadership breakdown can be applied to any leisure services agency.

EXECUTIVE

1. Superintendent of Recreation. The chief executive officer in charge of a recreation department or division and its personnel, responsible for planning, promoting, and administering a comprehensive recreation service for all the community.

2. Superintendent of Recreation and Parks. Chief executive officer in charge of a recreation and parks department and its personnel, responsible for the administration of a comprehensive recreation program for the entire community, and for the administrative management of the public parks, playgrounds, and other recreation facilities. (In communities utilizing a combined recreation and parks department, the superintendent of recreation heads the recreation division within this department.)

3. Assistant Superintendent of Recreation. Executive officer responsible for administrative planning, organization, and supervision of the recreation program as general assistant to the superintendent of recreation; acts for the superintendent in his/her absence.

SUPERVISOR

1. Recreation Supervisor (General). Responsible either for all recreation services for a district or a large subordinate geographic area of the community, or for all services or facilities of a similar type.
2. Recreation Supervisor (Special Activity). Responsible for the planning, promotion, development, and supervision of a specialized activity phase of recreation at a community-wide level. Programs could be music, sports, arts and crafts, outdoor recreation.

CENTER DIRECTOR

1. Recreation Center Director. Responsible for the direction of a comprehensive program for a single recreation center, which may include a recreation building or indoor center, playground, playfield, camp or day camp, or combination of any of these.
2. Assistant Recreation Center Director. Responsible for personal direction of assigned portions of the recreation program for a large or complex recreation center; serves for the recreation director in his/her absence.

DIRECT LEADER

1. Recreation Leader (General). Under close supervision, responsible for the promotion, organization, and personal leadership of a variety of recreation activities at an indoor and/or outdoor recreation center and for related work in the community.
2. Recreation Leader (Special Activity). Under close supervision, responsible for the organization, development, and personal leadership of one recreation activity or several closely related activities at one or more recreation centers.

TRAINEE

(The trainee positions that follow are for preparing young people for professional recreation leadership; they should not be considered substitutes for professional positions.)

1. Recreation Intern. Responsible for various administrative, supervisory, and leadership functions in a rotated work program under supervision of the superintendent. This is a professional internship for students of recreation curricula.
2. Student Recreation Leader. Under close supervision of a full-time staff member, responsible for the promotion, organization, and personal leadership of a variety of recreation activities in a field work program supervised by agency and college.
3. Junior Recreation Assistant. Under continuous supervision, assists recreation leaders to conduct games, special events, and other activities. Oversees free play activities and does routine tasks in both leadership and nonleadership work.[1]

A generalist direct leader or supervisor is responsible for all activity

1. *Recreation Leadership Standards* (New York: National Recreation Association, 1965), pp. 8–57.

areas (such as literary, drama, sports, and outdoor). The generalist is trained to lead a variety of activities in such positions as playground counselor, senior citizens center program specialist, and cruise ship youth activities director. Similarly, the generalist supervisor is equipped with the knowledge to program and oversee diverse activities. The specialist direct leader or supervisor is responsible for only one activity area (for example, sports or performing arts). For instance, a position as cultural arts supervisor would entail establishing a program in the fine and performing arts encompassing all age and skill levels. The dance specialist, under the cultural arts supervisor, would be hired to develop and instruct all dance programs wthin the cultural arts division (such as creative movement, aerobics, folk and square, social dancing, and so forth).

The following sample job titles reflect the distinction between generalist and specialist positions:

GENERALIST	SPECIALIST
Community Recreation Director	Administrative Specialist-Arts Division
Community Center Director	Special Programs Coordinator
Resort Manager	Supervisor of Athletic Activities
Parks and Recreation Director	Cultural Arts Coordinator

In terms of professional preparation, generalists are advised to take a liberal arts approach to education, enrolling for as many varied elective and activity leadership skills courses as possible. Exposure to a wide variety of field placement experiences is also encouraged. Specialists, on the other hand, should develop expertise in their specific area by pursuing the available courses and field placement experiences in that subject. For instance, a drama specialist would select such courses as puppetry, creative drama, directing, and set design and would pursue field placements such as children's theater director, acting instructor, and creative drama leader.

Thus, the college recreation major can choose to go either the generalist or specialist route at either the administrative or leadership/ programming levels. While there is a certain body of knowledge required of all recreation majors, curricula also have a built-in flexibility to individual career goals. Also, by minoring in recreation, it is possible for students in other disciplines to become recreation specialists in their particular fields. For instance, a music major with a recreation minor is employable as a music specialist in recreation settings. It is wise for recreation majors to explore their talents to determine if specialization in a particular activity area would be more satisfying than a generalist position. For example, a recreation major with an avid interest in guitar has the option to become a music specialist on an equally competitive basis with the music major/ recreation minor.

Career Titles

The following section provides a sampling of major career categories in recreation. The first types of organizations are nonprofit agencies or departments of institutions:

CHURCH RECREATION

Catholic Youth Organization athletic coach
Salvation Army director
B'nai B'rith Youth Organization leader
YMCA (Young Men's Christian Association) art instructor
YWCA (Young Women's Christian Association) music director
YMHA (Young Men's Hebrew Association) camp counselor
YWHA (Young Women's Hebrew Association) dance instructor
Mormon Mutual Improvement Association leader

ARMED FORCES RECREATION

(Employment for both military and nonmilitary personnel in Armed Forces positions; see Civil Service Bulletins for test announcements.)

Service club director
Red Cross area director
Special activities supervisor
Youth activities director

COLLEGE UNIONS

Campus facilities manager
Campus recreation director
Intramural sports director
College union program director
Faculty member in the leisure services department

VOLUNTARY RECREATION AGENCIES

(nongovernmental, nonprofit organizations with character-building emphasis)

YMCA/YWCA director
Boys Club/Girls Club leader
Boy Scouts/Girl Scouts camp coordinator
Settlement house activities director
Campfire Girls cultural arts coordinator
Police Athletics League outreach youth worker
Big Brothers/Big Sisters of America youth counselor
4-H crafts activity leader
Future Homemakers of America leader
Sierra Club director
American Cerebral Palsy Association recreation therapist
Office of Economic Opportunity outreach worker

Interestingly, these voluntary agencies have moved with the times in terms of their membership requirements. Future Homemakers of America members now include boys and the Boys Clubs accept girls. Girl Scouts in-

include senior citizen members. The former rural orientation of 4-H has been modified to include urban and suburban youth.

Commercial Recreation/Private Recreation

Career opportunities abound in both commercial and private recreation facilities as well. *Commercial recreation* centers are profit-oriented, privately owned recreation programs, such as a health club or a ski resort. *Private recreation* programs are those provided to a designated membership, financed by fund drives and fees—for example, a club-sponsored private fishing lake. Career opportunities include:

OWNER/MANAGER OF:

Hotel/motel	Casino
Sports track/arena/ball park	Billiard hall
Golf club	Video game arcade
Country club	Dance hall
Health club	Amusement theme park
Athletic club	Movie theatre
Dude ranch/riding stables	Theatre
Camp site/motor home site	Ice skating rink
Adventure trips	Roller skating arena
Travel agency	Bowling center
Sightseeing excursions	Tennis/racquetball complex
Ski resort	Shooting preserve
Boating/yacht club	Hunting guide
Marina	Vacation farm
Swimming pool	Cave/cavern
Private fishing pond/lake	

SALESPERSON OF:	**SOCIAL DIRECTOR/ACTIVITY INSTRUCTOR OF:**
Recreational equipment	Resort hotel
Boat canoe rentals	Cruise ship
Rental outfitters	Retirement community
Charter fishing boats	Singles apartment complex

Various businesses and industries also provide recreation for employees. Career opportunities include:

INDUSTRIAL RECREATION

Preretirement counselor (leisure counseling)
Facility manager (library, crafts, par course, nautilus)
Trip coordinator (theatre, special events)
Program coordinator (classes, tournaments, leagues, dances, banquets)
Camp director at company-owned lodge or camp
Resort or center director for union members

The basic premise behind industrial recreation programs is the belief that a contented employee is apt to be a more productive one. Industrial recreation is an employee benefit that attracts potential employees. And family recreation activities sponsored by the industrial recreation program appeal to the family-oriented employee. As a further benefit, in some cases employees are given a reduction in insurance rates for participation in company fitness programs. Others are given release time to pursue community volunteer work as a potential postretirement leisure pursuit. The employer's support of community service fosters good public relations with the community as does the provision of company recreational facilities for community use.

The industrial recreation program in any company assumes one of three management models: (1) administration by employees; (2) administration by management level staff; and (3) joint administration by managers and employees. The National Employee Services and Recreation Association, NESRA (formerly the National Industrial Recreation Association), was first established in 1941. Currently, it serves over 2500 members. In 1961, NESRA worked out a certification program for qualified industrial recreation administrators. On national and regional levels, NESRA conducts contests, conferences and workshops, community service projects, an intern program, and employment services. In recognition of the growing importance of employee tours, NESRA organized the National Industrial Travel Council consisting of transportation carriers, hotel chains, and tour operators. As an added service, NESRA publishes *Employee Services Management*. In 1964, a Research and Educational Foundation was established to conduct surveys and to collect information on the latest trends. Awards are given annually for outstanding member leadership achievement in employee services, recreation administration, and programming.

The student interested in a career in industrial recreation, private recreation, or commercial recreation should supplement the required core recreation courses with courses in business administration—including industrial psychology, accounting, personnel management, and public relations.

The government—federal, state, and local—provides recreation services also. This type of recreation is governmentally subsidized and designed to serve the general public's needs. Some typical jobs are:

GOVERNMENT-SPONSORED RECREATION

Community education supervisor
Playground director
Supervisor of county parks
Senior citizens center director
Cooperative Extension agent
Fish and Wildlife Services manager
National Park Services guide
County youth bureau director
Community center director
Federal conservationist
State area planner
Museum director

Professional positions vary from the leader level (for example, park ranger and naturalist in the National Park Service) through supervisor and administrator. Other federal agencies with recreation programs include the Urban Park and Recreation Program, the Department of Housing and Urban Development, Bureau of Land Management, Department of Education, and the Forest Service.

Recreation personnel are employed in municipal, county, state, and federal parks. They are also hired for community programs in community centers sponsored by municipal recreation departments and in community schools sponsored by Departments of Education. In the consideration of career options, it is desirable to understand the makeup of the municipal or county recreation commission or board as well as state and federal organizations.

GOVERNMENT-SPONSORED RECREATION

Each branch of government has an agreed-upon function to perform in providing recreation. With the evolution of recreation, a shifting of responsibilities has occurred in some instances. For example, the more direct and comprehensive involvement of the federal government in recreation has been accompanied by greater financial support to the states; consequently, the states have found themselves in a position to provide services that are broader in scope and more detailed in nature. The following sections analyze this shift of responsibilities in more detail.

Municipal Recreation

There are a number of ways municipalities administer recreation programs.

Recreation commission/board. A vast majority of recreation departments throughout the country operate under a board or commission setup. The primary function of this body is to oversee the work of the recreation administrator. Members of the board define the objectives of the department and develop policies for the purpose of realizing these objectives.

Recreation commissions or boards are usually comprised of between five and seven members, although they may have as few as three and as many as eleven. In Indiana, for example, the law stipulates a body of four with equal representation from each of the two leading political parties. Members are either elected by the general public or appointed by the city's chief executive. In either event, board members are usually selected on a staggered basis. This is done to enable a retention of a minimum of two-thirds of the board's incumbents, thereby providing for a greater degree of continuity.

The commission/board has its makeup and functions invariably spelled out by law. One of the most visible functions is that of an interpretation of the recreation department to the citizenry—and this includes justifying how the budget is spent. This function is becoming increasingly important as the struggle for municipal tax dollars becomes more difficult. Those boards made up of highly influential members are more likely to excel and flourish during the tug-of-war caused by the tax revolt.

Divided responsibility. Under this administrative plan, public recreational services are handled by more than one municipal agency. For example, New York City has divided control between the Board of Education and the Parks, Recreation, and Cultural Affairs Administration. The Division of Community Education of the Board of Education conducts programs in the schools and on athletic fields. The PRCAA operates designated recreation areas in conjunction with the Board of Education. They are arranged so that the school playgrounds are made available for community-wide use during the afterschool hours. These play areas are operated under PRCAA supervision. This cooperative policy is to be followed in future school construction.

Separate recreation authority. The task of administering recreation as a function distinct and separate from the rest of municipal government has staunch support for many reasons. By the authorization of a separate bureau or department of recreation, efficiency is enhanced. Cooperation with the private as well as the public agencies is simplified under a single authority so that a comprehensive recreation program can be achieved for the entire city. Moreover, the overlapping of duplicated programming resulting in wasted effort and funds is less likely. Efficiency is thereby heightened so that more valuable services can be rendered at minimal cost.

Community schools. There is increasing evidence of community recreation being provided under the auspices of community boards of education. The highest percentage of the capital investment of most communities is in school properties. Schools generally have facilities that can be utilized for recreational purposes.

The American Association of School Administrators and the Educational Policies Commission have long advocated that public school properties be kept open for public use during the afterschool hours.

However, the ever-increasing demands for expanded services upon boards of education have accounted for the willingness of some to yield the handling of community-wide recreation to another agency. In many cases where this has taken place, effective cooperation between the recreation agency and the school has occurred.

As illustrated by the following examples, school facilities can house a variety of community recreation programs: *auditorium* (entertainments, town hall meetings, speakers and forums); *gymnasium* (games, sports, dances); *shop* (carpentry, machine tooling, handicrafts, hobby groups); *pool* (swimming, diving, life saving classes); *music rooms* (instrument practice, band rehearsals, community chorus, community sing); *home economics rooms* (cooking, baking, sewing, interior decorating); and *classrooms* (club meetings, adult education).

Modern school construction plans often call for the placement of most of these facilities in a wing of the school plant so that the problems of winter heating, lighting, and policing are simplified. In Milwaukee, for example, the Department of Municipal Recreation and Adult Education operates under the direction of the Milwaukee Board of School Directors. The state law empowers the Board of School Directors to request a special tax to be used expressly for leisure-time activities for both children and adults.

The law also stipulates that the Milwaukee School Board may cooperate with any other municipal board or commission that has facilities usable for recreation. Under this arrangement, the School Board is to provide the instruction and supervision with the outside board furnishing the facilities. Pursuant to this provision, the public parks are used for athletics and playground activities, and the pools under the jurisdiction of the Board of Public Works are used for swimming instruction and aquatic meets.

Flint, Michigan is another city that is making around-the-clock use of its schools through its adult education and recreation programs. Funds are obtained through state support for adult education, board of education appropriations, the public-spirited Charles Stewart Mott Foundation, and other cooperating agencies.

By making fuller use of its schools for recreational purposes, Flint citizens are readily afforded the use of such "municipal luxury items" as swimming pools through the utilization of school areas that would otherwise go unused.

Community education. Community education—another aspect of leisure-time activities—received a significant boost with the availability of funds for development and implementation via Federal Community Education Legislation (HR 69, Title IX). An added stimulus has been the organization of the National Community Education Association with its headquarters in Flint.

The interagency cooperation of such agencies as the United Community Recreation Council, and the Welfare Council has resulted in more comprehensive and advanced programming. Furthermore, there has been repeated evidence of cooperation between the American Alliance for Health, Physical Education, Recreation, and Dance (through its American Association for Leisure and Recreation) and The National Recreation and Park Association. In addition, the National Joint Continuing Committee on Community Schools/Community Education has benefitted from financial support provided by the Mott Foundation.

On the federal level, the Model Cities Act (passed into law by Congress in 1967) also facilitated interagency cooperation in that it necessitated local comprehensive planning in order to qualify for grants from the federal government.

State Recreation

State governments are assuming an increasing number of recreation functions. Recreation, as an accepted member of the education family, is deserving of the same treatment accorded other disciplines. For decades, states have operated parks, forests, camp sites, winter sports, and picnicking, hunting, and fishing facilities—so recreation is hardly a newcomer.

The impact of state governments on the provision of leisure services has expanded greatly in recent years. Every state has by now a designated agency whose primary function is the assurance of recreation opportunities for its citizens.

Although the responsibility for this service may vary from state to state, all offer some type of technical and advisory assistance to their political subdivisions. Also, most states either provide grants-in-aid to cities and counties for the purpose of land acquisition or serve as a liaison between the federal government and municipalities in the administration of land and water conservation funds. Each state prepares a comprehensive outdoor recreation plan in order to qualify for land and water conservation funds.

Another vital state service is that of educating recreation professionals. This is accomplished primarily through state-supported colleges and universities. Professional curricula embracing leisure studies and parks and recreation management are available throughout the United States. In addition, several states actively stimulate professionalism by offering an accreditation mechanism that assures quality standards in professional preparation.

Federal Recreation

Traditionally, the federal government has exercised the role of assuring an adequate supply of outdoor recreation resources to meet the present and future needs of the American public. But significantly more involvement started with the issuance of the Outdoor Recreation Resources Review Commission report in January 1962. This was followed by the establishment of the Bureau of Outdoor Recreation by the Secretary of the Interior. The following year, the Bureau of Outdoor Recreation Organic Act provided the Secretary of the Interior with broad recreation planning authority. This was then implemented by the Land and Water Conservation Fund Act and the Federal Water Projects Recreation Act passed in 1965. Aside from federal revenue-sharing for acquisition and development of areas with outdoor recreation potential, it has provided management and technical assistance to states and municipalities as well as on-going planning, research, and environmental education.

Among the federal agencies with recreation functions are the following:

Corps of Engineers	Department of the Army
National Park Service	Department of the Interior
Fish and Wildlife Service	Department of the Interior
Bureau of Reclamation	Department of the Interior
Bureau of Land Management	Department of the Interior
Federal Extension Service	Department of Agriculture
Forest Service	Department of Agriculture
Council on Physical Fitness & Sports	Department of Health and Human Services
Public Health Service	Department of Health and Human Services
Public Housing Administration	Housing & Home Finance Agency

THERAPEUTIC RECREATION

In an earlier period, the recreation therapist was primarily a leader who offered direct recreation service of an activity nature within institutions serving the mentally ill and mentally retarded. Today, career options are broader and the roles more diverse. Recreation therapists assume such roles as administrators, consultants, counselors, community coordinators, educators, researchers, and leaders. Recreation therapists can pursue careers in any number of settings, including:

Hospitals (general, VA, psychiatric)

Schools for the blind, deaf, orthopedically disabled, neurologically impaired, and mentally retarded

Correctional recreation programs (jails, prisons, community-based programs, police community relations programs, probation/parole, and delinquency prevention programs)

Mental health centers (for outpatients, discharge patients, drug abusers, disturbed adolescents)

After-care centers for mental patients

Nursing homes (skilled nursing facility or intermediate care facility)

Hospice programs (for the terminally ill)

Group homes

Halfway houses (residences for discharged patients or inmates)

Alcohol or drug treatment programs

Rehabilitation centers

Sheltered workshops

Camps

Homebound outreach programs

Municipal recreation departments (As special populations coordinator, the recreation therapist facilitates mainstreaming, which is the integration of disabled individuals into regularly existing programs.)

National organizations for disabled persons

Architectural accessibility consulting firms (for example, surveying for compliance to regulations; installing ramps, hearing devices, braille signs)

Recreation therapists are also employed by voluntary associations created to serve the needs of individual special populations (such as National Foundation for the Blind, Easter Seal Society for Crippled Children) and philanthropic foundations committed to service to the disabled (such as Joseph P. Kennedy Foundation, Special Olympics).

Rehabilitation Team

In therapeutic recreation settings, the recreation therapist is usually a member of a treatment team including a physician, social worker, nurse, occupational therapist, physical therapist, speech therapist, recreation therapist, and so forth. The layperson is often unclear as to the distinctions between occupational therapy, play therapy, physical therapy, and therapeutic recreation and tends to use these terms interchangeably, which is incorrect; each of these professional areas has a unique orientation. To distinguish therapeutic recreation from the other therapies, definitions of those allied health professions follow:

> *occupational therapy*—a subdivision of physical medicine in which handicapped or convalescing patients are trained in vocational skills and activities of daily life through a program designed to satisfy the specific needs of the patient while providing diversion and exercise.[2]
>
> *physical therapy*—the treatment of disorders with physical agents and methods, as massage, manipulation, therapeutic exercises, cold, heat (including shortwave, microwave and diathermy), hydrotherapy, electrical stimulation, and light to assist in rehabilitating patients and in restoring normal function following an illness or injury.[3]
>
> *play therapy*—a form of psychotherapy in which a child plays in a protected and structured environment with games and toys provided by a therapist who observes the behavior, affect and conversation of the child in order to gain insight into his/her thoughts, feelings and fantasies. As conflicts are discovered, the therapist often helps the child to understand and work through them.[4]

While therapeutic recreation covers every type of recreational activity (arts and crafts, music, games, and so forth), physical therapy deals solely with motor activity. Similarly, while therapeutic recreation assists clients in a broad range of leisure skills, occupational therapy is confined to manipulative, physical skills related to occupational and maintenance activity. Since play therapy applies solely to children's play, it can be considered a subsidiary of therapeutic recreation.

2. Reproduced by permission from Laurence Urdang, ed., *Mosby's Medical & Nursing Dictionary* (St. Louis: The C. V. Mosby Co., 1983), p. 762.

3. Ibid., p. 845.

4. Ibid., p. 854.

As a member of the treatment team, the recreation therapist provides recreation activities for diagnostic, evaluative, and rehabilitative purposes within the context of a total treatment plan. Within this rehabilitation team, the recreation therapist must be cognizant of the client's needs, limitations, and overall treatment objectives. Concurrently, the recreation therapist must have a broad knowledge of recreational activities from which to select leisure pursuits that are amenable to client behavioral objectives.

It is critical that recreation be included in the context of the total rehabilitation approach, for unless leisure skills are developed, any other rehabilitative efforts are minimized. For example, concern for a parolee's vocational placement should be matched with equal concern for his leisure lifestyle, since stretches of empty nonproductive free time portend a return to criminal behavior and loss of that job. The role of recreation in any total treatment plan needs to be viewed in the context that recreation develops the social/physical/mental skills essential to a productive personal and professional life.

Training of the Recreation Therapist

Knowledge of leisure counseling techniques is an essential skill for the recreation therapist. Leisure counseling originated in a therapeutic recreation setting—a Veterans Administration (VA) hospital psychiatric ward in Kansas City in the 1950s. Leisure counseling incorporates knowledge of concepts of leisure, values clarification activities, and various counseling modalities. Upon first contact with the client, the recreation therapist conducts a leisure assessment that includes a personal history of leisure activities and present leisure needs. It is important that the recreation therapist expose the client to community leisure resources. In terms of institutionalized settings, clients need to be kept ever mindful of the community they will be returning to, so as to offset any tendency toward institutional dependency. This community exposure can be achieved through (1) slides of recreation facilities in the localities to which clients will be returning; (2) field trips to community facilities; and (3) speakers invited to the institution to discuss their leisure service agencies and personal hobbies. Once in the community, clients should be assisted by the recreation therapist in following through on leisure goals. For instance, in working with a mentally retarded adult, the recreation therapist may have to accompany him initially to the movies over a period of time to teach correct exchange of money, appropriate theatre behavior, and so forth.

Therapeutic recreation consists of prescriptive programming that involves the establishment of specific rehabilitative objectives for each client. To perform this function, every recreation therapist should be skilled in activity analysis and the establishment of behavioral objectives as discussed in Chapter 3. The recreation therapist must also be knowledgeable in all program activity areas as well as methods of adapting them to each disability, (for example, lighter equipment, shorter playing time, modified rules, shorter playing space). To do this effectively, the recreation therapist must also be familiar with the adaptive recreation materials that are available (such as braille scrabble, sound-producing balls for the deaf) as well as how to design original adaptations.

To insure compliance with high professional standards, the recreation therapist is encouraged to file for certification with the National Council for Therapeutic Recreation Certification of the National Recreation and Park Association.

Historical Overview of Therapeutic Recreation

Consideration of the field of therapeutic recreation should include appreciation of its historical development. As early as the late 1800s, Florence Nightingale and her nurses were introducing recreation materials into their service. In World War I the Red Cross sponsored recreation in military and convalescent hospitals. In World War II, skilled entertainers and specialists were employed in the Special Services division of the Armed Forces. The popular USO (United Service Organization) included the services of the YMCA, YWCA, Salvation Army, National Travelers Aid Association, National Catholic Community Service, and Jewish Welfare Board.

Over the years, key national developments have promoted the growth of therapeutic recreation. The Public Health Service sponsors a number of recreation programs at institutions such as St. Elizabeth's Hospital in Washington, D.C. and gives grants to NRPA for therapeutic recreation leadership training. The National Institute of Mental Health, a branch of the Public Health Service, assists research into the cause, prevention, and treatment of mental illness—research which incorporates therapeutic recreation. Legislation has also promoted the growth of such recreation: Section 504 of the Rehabilitation Act of 1973 mandated barrier removal to foster architectural accessibility for the handicapped. April 1977 saw the approval of a regulation requiring institutions receiving Department of Health and Human Services funds to provide equal access to services and employment to the disabled upon penalty of losing their funds.

Figure 2–1 highlights historical developments in therapeutic recreation.

APPLYING FOR RECREATION POSITIONS

The first step in acquiring a position in recreation is to get the message of your availability to a prospective employer via a detailed though not overly long letter. The letter should be accompanied by a resume and should focus on the highlights or prominent features of the resume. Your letter should also give a brief statement of your career goals.

Your initial contact with an employer should include the following:

FIGURE 2-1 Historical Developments in Therapeutic Recreation

1930s
Beginning of recreation service at St. Elizabeth's Hospital in Washington, D.C.

Menninger Clinic's stress on recreation as an aid to mental health

1940s
Expansion of recreation in military hospitals

Addition of Hospital Special Services Division to Veterans' Administration Recreation Service

Founding of Hospital Recreation Section of American Recreation Society

Formation of Leisure Time Committee in American Psychiatric Association

1950s
Establishment of Recreation Section of American Association for Health, Physical Education, and Recreation

Founding of National Association of Recreation Therapists

Creation of Council for Advancement of Hospital Recreation

Initiation of National Recreation Association's Consulting Service on Recreation for the Ill and Handicapped

Initiation of voluntary registration program for therapeutic recreation workers (over 1500 now registered)

1960s
First President's Panel on Mental Retardation

Formation of National Therapeutic Recreation Society as branch of newly merged NRPA

Passage of Public Law 90-170, which resulted in training grants and research for therapeutic recreation

Creation of Bureau of Education for Handicapped in Office of Education

First Special Olympics (Olympics for retarded)

1970s
Education of the Handicapped Act (PL 91-230)

Information and Research Utilization Center in Physical Education and Recreation for the Handicapped (IRUC), a service of AAHPER

Rehabilitation Act of 1973 (PL 93-113)

Education for All Handicapped Act (PL 94-142), which involves leisure education

National Therapeutic Recreation Society 750-hour training program

Standards for therapeutic recreation in psychiatric facilities through joint Commission on Accreditation of Hospitals

Source: Reynold Edgar Carlson, Janet R. MacLean, Theodore R. Deppe, James A. Peterson, *Recreation and Leisure—The Changing Scene* (Belmont, CA: Wadsworth, 1979), pp. 269-270.

1. *Resume:* Include a resume—a detailed listing of your education and experience (such as summer employment, field work, hobby pursuits, and related attainments). Mention resume highlights in your letter.

2. *References:* Provide a list of references (or include them on your resume). Select individuals who are familiar with the abilities relevant to the position for which you are applying. Choose professors and/or former employers who know you well. By all means, seek their permission to do so.

3. *Education and Experience:* In your letter, specify aspects of your education that qualify you more readily for the position. Similarly, state the features of your work experience that are pertinent to the opening for which you are applying.

4. *Particular Qualifications:* Single out particular skills in your letter. Do not sacrifice the truth in your eagerness for the position. Provide details on your strong points and weaknesses.

5. *Starting Time:* State the starting date of your availability as well as departure date if it is for seasonable employment (for example, start of college year.)

6. *Miscellaneous:*

    a. Be brief and to the point in your letter.

    b. Be precise as to why you are interested in this position; some advance insight as to the position and the employer may be of great value toward improving your chance of landing the position.

    c. Do not attempt to make misleading statements simply because you suspect the employer might desire to hear them. By trying to be something you are not, you will leave a poor impression rather than the good impression you think you are creating. The employer will see through falsehood.

    d. Indicate a willingness to learn and fill in any gaps in your qualifications for the job.

    e. Stand prepared to give (orally or in writing) the minimum salary you are willing to accept.

    f. Be prompt in correspondence or calling back.

    g. A stamped and addressed envelope should be inserted with the letter of application.

    h. Last, notify employer(s) upon accepting one position in order not to obstruct the chances of others.

Managing the Interview

The interview is an integral and vital part of the job application procedure. It can often tip the scale as to whether or not the candidate lands the job. Some contend that it is the single most important factor. The following are key factors to consider in preparing for an interview.

1. Clear up any uncertainty of the job requirements.

2. Point out why you are applying and how you qualify for the position. Be specific as often as possible (mention laboratory experience, volunteer and paid experience, honors, avocations, membership in organizations and offices held).

3. Square with the interviewer. Say "no" if a question locates a void in your experience. Every professional has a number of them. However, bounce back at the next opportunity with a strength. If applicable, give a valid explanation for the void in your background, but do not resort to excuses.

4. Secure information, such as salary range, later in the interview. First, answer the questions posed and sell yourself.

5. Permit the interviewer to establish the climate of the meeting. Do not upset the pace established.

6. Get as much information about the department or organization as you can prior to the interview. An advance visit or check can save your interview time for more significant questions.

7. An understanding of what is to be the next step and who is to make the next contact is an essential not to be overlooked. At no time should the interviewee give the impression of being overly assertive.

8. Don't leave the interview without asking the questions you have regarding the position and the agency itself. The employer will be more impressed with you if you are an active participant in the interviewing process rather than a passive recipient of questions.

Career Switching and Advancement

The job mart is subject to the vagaries of the economy. Also, it may fluctuate according to regional differences and the financial support given to leisure services.

Naturally it is professionally prudent to seek advancement when your qualifications warrant doing so. At times, a move upward may take place in the very department in which you are employed. In either case, the following guidelines may prove helpful:

1. Investigate the job mart carefully and in detail. Determine where the jobs are and know the key people to contact.
2. If applicable, do not leave one position before you have firmed up another.
3. Establish a number of contacts among colleagues, friends, and acquaintances who may ease the transition.
4. Graduate study on a part-time or full-time basis is one path to consider. Updating your schooling can result in expanding your skill capabilities. A "re-tooled" professional can be the outcome.

SUGGESTED READINGS

AMERICAN ALLIANCE FOR HEALTH, PHYSICAL EDUCATION, RECREATION AND DANCE. *Opportunities in Recreation and Leisure.* Washington, DC: AAHPERD, 1978.
AMERICAN ASSOCIATION FOR LEISURE AND RECREATION. "Leisure Today: Employee Recreation." Reston, VA: AALR, 1983 (Oct. 1983 *Journal of Physical Education, Recreation and Dance*).
THE CPC ANNUAL. *The Career Planning and Placement Guide for College Graduates.* Bethlehem, PA: The College Placement Council, 1984.
EPPERSON, ARLIN F. *Private and Commercial Recreation: A Text and Reference.* New York: John Wiley and Sons, 1979.
GUNN, SCOUT LEE AND PETERSON, CAROL A. *Therapeutic Recreation: Program Design Principles and Procedures.* Englewood Cliffs, NJ: Prentice Hall, 1978.
JENSEN, CLAYNE R. *Recreation and Leisure Time Careers.* Louisville, KY: Vocational Guidance Manuals, 1976.
NATIONAL RECREATION AND PARK ASSOCIATION, *Careers in Parks, Recreation and Leisure Services.* Alexandria, VA: NRPA, 1977.
O'MORROW, GERALD S. *Therapeutic Recreation: A Helping Profession.* 2nd ed. Reston, VA: Reston Publishing Co. 1980.
PETERSON, CAROL A. AND CONNOLLY, PEG. *Characteristics of Special Populations—Implications for Recreation Participation and Planning.* Washington, DC: Hawkins and Assoc., 1978.
SESSOMS, H. DOUGLAS, MEYER, HAROLD D., AND BRIGHTBILL, CHARLES K. *Leisure Services.* Englewood Cliffs, NJ: Prentice-Hall, 1975.
SHIVERS, JAY S. AND TAIT, HOLLIS F., *Therapeutic and Adapted Recreational Services.* Philadelphia: Lea and Febiger, 1975.
SMITH, RALPH. *Programming for Handicapped Individuals in Public Park and Recreation Settings.* Washington, DC: Hawkins and Assoc., 1978.

Figures 2–2, 2–3, and 2–4 show a sample cover letter and resumes provided by the Purdue University Placement Office.

FIGURE 2–2 Letter of Application Format

Your Address
Today's date

Mr. John Smith, Superintendent
Walton Recreation Department
Room 603H
1000 First Avenue
Newtown, IN 47001

Dear Mr. Smith:

Opening Paragraph: State the purpose of the letter. Where possible state why you are writing that particular agency; relate your interests to theirs. It is not necessary to know whether the agency has any openings in your field, but do state the area of work within that organization that you are interested in.

Middle Paragraph: Without repeating your resume, draw together from your resume, briefly and concisely, the strengths that qualify you for the position/area of work which you are seeking. Refer the reader to your enclosed resume.

Closing Paragraph: Encourage further contact by asking for an interview, or mentioning when you will be available for an interview. Thank the person for any consideration.

Sincerely,
(Signature)
Applicant (Full name, typed)

Remember to

1. Write to a specific person if possible. Check the University Placement Service [or professional directories] for current names and addresses. Include title (Dr., Ms., Mr.) and position (Director, etc.).
2. Check spelling and punctuation. Having a friend proofread it for clarity and errors is helpful. Do *not* mail a letter with uncorrected errors.
3. Use a resume to summarize your qualifications. The letters to specific employers should relate your background to the position in question.
4. Always sign in ink with your full name.
5. Reread your letter. It should include the important aspects of your college experience, a bit of your personality, and a summary of your pertinent qualifications. If it doesn't picture you as you are and how you want to look, rewrite.

FIGURE 2–3 Functional Resume Format

A functional resume allows you to highlight your transferable skills—those which you can apply to areas of work not directly related to your education or past work experience. You may wish to use this format if you:

- want to work in fields not directly related to your education
- have limited work experience but significant nonpaid experience
- have significant work experience in the same function where listing chronologically would be repetitive.

(*Name in Full*   )

Present Address (until)	*Permanent Address (after)*
date	*date*
Phone—include area code	*Phone—include area code*

Job Objective

Use this section to answer the question: What kind of work are you seeking? Specify immediate and ultimate goals (if known). Are you willing to travel, and/or relocate? Although stating a job objective on the resume is optional and may necessitate more than one resume, it is usually beneficial. If your job objective is not stated on your resume, it should be included in your cover letter (see cover letter format, Figure 2–2).

Skill Areas

This is a very important section of the functional resume. Examples of skill areas could be: "Managing and Organizing Skills"; "Human Relations and Interpersonal Skills"; or "Communication Skills". List skill areas which best describe your skills and which can be applied to the area(s) of work specified under "Job Objective" above. Example:
ADMINISTRATIVE AND MANAGEMENT SKILLS
- Supervised staff . . .
- Directed programs . . .
- Organized efforts to . . .
Include related skills from any area of your life, not just from paid jobs.

Education

List most recent first. Indicate graduation index and/or major index if you wish. It may be helpful to highlight course work, equipment familiar to you, skills, etc. Make this a section of what you know, not just where you went to school.

Work Experience

Most recent first. List employer (include military service and self-employment), under *job title*; describe duties but stress accomplishments and responsibilities. An added sentence regarding what you learned can be helpful. Include volunteer work if appropriate. Summarize summer and part-time work in one sentence unless particularly relevant.

Extracurricular Activities/Honors

Highlight the most appropriate activities and/or honors and list major offices held.

Thesis/Publications   Omit section if not appropriate.

Interests/Hobbies   If appropriate, and if you wish.

Personal Data

Strictly voluntary; may include factors such as: citizenship, age, marital status if you wish to bring to employer's attention.

References and additional information available upon request.

FIGURE 2-4 Chronological Resume Format

(_____ _Name in Full_ _____)

_Present Address (until ___)_   _Permanent Address (after ___)_
                        date   date
Phone—include area code   _Phone—include area code_

Job Objective   Use this section to answer the question: What kind of work
                             are you seeking? Specify immediate and ultimate goals (if
                             known). Are you willing to travel, and/or relocate? Al-
                             though stating a job objective on the resume is optional
                             and you may necessitate more than one resume, it is usu-
                             ally beneficial. If your job objective is not stated on your
                             resume, it should be included in your cover letter (see
                             cover letter format, Figure 2–2).

Education   List most recent first. Indicate graduation index and/or ma-
                             jor index if you wish. It may be helpful to highlight course
                             work, equipment familiar to you, skills, etc. Make this a
                             section of what you know, not just where you went to
                             school.

Work Experience   Most recent first. List employer (include military service
                             and self-employment); under _job title_; describe duties but
                             stress accomplishments and responsibilities. An added
                             sentence regarding what you learned can be helpful. In-
                             clude volunteer work if appropriate. Summarize summer
                             and part-time work in one sentence unless particularly
                             relevant.

Extracurricular Activities/Honors
                             Highlight the most appropriate activities and/or honors and
                             list major offices held.

Thesis/Publications   Omit section if not appropriate.

Interests/Hobbies   If appropriate, and if you wish.

Personal Data   Strictly voluntary; may include factors such as: citizenship,
                             age, marital status if you wish to bring to employer's
                             attention.

References and additional information available upon request.

Points to Remember

1. Please keep it short—one page is long enough for a personal resume, unless you
   have lengthy or unusual work experience.
2. If you are using this form for a job search through the mail, you will want to enclose a
   cover letter to the agency. Make the cover letter and your resume a coordinated, good
   looking introduction of yourself to the agency.
3. This form is flexible. It does not have to be kept in this order. For instance, if your work
   experience is your strong point, put work experience as the first major heading rather
   than education.

3

Program Planning—
Principles and Practices

The recreation program consists of those services provided by an agency to meet individual and community leisure needs and interests. The recreation program includes activities from such areas as arts and crafts, sports, music, drama, and outdoor. Recreation programming also includes making facilities, personnel, and other resources available to the community without the need for direct activity leadership. Since the provision of recreation programs is a foundation of the profession, knowledge of program planning principles is essential for the recreation professional.

Key steps in the program planning process include:

1. Establishment of agency philosophy, goals, and objectives
2. Assessment of community needs to determine program priorities
3. Program organization
4. Program implementation
5. Program promotion
6. Program evaluation.

AGENCY PHILOSOPHY, GOALS, AND OBJECTIVES

Guiding any program planning process is the agency's basic *philosophy* or purpose from which all programs assume their tone. The philosophy is a synthesis of the agency's goals and objectives. For example: The philosophy of an industrial recreation program might read "We are committed to the recreational needs not only of our employees, but of the community-at-large."

The agency philosophy is in turn reflected in the principles or aims of the agency such as (1) involvement of the community-at-large in program planning and facility usage and (2) encouragement of family recreation pursuits in the community.

Policies are guidelines on how these principles will be enforced. Policies cover such issues as administration, budgeting, programs, personnel, and maintenance. A policy to implement the industrial recreation program's principle of family recreation might be: "Priority will be given to making industrial recreation personnel available as consultants to family recreation programs in the community (for example, a family resort, YWCA)."

Finally, *procedures* are established to explain how the policies will be carried out. A procedure covering the policy cited here might be: "Industrial recreation personnel will be permitted full self-determination in arranging what portions of their week will be spent in the community."

Goals and objectives embody the philosophy of the agency. Program goals and objectives are the foundation of program planning and the criteria for program evaluation. A goal is: a long range, visionary end, not expected to be attained fully, usually written in lofty language. An objective is a step to achieve the goal—an attainable end; its achievement can be measured; it is written in clear, accountable terms. The success of a program is measured by how well the agency achieves its objectives. The program activity areas (for example, dance, outdoor recreation) are the tools to achieve the objectives aimed at the goals.

EXAMPLES OF PROGRAM GOALS AND OBJECTIVES

Municipal Agency
> Goal—We are committed to fostering appreciation of ethnic and cultural values.
> Objective—We will sponsor an ethnic festival monthly.

Youth Service Agency
> Goal—Our aim is to instill constructive leisure awareness in problem youth.
> Objective—In cooperation with the juvenile probation department, we will establish recreational programs as part of the court diversion program.

Industrial Agency
> Goal—We desire to improve the overall well-being of our employees.

Objective—We will make our recreational facilities accessible to employees on a flex-time schedule.

Therapeutic Agency

Goal—We will facilitate the patient's awareness of leisure choices upon reentry to the community.

Objective—A leisure counselor will maintain individual and group counseling sessions with the client during the initial phase of reentry.

Programming Philosophies

Recreation programs take on the perspectives of the individuals who initiate them. The philosophies behind these programming approaches are widely divergent as illustrated by the sample comments of the following recreation programmers. Each comment is followed by an analysis of the programming approach and the term coined to describe it.

Cafeteria Approach[1]

"Let's just offer a little bit of everything and they can pick what they want."
A smorgasbord of activities is provided, with those receiving strong response being maintained. If the programmer has not conducted an adequate assessment of community interests, the cafeteria approach is safer than offering scanty, inappropriate programs.

Traditional Approach[2]

"Why should we alter the program now? We've been offering this class for the last 5 years."
The traditional approach relies on past successes and ignores the products of current research and social change. It makes no effort to assess changing community interests and resources. Its rationale is that what worked then, must also work now.

Current Practices Approach[3]

"All the latest issues of *Parks and Recreation* highlight aerobic dance's popularity as a nationwide phenomena; we'd better join the bandwagon."
Programs are built around what is "in" instead of the actual interests of the constituents. The current practices approach ignores the fact that each community is unique and need not mirror the leisure activities in current practice elsewhere. The fact that a leisure activity flourishes in one habitat does not assure that it will be equally popular with the people of another locale.

Educated Guess Theory[4]

"I just have a feeling that roller-skating would be popular—don't ask me why, it's just an instinct."

1. James E. Murphy, *Recreation and Leisure Service: A Humanistic Perspective* (Dubuque, Iowa: Wm. C. Brown Co., 1975), pp. 51-52.
2. Howard G. Danford, *Creative Leadership in Recreation* (Boston: Allyn and Bacon, 1964), pp. 107-9.
3. Ibid.
4. Christopher R. Edginton and Carole J. Hanson, "Approaching Leisure Service Delivery," *Parks and Recreation*, Vol. 11, No. 3 (March 1976), pp. 27, 44-5.

Programs are based on conjecture in the hope that they hit the mark. The educated guess theory is a formal name for an attitude toward programming in which no effort is made to obtain community input.

Authoritarian Approach[5]

"Sports have been the greatest source of satisfaction in my life; this is where our program emphasis is going to be."

In the authoritarian approach, the programmer does not see beyond the blinders of his or her own views. This dictatorial style allows no programming input from staff or participants.

Prescriptive Approach[6]

"We must be accountable in our profession. Once we see the physical, mental, and social symptoms that need correction, we can recommend recreational activities that will help eliminate them."

Following an assessment of total lifestyle factors (such as health, income, living environment), leisure resources and activities are recommended or prescribed. As the term "prescriptive" implies, this is a very individualized programming approach. While it can be utilized in any leisure service setting, it is an essential in therapeutic recreation.

Expressed Desires Approach[7]

"We have to find out what the public wants us to offer this season. It's time to send out feelers."

Programs are offered on the basis of public preference. Efforts to obtain community input are good; however, since people tend to request programs that they already have some familiarity with, the expressed desires approach does not usually allow for much program innovation or experimentation.

Reaction Plan[8]

"Well, since no one has come in with any suggestions, we can gather that they are pleased with our program offerings."

This reflects a passive attitude toward programming whereby program alterations are considered only if a constituent initiates the approach. The programmer makes no effort to elicit programming input from the constituency.

Investigation Plan[9]

"Our surveys indicate that there are a large number of teens looking for after-school recreation programs."

The programmer conducts a needs assessment to determine leisure needs and interests. Surveys reveal demographic information such as age, income, occupation, and the individual's history of recreational activity. Of special importance is a section in which the individual indicates what he or she views as primary personal needs (such as achievement, self-expression, fitness). The programmer interprets how specific recreational activities could satisfy these

5. Danford, *Creative Leadership*.
6. Murphy, *Recreation and Leisure*.
7. Danford, *Creative Leadership*.
8. Albert Tillman, *The Program Book for Recreation Professionals* (Palo Alto, California: National Press Books, 1974), pp. 57-58.
9. Ibid.

needs. The survey results thus provide determinants of programs to be offered. The success of the investigation plan is the resident's ability to recognize and express personal needs and the professional's ability to analyze these data.

Indigenous Development Theory[10]

"Our youth outreach worker has helped the street gang on Maple Avenue follow through on their desire to repair the corner basketball lot."

This approach is characterized by the belief that the community must be approached on its own turf for any meaningful program development to occur. Grassroots leadership is mobilized with program development largely in the hands of the people themselves. While more time-consuming than other programming approaches, it produces effective results.

NEEDS ASSESSMENT TO DETERMINE PROGRAM PRIORITIES

Programs are designed in response to the agency's assessment of individual and group recreational needs. For instance, if constituents express a need for more physically stimulating activities, the agency can design a variety of active programs (for example, aerobic dance, athletics, hiking). To assess what people's recreational needs are, the agency must first have a complete understanding of the many physical, social, intellectual, and psychological needs met by recreational experiences. The scope of these needs is outlined in Figure 3–1.

As indicated in the chart, individuals pursue activities for a variety of reasons. As recreation professionals, we should be concerned with what each person is seeking from the activities so that we can better assure a quality experience for each individual. It is not enough to know that Mr. Jones is taking our weaving class; we should be interested in knowing what needs he hopes to fulfill through weaving. It is recommended that the recreation leader distribute a short questionnaire at the beginning of the class to assess these needs (see Figure 3–2). At the completion of the program, the questionnaire should be returned to the participants with the request that they express how the activity has or has not met the needs originally indicated.

Should an individual not initially be prepared to make a decision to pursue a specific activity, this same questionnaire is of equal use in helping the individual and recreation leader mutually arrive at some activity recommendations appropriate to the needs expressed.

Needs Assessment Survey

The assessment of community needs to determine program priorities is achieved by conducting a recreation survey. Depending on intent and

10. Edginton and Hanson, "Approaching Leisure."

Program Planning—Principles and Practices   **59**

FIGURE 3-1 Recreation is . . .

Accomplishment
Achievement
Acquired use of the senses
Aesthetic experience
Alienating boredom
Anticipation
Appreciating needs of others
Appreciation of new values
Awareness of spiritual, physical, and cultural aspects of the human sphere
Belief in a future for society
Better citizen participation
Better idea of where to go from here
Better perspective on life
Body achievement
Body awareness
Breakdown of minority and racial barriers
Bringing all people together
Broadened social feelings
Challenge
Challenging one's habitual patterns of mental and physical action to new experiences
Changes in self-esteem
Community working together
Community spirit
Concept of what kind of city (environment) I want to live in
Confidence
Coming down from an emotional or physical peak
Competing, struggling, overcoming challenges
Creative experience
Creative expression
Cultural sharing

Feeling of self-worth
Finding new talents
Friends
Frustration
Fun
Growth
Growth of interpersonal skills
Happiness
Health
Healthy relationship with mind and emotions
Helping others
Improved capacity of people to affect quality of their lives
Improved capacity to relate to children and young people
Improved community
Improved confidence in government and public service
Improved perception of own rationality
Improved self-confidence
Improved self-image
Improved sense of "community"
Improved skills
Improvement of mental health
Improving my city and neighborhood as a place to live
Increased imagination
Increased self-worth
Intensified skills
Interpersonal relations
Involvement
Injury
Inner peace
Joy
Knowledge

Promoting feeling of belonging
Providing channels for creative self-expression
Providing interrelationships to improve racial skills
Providing socially approved models
Recreated mind, body, and spirit
Re-creating
Recreation leadership which provides bridge between peoples' good ideas and actual achievement of ideas
Reducing tension by venting emotional drives
Refined cultural horizons
Reflection
Refreshed spirit
Rehabilitation
Rejuvenation
Relaxation
Release valve against pressure of living in poverty, ignorance
Relief and tension
Relief from the anxiety of fighting for self-image
Risk
Sanity
Satisfaction
Seeking and finding challenges and excitement
Self-actualization
Self-confidence
Self-discovery
Self-esteem
Self-expression
Self-fulfillment
Self-image

Dangerous challenges
Developing ability to be innovative
Developing ability to lose
Developing ability to win
Developing avocations
Developing new skills
Developing personal expressiveness
Developing teamwork values
Developing unique personal identity
Development of friendship
Development of "skills of living" in a pluralistic society
Diversity and pleasurable experience for all
Energizing the entire being
Enhanced communication
Enjoyment
Entertainment
Excitement
Exercise
Exhaustion
Expanded awareness
Expanded awareness of life
Expanded perspectives or views
Expanded understanding of people
Exhilaration
Exploring relationships
Exposure to new items
Family unity
Feeling at home with my environment
Feeling better about one's self
Feeling of belonging
Feeling of security in inner resources of one's lifestyle

Learning
Learning about environment
Learning about one's self
Less destruction in our facilities
Lessening tensions
Making a contribution
Making friends
Management or risk
Mastery
Mental achievement
Mental exhaustion
Mental health
Mental stimulation
More joy in personal and family life
Motivation
Muscle tone and coordination
Mutual trust
New adventure
New experience
New friendships
Oneness of body and mind
Opportunity for interaction
Opportunity to identify enjoyable activities by trial and error
Outlet of emotions
Participation with others toward common goals
Peer group relationships
Physical fitness
Pleasure from beautiful and well-kept surroundings
Positive feedback
Positive relationships

Self-satisfaction
Self-testing
Self-worth
Sense of achievement
Sense of control of one's destiny
Sense of human fellowship
Sense of reward
Separation from the mass
Service to people
Shared experiences
Simplicity in a complex/crowded urban life
Skills development
Skills in personal relationships
Socialization
State of mind
Status
Stimulating interests
Stimulating occupational goals
Stimulation of educational goals and objectives
Social skills
Strengthened personal competency
Success
Teamwork
Testing of body capabilities
Thrills
Understanding how I can help others
Understanding of other human beings
Understanding of potential to success
Use of time in interesting ways
Wider range of vision and comprehension of life

Source: David Gray and Sy Greben, "Wanted: A New Word for Recreation," *Parks and Recreation*, Vol. 9, No. 3 (March, 1979), p. 23.

FIGURE 3-2 Assessment of Recreation Needs

Name _____

1. List the needs you expect this activity to meet for you personally. Check all that apply:

_____ excitement		_____ exercise	
_____ accomplishment		_____ fun	
_____ challenge		_____ power	
_____ creativity		_____ competition	
_____ skill development		_____ knowledge	
_____ socialization		_____ relaxation	
_____ enjoyment		_____ adventure	
_____ entertainment		_____ mental stimulation	
_____ service to others		_____ rejuvenation	
_____ recognition		_____ responsibility	
_____ security		_____ vocational skills	
_____ wealth		_____ achievement	

_____ other

2. List your present leisure activities. Next to each activity, indicate which of the above needs are met by that activity.

Activity

(Example: hiking

Needs Met

exercise, adventure, challenge)

3. Followup Question (to be answered upon completion of the program): List each of the needs you checked in question 1. Next to each need give a brief explanation of whether this activity met this need.

Need

(Example: competition

(Example: socialization

(Example: relaxation

Program Result

The folk dancing class decided not to participate in the annual dance contest as they usually did. I was disappointed in this because I joined for the fun of competition.)

Yes, the folk dancing class was a great way to meet people.)

Yes, I found that while dancing, I forgot my worries.)

design, the survey can yield any or all of the following information pertinent to programming decisions:

1. *Demographic data.* These data provide factual information on population groupings and social factors within the community (such as age, sex, economic background, education, occupation, residence, ethnic background, marital status). This demographic information is significant to program planning; for instance, the survey's revelation of a large number of single parents suggests the need for expanding day-care recreation programs in the community.

2. *Personal interests and motivations.* Respondents reveal information pertaining to past leisure history, current leisure practices (such as recreational activities: type? frequency? where? with whom? skills required? needs met?), time use, and perception of free time available, projected leisure goals, and leisure values.

3. *Attitudes and opinions regarding existing programs and facilities.* Respondents state views on current program offerings (such as personnel, courses offered, facilities, accessibility, cost; what is the attitude toward increased fees for higher quality programs?).
4. *Current and projected resources in the community.* The survey assesses existing community recreation resources and determines levels of usage. From this community-wide perspective, gaps in services can be detected and corrected.

Most surveys appraise facilities and areas as to age, group, and population needs. Still others attempt to single out specific correlations such as delinquency reduction and recreation. Studies are also undertaken to compare the administrative setups or financial management of areas of comparable size.

The survey process is a form of positive public relations in that it pleases the public to know the agency is concerned enough about their views to poll them. The community, however, should feel there is a need for a survey, or much of the public support necessary for its success will be withheld. Informing the public of the survey through the media and speaking engagements will do much toward encouraging public support.

At the outset, a survey committee should be organized. Whenever possible, the survey should be sponsored by a responsible agency or group. Sponsorship can come from such groups as college recreation departments, boards and professional groups, park boards, and social agencies (community chests and councils, merchants' bureaus, and chambers of commerce and service clubs.)

The survey design should be easily read with unambiguous questions allowing elaboration of respondent's personal views. Books on experimental research and survey design should be consulted in the preparation of a survey. The surveys can be mailed, hand-delivered, or completed in one-on-one home interviews.

Ideally, the survey should precede the inauguration of a recreation program. However, there is ample evidence to substantiate the opinion that the survey is of inestimable value to recreation programs already in existence. Surveys as periodic agency appraisals may lead to programs that come closer to meeting the needs of the total community. If properly conducted and implemented, the survey is a powerful vehicle for strengthening leisure services. See Figure 3–3 for excerpts of a sample survey.

PROGRAM ORGANIZATION

Program organization refers to the guidelines followed in developing a program. The following paragraphs present key guidelines in program organization.

To function productively, an agency cannot operate in a vacuum, but must be aware of the goals and services of other community agencies. As the focus of a survey, the agency could assess the existing programs and

FIGURE 3-3 Sample Questions from a Needs Assessment Survey

Adult Questionnaire

Department of Parks and Recreation
Wooster, Ohio

1. Are you ☐ Married ☐ Single
2. Are you ☐ Male ☐ Female
3. What is your age _____
4. Are there children living in your home _____Yes _____No
   A. How many under 6 years of age_____C. How many 12 years to 14 years____
   B. How many 6 years to 11 years_____D. How many over 14 years of age____
5. How many years of education have you completed (circle number of years)

Grade School	1	2	3	4	5	6	7	8
High School	9	10	11	12				
College	1	2	3	4				
Graduate School	1	2	3	4				

36. Do you feel that existing parks are too far from your home
    ☐ Yes ☐ No
37. Do you consider that living near a park is an asset to the value ($) of your property.
    ☐ Yes ☐ No
38. Which of the following are representative of your opinions. (Check one or more)
    ☐ Parks should be used for active recreation only
    ☐ Parks should be used for active and passive recreation and should have beautiful qualities
    ☐ Some parks should be constructed that are conducive to passive recreation only
39. Which of the following facilities do you or your family use most. Place a 1 next to that facility, the next most, place a 2, third most place a 3, etc., and rank through 5.

☐ Freedlander Park	☐ Y.M.C.A.	☐ Wayne Co. Historical Society
☐ Christmas Run (City Park)	☐ Freedlander Pool	☐ Wooster College Facilities
☐ Knight's Field	☐ Knight's Field Pool	☐ Mohican State Park
☐ Jaycee Park	☐ Christmas Run Pool (City Park)	☐ Stark Wilderness Area
☐ Schellin Park	☐ Senior Center	☐ Pleasant Hill
☐ Cohan Park	☐ Youth House (Trinity Church)	☐ Charles Mill Lake
☐	☐ Public Golf Courses	☐ Clear Fork
	☐ Snow Trails	☐ Wooster Skateland
☐ Other (Specify)	☐ Country Club	☐ Out-of-Town Facilities

    _____
    _____

40. What other recreation facilities similar to those listed in Question 39 do you use other than those provided by the Department of Parks and Recreation, i.e., YMCA – Girl Scouts – School Activities. (List in order of greatest use first.)

    _____ _____
    _____ _____

41. Now here are some questions concerning specific recreation activities.

How often do you:	Not at all	Less than once a month	About once a month	Several times a month	Several times a week	Almost every day
Visit friends?	☐	☐	☐	☐	☐	☐
Go swimming outdoors (in season)?	☐	☐	☐	☐	☐	☐
Read a book or part of a book (do not include magazines)?	☐	☐	☐	☐	☐	☐
Paint or draw?	☐	☐	☐	☐	☐	☐
Spend time on crafts such as woodworking, model building, etc.?	☐	☐	☐	☐	☐	☐
Play a musical instrument?	☐	☐	☐	☐	☐	☐
Go dancing?	☐	☐	☐	☐	☐	☐
Work on the lawn, garden or around the house?	☐	☐	☐	☐	☐	☐
Play games such as cards, chess, monopoly, etc.?	☐	☐	☐	☐	☐	☐
Others (Be specific, but do not name more than *five*?	☐	☐	☐	☐	☐	☐

42. The following activities are some which you might do throughout the year.

How often do you:

	Not at all	Less than once a month	About once a month	Several times a month	Several times a week	Almost every day
Go shopping for pleasure?	☐	☐	☐	☐	☐	☐
Go swimming indoors?	☐	☐	☐	☐	☐	☐
Attend movies?	☐	☐	☐	☐	☐	☐
Attend plays and concerts?	☐	☐	☐	☐	☐	☐
Attend art shows or museums?	☐	☐	☐	☐	☐	☐
Play tennis?	☐	☐	☐	☐	☐	☐
Play golf (in season)?	☐	☐	☐	☐	☐	☐
Go bowling?	☐	☐	☐	☐	☐	☐
Attend sports events?	☐	☐	☐	☐	☐	☐
Attend adult education classes for enjoyment?	☐	☐	☐	☐	☐	☐

43. The following activities are more oriented to the outdoors.

How often do you: (in season)

	Not at all	Less than once a month	About once a month	Several times a month	Several times a week	Almost every day
Play softball?	☐	☐	☐	☐	☐	☐
Go fishing?	☐	☐	☐	☐	☐	☐
Go ice skating?	☐	☐	☐	☐	☐	☐
Go overnight camping?	☐	☐	☐	☐	☐	☐
Go driving for pleasure?	☐	☐	☐	☐	☐	☐
Bicycle for pleasure?	☐	☐	☐	☐	☐	☐
Go boating?	☐	☐	☐	☐	☐	☐
Go snow skiing?	☐	☐	☐	☐	☐	☐
Go on picnic?	☐	☐	☐	☐	☐	☐
Go hunting?	☐	☐	☐	☐	☐	☐
Go jogging?	☐	☐	☐	☐	☐	☐
Hike and walk for pleasure?	☐	☐	☐	☐	☐	☐

44. In what other recreation activities do you participate. List activities which were not mentioned in the questions.

How many days during year

_____   _____
_____   _____
_____   _____

45. Are there any activities in which you do not now participate but would like to.

Major reason for not participating now

Activities (Specify)	Do not know how	Facilities not available	Program not offered	Cost	No baby sitter	Other (specify)
_____	____	____	____	____	____	____
_____	____	____	____	____	____	____

46. Which of the following items does the family own at least one of

- ☐ Stereo or Hi Fi
- ☐ Automobile
- ☐ Home
- ☐ T.V.
- ☐ Camera
- ☐ Ice Skates
- ☐ Skis
- ☐ Archery Equipment
- ☐ Snowmobile
- ☐ Tape Recorder
- ☐ Bicycle
- ☐ Boat
- ☐ Camping Equipment
- ☐ Golf Clubs
- ☐ Snow Slide
- ☐ Toboggan
- ☐ Fishing Equipment
- ☐ Hunting Equipment

47. Is there a need for the Recreation and Parks Department to provide instruction in the use of this equipment.

_____ Yes _____ No   Specify _____

48. Now we would like to know how you feel about your community, its Park and Recreation system and other related items. Here are a few statements. Check the box which corresponds to how you feel.

	Completely disagree	Partially disagree	Partially agree	Completely agree
I am satisfied with the Parks and Recreation facilities in Wooster	☐	☐	☐	☐
The quality of leadership provided by the Department of Parks and Recreation is good	☐	☐	☐	☐
There are sufficient opportunities for children to use their free time constructively	☐	☐	☐	☐
There is a need to coordinate the existing Recreation Programs being offered by various organizations in Wooster	☐	☐	☐	☐
The type and quality of activities for teenagers is good	☐	☐	☐	☐
I would like to see an ice rink constructed in Wooster	☐	☐	☐	☐
The City of Wooster should acquire additional open space for Park and Recreation purposes	☐	☐	☐	☐
The quality of maintenance of Park and Recreation facilities is good	☐	☐	☐	☐

	Completely disagree	Partially disagree	Partially agree	Completely agree
The City of Wooster should update and install imaginative new playground equipment in the neighborhood parks	☐	☐	☐	☐
The Department of Parks and Recreation should expand its service to meet the demand of Wooster Citizens	☐	☐	☐	☐
I would be willing to pay additional taxes to provide more park and recreation services	☐	☐	☐	☐
Public park and recreation programs are well worth their cost	☐	☐	☐	☐
The Department of Parks and Recreation is spending its money wisely	☐	☐	☐	☐
There are not enough senior citizen activities	☐	☐	☐	☐
Wooster has better park facilities than most other communities its size	☐	☐	☐	☐
For activities which are expensive to provide and in which few people participate, those participating should pay a fee	☐	☐	☐	☐
I am properly informed about the activities offered by the Dept. of Parks and Recreation	☐	☐	☐	☐
More competitive athletics for females should be offered by the Department of Parks and Recreation	☐	☐	☐	☐
I would support the acquisition and development of a Green Belt (A park around the City)	☐	☐	☐	☐
If more Recreation Programs were offered in the City of Wooster, it would decrease Juvenile Delinquency	☐	☐	☐	☐
I would be willing to volunteer my time to help supervise Recreation Programs	☐	☐	☐	☐
Family recreation is important to our family	☐	☐	☐	☐

51. What improvements or changes would you recommend for existing Park and Recreation facilities and programs in the City of Wooster

_____

_____

_____

_____

Source: Joseph J. Bannon, _Leisure Resources: Its Comprehensive Planning_ (Englewood Cliffs, NJ: Prentice-Hall, 1976), pp. 418–426, Appendix C.

facilities in the community to prevent duplication of services. Agency recreation programs achieve maximum effectiveness if designed in a framework of interagency cooperation. Interagency cooperation efforts include:

1. Co-sponsorship of programs and special events
2. Facility sharing
3. Joint program planning and scheduling
4. Sequential programming by skill level among agencies (for example, beginning guitar at municipal recreation program, intermediate at privately funded arts center, and advanced at commercial music studio)
5. Contractual agreement to share personnel
6. Provision of technical assistance, leadership training, and publicity resources.

To be a well-rounded program, activities should reflect the following elements of balance:

Active/passive	Short range/long range
Individual/group	Indoor/outdoor
Single age or sex/mixed age or sex	Social/cultural/physical
Unskilled/skilled	Organized/unorganized
Special event/regular	Gradation in skills

For the purpose of providing a diversified program, it is necessary to provide such a balance in program activities. To maintain interest and involvement, program scheduling should be made with this balance in mind. For instance, in a camp program, midmorning would be appropriate for active games while passive activities such as storytelling or arts and crafts would be suitable for the "winding down" period prior to lunch.

Similar to the concept of short- and long-range activities is that of informal and formal activities. Informal activities refer to short-term, spontaneous activities requiring little practice; formal activities are those requiring an investment of time and practice. An informal arts and crafts activity would be fingerpainting; a formal arts and crafts activity would be quilting.

Where possible, use a theme to integrate your activity areas. For example, the theme "a trip to the zoo" could be initiated by an actual field trip to the zoo. Later, the storytelling group could devise stories about their trip. These could be shared with the art class who would design puppets suggested by the stories. The drama class could then stage the puppet presentation. By seeing how activities can be integrated for a unified purpose, it is hoped that the participants will be better able to integrate any disparate elements in their own leisure lifestyles. Thematic programming tends to have more of an appeal than regular programming due to its novelty approach.

Build continuity into your program by providing activities that build on previous skills and interests. Continuity includes the assurance that classes will go beyond the beginner level to include intermediate and advanced learning opportunities. Recreation leaders should aim for "carry-over value" in their programs whereby the participants see the application of program content to their daily lives. If participants desire to continue a recreational activity over time and can see the transference of its benefits to other parts of their lives, the activity is said to have carry-over value.

Examine your own concepts of recreation and consider how these are reflected in your programming priorities. For instance, a leader with a concept of recreation that is solely physical fitness may exercise an unhealthy zeal in trying to get the card player onto the dance floor or the chess player onto the tennis court.

Vary your program schedule in nontraditional ways to be accessible to the varied lifestyles in the community. For instance, family recreation programs should not be relegated to weekends because it was always so; families are sometimes together during weekdays and weekday nights due to school vacations, unemployment, extended employee vacation time, and so forth. Wherever possible, with any program, classes should be offered at more than one time period so as to reach the maximum number of participants and give an element of choice.

Be sensitive to how religious, ethnic, and regional factors influence the community's receptivity to programs. For example, certain religious groups ban dancing and card playing as offensive. The programmer should build programs around religious holidays celebrated by the community (such as Hanukkah, Easter). Ethnic practices should be noted and highlighted in classes, fairs, street festivals, parades (for example, Italian boccie ball, Caribbean steel band). Programs should spotlight the cultural traditions unique to that region (such as a southwest rodeo, midwest state fair).

Be prepared to make changes in the program due to unforeseen circumstances (personnel illness, weather change, unexpected turnout in terms of group size and/or population). Adaptation plans might include personnel substitutes, activities modified to the group, site changes and transportation to the sites, and publicity to inform the public of the changes.

Give attention to how you title your program; it may make all the difference in whether or not you attract participants. Write your titles with the educational level and value systems of your constituents in mind. The title "Group Counseling," for example, may inhibit attendance due to the stigma that some people attach to the word "counseling"; "Group Discussion" or "Rap Session," on the other hand, might keep the door of interest open.

In choosing a facility for your program, be sensitive to the following points: Is the space easy to maintain in terms of maintenance and cost? Is it safe, comfortable, accessible? Does it permit multi-use of short- and long-range activities? Is the space or facility adjacent to it conducive to the facility's purpose?

A policy covering fees and charges is an essential factor in programming. Recreation agencies are increasingly utilizing fees and charges to help subsidize the cost of services. These added funds can be put to use for more diversified program offerings. Activities that appeal to relatively few participants can be included and more readily justified if they are self-supporting through fees and charges, and thus not a drain on the tight budget. Though fees and charges have historically been a part of private and commercial recreation, they have been increasingly evident in public programs because people object to increased taxation for services. Overall, every effort should be made to keep fees and charges as low as possible in order to encourage maximum participation.

The recreation agency assumes liability for any accidents incurred by participants in their program. Therefore, it is essential to insure that all conditions under which the program is offered are safe and well-monitored. These include:

1. Maintaining safety of all facilities and equipment
2. Providing adequate supervision of all activities, particularly risk activities
3. Requiring first aid and CPR training for all staff
4. Completing accident forms even for the most minor injuries
5. Requiring medical release forms of all participants engaged in recreational activities that may pose a risk to their health or safety.

Play as a Developmental Process

In any discussion of age characteristics, the subject of play as a developmental process deserves attention. Play is a normal manifestation of children's growth and development. It is the laboratory in which the child experiments and learns of the world. While play is entered into for the sheer fun it provides, it need not stop there. It is also an avenue through which children express themselves, whether it be through blocks, clay, or construction sets. Success in a play venture will foster personality development and self-identity.

Since the child's whole personality is expressed during play, the recreation leader is provided with splendid opportunities for observation and teaching. Desirable personality traits can be encouraged and less acceptable ones discouraged. The self-centered child may benefit most from games calling for cooperation in group play, while a bashful child needs toys that build personal confidence. Make believe and imaginative play of adult situations can help the child rehearse life situations. It is important that the adult's attitude towards the child's play be one of respect and support to the point of even entering into the make-believe world. By seeing adults validate the importance of their play, such children grow with a more positive attitude toward leisure. If recreation leaders and parents constantly stress that all chores must be done before any play is allowed, then the child grows to be an individual who views leisure as something that must be "earned" after work. Thus, the child's "readiness to learn," or in this case play, is minimized and the inclination toward later spontaneity and exploration in leisure reduced. Adult influence is a significant factor in the development of the child's leisure attitudes: for instance, an emphasis on performance and achievement may lay the groundwork for the child's selection of solely competitive leisure pursuits. The recreation leader should provide parents with advice on recreational activities that they can do with their children. This provides an important "carry-over" from what children have played at the recreation agency to what they can also do in the home environment. Similarly, parents should inform the recreation agency of recreational skills they would like to see their children develop. For instance, a child whose parent reads to him, will desire access to reading material outside the home as well. Play permits the child to blow off excess energy. Also, many play activities serve an educational purpose by introducing the child to colors, shapes, numbers, letters, and skills.

The value of physical play is not to be overlooked in the development of the child. Manipulative toys help advance small muscle coordination. Balls and other games involve gross motor skills. Not only does vigorous play improve the general muscle tone, but it also strengthens the supporting structures of the internal organs as well.

Play Therapy

Play therapy, an aspect of the therapeutic recreation field, encourages children to play out their concerns through unstructured play. A variety of play materials are provided that can represent situations and feelings children wish to master. Through their use of dolls, clay objects, and other inanimate objects, children are able to work through the tensions these items evoke and represent. For instance, unusual roughness with a nurse puppet may represent a deep seated fear and resentment of a hospitalization experience. By observing children's choices of play materials and their methods of play, the therapist is able to determine their preoccupations and moods.

The objectives of play therapy include:

1. To assist children in adjustment to the hospital
2. To offer activities associated with normalcy
3. To foster opportunities for social interaction
4. To provide emotional support
5. To assist in providing medical information
6. To reduce anxiety about treatment procedures
7. To assist children in adjusting to physical conditions following a surgical procedure.

Resources for Play

Playthings that make it possible for children to alter their environment are highly desirable. Mural making or construction of an adventure playground, for instance, provide children with the ego-boosting experience of "leaving a mark" on their surroundings.

The availability of a playroom is an important part of many leisure service agencies. Commercial recreation establishments such as ski resorts and hotels provide children's activity rooms where children can occupy themselves while parents spend time together. The hospital playroom is the only place in the hospital environment where the frightened young patient can feel some sense of control over what is happening. Toys permit release of anxiety and provide a safe familiarity so needed in the general sterility and discomfort of the hospital setting.

Wherever possible, play should be conducted outdoors for the benefits of air and sunshine. An area should be made available where children can romp, dig, climb, jump, swing, and play table games in the open. Such fixed pieces as a table and bench, sandbox, swings, and slide should be available. A sheltered area to protect against inclement weather is a good location for dramatic activities, arts and crafts, rhythm band, and table games. In addition, a paved all-purpose area should be provided for activities requiring space, such as low-organized games, singing games, and rhythms.

Every leisure services agency that serves children should realize that opportunities for free play and low-organized games are an important part of the recreation program. Therefore, purchase of toys that will facilitate this free play deserves careful consideration. The degree of learning possible through play is largely dependent upon the success with which toys are chosen and put to use.

Factors to consider in purchasing a toy for a recreation program or family home use are:

1. Is the toy creative?
2. Can the child learn something from its use?
3. Will it hold the child's interest?
4. Is it safe to use?
5. Will it further the child's physical, emotional, and social development?
6. Does the toy suit the child's capabilities?

There are varieties of solo and group, active and sedentary playthings. Since the child's needs and interests cover a wide range and fluctuate at any given time, it is important to have a varied assortment of toys. Toys can be selected to meet the child's developmental needs for:

Creativity and artistry (blackboard, easel, modeling clay, pegboard, crayons, paints, water colors, basket making set)

Construction (blocks, tools, construction kit, workbench, mold set)

Rhythmical and musical development (tambourine, child's phonograph, piano, tom tom, xylophone, musical puzzles)

Imitative and dramatic play (miniature household appliances, doctor's kit, cash register, play suits, magic set)

Strength and skill development (ball, bicycle, hobby horse, roller skates, athletic supplies, archery set, jump rope)

Manipulative skill (peg sets, jigsaw puzzles, blocks, sound blocks, interlocking blocks)

Games (checkers, dominoes, lotto, croquet, chess, anagrams, target games)

Based on the developmental characteristics discussed earlier in this chapter, the following toys are recommended:

Infancy to 1-year: stuffed animals, rattles, washable balls, bath toys, beads, bells, musical toys

1–2 years: building blocks, pull toys, push toys, peg toys, stuffed animals, sandboxes, wagons, dolls, large blocks, kiddie cars

2–4 years: wheelbarrows, dump trucks, push wagons, hobby horses, kiddie cars, tricycles, housekeeping sets, floating toys, jigsaw puzzles, finger paints, sandboxes with appropriate toys

4–6 years: steam shovels, roller skates, simple construction sets, pegboard tables, coloring books, crayons, safety scissors, simple musical instruments

6–8 years: simple construction sets, doll equipment, simple science sets, jump ropes, craft work with tools, looms, paints, skates, musical toys, bicycles, elementary athletic gear

8–10 years: mold sets, puzzles, construction sets, printing presses, athletic supplies, dominoes, checkers, mechanical games, crafts (hand, loom), embroidery, bead looms, tool chests, work benches, magic sets, records, jigsaw and musical puzzles

10–12 years: chemistry, electrical, and mold sets; regulation size tools, sports equipment, construction sets, boats, airplane kits, bird guides, entomology, typewriters, scouting equipment, chess, checkers, and lotto games, wagons, musical instruments

Safety is a vital component of any toy selection. Toys with toxic colors or paint, sharp edges, or protruding parts should be avoided. Wooden toys should be checked for slivers. Toys with small parts that could be swallowed should not be part of a very young child's toy selection. Flammability of material and plastic is another reason for care. Electrical toys should be approved by the Underwriters Laboratories (UL) to help give assurance that they are safe; this certifies protection against defective construction that could be a fire hazard or result in electrical shocks.

Encouraging the child to devise original toys from natural materials is often preferable to commercial toys in terms of sparking the creative play spirit. The following items are appropriate for toy construction: paper cartons, crates, cereal containers, plastic bottles, barrels, and so forth. For those who love to play out different roles, costumes can be devised from clothing, sheets, hats, shoes, jewelry, blankets, and rugs. Through such role playing, children dramatize events from daily living and, in effect, rehearse for later life situations.

Lifespan Considerations

As an aspect of the Program Organization phase, the recreation leader is asked to consider the age level of the participant as an indicator of certain mental, physical, and social characteristics. It is felt that once age level is known, the leader can then determine those activities that would be appropriate to this developmental stage. However, it should be pointed out that the uniqueness of each individual precludes any age classification. There is no ideal standard of behavior to which each individual should conform. Variations in abilities and interests are the norm at any age level.

Age is undoubtedly a less influential factor than the time period in which the individual has lived. For instance, a 75-year-old individual of today has lived through different attitude-shaping events than will the 75-year-old of the year 2020. Attitudes towards leisure will vary greatly between an individual who has lived through the 1930s depression, which glorified the work ethic, and an individual who experienced the 1960s relaxed "Do Your Own Thing" philosophy. Also, rather than looking at age transitions as critical influences in one's life, it may be more realistic to highlight the lifestyle transitions themselves (such as graduation, marriage, widowhood). These transitions can occur at any age in a person's life; the recent college graduate may be a 21-year-old man, a 46-year-old woman, or a 68-year-old retiree. The influence of a graduation on one's vocational and avocational choices far outweigh the influences of one's chronological age.

Developmental characteristics, when considered, should be viewed only as general guidelines or behavior trends that provide an additional reference in the program planning process. This section describes developmental characteristics and their implications for recreation programming.

AGE CHARACTERISTICS	IMPLICATIONS FOR RECREATION PROGRAMMING
INFANT TO AGE 1-YEAR	
Dependency on others is paramount; need feeling of security to explore freely	In play, the presence of supportive parent or leader determines infant's positive attitude toward self and environment.
Need chance to learn about objects by grasping, feeling, hearing, and seeing, thereby aiding muscular control	Provide tactile play material (crib mobiles, rattles, balls, bath toys, squeaking musical toys, bells, stuffed animals.)
Need to develop muscular control	Play games that allow creeping and crawling, pushing and pulling, building (push and pull toys, blocks).
PRESCHOOL (AGES 3–5)	
Imitate those around them; enjoy make-believe	Program activities that allow a "trying on" of adult roles including dress up, storytelling, creative drama, singing games, puppetry.
Have a short attention span; restless	Recreation materials and neutral play apparatus should be available

AGE CHARACTERISTICS	IMPLICATIONS FOR RECREATION PROGRAMMING
PRESCHOOL (AGES 3-5)	for unscheduled play. Recreation activities should be diverse and of short duration.
Seek immediate gratification	Build in recreation experiences that help child learn some postponement of immediate satisfaction (for example, baking class).
Play side by side without interacting or sharing (parallel play)	Build in recreation experiences that require cooperation (such as rhythm band).
Have difficulty gauging own energy limits	Schedule rest periods and passive activities as needed.
Self-perception greatly influenced by "significant others" (influential people in their lives such as parents, siblings, recreation leaders)	Train significant others in child psychology and ways of playing with preschoolers including recommended play materials. Teach them to set guidelines and to praise wherever possible.
Seek sensory stimuli; anxious to explore environment	Recreation programs should include: sensory boxes (filled with different smells, tastes, and surfaces); nature study, hikes; finger painting, blocks.
Limited eye-hand coordination	This can be developed by such programs as creative movement, ball throwing, simple crafts, blocks.
Need to improve gross motor coordination (full body movement)	Activities to exercise this skill include ride toys, climbing, and rhythm activity (such as marching, running, skipping, and hopping to musical accompaniment).
Need to improve fine motor coordination (use of fingers)	Activities to exercise this skill include beads, digging, coloring, and so forth.
AGES 6–8	
Desire to excel; will practice	Activities that involve commitment have appeal (sports, arts, singing, science).
Eager for attention; seek approval	Activities are chosen for their ability to spotlight individual achievement (for example, a show, newsletter, team game).
Learning to share	Provide opportunity for group activities (camping, communal gardening, group relays).

AGE CHARACTERISTICS	IMPLICATIONS FOR RECREATION PROGRAMMING
AGES 6-8	
Constantly active	Recreation activities should provide physical outlets (such as tag games, New Games).
Muscle coordination improving	Program activities involving more fine motor skills (leathercraft, instrument making, and more gross motor skills, athletics, folk dances, hikes).
Inquisitive	Activities should offer opportunity for exploring the world (for example, nature study, history buff club).
Overestimate ability; concerned more with individual than team achievement	Downplay competition; help individuals set individual, realistic goals for themselves.
AGES 9–12	
Able to postpone gratification after work and practice	Recreation programs that require commitment are appealing (speech festival, team competition, band performance).
Developing teamwork attitude	Teamwork can be achieved through athletics, hobby groups, camps, teams, play casts, bands.
Growing concern for appearance	Such activities as dressmaking, grooming, and charm courses appeal to this interest.
Fine motor skills developed	This is demonstrated in such activities as needlepoint, construction sets, typewriters.
Improved depth perception	This is reflected in such activities as horseshoes, ring toss, softball, table tennis, hard ball.
Want responsibility to try on adult roles	Child can teach peers an activity or be responsible for certain aspects of the program (for example, set up of equipment, program publicity).
Developing values	Values awareness can be realized through such activities as discussion groups, values discussions, role playing, book reading groups.
Adventurous	Provide adventurous risk activities (such as Outward Bound, Project Adventure, backpacking).
Growing sexual identification as nearing adolescence	Opportunities for corecreational physical, social, and mental activity

AGE CHARACTERISTICS	IMPLICATIONS FOR RECREATION PROGRAMMING
AGES 9-12	
	should be offered (such as co-ed basketball team, dancing).
Like to store facts and classify information	Introduction to mental and collecting hobbies is especially suited to this age group (for example, public speaking, coin collecting).
Hero worship	Leisure values can be modeled by the recreation leader or distinguished role models in recreation fields (for example, a famous musician or tennis player).
Want rewards	Achievement can be recognized through praise or a reward and certificate. A "no-winner" attitude similar to the New Games philosophy should be fostered to downplay any unhealthy level of competition.
ADOLESCENT	
Strong peer pressure	In establishing team rules, downplay "choosing sides," which could cause self-consciousness. Outreach recreation workers earn the confidence of street youths and acquaint them with recreation pursuits as alternatives to negative peer influence.
Time of body changes, growing sexuality	Opportunities for release of physical tension are important (such as handball, tennis, bowling). There is need for corecreational activities in which the opposite sexes play with rather than against each other (such as social dancing, relay games, journalism clubs, band).
Seek adult roles; can question authority; desire responsibility	Wherever possible, adolescents should be involved in the program planning process. Peer leadership of activities is to be encouraged.
Striving for independence	Participants should be educated in lifetime leisure skills that can be self-initiated (for example, hobbies, fitness programs, musical instruments).
Emotional intensity; sensitive to failure	Competition should be deemphasized. Leisure counseling helps ado-

AGE CHARACTERISTICS	IMPLICATIONS FOR RECREATION PROGRAMMING

ADOLESCENT

Exploring career goals and values

lescent set realistic leisure goals. More opportunity is needed for values discussion, leisure, and vocation counseling.

YOUNG ADULTS

Lifestyle of this age group is varied dependent on employment, marital, and student status.

Married individuals are seeking a balance of activities to do individually and jointly. Young adult parents need exposure to activities that can be done with children as a home-based activity or in the community. This need has contributed to the growth of "parenting" courses (courses on how to be a good parent). College students are offered recreational activities through their student unions and clubs. Singles explore activities that promote self-improvement and socialization. A growing commercial sector is offering a variety of singles programs such as discussion groups, fitness centers, specialized activity groups like Singles Ski Club, and programs targeted to specific ethnic, religious, or age range groups, such as the Jewish Singles and the Catholic Alumni Club. The same agency can use different marketing approaches to appeal to the varied young adult population (for example, separate weekends for couples, families, and singles). Since the young adult lifestyle cannot be stereotyped, the recreation agency must be willing to tailor its services to the unique needs of its constituents (such as single parents, the unemployed, homosexual partners).

The group activities associated with school attendance are no longer easily organized as a single adult (such as basketball team, debating club); inclination is now toward individual,

Program offerings should include opportunities for individual, dual, or small group activities (for example, tennis, swimming, poetry writing, discussion group).

AGE CHARACTERISTICS	IMPLICATIONS FOR RECREATION PROGRAMMING

YOUNG ADULTS

dual, or small group activities easily integrated with one's schedule.

Interested in "carry-over" leisure skills (that is, activities that can be continued throughout one's life and whose personal benefits are far-reaching)

The carry-over value of an activity can be determined only by the individual according to his/her own needs and interests. The recreation leader should familiarize the participant with the concept of carry-over value and its importance in the selection of leisure pursuits.

Often a time of peak development in physical, intellectual, social, and civic interests.

These interests can be fostered through such recreational opportunities as Nautilus workouts, aerobic dance, choir, and community volunteering.

MIDDLE ADULTS

Like young adult, have continued concern for carry-over activities.

Carry-over value is individually determined. Recreation agencies should offer a variety of leisure pursuits with potential for carry over (such as interior decorating, photography). Recreation leaders help people assess those earlier recreational experiences that they wish to maintain and develop through the later years.

Like young adult, lifestyle is varied, dependent on employment, marital, and student status.

For those who work, preretirement counseling should focus on the development of positive leisure attitudes and interests for retirement. Family composition will affect leisure pursuits (for example, a middle-aged adult caring for an elderly frail parent may seek a respite program that allows for placement of the parent in a day-care program in order to have some free time for leisure). Couples with grown children may give more attention now to developing their own individual and dual pursuits (such as hobbies, travel, community volunteering).

Seek intellectual stimulation and maintenance of physical health.

A variety of programs are available to meet this need (adult education programs, health spa, diet centers).

AGE CHARACTERISTICS

OLDER ADULTS

Can be an interest in reflecting on the past in order to better synthesize life experience.

Physical abilities diminish; may be some mental loss; does not mean older adult is incapacitated.

Attitudes toward leisure will be affected by lifestyle circumstances.

Individual's personality is a product of a lifestyle evolution—not a radical change after 65. Despite what societal stereotyped thinking would have one believe, an individual does not automatically become cantankerous, close-minded, or withdrawn upon reaching the later years.

IMPLICATIONS FOR RECREATION PROGRAMMING

Oral history, journal writing, discussion groups, and ethnic festivals exemplify programs that draw upon personal reflections.

Recreation activities that incorporate physical exercise and sensory stimulation have been helpful in preventing further physical and mental loss.

For persons who have worked all their lives, attitudes toward leisure will be determined largely by attitudes towards retirement (Were work goals achieved? Have leisure goals and interests been established as alternatives to work goals? Do associates validate one's leisure or stress former work role? Is there a desire to adapt vocational skills to leisure skills?) Leisure counseling in industry and community preretirement counseling assist in retirement adjustment. Progressive retirement periods (for example, one month at a time) and miniretirement periods (sabbaticals) are advised to accustom the preretiree to the decision making accompanying expanded free time. Research indicates that the earlier in life the preretirement planning begins, the greater the individual's willingness to retire and the more positive the adjustment to retirement.

The recreation leader should ascertain the older adult's prior interests to determine those activities the individual may wish to further develop.

Organizing Recreation for Older Adults

Recreation can play a major role in assisting older adults to cope with the changes in their lives. In the present age, life expectancy has been much extended due to medical advancement, less work time, better knowledge of fitness and health, improved educational systems, and more productive lifestyle habits. The resultant expanded leisure time may inspire in some older adults the desire to explore latent interests. The recreation agency should expose the older adult to new pursuits not adequately explored over the lifespan.

Some older adults experience role loss due to change in family and job affiliations. New volunteer opportunities and social contacts are recommended to offset feelings of uselessness or isolation. An attraction of volunteerism for the older adult is that it makes a person feel useful and needed without imposing the obligations of work. As another approach, intergenerational programs meet the need of many older adults to nurture and pass on their knowledge to the young; this is also termed "the elder function". In turn, many young people today do not benefit from contact with grandparents and can have this gap filled by the wisdom and caring of other older companions.

Some older adults experience a fiscal loss that they mistakenly feel precludes their ability to have leisure in their lives. Those retirees who equate leisure with money may reason that they therefore have no leisure if they are subject to reduced pensions, fixed incomes, high housing and health costs. To prevent the disillusionment born of this distorted view of leisure, the recreation leader has the responsibility to expose the older adult to leisure pursuits not dependent on money and to conduct leisure education sessions exploring alternate leisure values.

Some older adults experience a physical loss that they mistakenly feel precludes their ability to maintain and develop leisure pursuits. However, "although 86% of older persons have one or more chronic health problems (e.g., diabetes, high blood pressure), 95% are able to live in the community. The conditions are mild enough to enable 81% of older persons to get around with no outside assistance."[11] Older adults with some form of physical limitation should be educated to ways in which leisure interests can be maintained with adaptations (for example, a bowling ball ramp to prevent bending, wheelchair square dancing).

Many behaviors are labeled as "senility" when in fact they are symptoms of other conditions including anxiety, depression, or grief. The word *senility* is actually a distorted, incorrect term for a condition known as organic brain syndrome. Organic brain syndrome, evidenced by such symptoms as disorientation, loss of memory, emotional imbalance, and poor reasoning is identified as either chronic brain syndrome (irreversible) or acute

---

11. Reproduced by permission from Robert N. Butler (M.D.) and Myrna I. Lewis (A.C.S.W., *Aging and Mental Health: Positive Psychosocial Approaches*, 3rd ed. (St. Louis: C.V. Mosby Co., 1982), p. 28.

brain syndrome (reversible). Chronic brain disorders refer to psychotic disorders caused by cerebral arteriosclerosis (insufficient blood to the brain due to hardening of the arteries) or by senile dementia and senile brain disease causing dissolution of the brain cells. Alzheimer's disease is a form of this latter senile psychosis. However, while this chronic brain syndrome is irreversible, acute brain syndrome can often be reversed through proper treatment. In acute brain syndrome, the psychotic behaviors can be due to any number of causes including congestive heart failure, malnutrition, infection and resultant fatigue, strokes, drugs, head trauma, alcohol abuse, and emotional instability due to change or loss.

Since the recreation therapist is very much guided by the doctor's diagnosis in determining the kinds of recreational activities suited to each client, it is important that the recreation therapist be aware of the fact that senility is often misdiagnosed. The recreation therapist should adopt a questioning attitude so as not to foster a recreational approach that unwittingly promotes deterioration rather than stimulation. It is critical that the recreation therapist provide this stimulation because physical and mental deterioration are fostered by inactivity and boredom.

Many older adults of today grew up in the Depression years that ascribed to the puritanical view that unless leisure was earned after work, it was undeserved, and therefore a source of guilt. The recreation leader should help older adults recognize and deal with the impact of the Puritanical work ethic on potential leisure satisfaction. Unfortunately, leaders have a tendency in their program planning to appeal to the work ethic, instead of encouraging a balanced work and leisure ethic. For instance, some leaders intentionally introduce a worklike, utilitarian quality into a recreational activity because they know it will attract participants (such as knitting for bazaars, baking for raffles).

There is often the tendency for persons to immediately take on a second career following retirement so as to avoid the prospect of confronting unscheduled free time and defining their leisure. This growing phenomenon points to the need for expanded leisure education programs for older adults. The recreation profession must educate the public to the attractiveness of leisure and retirement, so that it is something to anticipate rather than avoid.

Interest in pursuing new leisure interests may be accompanied by concern over the way "beginner classes" are taught. Older adults avoid recreation programs conducted by leaders who demonstrate low estimation of the elderly. The recreation leader needs to teach older adults in a manner that reflects respect for their years of life experience. An older adult pursuing an activity for the first time will resent being taught like a child instead of the novice he or she is.

Older adults may avoid senior recreation programs because their own negative views on aging cause them not to want to associate with their own peers. It is important for a recreation leader to be aware of this as a factor influencing attendance and involvement in age-segregated activities. The leader can help older adults alter these negative views by conducting open discussion of attitudes including values awareness exercises and individualized leisure counseling.

Approximately 5 percent of the nation's older adult population attend senior citizen centers. The demographics of women outliving men has resulted in a higher percentage of women attending centers than men.

The senior citizen center has not been fairly credited for the services it provides; instead it is projected as merely a place for bingo and cards. However, the senior citizen center is designed as a dynamic multipurpose center providing a variety of services including counseling, health services, recreational and educational programs, employment assistance, information and referral, nutrition, social action, tenant advocacy, and legal aid. The senior citizen center has been acknowledged by its participants as essential to the preservation of their mental, emotional, and physical health.

However, a major misconception pertaining to aging is the view that all older adults are lonely and in some dire need for socialization. Many recreation programs for older adults have been designed from this conceptual base and have resulted in a forced type of social recreation unresponsive to individual needs. Leisure satisfaction need not be derived from participation in social activities; many find enjoyment in home-based leisure.

Special Needs for Older Adults

Research indicates that the suicide rate for white males over 70 years of age is the highest of any age cohort; it is due, in large part, to social isolation, failing health, and depression. Recreation can play a role in helping to alleviate these conditions by providing opportunities for socialization and physical and mental stimulation.

In addition a growing number of older adults are partially or totally confined to their home. The need for home care will continue to rise as the number of older adults over the age of 85 is increasing at a higher rate of any other age group. A homebound individual is defined as one whose physical condition does not allow access to the community; unfortunately, of the approximate 13 percent of this nation's elderly who are homebound, many have unnecessarily assumed a homebound lifestyle due to ignorance of services, lack of transportation to services, or fear of crime occurring while going to and from services.

To provide the homebound with access to the stimulation of community recreation, recreation agencies have provided transportation assistance through such arrangements as agency vans, school buses, car pools, and transportation subsidies. Recreation agencies can help offset the fear of crime by providing more programs during daylight hours and in more localized areas, instituting crime prevention programs, and offering door-to-door transportation.

For those genuinely homebound due to physical limitations, the recreation agency can bring recreational materials to them. The addition of recreation to homebound services is a significant step since services were formerly limited to home repair, Meals on Wheels, shopping assistance, telephone reassurance, and so forth. Homebound recreation materials are individualized to clients' needs and include cassette tapes for correspondence with other homebound individuals, plants, crafts, music tapes, and so forth. Portable VCR units can provide the homebound with self-instructional tapes on recreational interests of their choice.

Approximately 5 percent of this nation's older adults live in nursing homes. Nursing homes fall within two categories: skilled nursing facilities (SNF) and intermediate care facilities (ICF) or health related facilities (HRF). As defined by the *Directory of Nursing Homes—A State by State Listing of Facilities and Services:*

> The skilled nursing facility is a facility that has been certified as meeting Federal standards within the meaning of the Social Security Act. It provides the level of care that comes closest to hospital care with 24-hour nursing services. Regular medical supervision and rehabilitative therapy are also provided. Generally, a skilled nursing facility cares for convalescent patients and those with long term illnesses.
>
> An intermediate care facility or health related facility is a certified facility that meets Federal standards and provides less expensive health related care and services. It has regular nursing service, but not around the clock. Most intermediate care facilities carry on rehabilitative programs with an emphasis on personal care and social services. Mainly, these homes serve people who are not fully capable of living by themselves, yet are not necessarily ill enough to need 24-hour nursing home care.[12]

Recreation is important to those who live in nursing homes since activities that encourage physical exercise and sensory stimulation may prevent further physical loss or mental deterioration. They also improve mental judgment and concentration while stimulating awareness of self, others, and environment. Sensory stimulation materials are easily created from available resources (for example, cloth books with textured pages, cloth pockets with manipulative items such as hooks and eyes, activity aprons that fit over wheelchairs and contain soft textures and fragrance bags). If residents appear restless or disoriented, it should not automatically be attributed to a physical cause, as it may in fact be due to a nonchallenging nursing home environment.

To reduce nursing home residents' feelings of isolation from the community, every effort should be made to bring the institution and community together. Community representatives can be invited to serve on the resident advisory council that contributes ideas for recreation programs.

Community field trips from the nursing home should be scheduled as much as possible. Resource people from the community should be invited into the facility as volunteer instructors and visitors. The nursing home facility can be made available to outside groups so as to facilitate interaction between residents and the townspeople. Families in the community can

12. Sam Mongeau, ed. *Directory of Nursing Homes—A State by State Listing of Facilities and Services* (Phoenix: Oryx Press, 1982), preface.

"adopt a grandparent" whereby they share their homes and lives with their surrogate grandparents whenever possible. The "real" families of the residents should be involved in the recreation program planning process, giving background on their relatives' prior recreational interests and receiving progress reports.

In her text *Leisure Activities for the Mature Adult,* Joan Moran outlines the following goals of recreation therapy in a nursing home:

1. To alleviate the resident's fears of loneliness, abandonment, and impending death.
2. To provide stimulation and pleasure.
3. To discourage potential tendencies of withdrawal by encouraging the residents to share activities and experiences with their peers in group situations, thus fostering a "we are not alone" feeling.
4. To reawaken the latent skills and interests of the resident, thus helping the person to revive normal life patterns.
5. To improve the resident's self-confidence and self-respect by encouraging him or her to communicate and function more effectively, thus lessening self-pity.
6. To help the resident feel a vital part of community life by bringing members of the community into the facility to entertain, instruct, and give volunteer service and by bringing the resident into the community whenever possible and feasible.
7. To encourage the resident's sense of responsibility toward others and demonstrate that the resident can still be a useful member of the community by providing opportunities to participate in civic projects.
8. To provide a variety of activities which permit the resident to be as alert and active as his or her individual physical, mental, and emotional health permit.
9. To help the resident function at optimal physical, emotional, and social level, thus maintaining or reattaining social and motor skills.
10. To assist the resident to achieve the most vital way of life commensurate with his or her abilities and disabilities.
11. To encourage residents toward individual and group enterprise and motivation.
12. To provide rehabilitation-oriented care on a short- or long-term basis to prevent further disability and to return the resident to a higher level of independent functioning in caring for individual needs and increasing the capability for independence.[13]

There is also another type of service provided to older adults. Many nursing homes and other service agencies sponsor day-care or respite programs that provide day programs to older adults while their caregivers, usually their middle-aged children, are at work or vacationing. The respite services include medical services, physical therapy, occupational therapy, nutrition, and recreation therapy. The day-care/respite program permits the older adult to be cared for at home rather than in an institution. Similar services are provided in hospice programs that are designed to care for the terminally ill in an atmosphere of dignity and comfort.

13. Joan Moran, *Leisure Activities for the Mature Adult* (Minneapolis: Burgess Publishing Co., 1979), p. 169.

Activity Analysis

The Program Organization phase incorporates use of activity analysis. In programming according to activity analysis, the recreation leader breaks each recreational activity down to its cognitive, psychomotor, and affective components. The individual's cognitive, psychomotor, and affective abilities are then matched against those of the activity to determine the activity's suitability for the individual. The *cognitive* domain refers to the mental/intellectual requirements of the activity; *psychomotor* refers to the physical/motor coordination requirements; and *affective* refers to the emotional/social demands.

Before programming an activity for an individual, it should be determined whether that individual has the coordination (psychomotor), intelligence (cognitive), and emotional maturity (affective) to engage in that activity. Since the recreational experience should be one of pleasure, it is important that participants are not referred to activities that are beyond their skill levels and therefore hold a potential for failure. Since activity analysis correlates individual skill levels with corresponding appropriate activities, the potential for success is maximized. Any deficiencies in cognitive, psychomotor, and affective skills can be specifically addressed by recommending activities that provide practice in those skills. For instance, if the individual reveals a weakness in directionality (a psychomotor skill referring to knowledge of left and right), the recreation leader can suggest recreational activities that develop directionality skills (such as drawing, folk dance, circle games).

Figure 3–4 indicates the types of competencies covered within the cognitive, psychomotor, and affective domains.

The cognitive, psychomotor, and affective domains do not exist in equal dominance within each given activity. For instance, an activity such as creative writing is high in the affective and cognitive domains because it revolves around emotional expression and intellectual reasoning. Should the creative writing be done within a group involving cooperation on a publication, the affective domain will be even more prominent due to the social interaction required. However, the psychomotor domain of creative writing activity is nonexistent.

Elliot M. Avedon in *Therapeutic Recreation Services* classifies the social interaction patterns within the affective domain as: intraindividual, extraindividual, aggregate, interindividual, unilateral, multilateral, intragroup, intergroup.[14] Definitions and examples follow:

LEVELS OF SOCIAL STRUCTURE:

1. *Intraindividual.* All the action is within person's own mind; person is an isolate.
     Example: daydreaming, meditation
2. *Extraindividual.* Person is involved with only an object.
     Example: working with clay

14. Elliot M. Avedon, *Therapeutic Recreation Service* (Englewood Cliffs, N.J.: Prentice-Hall, Inc., 1974) pp. 162–172.

FIGURE 3-4 Activity Analysis Rating Form

Activity: _____

Physical Aspects (Psychomotor)

1. What is the primary body position required?
   prone   kneeling   sitting   standing   other

2. What types of movement does the activity require?

bending _____	catching _____
stretching _____	throwing _____
standing _____	hitting _____
walking _____	skipping _____
reaching _____	hopping _____
grasping _____	running _____
punching _____	

3. What are the primary senses required for the activity?
   Rate: 0 = not at all; 1 = rarely; 2 = occasionally; 3 = often
   touch _____
   taste _____
   sight _____
   sound _____
   smell _____

4. Strength:
   Much strength   1   2   3   4   5   Little strength

5. Speed:
   Much speed   1   2   3   4   5   No speed

6. Endurance:
   Much endurance   1   2   3   4   5   Little endurance

7. Energy:
   Much energy   1   2   3   4   5   Little energy

8. Muscle Coordination:
   Much coordination   1   2   3   4   5   Little coordination

9. Hand-eye Coordination:
   Much hand-eye coordination   1   2   3   4   5   Little hand-eye coordination

10. Flexibility:
    Much flexibility   1   2   3   4   5   Little flexibility

11. Agility:
    Much agility   1   2   3   4   5   Little agility

12. How much of the body is involved?

_____ top half	_____ arms	_____ hands	_____ ears
_____ bottom half	_____ legs	_____ feet	_____ neck
	_____ torso	_____ eyes	
	_____ head	_____ mouth	

13. How much coordination of these parts is necessary?
    Much   1   2   3   4   5   Little
    Explain:

---

14. Rate degree of cardiovascular activity required.

Much
activity   1   2   3   4   5   Little
activity

15. Rate the degree of joint stress.

Much
stress   1   2   3   4   5   Little
stress

Social Aspects (Affective)

1. Interaction Pattern

   intraindividual _____
   extraindividual _____
   aggregate _____
   interindividual _____
   unilateral _____
   multilateral _____
   intragroup _____
   intergroup _____

2. How many primary participants does the activity demand? _____

3. Does the activity promote sexual homogeneity or heterogeneity? Explain:

4. Can everyone communicate with everyone else by nature of the activity?;
   Yes   No

5. What is the primary communication network?
   _____ 1 to 1
   _____ 1 to group
   _____ groups of 2–5
   _____ groups of 5–10
   _____ groups larger than 10

6. Does the activity demand that there be a leader in the group (does one person get most of the group focus)?
   Yes   No   Occasionally

7. Does the activity require cooperation or competition?
   Explain:

8. How much physical contact does the activity demand?

Much
physical
contact   1   2   3   4   5   Little
physical
contact

9. How closely spaced are the participants?

Close
together   1   2   3   4   5   Far
apart

10. What level of social relationship does the activity promote?

Intimate
relationship   1   2   3   4   5   Distant
relationship

11. How structured is the activity?

Highly
structured   1   2   3   4   5   Freely
structured

12. Type of interaction:

Verbal
communication   1   2   3   4   5   Nonverbal
communication

13. Inclusion-Exclusion

Inclusion   1   2   3   4   5   Exclusion

14.	Noise Level							
	High	1	2	3	4	5		Low
15.	Independence-Mimicry							
	Independence	1	2	3	4	5		Mimicry
16.	Independence							
	Independent	1	2	3	4	5		Dependent
17.	Inner-directed							
	Inner-directed	1	2	3	4	5		Outerdirected
18.	Rewards							
	Immediate	1	2	3	4	5		Delayed
19.	Maturity							
	Adult	1	2	3	4	5		Childish

Cognitive Aspects (Mental)

1. How complex are the rules which must be adhered to?

Complex	1	2	3	4	5		Simple

2. How much memory retention is necessary?

Much memory	1	2	3	4	5		Little memory

3. How much strategy does the activity require?

Much strategy	1	2	3	4	5		Little strategy

4. How much verbalization is required?

Much verbalization	1	2	3	4	5		Little verbalization

5. How much concentration is required?

Much concentration	1	2	3	4	5		Little concentration

6. How often are the following skills used?
   0 = never; 1 = rarely; 2 = occasionally; 3 = often
   Reading ————————————
   Writing ————————————
   Math ————————————
   Spelling ————————————

7. Skill required

Much skill	1	2	3	4	5		Chance

8. Rate the demands for the following identifications:

	Often				Never
Form and Shape	1	2	3	4	5
Colors	1	2	3	4	5
Size	1	2	3	4	5
Tactile	1	2	3	4	5
Objects	1	2	3	4	5
Classes	1	2	3	4	5
Numbers	1	2	3	4	5
Nonverbal Questions	1	2	3	4	5
Auditory Symbols	1	2	3	4	5

Visual Symbols	1	2	3	4	5
Concrete Thinking	1	2	3	4	5
Abstract Thinking	1	2	3	4	5
Body Parts	1	2	3	4	5

9. Check directionality required:
   Left/right _____
   Up/down _____
   Around _____
   Over/under _____
   Person/object _____
   Person/person _____
   Object/object _____

10. Complexity of scoring

Very Complex						Not Complex
	1	2	3	4	5	

Emotional Demands

1. Rate the opportunities for the expression of the following emotions during this activity.

	Often				Never
Joy	1	2	3	4	5
Guilt	1	2	3	4	5
Pain	1	2	3	4	5
Anger	1	2	3	4	5
Fear	1	2	3	4	5
Frustration	1	2	3	4	5

2. Rate the likely responses.

Success	1	2	3	4	5	Failure
Satisfaction	1	2	3	4	5	Dissatisfaction
Intrinsic reward	1	2	3	4	5	Extrinsic reward
Acceptance	1	2	3	4	5	Rejection
Confidence	1	2	3	4	5	Inferiority
Excitement	1	2	3	4	5	Apathy
Cooperation	1	2	3	4	5	Defiance
Patience	1	2	3	4	5	Impatience
Manipulation	1	2	3	4	5	Nonmanipulation
Awareness of others	1	2	3	4	5	Awareness of self

Administrative Aspects

LEADERSHIP: Minimum _____ Maximum _____
EQUIPMENT: None_____ Required _____
DURATION: Set Time _____ Natural End_____
Continuous _____
FACILITIES: None _____Required _____
PARTICIPANTS: Fixed Number or Multiple_____
Any Number _____
COMMENTS:

Source: Scout Lee Gunn and Carol Ann Peterson, *Therapeutic Recreation Program Design: Principles and Procedures* (Englewood Cliffs, NJ: Prentice-Hall, 1978), pp. 174–179. Reprinted by permission.

3. *Aggregate activity.* People are involved in the same extraindividual activity (everyone is together doing the same thing). Doesn't necessarily precipitate social interaction.

   Example: pottery class, exercise class

4. *Interindividual.* Persons involved one-on-one but don't have to communicate.

   Example: dual sport, chess

5. *Unilateral.* Attention is focused on one person.

   Example: dodgeball, tag

6. *Multilateral.* Activities of a competitive nature involving three or more people.

   Example: golf game, pinochle card game

7. *Intragroup.* Cooperative activity within a group.

   Example: group singing, pageant, drama

8. *Intergroup.* Two groups who have to cooperate within their groups to compete against the other group

   Example: football team, play competition

ACTIVITIES ARE SELECTED ON THE BASIS OF:

1. *Object tie.* Activities revolve around one object (water skiing, swimming, boating would revolve around water).

2. *Transference.* Activities allow us to transfer our feelings from one situation into the playing of the game (transfer hostility toward person to racquetball).

3. *Identification.* Activities are associated with a "people tie"; a person engages in an activity in order to associate with certain people (jog because it's popular with the local crowd and not because the person wants to). We associate certain classes or groups with different activities, often stereotypically (for example, shuffleboard is identified with older adults).

DIFFERENT TYPES OF EMOTIONAL MEANING DERIVED:

1. *Active games of anger/hostility/aggression.* These emotions are socially acceptable within the game structure.

   A. Anger taken out on object (golf ball, piano, clay)

   B. Anger taken out on another person's property (marbles, shuffleboard)

   C. Aggression released by propelling object toward person (racquetball, badminton)

   D. Aggression released by hitting person directly with object (dodgeball)

   E. Aggression released by body-to-body hitting (football, judo).

2. *Quiet games of anger.* The play provides aggressive conflict.

   A. Example of chess game: two warring armies. King represents male authority figure, bishop represents religion, the pawn represents the underdog, etc. Player may be revealing his/her antagonism toward the church if he or she always tries to beat the bishop. If he or she uses the pawn to beat the bishop consistently, this may reflect an identification with the underdog.

   B. Example of card game: poker involves outmaneuvering, bluffing. Some might not like bridge because they like to be independent in their strategies, while others might like partner games that allow them to project failure on another.

   C. Example of board game: monopoly urges you to aggressively build up an empire by reducing everyone else to poverty. War games like Blitzkrieg involve the annihilation of the opponent.

3. *Activities of a sadistic or destructive nature.*

   Examples: hunting, fishing, demolition derbies, pie in the face

4. *Activities of dominance and control.* Activities when we feel as we are in control. (These can overlap with other group categories, such as those mentioned in categories 1–3.)

   A. Examples: paragliding, tobogganing, gymnastics

   B. May have high risk involved (mountain climbing, cliff diving)

   C. May even be a form of a death wish (trapeze, parachuting).

5. *Activities of erotic/sensual pleasure.* Sublimated psychological way of satisfying sexual urges. Can also involve dominance and control.

   Examples: dancing, water sports, ballet, gymnastics

6. *Activities that allow us to express repressed feelings through identification.* Enable us to see ourselves or what we would like to be ourselves.

   Examples: Identify with characters and situations in plays, movies, books, TV. Identify with winners and role models in spectator sports, political campaigns.

7. *Constructive/life-extending urges.* Activities that will produce a product that will be lasting in our lifetime.

   Examples: gardening, writing, art, music composition, crafts

8. *Activities of a regressive nature.* Allow one to go back to a simpler lifestyle, as in childhood.

   A. Camping allows participant to regress in a social structure back to a simpler way of life.

   B. Spinning wool or whittling involve getting back to earlier, basic practices.

   C. Informal dramatics allow the participant to freely return to youthful state of imaginative play.

9. *Activities that allow us to express subordinated psychological/sex characteristics.* Activities that break traditional stereotypes but usually in a subtler, more socially acceptable way.

   Examples: Boy plays with a doll, but often within the context of a GI Joe character. Boy cooks but in a rugged camping situation. There is a need to go beyond the security of socially approved contexts and freely offer equal programming. (Girls take auto mechanics, boys learn to sew, etc.)

10. *Activities that allow us to deny reality.* Activities that allow us to get outside our own selves and our own situations.

    Examples: acting, "Clue," storytelling, music listening.

Figure 3–5 is an activity analysis worksheet format developed by Farrell and Lundegren in *The Process of Recreation Programming—Theory and Technique.*

Behavioral Objectives

The program planner demonstrates thoroughness and professionalism in program organization by individualizing behavioral objectives for participants. A *behavioral objective* refers to the behavior, skill, or insight the participant is expected to demonstrate following exposure to the program

FIGURE 3-5 Activity Analysis Worksheet

```
ACTIVITY:                                    Throwing a pot (ceramics)
BEHAVIORAL DOMAINS:   1. (Primary)                    Psychomotor
                         SKILL LEVEL:                                      X
                                      Low                              High
                                      Working the pot with the hands,
                         NATURE OF SKILL: wheel with foot
                      2. (Secondary)                   Cognitive
                         SKILL LEVEL:                      X
                                      Low                              High
                                      Planning pot design, processing
                         NATURE OF SKILL: steps in the procedure
                      3. (Tertiary)                    Affective
                         SKILL LEVEL:                      X
                                      Low                              High
                         NATURE OF SKILL:  Expression of self in pot


INTERACTION PATTERNS:
                X        X
```

Intra-individual	Extra-individual	Aggre-gate	Inter-individual	Uni-lateral	Multi-lateral	Intra-group	Inter-group

```
LEADERSHIP:            X

              Minimum                                        Maximum
EQUIPMENT:                                                      X

              None                                            Required
DURATION:                                X

              Set Time                 Natural End           Continuous
FACILITIES:                                                     X

              None                                            Required
PARTICIPANTS:                    Alone

              Fixed Number of Multiple                     Any Number
AGE:                     Any

COMMENTS:
```

Source: Patricia Farrell and Herbeta M. Lundegren, *The Process of Recreation Programming—Theory and Technique*, 2nd ed. (New York: John Wiley and Sons, 1983), p. 73.

activity. The establishment of behavioral objectives assures that the individual's personal goals for participation in that activity are considered and encouraged.

A behavioral objective includes:

1. Statement of the *behavior* to be attained
2. *Condition* under which to achieve the behavior (for example, time, space)
3. *Criteria* used to determine if behavior was attained.

An example of a behavioral objective is:

Program Planning—Principles and Practices   93

(Behavior) The participant will demonstrate mastery of folk dance steps
(Criteria) by carrying out the following dance steps as called out by the dance leader:

one-step	heel-toe polka
two-step	mazurka
polka	schottische
step hop	

(Condition) by the end of two dance sessions with no errors.

It should be clarified that a program objective and a behavioral objective are not the same. A program objective states what the *program* aims to accomplish while the behavioral objective states in measurable terms what the *participant* should be able to demonstrate through involvement in the program. For instance, a program objective for a youth drama program could be "to develop group cooperation skills among the participants through their participation in drama."

A behavioral objective for a participant in this drama group would have to indicate in measurable terms how the attainment of group cooperation skills could be demonstrated. Such a behavioral objective might read:

(Behavior) The youth will demonstrate group cooperation skills through drama
(Criteria) by creating and presenting an improvised, unrehearsed skit with three other class members
(Condition) within a 30-minute time period during the third drama class session.

PROGRAM IMPLEMENTATION

It is in the actual implementation of the program that all of the initial surveying, goal-setting, and organizing prove their worth. In carrying out a program, the recreation professional can adapt it to any one of a number of program formats. These include the following formats.

Drop-in. There is no leadership of organized activities. Physical resources are provided for participant's recreational use. Activity is primarily self-directed with personnel serving as resources. Equipment and materials may have to be brought by the participant. The drop-in format allows the individual to pick up an activity at any time, fostering independent leisure skills rather than program dependence. The drop-in format fits in with the variability of people's available free time. Its self-paced quality permits exploration at one's own tempo. (Examples are: ceramics studio, playground apparatus for child's free play, music headphones in rehabilitation center lounge.)

Class. Emphasis is on instruction, with the leader the primary teaching agent. Should a group be interested in the same subject, the class format is an economical way of delivering the same information to all simultaneously. Reinforcement and correction are possible in the class format. (Example: gymnastics class)

Workshop. Like the class, the emphasis is on instruction. However, the workshop is usually more casual and participatory than a class. It also focuses on more specialized topics than a class for shorter periods of time. (Example: puppetry workshop)

Club. The activity is pursued in the context of a mutual interest group. The general interest club is composed of members who join out of a commonality in social needs (such as age, sex, ethnicity, religion). The special interest club, on the other hand, is composed of members who join out of a commonality in subject interest (for example, cooking club, book review club). For more information on clubs, see Chapter 2.

Special event. The special event is a novelty program that stands out from the regularly scheduled activities. It is a "one-shot event" which can be a showcase, a culminating activity to a class or season, a civic celebration, or any other event that is broad in scope. Special events offer ideal opportunities for integrating program areas in thematic events. Information on special events and their organization can be found in Chapter 11.

Outreach. Outreach refers to programs brought to the people in their environment as opposed to a "facility-oriented" approach. The outreach program is designed in response to community input and environmental factors. Outreach efforts are achieved through such approaches as mobile recreation units and "roving leaders."

Competition. A competitive element is present in the activity. Competition can be against others (such as oratory contests) or the environment (competing against the elements as in white-water rafting). If organized as a contest, participants compete without interfering with each other's performance (for example, a singing contest, dart-throwing contest). In a game, however, there is direct contact with other competitors (such as a basketball game, hockey game). Contests and games can be organized as meets, leagues, or tournaments. In a meet, the player earns points for performance, the winner being the highest point scorer; individual scores can also be totalled for a combined team score. The league format involves each participant or team in an equal number of competitions against the other contestants. The winning team or individual is the one with the greatest number of points or winning competitions. The league format is often used in team sports.

Adapting the Program to a Format

Depending on the needs and interests of the group participating, a given program activity can be adapted to any of these formats: drop-in;

class; workshop; club; special event; outreach; competition. For the purpose of illustration, the program activity area square dancing will be discussed:

1. Dance hall and record player can be made available for *drop-in* use by square dancers.
2. Square dancing can be offered as a *class*.
3. A short-term square dancing *workshop* can be offered.
4. A square dancing *club* can be formed.
5. Square dancing can be highlighted in a "Wild West" *special event*.
6. Square dancing demonstrations can be brought to the shopping malls as a form of *outreach*.
7. A square dancing *contest* can be organized.

Figure 3–6 further illustrates how the various program activity areas can be adapted to these seven program formats.

Competition: Tournaments

One of the most important and popular program formats is competition. Since the success of competitive play is often dependent on the recreation leader's ability to organize tournaments, a specialized skill, this section is devoted to the structure and leadership of tournaments. To correct the general misconception that tournaments apply only to athletic events, it should be noted from the outset of this section that the tournament format is appropriate to any recreation activity—be it bridge or debates, pool or scrabble.

Seeding. To insure that all participants have fair advantage, the process of seeding is recommended. In seeding, the best individuals or teams are bracketed so that they will not eliminate each other early in the tournament. The judgment for seeding is based on the player's proven ability as revealed in previous play. Such an objective determination of seeding is preferable to any subjective judgment on the part of the recreation leader.

A minimum of two contestants is advised for seeding in a tournament of eight entrants, three for a tournament of 12, and four for 16. For recreational purposes, a maximum of four seeded entries is recommended. Caution should be exercised to place them well apart. For example, if there are but two seeded entries, place one at the top and the other at the bottom of the first-round bracketing; third and fourth seeded entries are to be inserted in the second and third quarters of the first round and so on depending on the number of entries to be seeded. On the basis of the eleven-entry tournament shown on page 100, entrants 1, 6, and 11 would be the seeded entrants.

Types of Tournaments

The most widely used tournament formats are the round robin, elimination, double elimination, ladder, and pyramid. Each will be discussed in this section, with attention being given to the strengths and weaknesses of each. The major factors in selecting the type of tournament to use are the number of participants and the availability of time, leadership, facilities, officials, and equipment. There is no set length for a tournament; depending on the activity's components and purpose, the tournament may consist of a summer-long league or an afternoon contest.

Round robin. One of the fairest and most highly recommended tournament systems is the round robin. It should be used at every possible opportunity so long as time and facilities permit. In the event the round robin tournament has so many entries as to warrant a division into leagues, the winner of each league can play off via an elimination tournament. Percentage is secured by dividing the number of games won by the number of games played.

$$\text{Percentage} = \frac{\text{Number of Games Won}}{\text{Number of Games Played}}$$

The number of games to be played is arrived at as follows: Number of games to be played = N(N-1)/2 (N = number of teams entered).

The advantages of the round robin tournament are: (1) Each team or individual has a chance to compete against every other. (2) It assures a maximum amount of play for all entrants. (3) If time permits, it can be run through more than once while sustaining interest. (4) Regardless of whether a team is strong or weak, it is given the opportunity of playing through to the end of the tournament. This is especially valuable for the weak ones who need the play even more than the others. (5) Interest in the tournament is upheld until its end. It is perhaps the most satisfactory of all tournaments.

The disadvantages are: (1) For effectiveness, it is restricted to a minimum of four and a maximum of ten entrants. For a greater number of entrants, dividing the team into leagues is recommended. (2) A greater amount of time and space is required for the larger schedule of this tournament as compared to the elimination tournament, for example.

Round robin tournaments may be conducted by the use of either the numerical or the square technique. In the numerical technique, as is demonstrated as follows, with an even number of entrants (six), each team or individual is given a number. The numbers follow each other as shown under #1 of the first diagram. In arranging #2, the numeral opposite 1 under #1 (in this case 6) is inserted in the vertical listing after which the nu-

FIGURE 3-6 Adapting Activities to Program Formats

PROGRAM AREAS	CLASS	COMPETITIVE	CLUB	DROP IN	SPECIAL EVENT	OUTREACH	WORKSHOP/ CONFERENCE
Visual Arts	Drawing Class	Pottery Contest	Miniatures Whittling Club	Visit to Art Museum	Art in the Park	Craft Sale at Residence for Elderly	Conference Teachers of China Painting
New Arts	Photography Class	Film Festival	Radio Club	Photography Lab	Computer Art Display	Photography on Display in Mall	Conference on Television as Art Form
Performing Arts (Dance)	Tap Dance Class	Dance Marathon for Charity	Square Dance Club	Juke-box Music for Dancing	Black Dance Troupe Concert	Teen Dance at a Shopping Parking Lot	Workshop on Ethnic Dancing
Performing Arts (Drama)	Puppet Class	Debate Contest	Dinner Theater Group—once a month	Costume Design Shop	Community Theater Production	Shakespeare in the Park	Creative Dramatics for Children
Performing Arts (Music)	Guitar Lessons	Battle of the Bands	Older Adults Kazoo Band	Classical Music Listening	Barbershop Concert	Christmas Caroling	Master's Workshop
Literary	Spanish Lessons	Topical Debate	Current Book Club	Library Reading Room	Rare Book Exhibit	Bookmobile	Workshop on the Works of Shakespeare

Sports, Games, and Athletics	Beginning Swimming Class	10-Mile Swim (in indoor pool)	Junior Lifesaving Club	Open Swimming for Families	County-wide Swim Meet	Mobile Swimming Pool	Workshop for Recreation Club Coaches
Outdoor Recreation	Orienteering Class	Cross Country Obstacle Ski Run	Gardening Club	Picnics	Winter Carnival	Day Camp	Family Conference on Boat Safety
Hobbies	How to Get Started on a Hobby	Matchbook Collectors Contest	Electric Train Owners Club	Hobby Shop Slot Car Racing	Hobbyists Trade Show and Sale	Mobile Display of Stamps and Coins	How to Know the Value of Book Workshop
Travel	Reading Topography Maps	Sports Car Rally	Antique Car Club	Sightseeing	Driving Along the Autumn Trail	Travelogs	How to See Europe by Train (workshop)
Social Recreation	Quilting Tips for Beginners	Pie Eating Contest	Saturday Group	Conversation	Progressive Dinner	Friendly Visitors	Bridge Club Workshop
Voluntary Service	Orientation to Working with Children	Taking a Sports Team to Play at Corrections Institution	Candy Stripers	Tutoring for Students	Recognition Dinner for Volunteers	Reading to Visually Impaired in Their Homes	Role of Volunteers in the Community Conference

Source: Christopher R. Edginton, David M. Compton, and Carole J. Hanson, *Recreation and Leisure Programming: A Guide for the Professional* (Philadelphia: Saunders Co., 1980), pp. 174–175.

merical sequence is followed. The same procedure is followed under #3, #4, and #5. Each team plays the team opposite it in the listing.

#1	#2	#3	#4	#5
1_76	1_75	1_74	1_73	1_72
2–5	6–4	5–3	4–2	3–6
3–4	2–3	6–2	5–6	4–5

To further exemplify this technique, an odd number of entrants is used. Herein, the letter B designates a bye. Otherwise, the procedure is the same as that demonstrated for six teams or, for that matter, for any number of entrants.

#1	#2	#3	#4	#5	#6	#7	#8	#9	#10	#11
1_7B	1_711	1_710	1_79	1_78	1_77	1_76	1_75	1_74	1_73	1_72
2–11	B–10	11–9	10–8	9–7	8–6	7–5	6–4	5–3	4–2	3–B
3–10	2–9	B–8	11–7	10–6	9–5	8–4	7–3	6–2	5–B	4–11
4–9	3–8	2–7	B–6	11–5	10–4	9–3	8–2	7–B	6–11	5–10
5–8	4–7	3–6	2–5	B–4	11–3	10–2	9–B	8–11	7–10	6–9
6–7	5–6	4–5	3–4	2–3	B–2	11–B	10–11	9–10	8–9	7–8

In the square technique (Figure 3–7) the letters denote the dates and each number signifies a different player or team. An X is placed where the horizontal and vertical boxes of a team or entrant meet. Starting with the second box of the horizontal row number 1, place the letter B and follow with the consecutive alphabet letters. The omitted letter A is placed under 12 since the letter X occupies its place. The last vertical row must be considered as the next consecutive regardless of the letter that appears in the space. Horizontal rows 1 and 2 illustrate the point as do the others.

Letter B is placed at the start of horizontal row 2. Since an X intercedes, the letter C which is displaced by the X is placed at the end of the row while D follows the X and so on. This procedure is retained right through horizontal row 11. The letters of vertical row 12 are placed on horizontal row 12. The completed square contains the complete schedule in codified form and ready for a double round robin. Let's imagine that letter A stands for July 1, B for July 3, and C for July 5. The sample listing in Figure 3–8 exemplifies how it can be worked out and listed.

The leader can graphically illustrate the standing of each team by placing a green color in the entrant's (horizontal) row when he or she wins and a red color in the same row when he or she loses. The second phase of the round robin can be illustrated by coloring the boxes below the X's similarly.

Use the same number of squares as there are teams entered. For an odd number of entries, add one vertical row. Follow the aforementioned procedure out to the last box. The last row indicates the dates during which a bye takes place.

	1	2	3	4	5	6	7	8	9	10	11	12
1	X	B	C	D	E	F	G	H	I	J	K	A
2	B	X	D	E	F	G	H	I	J	K	A	C
3	C	D	X	F	G	H	I	J	K	A	B	E
4	D	E	F	X	H	I	J	K	A	B	C	G
5	E	F	G	H	X	J	K	A	B	C	D	I
6	F	G	H	I	J	X	A	B	C	D	E	K
7	G	H	I	J	K	A	X	C	D	E	F	B
8	H	I	J	K	A	B	C	X	E	F	G	D
9	I	J	K	A	B	C	D	E	X	G	H	F
10	J	K	A	B	C	D	E	F	G	X	I	H
11	K	A	B	C	D	E	F	G	H	I	X	J
12	A	C	E	G	I	K	A	B	F	H	J	X

FIGURE 3-7

Sample Listing

Date	Teams	Scores	Teams	Scores
	1 vs. 12		4 vs. 9	
July 1	2 vs. 11		5 vs. 8	
	3 vs. 10		6 vs. 7	
	1 vs. 2		3 vs. 5	
July 3	3 vs. 11		6 vs. 8	
	4 vs. 10		7 vs. 12	
	1 vs. 3		5 vs. 10	
July 5	2 vs. 12		3 vs. 6	
	4 vs. 11		7 vs. 8	

Teams & Numbers

1. Browns
2. Cardinals
3. White Sox
4. Dodgers
5. Pirates
6. Cubs
7. Yankees
8. Red Sox
9. Giants
10. Indians
11. Phillies
12. Braves

FIGURE 3-8

Elimination. This tournament is not as popular as the round robin. Its disadvantages are: (1) The weak player who needs the play most is usually eliminated by the end of the first round. (2) One half of the players are eliminated after the first contest. (3) It fails to sustain interest, especially among those who are dropped. Nevertheless, this form of tournament does have advantages. (1) It is the fastest type of tournament to conduct and lends itself to play of short duration. (2) Less demand is made on the facilities. (3) It is relatively simple to administer.

Four types of the elimination tournament will be considered here: the single elimination, the standard consolation, the Bagwell-Wild version, and the double elimination.

In the single elimination (Figure 3–9) the number of games played is one less than the number of entries: $N-1$. A power of 2 is necessary in drawing this form of tournament. Assuming that eleven teams are entered in the tournament, the difference between the next higher power of 2 (2, 4, 8, 16) which is 16 and 11 yields five byes (do not play in first round). When there is an odd number of byes, in this case five, three are placed in the bottom half and two in the top half. Figure 3–9 illustrates how a single elimination with eleven entries is bracketed. As shown, all byes are taken care of in the first round with byes inserted at both ends. In this manner, a power of 2 is achieved going into the second round. When there is no seeding of players, the entries are placed in a hat and drawn to decide objectively where each entrant is to be placed. Should there be seeded players, the remaining entrants are to be placed on the basis of a drawing.

In the standard consolation (Figure 3–10) those who have lost out in the first round play-off the consolation phase. They are thus assured at least two contests. The defeated finalist is the winner of second place while the consolation winner takes third place.

Basically, the consolation tournament is a weak tournament. Dynamic leadership is required to sustain interest in the consolation portion. The single elimination or the double elimination (see Figure 3–11) are preferred. The double elimination (Figure 3–11) represents an attempt to keep from eliminating an entrant after one defeat; it takes two defeats to eliminate in this tournament. It is rarely used unless there are eight or fewer entries in the tournament.

The lowest bracketing can be explained best with the reminder that an entry is defeated as soon as two contests are lost. Since 3 has lost but one contest (to 7) she is eligible for another game. In this one, 3 is victorious and thereby wins the championship.

The Bagnell-Wild version (Figure 3–12) facilitates the selection of second and third places. However, it possesses the weakness of not permitting the start of play for the second and third places until the first-place winner is cleared. The illustration of the 11-entry elimination tournament diagrammed in Figure 3–12 is used again to show this adaptation.

As you will note in Figure 3–12 the single elimination is completed to arrive at the first-place winner. To decide the second-place winner, all de-

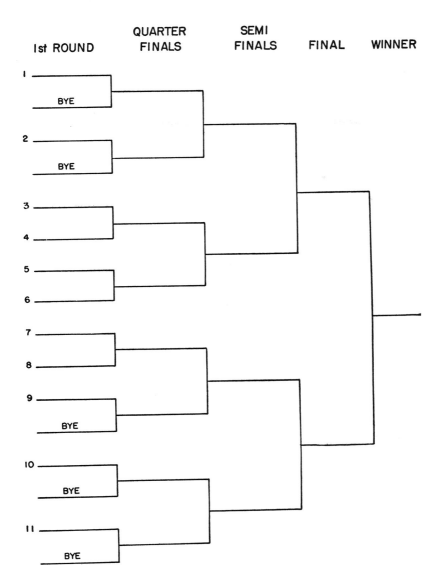

FIGURE 3-9

feated by the winner prior to the final round play each other in an elimination play-off. The loser in the finals (10) plays the winner of this elimination play-off to decide the second-place winner. The third place can be decided as follows: (1) When the entry that lost in the finals (10) of the single elimination is defeated in the second-place play-off she becomes the third-place winner; (2) Should she win second place, all who lost to her during the single elimination engage in a play-off. The winner of this phase plays the loser of the second-place finals to become the third-place winner.

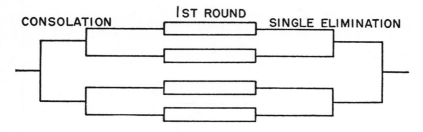

CONSOLATION   1ST ROUND   SINGLE ELIMINATION

FIGURE 3-10

Since Figure 3–12 shows no. 10 to have won second place, then all those she defeated in the single elimination (11 and 9) play one another, with the winner (9) opposing for third place the defeated finalist for second place (2).

Perpetual tournaments. The starting position in the ladder and pyramid tournaments (Figure 3–13) is decided by a draw. Starting and closing dates should be announced in advance. In the ladder tournament, the player is permitted to challenge either of the two directly above him. If it is a play area where the participants are there so seldom as to delay the tournament's progress, the leader may extend the challenge rights to any three above the challenger. Under the pyramid tournament, the contestant can challenge any one on the line above him. In both types, the challenger who wins exchanges places with the loser above him. The pyramid lends itself to more entries and more extensive challenging. Since fatigue may be a factor in one's defeat, the leader should limit the number of challenges that may be directed against anyone during a 24-hour period: restricting the number of challenges will be needed especially as the closing date approaches.

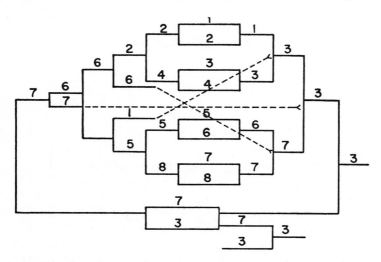

FIGURE 3-11

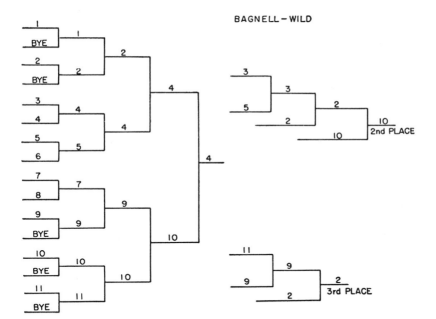

FIGURE 3-12

Tournament Leadership

The capable recreation leader will arrange and administer a tournament in way that reduces possible conflicts. Coordination of the tournament with other community agencies can result in improved community relations beyond the success of the tournament itself.

Organization of a tournament incorporates a number of important factors that will be discussed here.

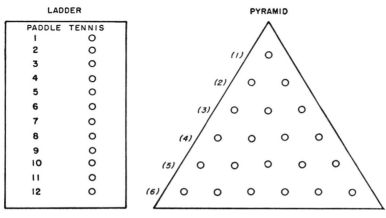

FIGURE 3-13

Selection of tournament dates. To insure probability of success, dates should be selected early and publicized thoroughly. (See next section on Program Promotion). The recreation leader can decide on a registration period sufficiently long to permit maximum enrollment in the tournament approximately 2 weeks prior to the start of play. Every effort should be made to adhere to the closing date selected for all entries. By the same token, the date established for the start of the tournament should be honored. The uncertainty created by changing dates does much to mar the effectiveness of a tournament. Holidays and other time conflicts should be anticipated in establishing dates for registration, closing entries, and tournament play. It is understood that the establishment of official dates is dependent on the advanced procurement of the necessary facilities and equipment to conduct the tournament.

Establishment of tournament policies and procedures. Participants should be placed in tournament play according to classifications appropriate to the tournament activity. Dependent on the activity's requirements, key factors to consider in placement may be age, mental activity, physical skills, height, weight, and so forth.

A major objective in organizing a tournament is to stimulate interest in the given recreation activity. Therefore, the tournament's eligibility rules should be few in number and simply stated. A rule should not be established unless it will be enforced consistently. Players should be advised that adherence to game rules and good sportsmanship are required.

Failure to report for play at the scheduled time should result in a loss of the game by forfeiture to the individual(s) or team(s) that did appear. In the event that all of the individuals or teams involved are late, the recreation leader may decide to permit them to play a shorter version of the game, providing it does not overlap with the playing of the regulation game scheduled.

Postponements should be viewed as a last resort in the scheme of tournament play. In the event of outdoor tournament play, poor weather conditions often necessitate a postponement. A period of time during the week can be set aside for the playing of postponed contests, or time can be tacked onto the end of the tournament. In the meantime, the tournament proceeds as scheduled, in the understanding that the postponed games will be integrated into the schedule.

If an eligibility fee has been charged to contestants to cover costs of personnel, prizes, and equipment or facility rental, all fees would be refunded in the event of tournament cancellation.

Recruitment of tournament personnel. It is advisable that the recreation leader solicits officials, referees, timekeepers, and scorekeepers as needed and does not attempt to cover any aspect of these areas personally; the recreation leader is needed to supervise the overall tournament program. The recreation leader should obtain medical personnel for those tournaments that require a preliminary physical exam and possible first aid responses during tournament play. An appeals committee should be established to rule on disputes and appealed decisions during tournament play. In relation to the appeals committee, the recreation leader serves ex-officio in a nonvoting capacity.

PROGRAM PROMOTION

No program, no matter how exemplary, can succeed unless the public is familiarized with it. Therefore, the program promotion process is critical to the full realization of program goals. Program promotion communicates the agency's services to the public in a creative, consistent manner. This portion of the program planning chapter will discuss the dynamics of program promotion.

Terms Defined

Public relations is the means by which the public perceives the agency's aims and objectives. Publicity, in turn, consists of the specific media techniques used in public relations. Promotion techniques cover the wide range of activities used to inform the public of the program (such as news, advertising, stunts.)

A good public relations program uses a combination of fundamental and routine publicity. Fundamental publicity gives interpretive reporting of the values of the program while routine publicity reports the routine facts surrounding a program. Examples of fundamental publicity might include an editorial on the need for more city parks or a human interest story on the effect of a music therapy program on local nursing home residents. Routine publicity, on the other hand, might include a news release on the new community center hours or a 60-second radio public service announcement on discount rates at the commercial bowling alley.

The public relations program of a leisure services agency is guided by a number of major aims. Jay Shivers in *Essentials in Recreation Services* outlines these aims to:

1. Develop public appreciation of recreational service.
2. Expose people to a wider variety of possible recreational experiences.
3. Disseminate information about the recreational system and develop knowledge and understanding of department functions.
4. Encourage genuine good public relations between the citizens and their department.
5. Modify negative attitudes and opinions which adversely affect the department.
6. Suggest a more precise survey and analysis of the community in order to determine needs and resources wherein the recreational agency can assume a more vital and rightful role.

7. Cooperate and coordinate activities with all other recreational organizations within the community to provide total community service.

8. Foster a definite desire on the part of employed personnel to understand the work of the department and effect better relations and closer contact with the public.

9. Clearly define the economic support necessary if the public system is to be enabled to carry out its ethical mandate.

10. Justify the necessity for the construction and maintenance of additional recreational facilities and areas in order to meet community needs.

11. Stimulate participation of citizens in utilizing existing facilities and areas and in taking part in planned recreational activities.

12. Remove political patronage from the public department.

13. Clarify and explain professional personnel standards in terms of more effective recreational offerings promoted in the safest manner.

14. Publicly explain the position of the recreational service system as the chief source of skilled and continuous provision of recreational experiences so that it may be widely understood that this service is available to the community.

15. Encourage volunteers to offer their time, talents, and skill in broadening recreational opportunities.

16. Avoid competition for the same participants among all agencies offering recreational opportunities in the community.

17. Promote voluntary contributions, endowments, gifts, and bequests.

18. Discover and list every segment of the public which may be of significance in shaping opinion favorable to the agency.

19. Encourage private citizens to consult the agency for information and program resources in seeking personal nonprogrammed recreational experiences.

20. Improve the relations between agency and mass media for a more valid and sympathetic presentation of departmental practices and policies.[15]

Outline of the Principles and Practices of Program Promotion

PROMOTIONAL BASICS

Know your product and your consumer—are you appealing to parents, councilpeople.

What are the community's customs, history, tastes, and economic, social, political, and religious outlooks? (For example, certain communities would not be receptive to belly dancing.)

Develop publicity plans a year ahead. Have a timetable based on all of your departments' programs. This will help on the advance budgeting of quality publicity.

Use a variety of media.

Ask yourself:

1. What are the objectives of the publicity?
2. What media will be used?
3. What money will be used?
4. What background and source material is needed?

15. Jay Shivers, *Essentials in Recreation Services* (Philadelphia: Lea and Febiger, 1978), p. 293.

5. How will the publicity plans be affected by agency policies and procedures, by interagency relationships?
6. How will the publicity be timed?
7. Is the plan feasible enough to meet emergencies?

Your publicity should show the deliverer and consumer of the service (for example, a picture showing a gymnastic coach assisting young gymnasts on the balance beam or an article containing quotes by a Recreation Department administrator and town participants).

Have a theme and logo. Keep it simple. A logo is a visual symbol that represents the organization (geometric designs, organic objects, animate or inanimate objects). A logo can be put on stationery, business cards, flyers, brochures, posters, press releases, forms, annual reports , novelty items, T-shirts, organizational vehicles, signs, uniforms.

Points to consider:

1. Aim your publicity at special groups for special purposes but don't miss the chance to do broad appeals occasionally.
2. Have your publicity reflect a wide range of recreational activities (make sure you do not just concentrate on the sports page).
3. "Piggy-back" on other community events to promote the recreation program. (For example, if a general topic of community concern is school construction, document the possible usages of the facility for recreation programs to achieve a community school concept.)
4. In your publicity, don't verbalize. Be direct. Call for action. Use direct phrases such as: "Send in coupon for course discount." "Contact us for information on our theater season.")
5. Your staff, programs, and participants are your best public relations.
6. The public should be involved in the design of your public relations (it allows you to discover their perceptions of what you're doing and make necessary modifications in your approaches).
7. Have one person in charge of publicity to eliminate departmental overlap.

ADVERTISING—ADVERTISING IS A PAID MESSAGE.

1. Direct action advertising encourages the individual to act immediately on the advertised information (for example, sign up now for judo lessons).
2. Indirect action advertising tries to create long-term interest in a service (that is, cites availability of services and programs on a long-term basis, advertising general facilities and classes).

Advertising includes: headline; illustration (photo); body copy; signature or logo.

CENTRAL IDEAS IN ADVERTISING

1. Bandwagon Approach: Appeals to desire to be part of the "in" crowd (for example: "Don't be a loner—come join the crowd and learn this new recreational activity").
2. Testimonials: Use locally or nationally well-known individuals to endorse the values of your program through pictures, word, or voice.

Two types are:

   a. direct endorsement—a direct quote or verbal commitment;

   b. indirect endorsement—a photo of a person engaged in an activity or using the facility.

3. Analogy and Association: This type of advertising implies by association that participation in the program will be beneficial (for example, a picture of a healthy, happy person engaged in a tennis program suggests that program produces fitness and fun).

4. Case Histories and Slice of Life: Show people in "real life" situations participating in your program (for example, a "man on the street" participating in a crafts class).

5. Service Uses: Show participants engaged in the activity or using the facility.

STATIONARY ADVERTISING

This includes: bulletin boards, posters, billboards, signs (including street signs).

Develop a permanent list of sites that will accept your posters and announcements.

Use these techniques for getting attention:

1. Display—two-dimensional inanimate objects;

2. Exhibit—three-dimensional objects (such as, schematic display of resort layout);

3. Demonstration—people demonstrating your program in action (for example, a gymnastics demonstration).

Determine:

1. How to adjust exhibits, traffic flow, etc.,

2. How much information to give within certain amount of time,

3. What kind of reaction do you want.

BROCHURES

A brochure is a printed work bound together to highlight programs, areas, facilities, and activities or present information that enables people to seek out desired leisure experiences.

Brochures come in all sizes, colors, shapes, and designs; they should be instructive and eye-catching and informative.

Points to Consider:

1. Brochure Content: What is the purpose of the brochure? to promote an activity? a set of activities? to disseminate information concerning other recreation and leisure opportunities? For example, a brochure promoting activities will include a description of the activity, its cost, the time of the activity, its location, its instructor. It may also contain application forms.

2. Brochure Timing: What timing will insure maximum visibility and impact? On a seasonal basis? weekly basis?

3. Layout and Design: Pictures? graphics? colors? sizes?

4. Cost: How much can be spent?

5. Methods of Distribution: Mailed? if so, to whom? left in facility to be picked up? sent to organizations—welcome wagon, service club, schools?

Brochures are important because they may be distributed cheaply (hand-outs, racks, counter tops) and they can tell a complicated story better than a 30-second broadcast, or graphs, charts, and maps. A recipient may file a brochure for future reference. You can get direct, immediate response from your brochure if you include an application or return card.

Important points to remember:

1. Unusual sizes, folds, die cuts may create interest, but cost more money.
2. Determine how a brochure will be distributed and design accordingly.
3. Work with a printer at beginning to determine the most economical way to go; know the due dates!!
4. Color is effective, but the more colors, the more it costs.
5. Changes, if any, which are made on the printer's proof will cost extra.
6. Avoid using information material that is subject to change (e.g., prices, board members, temporary addresses).
7. Make the brochure fit your visual image (e.g., flashing, rich, cute, dignified, serious).
8. Order as many as you need the first time—reprints cost more—but don't overorder.
9. Get bids in writing from printer in advance.

POSTERS

Posters may suit your promotional purposes in some cases. Remember:

1. Message must be simple—able to be read from a distance—8 to 10 words maximum.
2. Not very durable—great for target practice, may be stolen, vandalized, rained on.
3. May have multiple uses: stuck on windshields, stuffed in grocery bags, folder for brochure.
4. Best for name identity only.

Use these techniques in creating your poster:

1. Keep it simple—use a single concept.
2. Contrasting colors are best.
3. Keep type faces simple.
4. Use bold design.

NEWSLETTER

A newsletter is an informational booklet or flyer on the progress of the agency.

Points to consider:

1. To what audience: organization members? general public? certain geographic area or other type of population grouping?

2. Size and format: mimeographed sheet? magazine?
3. Newsgathering operation: entire staff? single contact individual?

FLYERS

A flyer is an advertising circular. It requires effective use of space in terms of layout, design, and color. Visual impact is of primary importance. Keep it simple. Use central theme.

Flyers should briefly state or display:

1. Name of the event or activity
2. Identification of the target audience—age grouping, sex, geographic location, competence/skill level, and perhaps leisure preference
3. The location, date, and time of activity (optional: enclose a map)
4. Sponsoring agency—name, address, telephone, contact person.

Methods of Distribution:

1. Individual collection—organizations distribute them
2. Mailing—to selected groups such as senior citizens, or to total population, or to existing membership
3. Displaying—post like miniposters
4. Personal distribution—put in schools for kids' programs, in stores for community-wide program.

DIRECT MAIL

The advantage of direct mail is that it is easy to target the market. However, several mailings are often needed to be effective.

Points to remember:

1. Must be unique so that recipient will bother to open it.
2. Make it easy to reply—enclose envelope, reply card, etc.
3. Follow up mailing with a personal call.
4. Personalized message gets more response.
5. Multiple mailings should be regular and planned initially—later mailings tie in to previous mailing.
6. Check postage regulations carefully.

SALES PROMOTION TECHNIQUES

Various gimmicks are useful in sales promotion:

1. Sampling: Try to presell the program by providing individuals with a sample experience such as a free first bowling class.
2. Use of Coupons: Offer reduced rates for participation, such as discount theater tickets.
3. Contests: Use competition to promote interest in a class (e.g., cooking contest promotes interest in cooking class—participants are rewarded in cash/services).
4. Demonstrations: Allow consumers to see a demonstration of the skills and benefits to be derived from the program (e.g., modern dance class demonstrates routines to mall passersby).

NEWSPAPER

The broad coverage of a newspaper makes it hard to target the market. Your material can be "lost" on the page. Know the editors and their policies, and their deadlines.

Figure 3–14 shows the *inverted pyramid format for press releases and public service announcements*. Excess is cut from the bottom up so the most important facts about the program belong in the first paragraph.

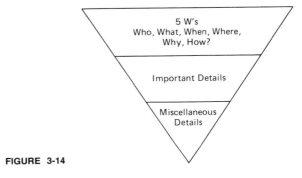

FIGURE 3-14

A sample news release form is shown in Figure 3–15.

A newspaper article, feature, or editorial usually allows more space than a press release.

You can also publicize the program through the community calendar.

Give reporters complimentary passes to your events so they can write reviews as a form of promotion. Have at least one open house yearly.

Write letters to the editor to thank individuals assisting your program or to express concern over issues affecting leisure/recreation.

You can send your article to regional or national special interest newspapers (for example, a special event or a hobby show could be advertised in a national trade newspaper).

Have a *press conference*:

1. When your event has someone prominent the reporters should meet;
2. When you have an announcement of broad significance to make, such as a fundraising campaign;
3. When a number of people or groups are participating in the event and their show of support demonstrates that this action is news. Have a prepared statement to give reporters.

As outlined by Shivers in *Essentials in Recreation Services*, news releases and press conference topics of a leisure services agency include the following sample subjects:

Significant events

Appointment of advisory council members
Meetings of the council, neighborhood councils, committees
Anniversary of establishment of the department
State or national occasions which can be tied into the agency's activities

FIGURE 3-15 Sample Promotional Press Release

Palm Gardens Municipal Roller Rink
35 Oakland Road
Palm Garden, New Jersey 07000
(513) 232-0197

News for Immediate Release

August 31, 1986
Contact: Susan Sawyer

Palm Gardens' Municipal Roller Rink opens its fall season with reduced rates for all roller skating sessions and open skating classes. Located at 35 Oakland Road, the rink is open Monday through Sunday from 9 A.M. to 1 A.M. For information, call (513) 232-0197.

The rink offers a wide variety of activities suited to every interest. Beginning, intermediate, and advanced roller skating classes are scheduled on an individual and group basis. Open skating periods allow individuals of all ages and skill levels to explore the excitement of roller skating at their own pace. The facility can be reserved for private groups for a nominal fee. The Friday night roller disco continues to attract a lively roller skating set.

Mr. Warren Bach, recreation director of the rink, indicates that since opening 2 years ago the rink has nearly tripled in membership. He attributes this success to expanded publicity, major facility renovations, and innovative programming. He praises the work of Ayers College recreation field work students who have provided valuable individualized instruction to novice roller skaters. Should you wish to contact Mr. Bach to request information, he can be reached at (513) 232-0197.

Annual banquets, dinners, celebrations
Annual national conference
Annual state conference
Annual district or regional conference
Local pageants, commemorations, or traditional events
Tournaments and program contests
Awards of merit to employees
Opening of an exhibition
Construction of a new or improved facility or area
Program demonstrations
National holidays, festivals, patriotic occasions
Special weeks, days, or months, e.g., Recreation Month

Reports on special studies

Reports on community recreational conditions
Reports on community surveys and master plans
Reports on construction
Reports on land acquisition
Reports on federal grants
Reports on institutes, workshops, and staff development program

Personalities

Visits by dignitaries
Personal accomplishments of participants
Visits by interested community groups
Winner of leagues, tournaments, games, contests

Employee advancement within the department

Interviews by departmental employees

Contributions to the community made by employees outside of the agency

Recognition and awards to individuals for voluntary service

Endorsements of the department by local officials and prominent citizens

Departmental policies

New rules and regulations governing certain events or facilities[16]

NEWSPAPER ADVERTISEMENTS

There are many problems to be aware of when considering newspaper advertising:

1. You will have no control of placement of the ad in the paper.
2. Quality of reproduction is often marginal to poor.
3. It is easy for an ad to get lost on a page if it's too small; the most effective size: 600 lines.
4. Color increases effectiveness by 70 percent—but it costs more.
5. Newspapers are not generally read by the poor and uneducated.
6. Frequency of ad is necessary for effectiveness.

Techniques for creating ads:

1. Use white space to make ad stand out.
2. Keep body copy short, easy to read.
3. Use good photography or none at all.
4. Line art reproduces best.
5. Use strong colors—avoid yellow.

TELEVISION

Some advantages of television advertising are:

1. Broad coverage—large ADI (area of dominent influence)
2. May target market with appropriate programming (that is, soaps, news, children's programs, and so forth).
3. Uses sight, sound, movement, color for most effective presentation of message

Techniques of creating a TV spot:

1. Keep production simple—studio time is expensive.
2. Be familiar with equipment capabilities.
3. Use professional talent.
4. Plan the spot before going to the studio.
5. Film is expensive—$200–$3000 minute.

A sample news release form for a TV video is shown in Figure 3–16.

16. Jay Shivers, *Essentials in Recreation Services* (Philadelphia: Lea and Febiger, 1978), p. 300.

FIGURE 3-16 Sample Video Promotion

Monique's Health Spa
83 Walnut Street
Spaulding, New York 27680
(619) 876-0985

News for Immediate Release

Video spot for TV

Video	Audio
Slide number 1	
Photo of people using fitness equipment	"Never thought working at looking good could be so much fun, did you?"
Slide number 2	
Photo of aerobic dance class	"At Monique's Health Spa, fitness and fun go hand in hand."
Slide number 3	
Photo of staff member monitoring client using a treadmill	"Our capable staff help each person devise an individualized fitness program based on an exercise regimen and nutritional guidelines."
Slide number 4	
Photo of people sitting at cafe tables around the pool	"After a session on our fitness equipment, enjoy a refreshing salad by our poolside, which becomes a lively disco at sundown."
Slide number 5	
Photo of outside of the building	"For your complimentary consultation and exercise session, contact Monique's Health Spa, 83 Walnut Street, Spaulding Phone (619) 876-0985 Hours: Monday through Sunday 9 A.M. to 1 P.M. Hope to see you there!"

RADIO

Opportunities for radio promotion include:

1. Newscasts
2. Public service announcements
3. I.D.'s (10-second announcement attached to station identification)
4. Personality spots (celebrity announces program)
5. Editorials
6. Public affairs panels
7. Talk shows—question/answer format.

Radio has several disadvantages; it can become background and it is harder to get attention. Also, radio cannot show agency logo or visual concepts.
   Points to remember:

1. Frequency is important—also time of day (rush hours).
2. You may target market depending on format of station (e.g., rock, country, easy listening).
3. Requires flexible scheduling—may add or change on short notice.
4. Stations may provide free production.

116 Program Planning—Principles and Practices

5. Jingles are effective and provide a tie-in with television.
6. Sound effects attract listener attention.

PUBLIC SERVICE ANNOUNCEMENTS (PSAs)

PSAs are free messages printed in newspapers or aired on radio or TV that promote the programs of nonprofit organizations.

Time Breakdowns:		if T.V.	
10 seconds	25 words	1–2	visuals
20 seconds	40 words	2	visuals
30 seconds	80 words	2–5	visuals
60 seconds	160 words	5–10	visuals

Format: Repeat phone number two times and slogan at beginning and end. Be short, concise, and snappy.

A sample public service announcement form is shown in Figure 3–17.

Timing is important. You can announce about general services with start and stop dates (from January to March). Or for a one-shot event, use one announcement, or one event can be covered over an extended period of time—a month ahead; for the first couple of weeks of the event; or for the last few days.

To arrange radio or TV interviews, send the producer documentation of your subject and a fact sheet.

IMPORTANT BASICS

Every agency should have a *press kit*, which is detailed information concerning the agency's operations and which is available to the press when requested. It contains:

1. History of the organization
2. Organizational chart listing employee positions
3. Biographical sketches of staff members

FIGURE 3-17 Sample Radio Public Service Announcement

Palm Gardens Municipal Roller Rink
35 Oakland Road
Palm Garden, New Jersey 07000
(513) 232-0197

News for Immediate Release

Radio Spot (Public Service Announcement)   August 31, 1986
60 seconds   Contact: Susan Sawyer

We're rolling out the red carpet at Palm Gardens Municipal Roller Rink! New registration extends from Labor Day through October 8th at the rink on 35 Oakland Road.

The rink fits into everyone's schedule, open 7 days a week from 9 A.M. to 1 A.M. The rink offers roller skating instruction at the beginning, intermediate, and advanced levels, as well as open skating sessions. Special roller disco night rolls around every Friday evening for our swinging skaters. The facility can be rented out for private engagements at attractive group rates.

So come join the fun at the Palm Gardens rink! Call (513) 232-0197. We're rolling out the red carpet!

4. Organizational services—programs and facilities
5. Annual report
6. Reprints of newspaper articles, editorials, or other media material
7. Photos of activities and services.

The *Annual Report* emphasizes the organization's strengths. It contains:

1. Review of financial position
2. Productivity (services rendered and behavioral outcomes produced)
3. Physical acquisitions and development
4. Management activities.

A *Publicity Kit* is designed around a specific program in your agency. It contains:

1. Fact sheet on agency
2. Backgrounder—several pages of information on special event
3. Photos
4. Extras (including poster, flyer, T-shirt, button, bumper sticker)
5. Background on individuals associated with the event
6. Invitations, complimentary tickets.

A *departmental* or *house organ* is a publication circulated solely among agency personnel themselves. It is an important means of keeping staff informed of agency developments they should know about if they are to be effective public relations ambassadors. The house organ, often written by the employees themselves, contains information on policies, programs, facilities, staff recognition, employee suggestions, letters to the editor, personal columns, research, program resource information, and so forth.

OTHER PROMOTION TECHNIQUES

Stage a publicity stunt—an event to focus attention on your agency (for example, a clown tricycle race to promote upcoming carnival).

Create "Leisure Week" with officials making public proclamations. Attract the public to a recreation site with a searchlight.

Carry the promotion theme through local school activities (for example, for a local centennial celebration, conduct a school essay contest on "Why I Like my Hometown").

Have information on recreation services circulated through: skywriting, Chamber of Commerce, Visitor Information Booth, speakers bureau, cruising loudspeaker, postage meter message, bus and subway ad space, church bulletins, industry publications, flyers with bills, menus, ads on marquee bulletin boards, and the tag line on telephone, weather service, and bank time and temperature readings.

PROGRAM EVALUATION

Program evaluation is a critical aspect of the program planning process as it measures the degree to which the recreation agency has achieved its goals and objectives. The evaluation process may reveal that the goals and objectives themselves need revision. The evaluation process is an ongoing one that continually provides input for further program decisions. Evaluation is not conducted solely at the end of a given program (summative) but is also conducted throughout the course of the program to monitor progress and developments (formative). Program evaluation can refer to a single program (a special event, a drama class) or the overall program itself (a ski resort or a summer camp, for example).

Need for Evaluation

Program evaluation is needed for the following reasons:

1. Data on the benefits of specific agency programs are needed to prove accountability and obtain further funding.
2. Input from the community is used as a basis for future programming decisions.
3. Public relations are enhanced by the fact that residents are pleased to be consulted for their program suggestions.
4. Involvement of the community helps assure that the agency's goals are synonymous with the community's goals.
5. The evaluation process encourages goal-setting and constructive self-appraisal among the staff.
6. The evaluation process upgrades recreation's public image as a profession.

Quantitative versus Qualitative Data

Since evaluation results are often utilized to justify the maintenance or cancellation of a program, there is often an undue emphasis on obtaining quantitative data (such as numbers in attendance or costs). This has led to a "head count mentality" in which the regularity of high attendance levels is used as an index of program success. A weakness of this quantitative base is that it does not examine the outside, uncontrollable factors that might have led to increased attendance (such as cancellation of a competitive local program). Similarly, drops in program attendance need not be due to weaknesses in the program planning process itself, but to external factors such as poor weather, transportation limitations, incomplete facility, staff turnover, and so forth. These outside factors over which one has no control are termed intervening variables. Unlike quantitative data, qualitative data are concerned with the participants' intrinsic motivations for participation including needs met and benefits derived. Since quantitative data deals with objective figures, it is easier to obtain and measure than participants' internal growth, and therefore the tendency has been to rely on this numerical information; increased efforts must be made to obtain qualitative data. The sample participant questionnaires in the needs assessment section of this chapter are examples of surveys for qualitative data.

The Evaluation Tool

The evaluation tool can take any number of approaches including:

1. Interviews with staff and participants
2. Videotapes of staff and participants engaged in the program

3. Staff and participant self-reporting devices (for example, diaries)
4. Staff anecdotal records of participant growth
5. Observation of staff and participants engaged in the program (observation conducted by an outside evaluator).

An evaluation can be completed by any or all of the following: participant, program administrator, leader, and outside evaluator. It should be noted that any criterion for program evaluation can be adapted to the frame of reference of any of the respondents above. For instance, the leadership criterion "ability to encourage leadership within the group" can assume the following distinct formats:

Participant: Do you feel that the leader gave you the opportunity to exert leadership when you wished to do so? If so, how?

Leader (of self): Did you provide opportunities for initiative and leadership within your group of participants? If so, how?

Leader's Administrator: Does the leader have a style that encourages leadership from the participants? If so, how?

Outside Evaluator: Did you observe the leader encouraging leadership from within the group of participants? If so, how?

The evaluation tool can be adapted to a variety of formats such as checklists, questionnaires, and rating scales. Case studies can be written to document the effects of a program on individual participants. Each case study gives a profile of how an individual's behavior or attitudes evolved throughout the program. If a more scientific, objective base is desired, experimental research can be conducted whereby, upon completion of the program, the behavior of preselected participants is compared to that of a preselected control group (nonparticipants). For example, a group of people with fairly similar characteristics (for example, nursing home residents) is divided into program participants and control group. The participants are exposed to a music therapy class to determine if their bodies' ranges of motion are increased through exposure to music therapy. At the end of a predetermined time period, control group and participants are evaluated as to their range of motion. Should there be an increase in range of motion among participants and not among the control group, the deduction is that music therapy produced these results.

Another evaluative approach is based on compliance with standards of a verified representative group. For example, the American Camping Association has published standardized checklists of conditions that should exist in a camping program. A weakness in the compliance with standards approach is that the standards themselves may not be pertinent to the agency. By relying on a checklist, the agency may neglect the very important process of goal-setting in response to its own unique needs and circumstances.

Areas of Evaluation

Depending on its purpose, the evaluation can study any one or all of the following topics:

Agency philosophy, goals, and objectives
Participant profile/community needs assessment
Program (specific or overall)
Administration/leadership
Facility and equipment
Evaluation (the process itself)

Evaluating Philosophy, Goals, and Objectives

Since the agency's philosophy, goals, and objectives form the basis for programming, it is essential that they represent an accurate perception of the community's needs and wishes. The changing needs of individuals and the overall community must be addressed through a dynamic program planning process. Community input is essential. For example, a goal for more intergenerational programming in a nursing home may have resulted in some very innovative programming, but the program will have less impact if the original goal was not one shared by the residents themselves. If there is dissatisfaction with a program, the question needs to be addressed as to whether the program itself needs revision or, on a more basic level, if the goal itself calls for reexamination. Respondents should have the opportunity in the evaluation to express their views on agency policies that affect delivery of services (for example, fees and charges, "recreation as privilege" in institutional settings).

Goal-setting is intended to be visionary and not necessarily fully attainable. The fact that an agency reaches all of its goals and objectives suggests that its range of vision is too limited. The evaluator does not only look at the number of goals achieved but also examines their scope. The evaluator is concerned with the quality of the goals, not the quantity. It is preferable to establish well-thought-out, challenging goals rather than to spin off shallow, easily attained goals "for effect."

Evaluation by Participants

Participants need to evaluate how programs can meet their individual needs. The "Recreation is . . ." table (Figure 3–1) at the beginning of this chapter outlines the many needs that are met by recreational experiences. The student's evaluation form (Figure 3–19) at the end of this chapter illustrates how participants can evaluate their own growth as a result of the program.

Every evaluation tool requests certain forms of demographic data (age, residence, occupation). When all of these demographic data are compiled, they provide a broad view of respondents' lifestyles; this serves as a basis for programming decisions. Participant evaluation can also include the perceptions of leaders regarding the needs and capabilities of their participants based on observation, interviews, and past program participation.

Evaluating Programs

This aspect of evaluation is concerned with respondents' opinions of the recreation programs currently offered. Participants can evaluate a program they have participated in (music class, carnival special event) or give their perceptions of the agency's overall program. The technical aspects of specific or agency-wide programs subject to evaluation include attendance level, suitability of scheduling, appropriateness of budget decisions, acceptability of leader-participant ratio, and effectiveness of publicity.

Key subjects of concern in program evaluation include the following questions:

In terms of time, staff, cost, facilities, and equipment, how cost-effective is the program in achieving its objectives?

Can other programs be more effective in achieving these objectives?

Does the program provide sufficient carry-over value? skill development? variety in learning situations? individualized approaches? balance? success experiences? integration with other programs? participant need satisfaction?

Evaluation of Administration/Leadership

Since the quality of leadership in recreation administrators and direct service leaders determines the quality of the recreation program itself, the evaluation of leadership is essential. A job description outlining mutually agreed-upon goals at the time of hiring forms the basis for evaluation later. The job description is vital to insure that the agency and staff person are working towards convergent goals from the outset.

The evaluation of administrators and leaders can be completed by the individual being evaluated (as a self-assessment), by participants, supervisors, and outside evaluators. As a part of their evaluation, supervisors and outside evaluators often look at the rapport between the administrator/leader and participants as a measure of leadership ability. The general atmosphere of the program is considered reflective of the leader's impact. At the end of this chapter is a sample of a leadership evaluation form to be completed by a supervisor or outside evaluator where observation is involved.

An administrator is evaluated on the basis of a number of issues including staffing decisions, scheduling patterns, budget determinations, public relations efforts, policy development, and so forth. The direct service leader, on the other hand, is evaluated on the basis of his or her ability to help participants achieve their program goals. A music leader, for instance, will be evaluated on the basis of how well he or she motivated and instructed the youth orchestra. Some leadership evaluation forms evaluate leadership on the basis of the number of participants who master the skill (for example, the number of successful orchestra players). In the case of both administrators and direct service leaders, evaluation forms usually include such factors as educational background, skills, work habits, work relationships, rapport with participants, organizational ability, and the like. The results of these leadership evaluations often provide the basis for recommending promotions, additional in-service training, and revised job descriptions and job classifications.

The evaluator should be discriminating in selecting a leadership evaluation tool that is pertinent to the individual's job description. For instance, it is unfair to rate a leader's writing ability when the leader has not been called on to do any writing in his or her particular leadership capacity. If a skill is not required of a leader, then that skill should not be one of the criteria used to evaluate that leader.

Evaluation of Facility and Equipment

The program's facility and equipment must be up to par to meet the goals of the program. The following factors should be considered:

Does the facility allow for effective programming? Does the equipment?
Have facilities been built in response to community requests?
Has equipment been purchased in response to community requests?

An example of a facility/equipment evaluation format follows in response to each of the evaluative criteria.

Facility/Equipment Evaluation

Indicate yes or no in the facility and equipment columns.

	Facility	Equipment
Safe		
Accessible		
Available		
Attractive		
Appropriate		
Suitable for multi-use		

Evaluating the Evaluation

The evaluation tool itself becomes an area of evaluation. Respondents rate the evaluation procedure in regards to the following factors:

Was the tool itself suitable for the purpose of the evaluation? for the clientele completing it?
Was the wording appropriate?
Were the program goals and objectives thoroughly and adequately presented?

Were the criteria reflective of the program?

Was the distribution procedure effective? (mailing? interview?)

Is the frequency of evaluation appropriate?

Were constituents and staff sufficiently informed of the need for the evaluation? Were efforts made to assure them of its importance?

Unless they are informed of the purpose to which the evaluation results will be put, staff will resent the time spent on the design and analysis of the evaluation, and respondents will resent the time they spend completing it. They should be made aware that the evaluation results will be used to upgrade the program being offered and revitalize the working environment.

Evaluation Process

After the evaluation tool is selected or designed and the public relations process is underway, the distribution procedure is determined and a collection timetable established. The evaluation data are then collected, analyzed, and translated into program goals.

The entire evaluation process can be conducted internally by staff or by an outside evaluator. Benefits of an outside evaluator include the point that an outsider is usually more trained in research design and inclined to be more objective than a staff evaluator from within the agency. On the other hand, the outside evaluator can also be viewed as more threatening than a staff evaluator and trigger a response that is not reflective of the program being evaluated. Outside evaluators are also usually more costly than staff, although it must be understood that one is paying for their specialized expertise in evaluation.

Benefits of the staff evaluator include ability to involve other staff in the evaluation process more naturally than an outside evaluator and the ability to see the larger picture of the agency's goals and practices than can be picked up by an outsider in a limited time frame. Disadvantages of the inside evaluator also exist. The already overworked staff person may have to sacrifice direct service to clients in order to accomplish the major task of evaluation. It is also very difficult for staff to be truly objective and self-critical of a program in which they have a personal investment in terms of emotional and financial security. Since there are pros and cons with either an inside or outside evaluator, the best solution is undoubtedly to blend both into the process. For instance, the outside evaluator could design the evaluation tool only after having been thoroughly briefed on the agency goals by staff. Then both outsider and staff could analyze and interpret the data.

As discussed earlier in this section, the program evaluation process is cyclical, whereby program evaluation results are constantly being fed back into the initial goal-setting step in the program planning process. The following statement from *Recreation Today—Program Planning and Leadership* by Kraus gives an illustration of this procedure:

In the study of a specific Milwaukee neighborhood center, the following findings and recommendations were reported:

Findings

1. This center is located in an area subject to racial tensions due to the migration of a new ethnic group to this area.
2. The new residents of this area are in need of recreation services but are inclined to be slow in availing themselves of the opportunities offered.
3. The decline in the evening attendance at this center is comparatively recent and has followed the pattern of other centers in which there has been a heavy migration of a new ethnic group.
4. There is not another public recreation center near this area; this center is well-located geographically. There are no private agencies operating in this area which conduct recreation programs; commercial recreation facilities are very limited.

After carefully considering all statistics and other evaluative data regarding the center, the supervisory staff made the following recommendations to the head of the department:

Recommendations

1. Continue the afternoon and Saturday programs and add at least one activity.
2. Continue the evening center for another year; then reevaluate and close the center if there is no better receptivity to the program.
3. Through questionnaires and conferences with adults and teen-agers, attempt to determine the desires and interests of the new constituency and program accordingly.
4. Improve the publicity program and publicize the availability of facilities for "permit" group meetings.
5. Request the PTA and leading citizens and neighborhood organizations to take an active role in promoting the center program, for there is a definite need for service in this area.[17]

Figure 3-18 is an example of a leadership evaluation form.

Figure 3-19 shows a sample participant self-evaluation form to be filled out upon completion of a recreation program.

17. Richard G. Kraus, *Recreation Today—Program Planning and Leadership* (Glenview, IL: Scott, Foresman and Company, 1977), pp. 557–558. Reprinted by permission.

FIGURE 3-18 Sample Leadership Form

FUNCTION	EXC.	GOOD	FAIR	POOR
Observed _____ Observer _____				
Session _____ Date _____				
Leadership Techniques				
1. Gained initial attention of group				
2. Used organized, effective method of initiating activity				
3. Rules, procedures clearly planned and explained				
4. Participation encouraged throughout activity				
5. Handled disruptive behavior effectively				
6. Voice projection loud and clear				
7. Evidenced knowledge of activity				
8. Showed ample preparation for activity				
9. Enforced rules and fair play				
10. Encouraged leadership in participants				
11. Exhibited patience				
12. Displayed enthusiasm throughout activity				
Activity Appraisal				
1. Set good climate for participant interaction				
2. Activity had flow, sequential buildup				
3. Participant interest sustained throughout activity				
4. Equal opportunity provided for all participants				
5. Sense of achievement instilled in participants				
6. Activity appropriate for age group				
7. All participants actively involved				
8. Activity appropriate for physical environment				
9. Activity offered:				
a) Physical activity				
b) Creativity				
c) Mental Activity				
d) Social Interaction				
e) Challenge				
Relationship With Colleagues				
1. Worked harmoniously				
2. Shared responsibilities equally				
Additional Comments: (Strengths and Weaknesses)				

This evaluation is to help you judge the nature of your experience and to help us improve the program. We appreciate the time and energy you take to fill it out completely and honestly.

What were *your* reasons for entering the program?

What specific insights about yourself did you learn while you were in the program?

Put an X in the areas where you feel you have made the most improvement. Put an 0 in the areas that you would like to work on.

_____ Is punctual and dependable
_____ Appears confident
_____ Is appropriately dressed
_____ Is attentive to others
_____ Is inquisitive
_____ Shows respect for group members, teacher, and assistant
_____ Has open mind
_____ Accepts constructive criticism and makes positive use of it
_____ Is cooperative and flexible
_____ Explores various areas and activities of group
_____ Demonstrates stability
_____ Seems happy about self
_____ Is able to interact openly with group members
_____ Is able to verbalize ideas to the group
_____ Is a good listener
_____ Refrains from using inappropriate conversation
_____ Is sensitive and helpful to others
_____ Shows ability to adjust to a variety of new circumstances and people
_____ Has coping skills
_____ Has personal insight
_____ Is able to channel energies in a productive way
_____ Can set own goals and follow through
_____ Shows ability to manage time and energy
_____ Shows talent in music or art

What new abilities, interests, and limitations did you discover about yourself?

What other progress occurred during the last few months?

Do you have any comments about your leader? Was he or she understanding and patient? Does he or she have a good sense of humor? Was he or she tolerant when you made mistakes or acted out? Can he or she relate well to young people?

_____
Student

_____
Date

Source: Community School of Music and Arts, Ithaca, NY.

ATCHLEY, ROBERT C. *The Social Problems in Later Life—An Introduction to Social Gerontology.* St. Louis: C. V. Mosby Co., 1977.

AVEDON, ELLIOT M. *Therapeutic Recreation Services.* Englewood Cliffs, NJ: Prentice-Hall, 1974.

BANNON, JOSEPH J. *Leisure Resources—Comprehensive Planning.* Englewood Cliffs, NJ: Prentice-Hall, 1976.

BUTLER, ROBERT N. (M.D.) AND LEWIS, MYRNA I. (A.C.S.W.) *Aging and Mental Health—Positive Psychosocial Approaches.* St. Louis: C. V. Mosby Co., 1977.

DANFORD, HOWARD G. *Creative Leadership in Recreation.* Boston: Allyn and Bacon, 1964.

DUNN, DIANA R. AND PHILLIPS, LAMARR A. "SYNERGETIC PROGRAMMING OR 2 + 2 = 5. *Parks and Recreation,* vol. 10, no. 3, March 1975, 24–26.

EDGINTON, CHRISTOPHER R., COMPTON, DAVID M., AND HANSON, CAROLE J. *Recreation ad Leisure Programming: A Guide for the Professional.* Philadelphia: Saunders Co., 1980.

FARRELL, PATRICIA AND LUNDEGREN, HERBERT M. *The Process of Recreation Programming: Theory and Technique,* 2nd ed. New York: John Wiley and Sons, 1983.

HORMACHEA, MARION N. AND CARROLL R. *Recreation in Modern Society.* Boston: Holbrook Press, 1972.

KRAUS, RICHARD G. AND CURTIS, JOSEPH E. *Creative Administration in Recreation and Parks.* St. Louis: C. V. Mosby Co., 1973.

KRAUS, RICHARD G. AND BATES, BARBARA J. *Recreation Leadership and Supervision—Guidelines for Professional Development.* Philadelphia: Saunders Co., 1975.

KRAUS, RICHARD G. *Recreation Today—Program Planning & Leadership.* Santa Monica, Calif: Goodyear Pub. Co., 1978.

MURPHY, JAMES F. *Recreation and Leisure Service—A Humanistic Perspective.* Dubuque, Ia: William C. Brown Pub., 1975.

MURPHY, JAMES F. AND HOWARD, DENNIS R. *Delivery of Community Leisure Services—An Holistic Approach.* Philadelphia: Lea and Febiger, 1977.

RODNEY, LYNN S. *Administration of Public Recreation.* New York: Ronald Press Co., 1964.

ROFOSZ, FRANCIS M. *Administrative Procedures for Conducting Recreational Sports Tournaments.* Springfield, IL: Charles C. Thomas, 1982.

SHIVERS, JAY. *Essentials in Recreation Services.* Philadelphia: Lea and Febiger, 1978.

TILLMAN, ALBERT. *The Program Book for Recreation Professionals.* Palo Alto, CA: Mayfield, 1973.

4

Leisure Education in Program Planning

The recreation professional's responsibilities are not restricted to the provision of programs. Beyond this, the professional must be concerned with the individual's achievement of qualitative leisure experiences with carry-over value. With this as the priority then, the professional places importance on helping individuals make independent leisure choices to the point that participants' leisure satisfaction takes precedence over whether they can be encouraged to register for programs. In this way, professionals perform their functions as facilitators and enablers rather than as programmers and providers. Through the leisure education process, professionals engage participants in an ongoing process of assessing leisure attitudes, values, decision-making skills, capabilities, and options. This chapter presents concepts and practices to assist recreation professionals in the integration of leisure education into their respective leisure service delivery systems.

LEISURE EDUCATION DEFINED

Through leisure education, individuals explore attitudes towards leisure and its significance in their lives. In the process of setting leisure goals, individuals assess their needs, interests, skills, and past leisure experiences.

They explore options and consider the outcomes of leisure choices.

In the book *Leisure Education—Theory and Practice,* Jean Mundy and Linda Odum define leisure education in a number of ways as:

- a total movement to enable an individual to enhance the quality of his/her life in leisure.
- deciding for oneself what place leisure has in his/her life.
- a process to enable the individual to identify and clarify his/her own leisure values and goals.
- an approach to enable an individual to enhance the quality of his/her life during leisure.
- coming to know oneself in relation to leisure.
- a lifelong process encompassing pre-kindergarten through retirement years.
- increasing the individual's options for satisfying quality experiences in leisure.
- a movement in which a multiplicity of disciplines and service systems have a role and responsibility.[1]

As additional points of clarification, Mundy and Odum add that leisure education is *not:*

- attempting to replace an individual's set of leisure values with "our set" of leisure values.
- imparting standards of what is "good or bad" use of leisure.
- a focus on getting people to participate in more recreation activities.
- only teaching skills and providing recreation programs.
- a program to undermine the work ethic.
- advocating a leisure lifestyle for everyone.
- restricted to the American educational system.
- a subject to be taught.[2]

Leisure education is achieved through a variety of program approaches, including role playing, discussion, and values clarification exercises. Leisure education concepts can be incorporated into program activity areas (such as social recreation, music, dance). An extensive list of such leisure education activities is included at the end of this chapter.

Leisure education can be introduced into any setting. For example, the Camp Fire Girls of Buffalo County, New York, developed an "I Can Do It!" series, which is basically a leisure skills development course covering such areas as cooking, pet care, bicycle safety, and so forth. Schools can introduce leisure content into their courses (for example, a business class could price commercial recreation equipment, a geography class could practice orienteering for hiking).

1. Mundy, Jean and Odum, Linda, *Leisure Education: Theory and Practice* (New York: John Wiley and Sons, 1979), pp. 3–4.
2. Ibid, p. 4.

LEISURE EDUCATION IN LEADERSHIP APPROACH

An important aspect of leisure education is the recreation leader's leadership style. The aim of the recreation leader as leisure educator should be to facilitate independent decision-making skills in participants. The following checklist specifies facilitation techniques for the leader.

1. As a leisure educator do you acknowledge the distinct learning patterns among your participants, and attempt to individualize leisure skill instructions?
2. Do you provide opportunities for people to learn in different ways? Examples: Are participants allowed to
    * choose reading, observation, aural, or "hands on" instruction?
    * choose individual or group instruction?
    * select, from variable schedules, one that corresponds to their peak learning periods of the day?
    * move from project to project—or must they complete one at a time?
    * choose from short- and long-term projects?
    * engage in spontaneous as well as structured learning processes?
    * engage in an activity without the imposition of a performance objective?
    * make own determinations regarding such issues as sharing equipment without relying on leader's supervision?
    * explore a multitude of activities so as to be better exposed to leisure options for the future?
    * consider home-based, independent leisure pursuits that in no way foster the attendance level of the agency?

Since recreation leadership training stresses group leadership skills, it is often difficult for the leader to acknowledge and accept the value of disparate, spontaneous leisure interests among clients. In the focus on group instruction the leader may miss the "teachable moments" for individual leisure education. For instance, in conducting a current events discussion group, the leader may note that a participant is doodling on a note pad instead of following the discussion. In the midst of a formal leisure activity—in this case the current events group—an individual is engaged in an informal leisure activity, the doodling. The doodling is no less significant than listening to the discussion. As a leisure educator one places no value judgments or hierarchy of importance on individuals' leisure activities. In this particular situation, the recreation leader could seize the opportunity to help the individual see the value of such spontaneous informal leisure the doodling represents. Often, individuals are barely conscious of their miscellaneous leisure moments and thus are not able to explore the significance of them in their lives. When asked what they view as their leisure, they may instead list a series of formally planned activities (such as tennis, crafts, bowling) and completely overlook the informal unplanned leisure moments of their lives (such as combing and brushing their hair, joking with friends, watching the sunset). By promoting this individual self-awareness of leisure experiences, the recreation leader is acknowledging that the individual's leisure education process takes precedence over the agency's activity-registration process.

As leisure educator, the recreation leader helps clients identify what elements appear necessary to constitute their qualitative leisure experiences. This requires that the leader go beyond provisions of any activity to include guided explanation of leisure values. For instance, through discussion and experience over time, an individual may discover that he or she does not derive leisure satisfaction from cooking unless he or she can cook for others, can experiment with the recipe, and can do so with a low cost factor. Thus, the individual learns that leisure satisfaction is inextricably related to leisure values of service and sociability (cooking for others), self-expression (recipe experimentation), and economy (low cost). Prior to this self-realization, the individual may not have realized why he or she was experiencing such variable levels of enjoyment from cooking.

In addition to discovering how personal values affect leisure satisfaction, the individual also needs to identify how external factors exert a critical influence. For instance, the same activity—in this case cooking—can take on different levels of enjoyment in relation to any number of outside factors. Examples include where the cooking is done, how it fits in with the other events of the day, the availability of necessary ingredients and utensils, and the positive and negative influence of people present including family, friends, and cooking instructor.

By guiding the individual through this self-discovery process, the recreation leader fulfills the leisure education role of activity enabler rather than solely being activity organizer.

In the case of children, recreation leaders should inform the family of recreation interests the child has displayed in the program, be it crafts, dance, or any other activity. Contact can take the form of phone calls, correspondence, or notes sent home. This communication makes it possible for the family to encourage their child's development of leisure skills. The activity may even be one that the entire family chooses to enjoy together. This communication between agency and home is vital in helping the child develop an integrated leisure lifestyle in home and community. Recreation professionals have been lax in developing these contacts and should demonstrate a renewed commitment to this effort.

LEISURE DEFINED

Leisure is a state of mind marked by the feeling that one is freely choosing one's present experience. External obligations are nonexistent or, more important, are *perceived* as nonexistent. As long as the individual feels that sense of freedom and personal investment, leisure can exist in any situation, even in those characterized by obligations or external expectations. A photographer who eagerly throws herself into her newspaper photographer job, comes home to take slides of her children, and later volunteers as a photography class instructor, would find it difficult to state when her work and leisure began and ended—there is a holism that permeates her lifestyle. Since leisure is a state of mind, it can be determined only by the individual himself or herself.

INFLUENCE OF WORK ETHIC ON LEISURE

Recreation is defined as a personally satisfying activity engaged in during leisure. Many people do not allow themselves the full benefit of leisure and recreation because they are dominated by a work ethic that instills guilt over nonwork pursuits. The influence of the work ethic has historical roots. The Puritans believed that spirituality demanded rejection of recreational pleasures. They felt that due to original sin, humans were unworthy of any forms of enjoyment. Their condemnation of "pleasure pursuits" was also due to their resentment of the upper class's pleasurable lifestyle; if they, the Puritans, chose to work diligently, they expected all classes of people to do the same.

As a by-product of harsh economic and environmental conditions, Calvinistic doctrine required hard work for survival and eternal reward—and thus rejected leisure. In Colonial America, a barn dance was permitted only because it occurred after a work project such as a house raising; in no other way would it have been justified. Sayings such as "Idleness is the devil's workshop" were embroidered on samplers and were simultaneously being etched into the collective consciousness; these ideas remain a part of our contemporary attitudes. The severity of American society's inability to accept nonwork hours is reflected in a condition termed "the weekend neurosis." Alexander Reid Martin, psychiatrist, coined this term to describe the anxiety exhibited by clients unable to cope with the challenge of free unscheduled hours. These clients would typically be the first to grab a second job or work overtime rather than alter their negative leisure attitudes and lack of recreational interests.

Work's influence on leisure attitudes is reflected in the many views and theories of leisure that have work as a reference point. Examples of these various viewpoints are:

1. *Task generalization (spillover) theory*—individuals select leisure pursuits similar to work activity (e.g., teacher volunteers as an adult literacy tutor).
2. *Compensation theory*—individuals select leisure pursuits that provide compensation for what they are not receiving at work (e.g., secretary seeks nonsedentary recreation such as racquetball). (Harold Wilensky proposed both 1 and 2.)
3. *Quantitative or discretionary time view of leisure*—most prevalent concept of leisure; considers leisure to be free-time hours available after work. Advocates of this view associate increased blocks of free time with increased leisure. The

question to be asked is if an individual has large blocks of free time but exhibits restlessness, boredom, or destructive behavior in that time, is the individual truly "at leisure"? "Do free hours a leisure experience make?"

4. *The qualitative view of leisure*—states that it is the quality of the experience and person's perception of it that determines if it is leisure. Leisure can not be measured in relation to time.

5. *Deferred leisure*—views leisure as something earned or saved up for after work; subscribes to the work ethic which permits leisure only after work completion. Deferred leisure can also be termed delayed satisfaction, for it causes individuals not to look for the leisure potential in every day. Viewing leisure as the Golden Age of Retirement is an example of deferred leisure.

6. *Compensatory or recuperative leisure*—justifies leisure as a rest from work and rejuvenation for more work.

The work ethic has infiltrated our leisure pursuits themselves. The predominant feeling that one has to be productive leads many individuals to pursue only those activities that are utilitarian (for example, knit for the bazaar, volunteer for the hospital). Emphasis on performance and perfectionism makes leisure activities more like work than recreation. The Little Leaguer being pressured by the parents to win at all costs is being instilled with a work orientation to leisure. The feeling that one needs to be always occupied in some form of activity ironically leads many to "work at leisure."

LEISURE COUNSELING

Leisure counseling, a leisure education approach, employs verbal techniques to facilitate client awareness of leisure values and interests. Chester McDowell has defined leisure counseling as "a helping process that facilitates interpretive, affective and/or behavioral changes in others toward the attainment of their leisure well-being."[3]

Since individuals' leisure needs and problems vary in severity, there are a variety of leisure counseling modalities suited to each situation. McDowell has defined these modalities as:

1. Leisure-related behavioral problems
2. Leisure lifestyle awareness
3. Leisure resource guidance
4. Leisure skills development.[4]

Leisure-related behavioral problems. McDowell states that in this modality, "the primary counseling focus is on therapeutic facilitation."[5] This

3. Chester F. McDowell, *Leisure Counseling: Selected Lifestyle Processes* (Eugene, OR: University of Oregon, 1976), p. 9.
4. Chester F. McDowell "An Analysis of Leisure Counseling Orientations and Models, and Their Integrative Possibilities," in David M. Compton and Judith E. Goldstein (eds.), *Perspectives of Leisure Counseling* (Alexandria, VA: National Recreation and Park Assoc., 1977), p. 6.
5. Ibid.

counseling is used in the treatment of already existing leisure problems (poor self-image, boredom, maladaptive behavior, and so forth) and requires training in counseling theory (Gestalt, transactional analysis, behavior modification, individual, group, and family counseling).

Leisure lifestyle awareness. In this modality, states McDowell: "The primary counseling focus is educational and preventative."[6] Techniques such as values clarification, goal-setting, contracting, and time budgeting are employed. Leisure lifestyle awareness should be a continuum over the entire lifespan from preschool to older adulthood involving every social agent concerned with the individual's welfare (parents, school, recreation program).

Leisure resource guidance. This modality uses avocational interest inventories.[7] Also known as avocational counseling, activity counseling, or recreation counseling, leisure resource guidance is concerned with helping individuals find self-satisfying recreational activities.

Avocational counseling can include the:

1. Completion of activity interest inventories
2. Selection of activities based on viewing of videotapes, photos, films
3. Hobbyists and speakers on recreational activities
4. Availability of reading material, self-instructional tapes, and trial basis recreational equipment swapping
5. "Dial a leisure" telephone line and community calendar for up-to-date local recreational news
6. Field trips to see people engaged in recreational pursuits (particularly helpful to the institutionalized in easing community reentry and fostering positive leisure skills upon release)
7. Review of activity cards containing relevant information on each activity (cost, location, rules, duration, equipment needs, benefits).

Leisure skills development. According to McDowell, in this modality: "The primary counseling focus is on developing integration, normalizing, leisure-related skills"[8] for clients with some form of disability (for example, stroke victim, mentally retarded child). Skills include instruction in physical activity appropriate to a physical disability, socially acceptable behavior, motor skill development, time budgeting, and so forth.

Delivery of Leisure Counseling

The term *leisure counseling* should not give the false impression that leisure counseling is restricted to therapeutic recreation agencies; on the contrary, it is applicable to any leisure services setting. The Milwaukee Mu-

6. Ibid.
7. Ibid.
8. Ibid.

nicipal Recreation Department has a model leisure constructive counseling program. Constructive Leisure Inc. in Los Angeles and Creative Leisure, Inc. in Katonah, New York are examples of commercially established leisure counseling.

It should be noted that one is not a leisure counselor by nature of being a graduate of a recreation curriculum; specific coursework is necessary. The training generally agreed upon for leisure counseling includes coursework in vocational counseling, clinical psychology, counseling theory, educational psychology, interviewing skills, assessment techniques, philosophy of recreation and leisure, and human behavior.

The leisure educator/leisure counselor helps participants understand how their leisure choices are influenced by the following factors:

Economic background	Family influence
Educational background	Ethnic background
Age	Religious background
Occupation	Media impact
Sex	Laws
Residence	Transportation
Self-concept	Climate
Values	Knowledge of options
Skills	Surrounding environment (natural: e.g.,
Emotional and physical health	lake; constructed or manmade: e.g.,
Expectations of leisure	bowling alley).
Peer influence	

A leisure services delivery system, be it hospital, resort, camp, or municipal recreation department is one that recognizes that leisure satisfaction is not possible unless recreation is viewed in the context of all factors cited in the preceding list. This view, otherwise known as *holism,* sees the integration of lifestyle factors as contributing to the total quality of life. Figure 4–1, an assessment conducted in a nursing home, illustrates the importance of considering the individual's total lifestyle in leisure education/leisure counseling.

Examples of leisure behavior that requires more therapeutic intervention on the part of the leisure counselor include:

Compulsive behavior (e.g., gambling)	Procrastination
Excessive competition	Fear
Materialism	Poor self image/poor body image
Obsessive behavior	Negative attitude
Poor time budgeting	Inability to deal with peer pressure
Inability to compensate for disability	Inability to anticipate consequences of lei-
Guilt	sure choices
Regression (avoidance of present)	Excessive sense of obligation
Anxiety	Dependency on people or objects
Boredom	Inability to sift through media barrage
Uncertainty	Lack of confidence
Social isolation	Unrealistic self-expectations

FIGURE 4–1 Leisure Service Delivery

Work/Leisure Orientation

Ideal: holistic life; work/leisure/family viewed as one; purposeful and meaningful activity; leisure is earned.
Present: segmented life; lack of meaningful activity, no work, therefore no leisure.
Possible Solutions:
  1. Less specialization of care services, more integrated approach.
  2. Provision of work, service activity.
  3. Earned leisure involvements.
  4. Leisure counseling to effect attitude change.

Time

Ideal: live by the seasons and the sun; normal rhythm of day; evenings and weekends spent in leisure.
Present: scheduled by the clock; early rise, early to bed, no choice; leisure services lacking in evenings and on weekends.
Possible Solutions:
  1. Allow more freedom—open breakfast, freedom to fix own breakfast.
  2. Hire more staff to enable normal time routines.
  3. Reschedule leisure services to provide evening and weekend activities.

Living Environment

Ideal: own home and furnishings; household responsibilities; privacy; accessibility to community.
Present: shared room; little space; few personal belongings; housekeeping services; usually isolated location.
Possible Solutions:
  1. Apartment-like areas for more independent living.
  2. Individualization of room, with personal furniture, plants, pets, etc.
  3. Larger rooms to provide feeling of "own space."
  4. Opportunities to do household chores (gardening, cleaning, etc.).

Leisure Interests: Family

Ideal: primary source of socialization; intimate social-sexual involvement; major portion of free time spent with family—4 to 18 hours daily.
Present: limited family interaction—one hour per day maximum.
Possible Solutions:
  1. Provide more opportunities for spouses to live together in the care home, or conjugal visits.
  2. Educate family to the importance of their involvement.
  3. Organize family leisure events in and out of care home.
  4. Refer residents to care homes in close proximity to family.
  5. Provide aid needed to make weekend home visits possible and desirable.
  6. Facilitate adopted family, adopted grandchild, and adopted grandparent programs.
  7. Strive to involve staff in making meals and evening activities homelike.

Leisure Interests: Group

Ideal: card playing; clubs; sports; church (sources of socialization and worship); community based; minor part of free time spent in these activities—2 to 8 hours a week on the average.
Present: entertainment; chapel services; three B's—Bible, bingo, and bowel movement; crafts, institutional group activities; 2 to 8 hours daily; scheduled activity; community special events.
Possible Solutions:
  1. Use all available community resources: senior centers, adult education, special events, clubs, private and commercial.

2. Facilitate continued attendance at church of choice in the community where residents lived.
3. Focus majority of services toward fostering family and one-to-one social relationships rather than large group activities.

Leisure Interests: Individual

Ideal: sewing, knitting, collecting, reading, music, TV.
Present: limited involvement due to health problems.
Possible Solutions:
1. Begin preventive leisure education before sensory impairments and other physical involvements become severe—that is, redirect clients to other interests, teach them about talking books, blind knitting, etc.
2. Provide motivation to continue a hobby—volunteer aid, clubs, art shows, sewing circles, gift sales, etc.

Source: Carol Stensrud, "Helping Meet the Needs of the Institutionalized Aged," *Leisure Today*, (Reston, VA: AAHPERD, Vol. 2, April, 1977), pp. 22–24.

HOBBIES

Hobbies are an encouraged by-product of leisure education because they are lifelong leisure skills chosen because of their natural integration into the individual's lifestyle. A person chooses a hobby for its ability to satisfy unique personal needs—whether those needs are physical or mental development, recognition, monetary gain, or others. One individual might choose photography as a form of self-expression, while another is attracted by its potential for profit-making. A hobby's appropriateness for an individual is largely related to how the nature of the activity is agreeable to that individual's personality. For instance, doll house furniture making as a solo activity might appeal to an individual who possesses self-discipline and powers of concentration; however, a person less inclined to detail and perseverance might not find this such an attractive hobby. In selecting a hobby, the individual considers a number of factors including the space, equipment, time, local resources, money, skills, and level of social contact needed to pursue it. For instance, having limited money and space might reduce the feasibility of antique collecting as a hobby.

Hobbyists (persons engaged in a hobby) do not become dependent on the local leisure services agency to program their free time hours—the possession of a hobby acknowledges people's ability to pursue a self-directed leisure activity over an extended period without any agency dependency. In the true essence of leisure education, the leisure services agency becomes a resource for hobbyists rather than a filler of frenzied leisure hours. Therefore, recreation agencies are encouraged to schedule hobby fairs/exhibits that educate the public to the variety of hobbies they can choose.

Participants can explore potential hobbies by viewing films on activities, visiting activity centers, and speaking with hobbyists themselves on the dynamics of their hobbies. In addition, avocational interest inventories (also called activity interest inventories) are leisure education tools for revealing individual hobby interests.

Hobbies are often mistakenly viewed as activities for shut-ins or for individuals in the privacy of their attics. On the contrary, hobbies can be active and group-oriented, such examples being gardening, camping, sailing, travel, dramatics, and folk dancing. The development of common hobbies among family members increases family cohesiveness.

There are countless hobbies that can be conveniently categorized into creative, educational, collecting, or performing hobbies. Creative hobbies involve the personal creation of art or utilitarian objects. Educational hobbies involve the investigation of information and learning of material. In a collecting hobby, the hobbyist is absorbed in gathering items of interest. In a performing hobby, the individual is engaged in an activity that involves some physical performance. Some examples of the various types of hobbies are listed here:

COLLECTING	EDUCATIONAL
Coins	Botany
Stamps	Geology
Bottles	Homemaking
Dolls	Philosophy
Buttons	Interior Decorating
Antiques	Art
Shells	History
Books	Music
Butterflies	Classical Books
Leaves	Astronomy
Insects	Psychology
Match Covers	Sociology

CREATIVE	PERFORMING
Sculpture	Camping
Creative Writing	Sailing
Drawing	Cooking
Model Furniture	Folk Dancing
Music Composition	Archery
Nature Crafts	Bowling
Sewing	Band
Set Designing	Acting
Musical Instrument Making	Fishing
Painting	Hiking
Pottery	Social Dancing
Puppet Making	Chorus

Hobbyists quite often are interested in more than one hobby. For example, an interest in art may not only take the form of creating through painting, but also may entail studying the mixing of colors, collecting postal card size reproductions of artistic works, and studying the styles of eminent artists by visiting museums, exhibits, and doing research on the subject.

LEISURE EDUCATION ADVANCEMENT PROJECT

A concrete and creative approach to leisure education has been provided through the Leisure Education Advancement Project (LEAP) Kangaroo Kit, a kindergarten through twelfth grade curriculum guide developed by the National Recreation and Park Association. As a result of funding from the Lily Endowment, the Society of Park and Recreation Educators (SPRE) of the NRPA developed the LEAP materials in 1975. The Kangaroo Kit's curriculum format is not intended to limit its use to school settings; on the contrary, its objectives and correlary activities belong in any recreation setting due to their broad conceptual range.

The twelve general learning objectives that served as the basis for the Kangaroo Kit include:

1. The student will appreciate that the dimensions of leisure in a world with the potential for increased discretionary time may affect not only the quality of life, but its survival.
2. The student will recognize that discretionary time is inherently neither good nor bad, that the value assigned is a matter of personal and societal judgment.
3. The student will understand that any life experience can be a leisure experience; it is a matter of personal choice and attitude. It may be the result of social integration or private thoughts, can occur while one is physically active or passive, includes anticipation and reflection, may be structured or unstructured, planned or spontaneous.
4. The student will understand that effective leisure living and leisure choices will be dependent upon the development (acquisition) of skills, knowledges, and attitudes learned through study, experience, and practice.
5. The student will understand and appreciate the dynamic relationship which exists between and among environment, social institutions, and individual life-styles as they affect leisure behavior and opportunities, and to identify sources which influence leisure attitudes and choices.
6. The student will understand the potential of leisure for personal growth and personal satisfaction and the relationship among work, family, leisure, and other social roles in the evolution of a life plan.
7. The student will recognize that there is general understanding of the importance of work in American society, that the potential contribution of leisure is not well understood and that work and leisure are both possible sources of feelings of dignity and self-worth and can be mutually supportive.
8. The student will appreciate those intangible qualities of the leisure experience which transcend an individual's physical existence, but are experienced on the emotional and spiritual plane.
9. The student will recognize that the use of discretionary time has meaning which extends beyond the individual's satisfaction and has implications for the total environment (social, human, physical, and natural).
10. The student will understand and demonstrate that a leisure experience is self-motivated in response to personal perceptions of an appropriate pace, natural rhythms, interest, and opportunities (e.g., laws, peer pressure, etc.), and that the choice of leisure experience is often limited by social control.
11. The student will identify, understand, and evaluate leisure resources, choices,

FIGURE 4–2 Kangaroo Kit Activity: Leisure Choices

TARGET: The student will recognize and evaluate the consequences each person's use of leisure has on human, social-constructed, and natural environment: The student will recognize that each person is ultimately responsible for his/her own leisure as well as for influencing the community to suggest leisure opportunities.

FOCUS: Observe and weigh relative values of leisure choices and their consequences in daily experiences.

SUPPLIES: One large chart to show how differently students feel about similar experiences. Copies of charts on which students may keep their personal feelings.

ACTION Have students record how they and other people view their leisure choices. Put up a chart to record how similar leisure choices are viewed by different children.

SAMPLE CHART

KEY:

 Wow!   So-So/Didn't Notice (Example)   Ugh   Anger

Activity	Self	Friends		School Adults	Parents
		Girls	Boys		
Mud pies				Custodian	

THEN: Discuss rewards or costs of these choices. Were they worth it anyway? How did they know the way others felt?

Source: National Recreation and Parks Association, *Kangaroo Kit Leisure Education Curriculum*, Vol. 1, Grades K–6 (Alexandria, VA: NRPA Publications Office, 1977), p. 724.

and environments available in the community, state, and nation, and develop appreciation of various modes that individuals may have of utilizing these resources.

12. The student will recognize and evaluate the consequences of leisure choices to oneself, to others, and to the environment; and to accept that both the individual and the community are ultimately responsible for one's leisure behavior and experiences.[9]

The Kangaroo Kit contains many inventive, effective activity suggestions for achieving these objectives. Recreation leaders would be wise to use the Kangaroo Kit as a programming resource. Figures 4–2 through 4–5 show samples of Kangaroo Kit leisure education activities.

---

9. National Recreation and Park, Association. *Kangaroo Kit Leisure Education Curriculum*, Vol. 1, Grades K–6 (Alexandria, VA: NRPA Publications Office, 1977), pp. 31–32.

FIGURE 4–3   Kangaroo Kit: Leisure Planning for a Day

TARGET: Make it happen! The student will understand the potential of leisure as well as work, family, and other social roles in developing a life plan to ensure continued personal growth and satisfaction.

FOCUS: To develop an ability and responsibility to plan and use leisure and work opportunities.

SUPPLIES: Chart, similar to one below, for each student.

ACTION Have student complete chart at start of day.

NAME _____ (Check off those things you will do)

MY PLAN FOR ONE DAY

Read	Puppets	Handwriting	Art Table
Math Book	Clay	Music	Science
Special	Records	Painting	Cut and Paste

EVALUATION: (i.e. how I felt about the things I did)

THEN: At end of day, discuss with student reasons why they selected certain activities, and how they felt about each activity.

Source: *Kangaroo Kit Leisure Education Curriculum,* Vol. 1, Grades K–6, p. 817.

VALUES CLARIFICATION IN LEISURE EDUCATION

Values clarification exercises are self-assessment activities that facilitate knowledge of personal values and leisure attitudes. Values clarification plays a critical role in leisure education and leisure counseling. As leisure educators, recreation leaders are encouraged to develop a resource file of values clarification exercises that can be implemented in the various program areas (such as music, art, drama). Values clarification exercises are particularly appropriate for the mental recreation area, which involves writing and discussion.

FIGURE 4-4 Kangaroo Kit: Achieving Goals

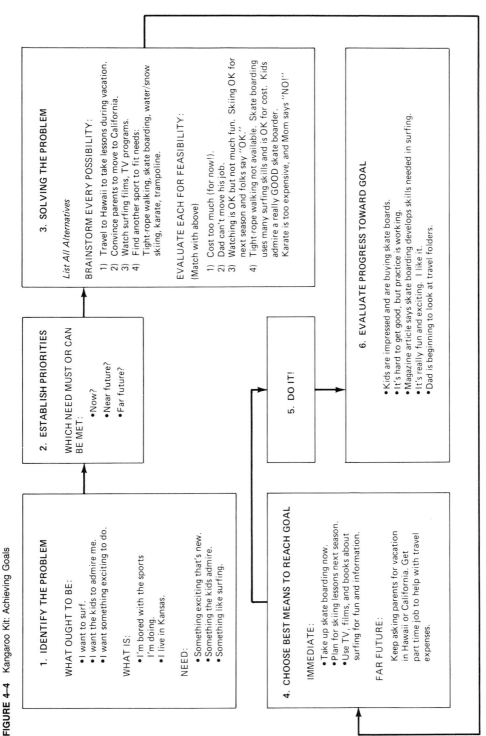

1. IDENTIFY THE PROBLEM

WHAT OUGHT TO BE:
- I want to surf.
- I want the kids to admire me.
- I want something exciting to do.

WHAT IS:
- I'm bored with the sports I'm doing.
- I live in Kansas.

NEED:
- Something exciting that's new.
- Something the kids admire.
- Something like surfing.

2. ESTABLISH PRIORITIES

WHICH NEED MUST OR CAN BE MET:
- Now?
- Near future?
- Far future?

3. SOLVING THE PROBLEM

List All Alternatives

BRAINSTORM EVERY POSSIBILITY:
1) Travel to Hawaii to take lessons during vacation.
2) Convince parents to move to California.
3) Watch surfing films, TV programs.
4) Find another sport to fit needs:
   Tight-rope walking, skate boarding, water/snow skiing, karate, trampoline.

EVALUATE EACH FOR FEASIBILITY:
(Match with above)
1) Cost too much (for now!).
2) Dad can't move his job.
3) Watching is OK but not much fun. Skiing OK for next season and folks say "OK."
4) Tight-rope walking not available. Skate boarding uses many surfing skills and is OK for cost. Kids admire a really GOOD skate boarder. Karate is too expensive, and Mom says "NO!"

4. CHOOSE BEST MEANS TO REACH GOAL

IMMEDIATE:
- Take up skate boarding now.
- Plan for skiing lessons next season.
- Use TV, films, and books about surfing for fun and information.

FAR FUTURE:
- Keep asking parents for vacation in Hawaii or California. Get part time job to help with travel expenses.

5. DO IT!

6. EVALUATE PROGRESS TOWARD GOAL

- Kids are impressed and are buying skate boards.
- It's hard to get good, but practice is working.
- Magazine article says skate boarding develops skills needed in surfing.
- It's really fun and exciting. I like it.
- Dad is beginning to look at travel folders.

Source: *Kangaroo Kit Leisure Education Curriculum*, Vol. 1, Grades K–6, p. 44.

FIGURE 4–5 Kangaroo Kit: I Need to Try . . .

TARGET: Make it happen! The student will understand the potential of leisure as well as work, family, and other social roles in developing a life plan to ensure continued personal growth and satisfaction.

FOCUS: To have the student experiment/sample a great variety of leisure activities in a variety of forms in a number of different leisure categories.

SUPPLIES: Mimeo chart for each student as per sample on the back of this page.

ACTION: Have students list experiences they have during a week (including the weekend) that are satisfying to them, bring them pleasure, and make them feel good about themselves.

THEN: Using this information, have them determine what kinds of experiences they've missed.

Have them make a list of the kinds of activities they need to try.

Example: I NEED TO TRY . . .
- something that involves service
- something that results in a product
- something I do ALONE.

These can be things that last only a moment or that take a long time. They can be either work or leisure.

- Identify the characteristics that each has.

- Try to figure out which parts of the experiences made them satisfying to the student.

* Follow-up with the student in planning a program for their leisure that will include those missed categories for a period of at least two weeks!

SAMPLE CHART OF EXPERIENCE

SATISFACTION
RATING   GREAT!   O.K. (nothing to write home about)   UGH! (not my style)

ACTIVITIES	Movie Date	Talking with Gang	Water Skiing	Stamp Collecting	Car Washing	Sun Bathing					
CATEGORIES											
Provided a Service											
Resulted in a Product											
Was aesthetic (beauty, form, color, texture)											
I was Active											
I was Passive											
It was Physical											
It was Mental											
I used my Senses (smell, taste, touch, etc.)											
I was a Spectator											
I was a Participant											
I did it Alone											
I did it with Others											

Source: *Kangaroo Kit Leisure Education Curriculum,* Vol. 2, Grades 7–12, pp. 324–325.

Figure 4–6 shows a leisure values inventory that is ideal for use in leisure education workshops and individual leisure counseling.

Figure 4–7 shows a values clarification exercise that appears in the text *Leisure—A Resource for Educators* which contains leisure education activity suggestions.

The text *Values Clarification—A Handbook of Practical Strategies for Teachers and Students* is a valuable resource for the recreation leader seeking leisure education activities. See Figures 4–8 through 4–11 for examples of values clarification exercises to be found in this text.

Figure 4–6 How Do You Rate Your Leisure Lifestyle?

Please complete the following leisure inventory ("at your leisure!") when you are freely able to give it your full consideration. It will provide you with some exciting insights on how to achieve new leisure satisfaction.

Values—Your personal values reflect what will bring you the greatest happiness and satisfaction in your life. If you are guided by a knowledge of these values in making your leisure choices, the results will be more enriching. For instance, a person who acknowledges how much he or she values recognition will be motivated to choose a leisure activity promising success and achievement. Those who are not consciously aware of their values tend to choose leisure activities at random, thus resulting in experiences that are empty and shallow in meeting their personal needs.

To become more aware of your personal values so that you can select leisure activities in symmetry with those values, please complete the following:

On a scale of 1–5, with 1 being the lowest and 5 being the highest, rate the importance of each of the following values to you by circling the corresponding number.

physical fitness	1	2	3	4	5
creativity	1	2	3	4	5
socialization	1	2	3	4	5
mental stimulation	1	2	3	4	5
spiritual growth	1	2	3	4	5
family	1	2	3	4	5
friends	1	2	3	4	5
recognition	1	2	3	4	5
service to others	1	2	3	4	5
adventure	1	2	3	4	5
self-expression	1	2	3	4	5
economic security	1	2	3	4	5
self-esteem	1	2	3	4	5
entertainment	1	2	3	4	5
affiliation with a course	1	2	3	4	5
affiliation with a group	1	2	3	4	5
skill development	1	2	3	4	5
enjoyment, fun	1	2	3	4	5
contemplation	1	2	3	4	5
appreciation of beauty	1	2	3	4	5
competition	1	2	3	4	5
cultural enrichment	1	2	3	4	5
power	1	2	3	4	5
personality development	1	2	3	4	5
status	1	2	3	4	5
self-sufficiency	1	2	3	4	5
responsibility	1	2	3	4	5
new learning	1	2	3	4	5
sexual expression	1	2	3	4	5

1. Next to each one of the values you rated 4–5, indicate what role or roles you now hold enable you to satisfy these values. (Example of roles include friend, parent, spouse, sibling, grandparent, church member, citizen, student, consumer, employer.) In the months and years ahead, these roles will increase or diminish by necessity or choice. Therefore, think how remaining roles might be utilized to satisfy these value needs.
2. Next to each one of the values you rated 4–5, indicate what activities you do to meet those needs and with what frequency.
3. Review your responses to see what strong personal values emerge.
4. Have these values changed much over your lifetime?
5. As you get older, are you substituting new ways of meeting these value needs?
6. What present and future leisure activities will satisfy the values you so highly prize? Jot some of these activities down.

As a starter on leisure activities, answer the following questions here:

1. What have you done in the past year that was new or different?
2. Do your leisure activities provide the same, more, or less satisfaction as those derived from work activities? (Use former work activities if retired.)
3. If your work activities are or were pleasurable, can any be adapted to leisure activities?
4. With whom do you like to do things? Do you prefer an age mixture?
5. What do you have planned for the near future that is new or different?
6. If married, what do you and your spouse do in leisure separately? Jointly? What changes would you like to make in this pattern?
7. Would you rather do something or learn about it?
8. Do you plan to develop any new hobbies? Do you feel you "outgrew" some? Are some "just for kids"?
9. Do you plan to develop any new hobbies?
10. Do you avoid beginning a new activity because you fear you won't excel in it?
11. Do you put spouse or family requests ahead of personal leisure interests?
12. Do you choose leisure activities involving social interaction?
13. Are your leisure activities limited by the facilities or human resources in your community?
14. Is money a factor in limiting your ideal leisure lifestyle?
15. Is transportation a limitation to your leisure goals?
16. Is some physical disability limiting your leisure activities?
17. Are seasonal or geographical conditions posing obstacles to your leisure goals?
18. Would you like to volunteer as a leisure choice?
19. How does your culture "celebrate" its holidays?
20. What makes you proud of yourself?
21. Do you think that certain leisure activities are more "worthy" than others?
22. Where do you feel most at leisure? When do you feel most at leisure?
23. Do you dread or anticipate holidays such as New Year's Eve, Valentine's Day, and so forth?
24. Make a list of some sample activities you pursue each day and label them work or leisure. Look back and decide what makes them work or leisure for you.
25. Do you have a balance in the leisure activities you now pursue or plan to pursue? Check this against the following balance factors:

planned/spontaneous
inexpensive/expensive
home/outside home
spectator/participant
solitary/group
mental/physical
family/outside family

Do you feel you need to correct any imbalances? If so, how?

This questionnaire has helped you establish your leisure goals, yet perhaps you are still hampered by misconceptions or self-doubt. What obstacles are standing in your way? With every "but" in "I'd like to do this, *but . . .*", you're building the "*But*tress" or wall against your leisure goals. You need to examine the "buts" in this buttress to see whether you have a real or imagined wall. Imagined obstacles are those self-defeatist messages that hold us back from our desired goals. They are often societal stereotypes that become our personal crutches. Examples of imagined obstacles would be "I can't learn that at my age," "Older people aren't supposed to do that," "I don't have the ability," "I'm not good enough," "I'll hold the rest of you up if I try it," etc. Real obstacles, on the other hand, are extrinsic factors over which one has little control and which impede leisure choices, such as limited income, lack of transportation, physical limitations, seasonal or geographical conditions, etc. Yet, once identified, the real obstacles can be dealt with and necessary adjustments made. It is important for you here now to frankly inventory what are the real obstacles to your ideal leisure and what are the imagined obstacles. Then explore how you could possibly eliminate these obstacles.

Imagined Obstacles: *Real Obstacles:*

Methods of Elimination:

In summary, the challenge of leisure is exciting for it invites us to explore new vistas of self-expression and quality experiences. It is hoped that this leisure inventory has provided you with new insights into how to meet the ongoing leisure challenge. Best wishes in your continued growth! Be all you can be!

FIGURE 4–7   Values Clarification Exercise

Put a check beside those needs that are important to you.
It's Important to Me:

_____ to do something meaningful	_____ to make use of my skills
_____ to be physically active	_____ to improve my skills
_____ to be committed to something	_____ to develop my skills
_____ to keep busy	_____ to have something to show for my efforts
_____ to do lots of different things	_____ to get approval for what I do
_____ to relax and take it easy	_____ to be a success at what I do
_____ to do something different from work and/or school	_____ to have feelings of personal worth and confidence
_____ to be entertained	_____ to learn more about myself
_____ to be able to do what I want	_____ to develop interpersonal relationships one to one
_____ to be spontaneous	_____ to be with groups, teams
_____ to make and carry out plans	_____ to meet new people
_____ to try my own methods of doing things	_____ to develop friends
_____ to compete with others	_____ to help others
_____ to compete with myself to do better	_____ to laugh and enjoy
	_____ to be in attractive surroundings

List the five most important needs for you (in order of priority). Are you presently meeting these needs through your leisure? if yes, state how. If not, state how you could meet that need.

Source: Ministry of Culture and Recreation, *Leisure—A Resource for Educators,* (Toronto, Ontario: 1978), p. 64.

FIGURE 4–8 Twenty Things You Love To Do

List twenty things that you love to do.

1. Place a dollar sign ($) next to any item that costs more than $3.00 each time it is done.
2. Place the letter A beside those items you prefer to do alone, the letter P beside those activities you prefer to do with other people, and the letters A-P next to activities you enjoy doing equally alone or with other people.
3. The letters PL are to be placed beside those items that require planning.
4. The coding N5 is to be placed next to those items that would not have been listed five years ago.
5. The numbers 1 through 5 are to be placed beside the five most important items, 1 being the most important to you.
6. Use the letter R for those things on your list that have an element of RISK to them.
7. Mark with an S any item that can only be done in a particular season of the year.
8. Put the letters IQ next to any item that you think you would enjoy more if you were smarter.
9. Place the letter U next to any item that you think other people would find unconventional.
10. Use the letters MT for items you think you will want to devote more time to in the years to come.
11. Put the letters CH next to the things you have listed that you hope your own children will have on their lists some day.
12. Put an MI next to items you would not be able to do if you moved 1000 miles from where you are now.
13. Put a B next to those items you would like to be able to do better.

Source: Reprinted by permission of Dodd, Mead & Company, Inc., from *Values Clarification* by Sidney B. Simon, Leland W. Howe, and Howard Kinchenbaum. Copyright © 1972, 1978 by Hart Publishing Company Inc., pp. 30–34.

FIGURE 4–9 Rank Order

Rank order each of the following choices according to your value preferences.

1. Where would you rather be on a Saturday afternoon?
   _____ at the beach
   _____ in the woods
   _____ in a discount store
2. If I gave you $500.00, what would you do with it?
   _____ save it
   _____ give it to charity
   _____ buy something for myself
3. Which do you like best?
   _____ winter in the mountains
   _____ summer by the sea
   _____ autumn in the country
4. Which would you least like to do?
   _____ listen to a Beethoven symphony
   _____ watch a debate
   _____ watch a play
5. Which would you most like to improve?
   _____ your looks
   _____ the way you use your time
   _____ your social life
6. Which would you find easiest to do?
   _____ campaign for contributions to a Thanksgiving food drive
   _____ tutor students
   _____ be a hospital volunteer

Source: Reprinted by permission of Dodd, Mead & Company, Inc., from *Values Clarification* by Sidney B. Simon, Leland W. Howe, and Howard Kinchenbaum. Copyright © 1972, 1978 by Hart Publishing Company Inc., pp. 58–93.

FIGURE 4–10 Either-Or-Forced Choice

> From each set of alternatives, choose that characteristic you most identify with.
> Are you
>   more of a saver or spender?
>   more likely to walk on thin ice or tiptoe through the tulips?
>   more like a clothesline or kitestring?
>   more yes or no?
>   more like breakfast or dinner?

Source: Reprinted by permission of Dodd, Mead & Company, Inc., from *Values Clarification* by Sidney B. Simon, Leland W. Howe, and Howard Kinchenbaum. Copyright © 1972, 1978 by Hart Publishing Company Inc., pp. 94–97.

FIGURE 4–11 Pie of Life

> Draw a circle to represent a day in your life. Divide into four quarters, each representing 6 hours and totalling 24 hours. Draw slices in "your pie" to represent proportionately the amount of time you spend on: sleep, school, work, alone, with friends, with family, home-work, on chores (maintenance activities), and miscellaneous (other pastimes). Your pie may look something like this:

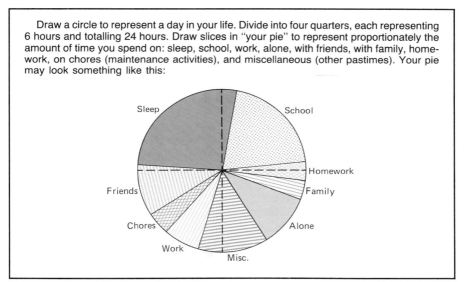

Source: Reprinted by permission of Dodd, Mead & Company, Inc., from *Values Clarification* by Sidney B. Simon, Leland W. Howe, and Howard Kinchenbaum. Copyright © 1972, 1978 by Hart Publishing Company Inc., pp. 228–233.

LEISURE EDUCATION THROUGH PROGRAM ACTIVITIES

Each of the following program areas contains activity suggestions for integrating leisure education concepts.

Outdoor Recreation

1. While on a hike, make a list of as many leisure activities as you can associate with the things you see (for example, (a) leaves: leaf printing; (b) rocks: rock collecting; (c) sticks: whittling; (d) plants: gardening).
2. After a camping experience, discuss how the absence of mechanical technology affected quality of leisure. For instance, the absence of the stereo may

later be viewed as a blessing since it motivated the spontaneous creation of original music around the campfire.

3. Keep a journal of outdoor recreational activities you engaged in which technology has replaced with labor-saving devices (for example, (a) making own fire: microwave; (b) hand-stirring: electric mixer; (c) hand-washing: washer/dryer). In light of this technology, discuss what you feel has been gained and lost in terms of quality of life.

4. Using available materials in the natural environment, construct a miniature setting that you feel to be most conducive to your leisure satisfaction. Design an environment that would allow you to pursue your areas of recreational interest. For instance, one interested in water sports could create a body of water (natural environment) and a marina (constructed environment). This learning activity illustrates that leisure choices are largely circumscribed by the available resources of the constructed environment (architecturally designed resources such as recreation centers, resorts, libraries) and natural environment (environment created by nature such as mountains, streams).

5. Tour the local area and record natural and constructed environments and their potential leisure uses (for example, natural: shaded area for storytelling; constructed: miniature golf course).

6. Set up a nature trail in your backyard. Label all the flora and fauna and print up guides for neighborhood visitors.

7. Take a tour throughout the community to find examples of a leisure choice's negative influence on the environment (for example, discarded soda cans, tire treads on gardens).

Sports/Games

1. Adapt games to contain leisure content. For example instead of "This is the way we wash our clothes" in the *Here We Go Round the Mulberry Bush* game, substitute "This is the way we play our flutes." Players originate the leisure activities and lead the group in pantomime.

2. In any game, remove the competitive element so that participation is truly determined by intrinsic motivation rather than the extrinsic motivation of competition and awards.

3. Run a *Lifelong Leisure Sports Day* which exposes participants to individual and dual sports. These sports, such as tennis, racquetball, golf, bowling, and jogging, are more easily maintained over a lifetime than group sports which require team affiliation together with group planning and organization. The team-sports orientation is more often indigenous to a school system and does not meet the need of the individual who seeks to incorporate a fitness activity into his or her nonacademic lifestyle.

4. To demonstrate that each person can control the quality of his or her leisure experience, have participants alter the rules of a game to correspond to their own group needs.

5. Make up creative adaptations for games. For instance, create a miniature golf course with human obstacles, such as people on all fours for tunnels, and cupped hands for holes.

6. Tug-of-war teams are established. Each team selects one of the following factors which can affect leisure: constructed environment, natural environment, family influence, peer pressure, age and sex stereotypes, ethnic beliefs, religious influences, economic conditions, education, and media impact. The teams decide on an individual case study, with each side representing a conflicting leisure influence. For instance, a 12-year-old may want to be with

his or her friends in summer resident camp (peer influence) but his or her family may wish to have him or her to travel with them to see relatives across the country (family influence). As each side tugs, it shouts out its viewpoint. The point of the game is to have participants physically experience conflicting influences which affect leisure choice.

Social Recreation

1. Pin a piece of paper to your clothing that indicates a leisure activity you are pursuing and a need you still have to meet in your leisure (for example, need: adventure, activity: chess). Everyone mingles throughout the group, reading people's tags to see how they can meet each other's needs by sharing recreational experiences. For instance, the person with the chess player tag might agree that he or she would be a likely match to the person seeking intellectual stimulation. Similarly his or her need for adventure could be met by the individual labeled as a white water rafter. It is hoped that some individuals will actually be interested in pursuing shared leisure activities beyond the social event.

2. Create a board game in which the players must avoid landing on the blocks that pose obstacles to their intended leisure pursuits (for example, time, weather, safety, cost, environmental factors, social obligations).

3. Players move in two concentric circles. Upon a signal they stop. Each person faces the person opposite and explains what he or she perceives to be the other person's leisure lifestyle based on appearance and personality.

4. Create a board game in which the player picks up a "Benefits" card every time he or she lands on a Leisure Activity block. If the benefit appears to be appropriate to the activity landed on, the player moves ahead a number of spaces. If the benefit does not match, the individual moves back a number of spaces. For instance, if the player picks a Benefit Card reading "physical fitness" for landing on an activity block reading "card playing" then the player moves back.

5. Play TV game *Dating Game* with all questions pertaining to candidates' attitudes towards leisure and their activity preferences.

6. On a human size board, players roll dice and move to a station that is labeled with one of the elements of activity balance (for example, active/passive, solo/ group). Pantomime an action that illustrates the element (for example, solo could be illustrated by reading).

7. Participants must guess the leisure activity pinned on their backs by asking group members Yes/No questions (for example, Would I do this outdoors?).

8. *Meet Your Match.* As each question is asked, players hold up their responses and mark on their tally sheets who else in the group has a similar response. From the total tally at the end of the game, each person can determine who else in the group has recreation interests. For example:

Round 1. How do you feel when fishing? dancing? reading? backpacking?

Round 2. What leisure activity makes you feel adventurous? proud? happy? cautious?

Round 3. On a scale of 1–3 (1 being the lowest, 3 the highest) rate the following activities in terms of your level of interest:
   cooking
   gardening

skiing

playgoing.[10]

Additional examples can be added by the players.

9. Each team is given the name of a commercial product or slogan and must identify the leisure activity associated with it (for example, frankfurters—baseball; "We try harder"—travel [Avis Car Rental]). The team to guess the correct leisure activity first wins a point. The game is repeated until 20 points are achieved by a single team.

10. Develop a set of cards with leisure activities on them. On another set, write "large" or "small" representing muscle skills. Each player selects a card from each pile. If the activity requires large muscle skills (such as "football"), but the other card reads "small muscle skills," the player must hold on to the cards. However, if the skill card agrees with the activity, such as small muscle skills for sewing, the player can discard the cards. The player with the least number of cards at the end of the game wins.

11. *Intervening Variable Board Game.* Players develop a board game with leisure activities marking various blocks. When a player lands on an activity block, he or she picks an intervening variable card, which explains a condition that may or may not affect his or her ability to participate in the activity. Intervening variable cards include age factors, environment, weather conditions, physical limitations, and so forth. The aim of the game is to have players realize that a leisure activity may require adaptation in the face of an intervening variable, but that it should not automatically be rejected. The game impresses players with the importance of creative, flexible decision-making in leisure. For instance, although one lands on a dance activity block and picks a card reading "broken leg," it is still possible to engage in wheelchair dance arrangements. Should a person be unable to explain how an activity can be modified in light of an intervening variable, he or she moves back a space.

Creative Movement/Dance

1. Move so as to suggest how you feel when at leisure, when at work.

2. As the leader calls out outcomes of leisure experiences, move in response to the moods they suggest (for example, boredom, relaxation, exuberance, stimulation, frustration).

3. Participants develop an ethnic dance festival, and in the process learn how ethnic beliefs and characteristics are reflected in the movements.

4. The group identifies ephemeral moments when they felt at leisure (for example, the touch of a lover's hand, smell of lilacs, feel of cool sheets against a warm body). As each phrase is called out, the group individually or collectively interprets the meaning through movement.

5. Our leisure choices do not occur in a vacuum but affect (1) oneself; (2) other people; (3) natural environment; (4) constructed environment. Players stand in a row, each one representing one of these four factors. As the leader calls out an activity, individuals respond with a gesture and explanation of their response. For example, sand dune buggy racing might elicit a raised fist and the statement, "Don't destroy me!" from the individual representing the natural environment, the sand.

10. Jean Mundy and Linda Odum, *Leisure Education: Theory and Practice* (New York: John Wiley and Sons, 1979), pp. 189–190.

Arts and Crafts

1. From objects in a bag, create an ingenious piece of recreational equipment.
2. Using colors, illustrate how different leisure activities have resulted in different levels of satisfaction for you.
3. Create an inanimate object that reflects your leisure lifestyle (for example, a shoe made of canceled plane tickets represents a physically active leisure. Hearts painted on the shoe represent the importance of family and friends in this individual's leisure happiness.)
4. Make a collage or quilt of your leisure lifestyle.
5. Paint or fingerpaint your mood when at leisure.
6. Construct a leisure mobile that illustrates how you are working for balance in your leisure choices. (for example, physical/mental, solo/group).
7. Develop a brochure with illustrations and written copy describing your fantasy leisure setting.
8. Make a banner that stands as a trademark of your current leisure lifestyle. For instance, a tent symbol may represent an outdoor recreation interest, a pair of crutches the weekly volunteer work at the hospital.
9. Cut out magazine pictures or take photos of people engaged in various leisure activities. Make an album. Discuss the benefits each of these pictured activities offers.
10. Develop a collage of pictures or photos of leisure environments (for example, beach, pool room).
11. To deemphasize the association of consumerism with leisure satisfaction, construct a craft made solely of available materials (such as egg cartons, bottle tops, pipe cleaners, cans, straws).
12. Make a collage or picture of how you feel others view you at leisure, how you presently view yourself at leisure, and how you would like to view yourself at leisure.
13. To show how a leisure interest can be satisfied from any number of local resources, take slides of various leisure settings in your community (for example, museum, bowling alley, health spa, park, skating rink).
14. Make a collage of pictures showing celebrities engaged in leisure activities or endorsing leisure products. Ask group if their heroes' or heroines' leisure lifestyles influence their own leisure choices.

Music

1. Conduct a "Name That Tune" contest in which all the songs contain reference to a leisure activity (for example, "Row, Row, Row Your Boat," "Color My World," "Sittin' on the Dock of the Bay").
2. Select music that captures the moods suggested by slides of leisure activities. Play the music as accompaniment to the slides.
3. To the song "Happiness Is" from *You're A Good Man, Charlie Brown*, have participants contribute lines that state what leisure activity brings them happiness.
4. Incorporated within a music appreciation class, discuss in small groups all the leisure activities that can be associated with a song title (for example, "Moon River"—white water rafting, fishing, sailing, canoeing, swimming).
5. Play different types of music, and discuss how each does or does not contribute to a leisure atmosphere.

6. Bring in songs that you associate with a leisure experience (for example, "Blue Danube" might recall a feeling of relaxation while painting).

7. As the song "Up, Up, and Away" is played, have participants write on the kite strings the personal obstacles to leisure that they want to send off into oblivion (for example, lack of confidence, lack of transportation).

8. To the accompaniment of the song "Anything You Can Do I Can Do Better," have participants add lines reflecting personal examples of when competition overshadowed leisure enjoyment.

9. To the accompaniment of the song "My Favorite Things," have participants add lines pertaining to personal moments of leisure satisfaction (for example, picking flowers, watching a sunrise, hugging a child).

Literary/Mental Activities

The following leisure education exercises can be discussed or written about as part of the mental recreation program.

1. If, due to some monetary bonus, you did not have to work any more, would you still do so?

    Is there a personal investment that you feel in your work? Could leisure be a satisfactory alternative?

2. Create a story with other members of a group in which each of you is pursuing the same leisure activity for a different reason (for example, woodworking class attracts a retired carpenter who needs to continue to feel useful in his or her trade, a youth interested in selling crafts for profit, and a middle-aged scholar who feels a need to use his or her hands after a day of mental activity).

3. Along the same lines, create a story in which each of you is pursuing the same leisure activity for one of the following reasons: (a) feeling of anticipation; (b) actual doing of the activity; (c) its ultimate benefits; (d) social prestige.

    For instance, in terms of jogging, one may primarily enjoy the prospect of the jog, another relishes the running experience itself, another jogs because of the physical and mental benefits, while another is motivated by the social approval of eventual weight loss.

4. Discuss the effects of an individual's leisure choice on other people or the environment (for example, a motorcycle-riding group may create an unacceptable noise level for the community in which they live).

5. Discuss what each of you would bring to an isolated island if only one item were possible. The choices reflect the predominant life values, which gives good indication of how leisure satisfaction would be derived. For instance, choosing to bring a musical instrument indicates creative expression to be a source of one's leisure satisfaction.

6. Discuss which of the following people you would most like to have in your neighborhood: (a) one of the most popular athletes in town; (b) a family with a house at the beach; (c) an expert in your favorite subject of study.

    How does your choice reflect a leisure value of yours? For instance, preferring an intellectual neighbor above one with prestige, money, or physical ability indicates that intellectual stimulation is an important leisure value for you.

7. Which of the following would you be best able to cope with: (a) deafness; (b) blindness; (c) amputation.

    Discuss your answer in terms of what it indicates about the leisure activities you value: (for example, a lover of music might find deafness more difficult than blindness or amputation).

8. In a short story, create your vision of full leisure satisfaction. Describe the place, activities, season, climate, and people that make up that experience.

9. For a future group discussion, carefully observe the media to note their attempts to sell you leisure satisfaction through consumerism.

10. Interview individuals about their leisure activities and print results in a newsletter or post on a bulletin board.

11. Play TV games, with all references pertaining to leisure outcomes (adventure, relaxation, and so forth), and leisure activities (sailing, dancing, and the like). This can be adapted to such game formats as Jeopardy, Family Feud, To Tell the Truth, Password, and $25,000 Pyramid. An outline of $25,000 Pyramid is included as an illustration.

$25,000 LEISURE PYRAMID GAME

Adapted from the $25,000 Pyramid TV game, the $25,000 Leisure Pyramid Game is designed as a leisure education game. The six categories deal solely with leisure, the focus being on individual leisure skills and attitudes, the implications of leisure choices on society, and leisure education methods.

The six categories are "Voice of the Heart," "Roadblocks," "Is That All There Is?," "There's No Such Thing As Leisure Island," "The Ways and the Means," and "Give Me Options." Write each of the six categories on an 8½ in. by 11 in. piece of paper, Place a bonus number "7" behind one of these categories to indicate a double score. Then arrange the categories on posterboard or against the blackboard in pyramid form: put three on the bottom level, two in the middle, and one on top. Choose an emcee, scorer, timekeeper, and two teams of pairs.

The first team chooses one of the six categories, which is then removed from the board. After the emcee reads the general description of the category (see emcee information at end of this game description), one member of the team is given a packet of seven words corresponding to the category title. The object is to get the partner to guess the seven words by only giving one-word clues. For example, in the category "Give Me Options," the aim is to correctly guess specific leisure activities suitable for a teen seeking socialization. Thus, to get across the first word, "waltz," the giver might use one-word clues like "dance," "graceful," "sophisticated." For each of the seven words guessed, one point is received. After going through what they can of the category in 1 minute, the other team chooses a category. The teams alternate until the categories are completed, with the team choosing the Bonus 7 category doubling its score for that round. Throughout all of the rounds of the game, it is expected that members within each team pair will take turns being giver and receiver.

The team with the highest score is then given the opportunity to play the $25,000 Pyramid. In this there are also six other leisure categories arranged in pyramid form, with the difference being that the team member must guess the overall category from one word clues related to the subject area. For example, if the leisure category was "Things You Do Alone in Leisure," the giver would relate words relevant to that such as coin-collecting, solitaire, knitting, and so forth, until the partner guessed it. Again, there is a 1-minute time limit. It is the giver's job to think up all the possible one word clues related to the overall category in order to help the partner guess it.

The six categories are "Tourism," "Things You Do Alone in Leisure,"

"Leisure Entertainment," "Spectator Sports," "Leisure Activities Requiring Money," and "Home-Centered Leisure."

It is suggested that an easel containing the correct answers be shown to the audience throughout the game so that they are more involved in the educational process. If there is a large group interested in becoming players, you may wish to divide the entire group into two teams and let different representatives come up for each round. Should the group wish to remain as audience cheering on the pairs, you may wish then to direct the words that were missed to them and see if they can guess them without reference to the easel.

As part of the leisure education process, it is encouraged that the players continue to develop further game categories pertaining to leisure.

The following describes the various categories and lists the words to be guessed in each category. After a player selects a category the emcee should give the description (in quotation marks). The words to be guessed should be handed to the player who will "give" the clues.

Emcee Information:

Category 1. *Voice of the Heart*—"These are feelings one may experience during leisure."
Words to guess: (1) boredom; (2) freedom; (3) relaxation; (4) happiness; (5) anxiety; (6) guilt; (7) satisfaction.

Category 2. *Roadblocks*—"These are reasons why an individual may say he or she doesn't have leisure."
Words to guess: (1) poverty; (2) school; (3) job; (4) laundry; (5) commuting; (6) family; (7) sick.

Category 3. *Is That All There Is?* "These are outcomes you may be looking for in a leisure activity."
Words to guess: (1) exercise; (2) creativity; (3) friendship; (4) skill; (5) employment; (6) adventure; (7) achievement.

Category 4. *There's No Such Thing As Leisure Island*—"These leisure choices show the effects of our choices on society and environment."
Words to guess: (1) volunteering; (2) hunting; (3) vandalism; (4) drugs; (5) choir; (6) littering; (7) tutoring.

Category 5. *The Ways and the Means*—"These are means of helping people discover their own leisure interests."
Words to guess: (1) role playing; (2) media; (3) inventory; (4) interviews; (5) questionnaire; (6) counseling; (7) discussion.

Category 6. *Give Me Options*—"These are suggestions for leisure activities you might make to a teenager seeking more socialization."
Words to guess:
(1) disco; (2) drama; (3) athletics; (4) chorus; (5) club; (6) camp; (7) band.

12. Complete unfinished phrases that will reveal leisure goals and attitudes. For example: In my wildest dreams I see myself _____.
I realize that my leisure is _____.
I am happiest when _____.
I would consider it dangerous to _____.
I feel most truly myself when _____.
It is important for me to _____.
In my leisure I need to improve _____.
A leisure activity I'd like to try is _____.

13. In 10 minutes see how many community leisure resources you can list (for example, Ella's Bowling Lanes, Von Tapier Park, Ed's School of Dance).

14. Discuss how one person's maintenance activity can be another's leisure (for example, for some, shopping is a necessity; for others, a leisure activity). How can a maintenance activity take on more of a leisure quality? (for example, through change of location, time, company, musical accompaniment.)

15. Write down leisure activities you would like to try but feel you do not have the skills for. Are you sure you are not being too hard on yourself? If not, how can you develop those skills?

16. Observe ways in which the media foster age or sex stereotypes regarding leisure pursuits (for example, granny knitting in rocking chair, little girl playing with tea set).

17. As a group, investigate how local laws impact on leisure choices (for example, regulations regarding snowmobiles, gambling).

18. Discuss how the same activity can be appropriate or inappropriate depending on local laws, space factors, time factors, and effects on others. For instance, singing in the streets will be greeted differently by residents and lawmakers if carried out at 3 A.M. rather than 11 A.M. Local ordinance laws and a limited facility space may prevent a casino night in one town but not in one adjacent.

19. Interview your predecessors as to how they viewed leisure in their lives and what activities they pursued.

20. Have classes in time budgeting.

21. Discuss how the salary, schedule, and location of your occupation is or is not conducive to the leisure you desire.

22. Play *Concentration*. The object of the game is to get enough words to determine the hidden phrase. The leader asks a question regarding a leisure activity (for example, What is tai chi?). The person who answers correctly gets two cards. If they match, the player is given a word from the sentence to be guessed (for example, in a match, the player is told the word "penny," and putting that together with previous word clues ("save," "a") determines the phrase to be "a penny saved is a penny earned."

23. Write your own obituary. An obituary is intended to summarize the life of an individual, but most often only occupation and family status are cited, with no mention of leisure pursuits. In your obituary, include what you expect to have experienced in leisure by the end of your life.

24. Research and debate a controversial issue pertaining to leisure (for example, the National Rifle Association versus gun control advocates).

Drama

1. Do charades of leisure activities.

2. One person pantomines a leisure activity such as swimming. Others join in the scene if the setting suggests a leisure activity that they enjoy doing and can pantomine (such as collecting sea shells, bathing).

3. Develop a skit on how a personal need was met by a leisure activity (for example, need to be of service met by volunteering in a hospital).

4. Role play leisure lifestyles of the past and present. How did past recreational pursuits and leisure attitudes differ from those today? How are they the same?

5. Dramatize a scene in which peer pressure results in an individual's making a leisure choice against his or her better judgment (for example, drug-taking, vandalism).

6. Have two puppets represent the two sides waging war within a person regarding a potential leisure choice (for example, "I'd love to paint."/"Oh, but I don't have the skill.").

7. Use puppets to dramatize a family recreation experience. The use of puppets is a therapeutic medium for revealing and dealing with emotional problems. The way in which the individual has puppets interact reflects interpersonal dynamics that might not normally emerge in regular discussion. For instance, if an overbearing parent stressed achievement in any recreational activity, this might be evidenced in the way the puppeteer makes the father puppet shout insults to the son puppet, a struggling Little Leaguer.

8. Dramatize how an individual's insecurity leads him or her to go along with leisure fads.

9. Act out the contrast between someone who has achieved balance between work and leisure and another who derives his or her total identity from work.

10. Dramatize how one's childhood experiences with a leisure activity can be a positive or negative influence on later adult involvement.

11. Act out how a person's insistence on perfection jeopardizes his or her enjoyment of leisure.

12. Act out how always projecting for that "ideal leisure" in the future can blind one to present leisure possibilities.

13. Role play what you feel to be your leisure lifestyle 5 years from now, 10 years from now.

14. Role play an example of how people can pursue the same leisure activity out of different motivations. The person operating out of intrinsic motivation is concerned with satisfying personal needs; the person operating out of extrinsic motivation is attracted to the prospect of external recognition and rewards. One of the aims of leisure education is to foster intrinsic motivation.

15. Role play a leisure counseling session according to the following format:

ROLE PLAYING LEISURE COUNSELING

This leisure education exercise is concerned with leisure counseling and is an example of how an expressive art—role playing—can be utilized to achieve a leisure education objective. The group will split into pairs, with one person being the individual going to a community center for leisure counseling, the other person being the leisure counselor. The role playing involves the counselee expressing to the counselor a desire for more qualitative leisure experiences, thus leading the counselor to respond with helpful suggestions.

To help each counselee develop his or her fictitious character, each will select a slip indicating a given characteristic from each of the following five category envelopes: "Who Am I?" (age and marital or family relationships), "My Income and Residence," "A Favorite Leisure Activity," "My Work Life," "What I'm Seeking in Leisure." The counselee will incorporate all of these characteristics into developing his or her role. It is imperative that the counselor not see any of these slips for this would diminish the "real life" quality of an interview in which the counselor gradually discovers the many dimensions of the counselee. It is natural and desirable that some of the resulting character combinations be challenging and unsimplified for this better illustrates the complexity of human beings and serves as a more realistic example of the factors of which a leisure counselor must be aware.

The character's age is an indicator of the developmental capacity for certain leisure experiences. Residence is another characteristic that will often determine leisure options. For instance, a person from the plains area who is seeking physical exercise would be frustrated by the leisure counselor's suggestion to try mountain climbing. Similarly, income is a factor for the leisure counselor to consider before recommending expensive travel or commercial recreation for the person seeking adventure. Work life is of importance to the leisure counselor for it may indicate whether the individual is seeking leisure for compensatory reasons or for further exploration of job-related skills and interests. The category of favorite leisure activity is of significance, for in examining what makes this a favorite for the individual, the counselor has some basis for suggesting further leisure experiences. The marital-family relationship is of consideration in exploring joint or individual activities and in knowing which type of activity would enhance or disrupt this relationship. Some leisure activities, such as an extended camping trip, may not be possible in light of family commitments. The category of "What I'm Seeking in Leisure" is the aspect to be focused on in the counseling session for this leisure attitude will determine what leisure activity is suitable or if activity is even the desired outcome. Perhaps a modification of a current leisure attitude or activity is all that is needed to supply what the individual is seeking in leisure.

In beginning the dialogue, it is suggested that the counselor direct the interview toward what the person is seeking in his or her leisure. This will diminish the too frequent emphasis on activity and recreation program quotas and put it on the individual's needs. The phrase "leisure experience" should be used instead of "leisure activity" to help the counselee see leisure as an attitudinal phenomenon occurring anywhere and not merely free time participation in the community center's programs.

In the role-playing, the counselee is not to feel a compulsion to make known all of his or her characteristics at once, but should take clues from the counselor's questions and gradually reveal a personal composite picture. When the counselor is satisfied that the individual has received some constructive guidance, the role playing can terminate. It should be followed by a discussion of what approaches did and didn't work during the counseling as well as the feelings experienced by both individuals in their roles. Questions to be considered would include: Did you find the leisure counselor judgmental of your interests? Were you honestly pleased by his or her suggestions or just being polite? Did the counselor help the character you played discover more about himself or herself in regards to leisure attitudes? The leisure counselor in turn could be asked: Did you feel that the counselee was open to new views of leisure and leisure experiences? How did you feel that the leisure experiences decided upon would be beneficial to the counselee?

After evaluating how their characters responded during the role playing, they should reverse roles to experience the other viewpoint. This second role playing and discussion should then be followed by a general group discussion of the entire leisure counseling role-playing experience as a leisure education approach. The group should be urged to add any additional character categories they feel are necessary as well as individual slips with each category.

It should be noted that music, art, dance, drama, and literary arts are ideal media for projecting leisure education content. The activities described in the following chapters need not be restricted to small group participation, but can be designed as presentations to elicit audience involvement. For example, a leisure education troupe could tour the community requesting that audience members become actively involved in the leisure education content of the songs, skits, dances, and art work. The song "My

Favorite Things" can vary with each performance as the audiences contribute different recollections of happy leisure moments. The audience might also be involved in the creation of a group mural to form a backdrop of their ideal leisure settings. They can be involved in any leisure education skits outlined in the drama section as in the dramatization of peer pressure situations. As an example of possibilities for group collaboration in dance, the audience can interpret through movement their feelings and moods while at leisure.

SUGGESTED READINGS

BRIGHTBILL, CHARLES K. AND MOBLEY, TONY A. *Educating for Leisure-Centered Living.* New York: John Wiley and Sons, 1977.

CORBIN, H. DAN AND TAIT, WILLIAM J. *Education for Leisure.* Englewood Cliffs, NJ: Prentice-Hall, 1973.

CURATIVE WORKSHOP. Avocation Activities Inventory. Milwaukee, WI: Curative Workshop, 1973.

EPPERSON, ARLIN, WITT, PETER A. AND HITZHUSEN, GERALD. *Leisure Counseling: An Aspect of Leisure Education.* Springfield, IL: Charles C. Thomas, 1976.

JOSWIAK, KENNETH FRANCIS. *Leisure Counseling Program Materials for the Developmentally Disabled.* Washington, DC: Hawkins and Assoc., 1976.

LOESCH, LARRY C. AND WHEELER, PAUL T. *Principles of Leisure Counseling.* Minneapolis: Educational Media, 1982.

McDOWELL, C. P. *Approaching Leisure Counseling with the Self-Leisure Interest Profile.* Salt Lake City, UT: Educational Support Systems, 1973.

McKechnie, G. E. *Leisure Activities Blank Booklet.* Palo Alto, CA: Consulting Psychologists Press, 1974.

MIRENDA, JOSEPH J. *Leisure Interest Finder.* Washington, DC: American Association of Health, Physical Education, and Recreation, 1973.

MUNDY, JEAN AND ODUM, LINDA. *Leisure Education: Theory and Practice.* New York: John Wiley and Sons, 1979.

MURPHY, JAMES F. *Concepts of Leisure. Philosophical Implications.* Englewood Cliffs, NJ: Prentice-Hall, 1974.

NATIONAL RECREATION AND PARK ASSOCIATION. *Kangaroo Kit Leisure Education Curriculum.* Volume 1—Grades K to 6; Volume 2—Grades 7 to 12. Alexandria, VA: NRPA, 1977.

NEULINGER, JOHN. *Psychology of Leisure.* Springfield, IL: Charles C. Thomas, 1974.

OVERS, R. P., TAYLOR, S. AND ADKINS, C. *Avocational Counseling Manual: A Complete Guide to Leisure Guidance.* Washington, DC: Hawkins and Associates, 1977.

WITT, JUDY, CAMPBELL, MARILYN AND WITT, PETER A. *A Manual of Therapeutic Group Activities for Leisure Education.* Washington, DC: Hawkins and Associates, 1979.

5

Drama

The recreation professional who is trained in drama leadership skills is equipped to provide participants with countless opportunities for self-expression. This chapter is designed to familiarize recreation professionals with the wide spectrum of drama activities and the values to be derived from them.

VALUE OF DRAMA

The many benefits to be derived from participation in drama strongly support the inclusion of drama in recreation programs. These benefits include the following:

1. Drama develops the participant's sensory awareness and listening skills.
2. Drama increases the participant's powers of concentration and memory retention.
3. The participant develops better understanding of body movement through pantomime, the use of gestures, creative movement, and the development of characterizations.
4. The opportunities for socialization, emotional release, and use of the imagination are enjoyable and therapeutic.

5. Drama fulfills our basic need to communicate feelings.
6. Involvement in drama increases one's poise and self-confidence.
7. Drama offers the opportunity for self-expression and creativity.
8. Participants learn more about themselves as their responses to reality situations are tested in spontaneous improvisations.
9. Since the subject of drama covers the entire realm of human experience, participants increase their sensitivity to people and the lives they lead.
10. In confronting the various options in dramatized situations, participants improve their decision-making skills.
11. As players or audience members, the individuals expand their appreciation of art and beauty.
12. Drama, as a mirror of life, causes participants to observe the life around them as they study details to dramatize.
13. Drama can highlight individual or community problems through such vehicles as role playing or street theater.
14. Drama is a dynamic way to explore a group's conflicts and interpersonal relationships, perhaps arriving at alternative behaviors.
15. Drama integrates the arts (dance, music, art, literature), creating a unified whole that makes each of the arts more meaningful.
16. By participating in the communal experience of drama, individuals learn the value of cooperation and responsibility.
17. Drama in education allows students to experience the concepts they study (for example, dramatize historical event, bring paintings to life, do addition as a bank teller).
18. Drama allow one to make fantasies real, to truly become other people in other places.
19. Drama increases facility in speaking and reading.
20. Performing for others, the participants reap the rewards of the audience's praise and support and are reinforced in their artistic pursuits.

DRAMA IN RECREATION LEADERSHIP

In their professional development, recreation students may choose to concentrate primarily on the area of drama to prepare for positions such as cultural arts specialist for municipal programs, special events coordinator for shopping malls, drama therapist for special populations, creative dramatics instructor, children's theater director, and community theater director. On the other hand, recreation students may also choose to utilize drama skills in conjunction with other job responsibilities. For instance, the social director of a cruise or resort may employ drama in a "get-acquainted mixer"; the nursing home recreation therapist may use creative movement and sensory exercises to stimulate residents' responses; the camp counselor may stage a colorful pageant that integrates the camp's programs in folklore, crafts, and nature study. In any recreation setting, the recreation professional's possession of drama skills will enhance the leisure services program.

Those readers interested in additional leadership instruction beyond the scope of this chapter should consult the many reference texts available on acting and directing; additionally, technical theater production covers such areas as costume, makeup, set design, sound, lighting, and stage management. The aspiring creative drama leader also has a wealth of resources to explore: texts on theater games, pantomime, creative movement, puppetry, improvisation, storytelling, and more.

Informal drama is the focus of this chapter. It is more applicable to the informal, participatory nature of most recreation settings than is theater. However, the basic terminology of theater will also be discussed.

CREATIVE DRAMATICS AND THEATER

At the outset, it is important to distinguish between the terms "theater" and "creative dramatics," for each possesses unique characteristics and requires different leadership approaches. Theater involves the presentation of drama before an audience and requires rehearsal to achieve the performance goal. The person directing formal drama must be trained in acting and directing styles and understand conventions of staging. Creative dramatics, on the other hand, consists of drama activities that encourage and endorse individual self-expression without concern for audience approval. Creative dramatics stresses the benefit of the dramatic process itself rather than the benefit of the dramatic product—a performance. Creative drama provides greater acceptance of individual interpretation whereas theater tends to guide the individual toward achievement of a preconceived ideal.

Any dramatic form can become formal or informal depending on the leadership approach taken by the recreation leader. For instance, role playing becomes informal drama when the situation allows for spontaneous improvisation and is centered on present enjoyment, as in the case of a free-form skit on family life. However, were that same family skit to be approached for its presentational possibilities, and the players become actors who rehearse for performance before an audience of any size, then formal drama has occurred.

CONCEPTS IN CREATIVE DRAMATICS

Creative dramatics has mistakenly been associated with children, the notion being that creative dramatics was a way of rehearsing for the later "adult" form of drama, theater. This is a false idea because the need to play out ideas through drama transcends age; this fact is supported by the number of senior-citizens' drama clubs enjoying lively, informal sessions that incorporate movement, dialogue improvisations, and other dramatic forms. One does not "graduate" from creative dramatics to theater; each approach has value in and of itself. From youth to old age, we all should be exposed to both creative drama and theater.

The success of a creative dramatics activity is due in large part to the atmosphere created by the leader. The creative dramatics leader does not push the players to any standard of performance but rather leads them to the exploration of their own creativity and imagination. To guide this learning process effectively, the leader must be familiar with several key leadership principles of creative dramatics.

Since creative dramatics strongly deemphasizes any semblance of audience, the structure of the creative dramatics session is important. For example, in "unison playing" all participants are involved in the dramatic activity at the same time and no one is highlighted for observation. The impetus for the dramatic activity usually comes from the leader's sidecoaching—narration that sets the scene, suggests possibilities for action, and guides the dramatic progression. For example, the leader might sidecoach, "You are shivering campers attempting to start a fire in the bitter wind." Unison playing would allow each player to interpret that action in his or her own way. Unison playing allows for greater freedom and spontaneity; individuals need not wait till they are called to demonstrate for the group. An audience might have caused reluctance in shyer individuals, and for others it would have encouraged the tension and artificiality of rehearsal.

In unison playing there are three formats: individual, paired, and group play. In individual play, the player interacts with no one, in paired play with a partner, and in group play with any number of other people. Depending on the format used, the dramatic activity can take on a wide variety of meanings. Let us refer back to the situation of the campers seeking warmth: In individual play, the player might assume the role of a solo Outward Bound member battling nature's elements. In paired play, two might join as cowboy partners stopping to camp out during a rugged westward journey. In group play, the entire ensemble could assume the identity of shipwrecked crew members seeking a source of warmth.

Each format has its distinct advantages. Individual play builds greater concentration and allows for more privacy. For a situation in which the leader feels more group control is needed, individual play is more appropriate as it allows a one-to-one relationship between leader and player with no distraction by other players. It also affords the player the opportunity to play all of the characters and actions in the scene as the entire sequence is in the realm of his or her own interpretation. Paired play develops sensitivity between players through the blending of movement and the exchange of dialogue, and serves as a stepping stone from solitary, individual play to the interpersonal skills required in group play. Group play provides the benefits of socialization and cooperative play as well as insight into the motivations behind others' responses.

The use of each format will depend in large part on the age and size of the group and the space to play in. In some instances, limited space may prevent free-form unison play and other approaches must be devised.

However, space restrictions should not be viewed as obstacles but as creative stimuli. Desks bolted to the floor, for example, can become computer terminals or pilots' cockpits. In fact, large spaces can have drawbacks: the person overwhelmed by a lack of boundaries may tense up; and conducting a creative dramatics session on the stage of a large gym may be poor judgment, for despite the leader's assurance that there will be no eventual performance, the players still experience the sensation that comes from being elevated for public view.

Before engaging in a particular drama activity, it is often advisable to have players try out various approaches through "preview playing." For example, in "previewing" a space journey, players could try various means of space travel before actually entering into the scene. Preview playing helps develop the players' confidence and gives the leader the opportunity to assess their level of enthusiasm and readiness.

The effective creative dramatics leader will be equipped with a variety of activities that can be tailored to the nature of the group and setting. These activities have a thrust toward one or more of the following aims: *sensory exploration, creative movement/pantomime, characterizations,* and *improvisation (movement* and/or *dialogue).* These aims are not to be viewed as separate entities, for by the very nature of drama there is a dynamic blending of the elements. For instance, to achieve a believable character, the individual must develop an understanding of how this character responds physically to the environment through movement and sensory awareness. Sensory exploration often overlaps with pantomime, as does pantomime with characterization; the interrelationships are inherent to the fluidity of drama. In reviewing the leadership examples given in this chapter, the reader should discern the interrelationships between these dramatic aims. For the purpose of instruction, however, each of these aims will be discussed individually, with leadership examples given for each.

SENSORY EXPLORATION

Sensory exploration involves activities designed to heighten awareness of the five senses. By concentrating on the experiences of taste, smell, touch, hearing, and sight, players put themselves in touch with the world of imagination. In focusing on these sensations, whether recalled or real at present, the player creates an immediacy and believability that is primary to the creative dramatics process.

The following exercises are designed to stimulate sensitivity to the five senses.

Sensory Exploration Activities

Let your face show that you are: swallowing a bitter pill, eating a pizza with extra cheese and chili peppers, eating a drippy double-scoop ice cream cone, drinking coffee with salt instead of sugar.

Close your eyes and identify sounds. Distinguish between sounds that are part of your immediate environment, that are nearby, and that are far away. Link these sounds together to form the basis of a story to dramatize.

Blind Walk. One member of each pair is blindfolded or has eyes closed while the other partner leads him or her around the environment. In addition to heightening sensory awareness, this exercise builds the mutual trust necessary among fellow players in drama.

While your partner gives you a message in gibberish or nonsense language, guess the message by listening to his or her tone of voice.

React with your body as if you are touching different substances with your whole body (e.g., cotton, pine needles, fur, sandpaper, lace, satin, dried-up leaves, sand).

You are in a strange place where you must push yourself through different substances. Feel how the different pressures against your skin affect your movement (e.g., honey, swampland, hailstones, spaghetti, clay, cobwebs, velvet).

Savor the flavors of a fantasy eight-course meal. Relish each bite. Take the same meal and eat it now as if you were a poor vagrant; next, as a fastidious socialite.

While your partner makes a sound, imitate and expand upon it.

Observe your partner's appearance, for in a moment your partner will turn away from you and change three things about his or her physical person. You will have to try to guess what has been changed.

Listen to the sounds around you. Focus on one and think of it in a larger sense. For instance, if you hear a motorcycle, imagine who is riding it, where the rider is going, etc. Think of elements of conflict and develop a scene to dramatize.

Create sounds from objects and your own vocal mechanisms, then incorporate these into a scene. For instance, swaying gravel in a tin pan creates a windshield-wiper sound that suggests a scene involving a car driving in a storm.

As a group, follow in unison with your eyes, heads, and bodies the progress of a tennis match, a plane in the sky, etc.

In pairs, each person takes turns sculpting his or her partner nonverbally. The sense of touch is accentuated. The end-product may be a realistic sculptured figure engaged in a discernible act or a free-form sculpted figure in which the individual's position suggests an abstract idea or symbol (e.g., peace).

Observe the contents of a room closely. Then, in another setting, reproduce that room as nearly as possible by establishing its contents through pantomime and movement.

Move the way you feel when you hear sounds as they are made (e.g., bell, hammer pounding table, alarm clock, whistle).

Move the way you feel when you hear the names associated with sounds (e.g., crunch, splat, growl, mumble, splash).

Explore a sensory box—which contains items that you cannot see but experience solely through taste, touch, and smell. Taste items might include lemon, garlic, candy, onion, and anchovy. Touch items could be gravel, chiffon, sandpaper, and tissues. Smell items could include pine, lilac, oregano, and orange. Your reaction to these items should reveal itself in your facial expression and interpretive movement. Select a few of the sensory items that elicited the strongest response from you. Create a dramatized scene in which you link your sensory impressions together. For instance, the smell of pine may create the location of a log cabin where you experience the rough feel of gravel on the roadway pressing through your sandals. Later that night, you and your companions cook over the open hearth and enjoy a stew laced with tangy garlic.

CREATIVE MOVEMENT AND PANTOMIME

Body movements take on more energy and meaning when prompted by a dramatic impulse. For example, the leader's sidecoaching to "Reach and grab a star" is far more evocative than the flat statement, "Raise your arms." Thus, creative movement involves physical activity that is associated with a dramatic idea and serves as a means of creative expression.

Locomotor movements (traveling movements such as walking and running) become charged with new interest if one is, for instance, suddenly walking in a vat of peanut butter or running up a moving escalator. Likewise, while standing in place, the player can be prompted to do nonlocomotor movements (such as bending and bouncing) with a dramatic motivation such as, "You are bending down to get into a girdle that is so tight you must bounce yourself into it." Creative movement can be approached as an individual activity or be linked to the development of characterization through gesture, posture, and walk. Creative movement can also be linked with sensory exercises for a fuller dramatic experience, as illustrated in the previous section.

Many creative movement exercises could fall under the category of warmups. A "warmup" is any creative physical activity intended to prime players for participation in the drama session. Often, the most productive warmups are those that are linked thematically to the purpose of the session. For instance, a creative dramatics session on underwater exploration might begin with a warmup of slow-motion "underwater" movement.

Creative movement also includes the area of pantomime (the expression of ideas solely through actions). Because pantomime does not involve any verbalization, many leaders make the false assumption that it is one of the simplest forms of drama and use it as a first activity with their groups. In actuality, however, pantomime is one of the more complex forms of drama; it requires great concentration and physical coordination to communicate an idea without the assistance of speech. One of the most common blunders made by creative dramatics leaders is to ask a player to pantomime an activity for a viewing audience to try to identify. It is very likely that the audience will not perceive the action the way the player feels it is being presented. The establishment of such an actor-audience situation is contradictory to the philosophy of creative dramatics because the player must be concerned with results and audience endorsement instead of enjoying the process itself. Individuals may choose to share their personal interpretation, but that is much different from being expected from the outset to perform.

Action Games and Songs

Pantomime is integrated into many dramatic activities. It highlights the narration of stories and adapts itself also to children's games and songs. In "action songs," players pantomime actions that correspond to the words of songs. For instance, in "Kum Bay Yah" they do the actions associated with the repetition of lines such as "Someone's praying, Lord, Someone's dancing, Lord", and so forth. The song "Here We Go Round the Mulberry Bush" allows the players to pantomime actions to such cues as "This is the way we wash our clothes," and so on. In the songs "Old MacDonald Had a Farm" and "The Farmer in the Dell," the players are prompted to give their movement interpretations of the characters and animals. The words to "Take Me Out to the Ballgame" can be enlivened through pantomime of the baseball fans' actions.

Action songs do not only apply to children; any song can be selected and interpreted that is suitable to the age range. To illustrate, one pantomime game done to song is quite appropriate as an adult mixer. As one team sings a song—which they have chosen because of a particular occupational reference—the other team collectively pantomimes occupations until they hit on the right one. For example, hearing the song "White Christmas," they might pantomime the actions of Santa Claus, a skier, and a snow-plow operator before hitting on the predetermined occupation, skater. The creative leader will select those songs for pantomime and creative movement cues that are appropriate to the group.

Games, like songs, also lend themselves to cues for pantomimic action. For instance, rather than just the standard cues, "Touch your toes . . . Simon Says clap your hands," and so on, the creative dramatics leader gives cues that allow for more creative interpretation. "Simon Says fly a kite lazily," "Simon Says be the man on the flying trapeze." In the games "Follow The Leader," the players can take turns leading their companions not just in movement, but in creative narrated movement, such as "Let us move like happy clowns . . . Now we're planes flying high in the sky . . ." In the game "Red Light, Green Light," players should be given the additional motivation to move the way their favorite cars do.

Finger Play Games

Finger play games are particularly appropriate for preschoolers as they appeal to their sense of rhythm and need for simplicity. In finger play the fingers act out the movements suggested by simple nursery rhymes and poems. Examples would be "The Itsy Bitsy Spider" and "Hickory Dickory Dock."

Story Play

Story play involves line-by-line pantomimic cues to develop a story line. The leader's sidecoaching builds up sequentially to create a story similar to the following: "You put on your snowshoes. Open the door and feel the cold air against your face. Walk through the deep snow. You decide to build a snowman . . . ". This type of sidecoaching is appropriate to the group that needs additional guidance, but at no point should the sidecoaching become directive. The purpose of sidecoaching in any situation is to facilitate the individual decision making of the players, so at no point should it be used excessively or without discretion.

Creative Movement and Pantomime Activities

Mirroring: In pairs, partners take turns following each other's gestures and facial expressions as closely as possible.

Move about the space according to the action and adverb called out by the leader: "Walk briskly," "Drive carelessly," etc.

As a beginning warmup, think of creative ways to do tension-relaxation exercises. Example: "You are stiff cubes of ice. But the sun hits you and you begin to melt. You are a puddle of water. Suddenly the sun disappears and the air grows cold. You form into blocks of ice again." Other examples include bacon frying, a rubber band stretching, a seed growing . . .

Machines: One person starts a movement with a corresponding sound. Gradually more people join in, synchronizing their movements and sounds. Think about what kind of machine you are.

Toss around an imaginary ball in a group circle. Notice how the position of your hands and body change as the ball becomes a medicine ball, a tennis ball, a basketball, a ping-pong ball . . .

The group passes along an imaginary object in a circle. From the way the players hold it, you get a clue of when it has been changed to something else. You may start sending around a hot potato that becomes a kitten, which becomes a gem . . .

You are surrounded by a thick murky substance that you have to keep pushing away on all sides or it will fill up your space.

All players sit in a circle. One brings an actual object and through imaginative action makes it into something else. For instance, the player places a rope in the middle of the circle and steps into it like a manhole. The person who correctly guesses the use of the object, then changes the interpretation of the object.

Pantomime sports movements in slow motion. This points up the grace of the movements and helps control unregulated behavior.

Each player brings one imaginary object into the playing area and begins to pantomime its use. When entering the playing area with the object, each player must remember where each object is so as not to destroy the established space. Players must use some of these established objects in the course of their pantomime.

Become Raggedy Ann and Andy and hang limp, feeling different parts of the body relax. Swing from the waist, let your knees flex. Swing your arms from side to side. Slowly feel yourself rising . . . until you feel yourself standing tall.

Move like various inanimate objects. Become an electric mixer, a vacuum, etc.

All stand in a circle. One person begins a sound and a movement that the others follow. Each, in turn, evolves his or her own sound and movement from the one preceding.

All join in a cooperative effort on the same action, such as a tug of war, a rowing expedition, etc.

Let your hands talk to each other. Let your hand talk to your foot, your elbow to your toes, etc. Have them express how you are feeling, what you are concerned about.

Spell out each other's names with your bodies.

Start telling a story and, at the snap of the leader's fingers, continue telling the story only in actions.

Join with a partner to become inanimate objects that are paired for their use (a popcorn popper and a popcorn kernel, for example).

Begin a pantomime, to which the leader adds conflict: "You are driving a car. Your brakes fail."

Show changes in weather by the way you walk down the street.

Pantomime rhyming words.

Line up and start a pantomime. See if the pantomime is the same by the time it gets to the end of the line. This exercise points up the importance of encouraging preciseness of movement so as to accurately project the idea. For instance, hands should not be clenched tightly around an imaginary rope sliding through your fingers, for there is no room for the rope to pass through!

Charades

In charades, a team pantomime game often used as a party mixer, players pantomime a word or a phrase as team members try to guess it within the allotted time period. The leader has slips containing the titles of books, movies, songs, plays, radio and TV shows, or of famous slogans, proverbs, or quotations. In acting out the term, one may point to a part of the body but not to a prop. Since there are a number of rules associated with charades and many variations on the game as well, it is recommended that the interested leader consult a reference detailing these features. However, the following hand-signal terms serve as the basis for conducting most charades.

1. Film—Simulate cranking motion of operating a movie camera.
2. Book—Palms held open like an open book.
3. Play—Pull curtain ropes.
4. Radio or TV—Turn a knob.
5. Song—Bring palms of cupped hands from mouth outward.
6. Proverb or slogan—Two fingers of each hand held in air to indicate quotes.
7. Number of words in the title—Hold up number of fingers corresponding to number of words.
8. Number of syllables in the word—Lay corresponding number of fingers across the back of wrist.
9. Small word—Bring thumb and forefinger together.
10. Shorten the word—Bring thumb and forefinger together.
11. The word sounds like another—Pull on ear lobe.
12. Change word to past tense—Throw invisible object over the shoulder.
13. Start all over—Wave hands in front of body.
14. "You're very close" or "Give me more"—Vigorously wave hands from player to self.

CHARACTERIZATION

Characterization—or the creation of a believable character—can be accomplished through creative dramatics activities that develop the physical and emotional qualities associated with playing a role. As a result, the players assume new identities, becoming sensitized to the attributes of the characters they play. The development of a role may lead into dialogue activities, the verbal interaction between two characters.

The following offers some valuable exercises that will stimulate participants to grasp and command the idea of characterization.

Characterization Activities

This activity stresses the importance of tone of voice in projecting a character's feelings: Each individual player will be given the same words but with different frames of reference. This can be done in a circle. The leader turns to each player and asks, "How would you say 'Is that true?' as if you had just been given sad news?" "As if you had just been told an outlandish tale?" And so on.

Order a meal as different characters would (a company president, a nutrition expert, a fussy old lady). How does your behavior change with each role?

Each time the drum is hit, freeze in a different position. On the last beat, bring your freeze position to life by becoming the character that the pose suggests.

Pantomime a simple daily activity that you yourself do. Now, do this activity as another character for whom the action is difficult. (e.g., putting on a girdle; a fat woman putting on a girdle).

Each time the drum is hit, freeze in a different position. Connect the last three freeze positions into an action sequence that suggests a character.

As the leader calls out different character roles, shake hands with your partner the way that character would (e.g., your boss, your grandmother).

Select a picture of a character that interests you. Develop a profile around this character. What is the character's personal life? professional life? educational background? residence? age? financial situation? physical attributes? Assume these characteristics. Turn to the person next to you and initiate dialogue in character.

Develop a character based on the emotions suggested by the percussive rhythms of the drum. For instance, a staccato beat may suggest a nervous, flighty character. Begin walking as your character. Move to the space that your character would most likely occupy (e.g., office, bakery, health spa) and begin pantomiming your occupation. This can lead into dialogue with nearby characters with whom you would be likely to interact.

The leader attaches the name of a role to the back of each player. All players move about the room and address each other according to the role they see on each other's backs. For instance, a waiter might be addressed by the words, "What is your special today?" Once the player has determined what his or her identity is by the way he or she is addressed, the player enters into the role. Players interact in character, building scenes of conflict and resolution.

Become a person of another time period, real or fictional. Project that character through speech and action.

Physically show the aging process of a given character.

Portray a popular figure who is being interviewed for TV.

Try on different shoes and hats, assuming the characterizations they suggest. When you have found a role of particular interest to you, evolve speech and action for that character, interacting with those around you.

Create a character from the mood suggested by a color of your choice. For instance, green might suggest a calm and cool personality. Put your color with that of the person next to you. The resulting color will determine the mood of your interaction with this person. (e.g., yellow would suggest a happy situation, black a sad one).

Create a character from a prop (a comb might suggest a beautician, for instance). Show your character's emotions by the way you use that object.

Walk about the room. At the sound of the drum, turn to the person next to you and say the first line you think of. Your partner and yourself must blend your disparate comments into a viable conversation that defines your characters' roles.

Experiment with vocal and physical impersonations of well-known characters.

Develop your own monologue for a real or fictional character. You may choose characters from literature or real life. Based on what you know about the character, spontaneously begin speaking as that character, using the first person "I."

As the leader calls out different characters, interpret them through your walk and facial expressions as well as gestures (e.g., politician, nurse, stunt man).

IMPROVISATION (MOVEMENT AND/OR DIALOGUE)

Improvisation is the spontaneous interpretation of creative thought through physical and/or verbal expression. Improvisation builds on and incorporates the skills discussed in the aforementioned sections on sensory exploration, creative movement/pantomime, and characterization. It can involve movement, dialogue, or a combination of both. For the purpose of definition, "skits" are those improvisations having a plot line, most often humorous but not necessarily so. "Stunts" are improvisations having a more slapstick, physicalized quality. The stunt is characterized by originality of plot and the creative use of available resources. Stunt props are symbolic, not realistic; for instance, curtains can be simulated by two "human poles" opening and closing bed sheets. To further encourage spontaneity, a prop man can hand the players nearby objects to further the plot. For example, a yardstick can become a horse, a wand, or anything that can be imagined.

Melodrama Stunt

Melodrama, a popular stunt format, is characterized by exaggerated gestures and physical humor. Many conventions are employed to encourage the humor; the players are often involved in "booing" the villain and cheering the heroine. Players can portray the scenery (e.g., lifting their arms as tree branches) or existing scenery can be labeled as something else (the sign "tree" placed on a coat rack). It is humorous to have the players speak not just their lines but also the stage directions that accompany them; thus the line "It is hot" might become: "It is hot, Susie Mae cried in dismay." The following sequence illustrates melodrama's reliance on improvised actions to accompany the narrator's words. In the narrative, the numbers in parentheses correspond to the actions in the list below it.

As the curtains part (1) a shady character (2) enters the room. He is draped in black (3) as all villains are. He is suddenly struck (4) by the sight of a beautiful woman who is tied up in work at the sink. (5) He is so enamored of her that much time goes by (6) before he begins to speak.

"Ah, my dear! You are the love of my life. I must have you!" He tears across the room passionately. (7)

"Leave me be (8) I beg of you!" pleads the lovely lass. "I am betrothed to Lance Butler who is expected any moment. You are no match for him." (9)

True to her word, Lance stalks into the room (10), a demanding presence. (11) He immediately sizes up the situation. (12)

"Alright, Vernon Villain, you'll get no further in your evil plans. Pauline is mine forever. You are a cad and I will personally see that you are driven out of this town." (13)

Footnotes for accompanying actions:

1. Two people with signs marked "curtains" stand in the middle of the scene and move away from each other to opposite sides.
2. He puts a lamp shade on his head.
3. He rips the black drapes from the window.
4. The curtain rod falls and hits him on the head.
5. She is wrapped in rope from the waist down.
6. "Time," written on paper towelling is unraveled at length across the playing space by two players.
7. He tears up pieces of paper as he crosses the playing space.
8. She swats at an annoying bee buzzing around her ear.
9. She hands him a match.
10. He throws corn stalks on the floor ahead of him.
11. He shouts demandingly, "So where are my presents?"
12. He takes out a tape measure and wraps it around Vernon's wrists like handcuffs.
13. He grabs his car keys, saying casually, "Come on, I've got my Ford out back."

In using this sequence with a group, the creative dramatics leader can retain the footnoted actions. However, for the creative development of the players, it is preferable to have them devise their own sequences with the freedom to create actions spontaneously from the objects at hand.

Shadow Play

The shadow play is another form of improvisation popular with groups interested in informal drama. In shadow play, the players engage in dramatic action behind a sheet or window shade with a light behind it, creating a silhouette effect. Depending on the setting, the screen can be framed or stretched between two door posts or two trees (the effect outdoors is particularly striking). For a 7 foot by 12 foot screen, a single 150- to 200-watt bulb placed 4 to 6 feet behind the screen provides a sufficient light source. Colored cellophane can be placed on an overhead projector or before the light source to create interesting scenic effects. Scenery can be established by tacking black cardboard or construction paper on the screen. Since shadow play involves visual effects, it is important that the players emphasize large, clear movements in their dramatization. There are a number of dramatic activities possible within shadow play. The players can pantomime a sequence to accompany a narrator's story; the pantomimed sequence can also be done without any accompanying narration. The players can use both movement and speech to tell their own story. The stylized effect of shadow play also lends itself to the use of a chorus whose words or songs highlight the impressive silhouette action. Players can also project their ideas and emotions into profile puppets pressed close to the screen. Made of cardboard or poster board and controlled by rods made of coat hangers, the puppets create a mesmerizing image.

Puppetry

Puppetry, in general, provides a rich source for improvisational material. Puppets act out our stories, play out our roles, move to our music, reveal our innermost feelings. . . . Emotions one might normally find too threatening to express directly as oneself are magically released through the character of one's puppet. Puppetry runs the gamut from spontaneous dialogue between two felt fingers to a staged production with puppets of sophisticated design. Puppets that represent various characters and roles (e.g., policeman, doctor) allow players to try on different identities. Besides these role-assigned puppets, it is recommended that there be a number of "neutral" puppets that are vague enough to assume the projected fantasies and concerns of the players. While many commercial puppets are available, the making of original puppets is encouraged; in this way individuals establish a special bonding with a character of their own creation.

Puppet making is an excellent example of the value of program integration, for here the art and drama departments join in the accomplishment of a common project. Puppets can be made from any number of materials including styrofoam balls, papier-maché or clay, stuffed socks, felt, gloves, tongue depressors, tissue rolls, tin cans, vegetables, and paper bags. More sophisticated puppets known as marionettes can be made; multiple strings are attached to the body parts of the puppet and suspended from a T-bar. Puppet stages, like the puppets themselves, can be devised from whatever is at hand including blocked up doorways, table tops, overturned boxes and crates, dutch doors, and curtains on rods suspended between two chairs.

Puppetry is especially appropriate to recreation settings because it adapts easily to unique space, time, and budget factors. Those interested in using puppetry with their groups should refer to the many available books on puppet construction and the art of puppetry. Examples of puppet construction are included in the arts and crafts chapter.

Story Dramatization

Another major area of improvisation is story dramatization. Story dramatization is the improvised interpretation of a literary work, and it gives life to characters that were once just words on a page. Stories become memorable because the players live them instead of just reading about them. To be suitable for dramatization the literary piece should have several important elements: an interesting idea, a conflict, essential action, realistic characters, and stimulating dialogue.

Depending on their ages and abilities, the participants can have the story read to them or can read it themselves. If the story is read aloud, the reader must be enthusiastic and feel free to delete passages that might reduce the immediacy of the action. A vibrant voice and facial expression can be augmented by the use of pictures, props, felt board characters, and music to set the mood.

In all cases, the recreation leader must determine if there is a sufficient level of interest in the subject's content before proceeding to dramatization. Based on participant response to the literary piece, the leader and group mutually decide whether all or only parts of the story should be dramatized. For instance, there may be interest in improvising only the action scenes and omitting dialogue sequences. It is also acceptable to give a brief synopsis of the piece without covering it in its entirety. For young groups and beginners, story dramatization often consists of narrative pantomime in which the players pantomime the actions suggested by the story. Additional narrative details of action as well as sensory stimuli are frequently added by the leader in order to provide participants with more opportunities for dramatic involvement. The underlined portion of the following passage indicates where the creative dramatics leader has added to the story some additional pantomimic cues: "While Fritz stayed at home to do the housework, Hans did the work in the field, *cutting and stacking the brittle hay in the blistering heat.*" The narrative details of action (cutting and stacking) give players specific actions to interpret, while the sensory details (brittle and blistering) enable players to truly immerse themselves in the sensations of the environment. The story thus becomes much more real in the process.

In narrative pantomime, unison playing allows all participants to become whatever character(s) they please. In individual, paired, and group playing, each individual can choose to play one character consistently throughout the story or try on different roles as they appear.

Most often, older children and adults will be interested in dramatizing only certain aspects of the story, and so will find narrative pantomime too directive and confining. They may wish to work through dialogue sequences of the story and ultimately link them together. They may read up to only a certain portion of the story and then devise their own improvised endings. They may write their own stories and adapt them to dramatization. They may be more interested in dramatizing what happened before or after the story's plot. Props, setting, and costumes may be added to reinforce the characterizations.

The leader of story dramatization needs to be attentive to the signals the group projects. The session can be adjusted according to their responses to the material. For instance, if the group seemed to be more interested in the subplot than the main one, that should be the subject of the dramatization.

If shy, reluctant individuals would find acting too threatening a prospect, integrate them into the dramatization by having them create sound effects to signal the appearances of different characters (such as cymbals for the king). In using the characterization exercises mentioned in the previous section, the leader may note a player's enjoyment of a particular role and find a way to add that character to the story.

The success of story dramatization is due in large part to the choice of material and its appropriateness to the age group. For instance, stories for young children should have repetition of action (such as "The Three Little Pigs") so that the children are not overwhelmed by stimuli they can't assimilate. Through repetition, the child comes to associate certain expressions with certain characters and comes to act them out with increasing confidence. If the children form groups representing separate characters, they can respond with collective sound and gesture to the mention of their characters' names in the story. Preview playing allows the leader to determine individual players' understandings of vocabulary words and context clues in the story; for instance, if someone is portraying a "slothful" character as an energetic one, the error is visible and can be corrected.

The literary subjects for story dramatization are endless and each suggests multiple choices for improvising characters, scenes, settings, and conflicts. Stories written in the past tense can be put in present tense for more dramatic effect. Portions of stories, poems, letters, essays, and lyrics can be linked together to dramatize a common theme such as adventure or justice. Keeping with the philosophy of creative dramatics, all of these scenes can be improvised for the sheer enjoyment of creating them, and not for audience feedback unless desired by the players.

Radio Play

The radio play is a form of improvisation in which the players express dramatic action through speech, sound effects, and music. Since visual action cannot facilitate the drama, it is especially important that the players exercise vocal variety and expressive tones of voice. The players can create their own script, use a published radio play, or adapt short stories or plays to the radio-play format. A set script need not be established on paper; it is acceptable to have the basic outline of a plot around which the dialogue and narration is improvised. Since the who, what, and where of the radio play can only be expressed orally, the situation should be one that is easily visualized.

In radio-play production, voices, sound effects, and music are recorded on a tape recorder. The ideal taping site is a studio or small room without windows, with walls and floor carpeted; however, for the informal recreation setting a tape recorder is sufficient. Players should be huddled around the microphone with no rustling of scripts to disturb the taping. If your recorder has two microphones, one should be used for actors and the other for sound effects. If you have two recorders, one recorder can be used to tape additional sounds and group voices to create a more realistic background. In the final tape, background sounds will set the scene and gradually dim as the actors speak.

Perhaps one of the most enjoyable aspects of radio play production is the improvisation of sound effects. The players may choose to build an entire creative dramatics session around a demonstration of their original sound effects. This creative transformation of objects should be encouraged, particularly when the resources on hand at the moment can be used imaginatively. Examples of original sound effects have included the following:

Footsteps—Hit wooden platforms or a box of gravel.
Sloshing footsteps—Swirl a stick through water.
Door—a box that creaks.
Squeaky door—scratch metal nail against glass pane.
Eggs frying or fire crackling—Crinkle cellophane.
Hoofbeats—Hit styrofoam cups against table.
Locomotive—Rub sheet metal or snare drum with a drummer's wire brush.
Water effects—Blow through a straw into water near a microphone; for splashes, pour water from one pail into another.
Rain—Shake dried beans into large round tin pan.
Movement through the woods—Rustle dry shrubs near microphone.
Arrow shot from a bow—Twang a rubber band from a yardstick, then stick penknife through cardboard.
Jet sound—Move vacuum across the face of the microphone.

Sound-effects records can also be taped, but the creation of original sound effects is more in keeping with the goal of creative dramatics. Players can learn more about the radio play format by listening to such classic recordings as "War of the Worlds," "Inner Sanctum," and "The Shadow." Do not interpret "radio play production" to mean a formal, polished product is expected; on the contrary, like all creative dramatics activities, radio plays should be sources of experimentation and pleasure. Some common terms used in the creation of a radio play are:

1. Sound Up and Under—Sound comes on, then fades.
2. Tagging the Sound—Through dialogue, the character identifies the sound as a place.
3. Tagging the Character—Through dialogue, people call each other by name to identify character.
4. Sound Perspective—Sound moves from far to near—change in volume.
5. On Mike—Speak away from microphone to suggest distance.
6. Off Mike—Speak away from microphone to suggest distance.
7. Use of Narrator—Describes what can't be explained through sound or dialogue. It is used for transitions between scenes. Use only when necessary; dialogue is preferable.
8. Fade with Sound—Go down in one sound and up in another to show change of scene.
9. Bridge—Music used in transition.
10. Sting—Crash of music used for emphasis.
11. Noodle—Funny sting.
12. Remote—Broadcast originating on site away from the studio.
13. Segue—Transition, usually musical, from one mood to another.
14. Background—Music or sounds used to establish atmosphere.
15. Theme—Music identifying a particular program.
16. Cut—Stop.

The radio play adapts itself to many innovative programming ideas. Homebound individuals can organize a tape correspondence club in which members personally create and mail radio play cassettes to each other. Institutionalized residents can tape radio plays and air them over the institution's public address system, achieving a communications network that transcends whatever physical limitations they might have.

Role Playing

The term "role playing" in this context refers to improvisations that explore characters' responses in dramatic situations. The role-playing scene is improvised in that the players respond to the dynamics of the moment and do not anticipate in advance their response. In role playing, players can either play themselves in the context of a given dramatic situation or assume another identity. Playing oneself has the benefit of enlightening individuals to their personal motivations and patterns of response. Assuming another identity prompts players to look at life outside of their mental framework and become sensitive to others' needs. The following activities provide opportunities for role-playing improvisations:

Role-playing Improvisations

One person begins pantomiming an action set in a particular place, such as shell collecting on the beach. As soon as others recognize the setting, they join the scene and add an action (e.g., swimming, sand-castle building). If you wish, dialogue can be added as soon as all people have joined the scene.

Role play conflict situations between two or more people (e.g., husband wants to go on vacation, wife wants to save money and stay home).

Jostle the imagination by dramatizing the "Magic If" (e.g., What would you do if you left home tomorrow? if you won the lottery? if an old friend was to reenter your life?).

Each group is given a skeleton story or a basic plot upon which to build an improvisation (e.g., solving of a mystery or a journey of adventure).

Role play situations in which the same characters act differently when placed in a different setting (e.g., how does behavior differ when a teacher is in front of the classroom? in the laundromat? at home?). Show these variations by connecting these scenes into one situation.

Prepare one set of cards with places, another for props, another for characters. Groups pick the three cards and combine the three into a scene.

Players act out their versions of the discovery of inventions such as paper clips, bubble gum, and pogo sticks.

Develop a scene in which characters conflict in their opinion of the value of a certain element. For example, in a scene concerning the subject of snow, there is disagreement between a ski resort operator who likes it for business and a mailman who dreads it for incovenience to delivery.

Listen to a song and imagine what is happening in the music. Where is the setting? Who is involved? Plan an improvisation and play it, with the music perhaps playing in the background.

The pair or group of players is given a set of props that they must integrate into a scene.

Create an improvisation around proverbs such as "Make hay while the sun shines."

Improvise what might have led up to the scene you see depicted in a painting or photo, or what might occur after it.

Play a movie through until just before the ending, then shut it off and improvise your own ending.

Improvise a scene involving conflict between people who each want something different from one another (e.g., an aunt wants affection from her nephew, while he wants her financial assets only).

Improvise a "campy" version of a fable, as in a fractured fairy tale. For instance, "Snow White and the Seven Dwarfs" might become a singing group.

Create a scene in which you physically become parts of the environment (e.g., simulation of a table, mountain, tree, or bench).

Improvise a scene around the situation suggested by a design:

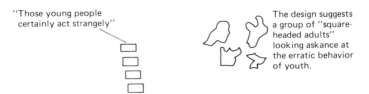

"Those young people certainly act strangely"

The design suggests a group of "square-headed adults" looking askance at the erratic behavior of youth.

Improvise a scene suggested by the way the furniture is arranged (e.g., rows of chairs might suggest a plane).

Magazine photos are cut in half and the sections divided among the group. Individuals circulate to find the sections that match their pictures and improvise the dramatic situation suggested by the completed pictures.

Dramatize a historical event as if it were happening in the present.

One group improvises actions that tell a story while another group provides the dialogue and narration to accompany the action. Close observation and cooperation is necessary. This activity is referred to as "drama dubbing."

Put themes in one box and locations in another. The group selects one from each box and must put them together to form a scene (e.g., the theme "It is better to give than to receive" combined with the location of a supermarket might suggest a scene in which an individual lets a more needy customer get the last sale item).

Players create scenes spontaneously as others call out the "who, what, where and when."

The players are divided into two groups: the present and the past. As the "present" group reaches a point in their improvisation that suggests a reference to the past, the other group steps in and dramatizes that selection. For instance, as a husband and wife begin to discuss their wedding, they relinquish the scene to another couple who actually dramatize the wedding event.

Each player is matched with another player who portrays his or her subconscious. At appropriate points in the scene, the subconscious speaks out loud, revealing the inner thoughts and motivations of the character. This is called "doubling."

Improvise scenes that demonstrate the need for cooperation between individuals to achieve a goal (e.g., pilot and copilot, mountain climbing crew).

Explain the beginning and end of a scene and request the players to improvise the middle.

Create a simulation game (role playing adapted to a game format). Sample simulation games have dealt with the ecology, race relations, urban development, tenant-landlord relations, and other social issues. Players assume the roles of community representatives having their own self-vested interests. Guidelines are established for determining the successful resolution of the game's dramatic conflict. Point values can be assigned to goal setting and goal accomplishment within the role play.

Create a total environment for a scene, making it as close to the actual physical layout as possible. For instance, to get players in the mood for acting out a museum scene, it is best to have them walk into a room already set up like a museum. A receptionist might welcome them and a tour guide begin to take them around the rooms filled with paintings. Do not preface the occasion with any explanation—just draw them right into the scene as if it were "real life."

The newspaper suggests many ideas for improvisation. Give players headlines and ask them to improvise the scenes the titles suggest. The balloons above cartoon characters can be blocked out and the players asked to devise their own dialogue. A photograph can be brought to life. From the horoscope section, scenes can be developed in which two or more people's predictions overlap in conflict or agreement. From the classified ads, select those which suggest interesting characters and dramatize the stories leading up to the ads. Questions might include: Where did this individual ever obtain such an item to sell? Why does this individual seek such a job? Perhaps an entire flea market scene could be arranged around the classified ads from the newspaper. New stories can be explored for their human interest elements and dramatized. Portions of stories can be given to the players who must then improvise the missing section.

There is a wealth of resources available for stimulating ideas and participation in creative dramatics. It is recommended that the creative dramatics leader begin accumulating a file of activity motivators: A sensory box of smells, textures, and tastes can easily be created from available materials. Musical instruments (e.g., rattles, wood blocks, triangles, finger bells, tambourines) suggest moods for situations and characters. Music can also be an important motivator in that it sets the rhythm of movement and can initiate and terminate action. Recorded music, tapes, and recorded sound effects also prompt ideas for dramatic situations. Should recorded sound effects not be available, sound effects can be created manually with everyday materials. A collection of objects should be available as neutral props (props that can be transformed by the imagination into various uses, such as a yardstick that becomes a wand, a walking cane, or a kite string). A variety of puppets, including neutral puppets, are ideal for motivating improvisations and scene development. A box full of hats, shoes, costumes, masks, and makeup provides stimuli for characterization as participants "try on" various personalities as they change accessories. Fabrics can be used for costumes (e.g., Indian shawls, cloaks) as well as for the creation of scenic effects (e.g., rippling water if shaken between two people, mountains if draped over furniture). A file of photographs from family albums, magazines, and newspapers gives rise to ideas for characterization and plot. Films, literature, and personal recollections all become sources of thematic ideas for creative dramatics. Be sure to link creative dramatics to the outside world; ask participants to be attentive to the sensory details and people they observe, so that they can dramatize these impressions upon their return.

This file of activity motivators should be organized for easy reference so that leaders are equipped to vary their approach according to participant response. The knowledge of many different activities enables leaders to be more flexible in their leadership. It is recommended that a session's activities all contribute to a thematic unity. To achieve this, prepare a lesson plan that outlines the direction of the creative dramatics session. This provides leaders with a better perspective on their intended aims and techniques, and gives focus to a session that might otherwise be a series of unrelated exercises. A lesson plan is a reference for the leader and is not to be shared directly with the participants.

LESSON PLAN

The following sample illustrates the format to be followed in developing a lesson plan for a creative dramatics session. First, goals are listed to define the intended aims of the activities to follow. These aims refer to the psychosocial and physical benefits to be derived by the creative dramatics participants. Second all of the leader's narration (motivating remarks and sidecoaching) as well as activities are designed to advance the achievement of these aims. Each narration throughout the session serves, third, as a motivational lead-in to a dramatic activity. Finally, each activity is then usually followed by a discussion to help players synthesize insights derived from the dramatic experience. Each element of the session, from initial warmup to concluding narration and/or discussion should serve as a building block toward the attainment of the session's aims. In this sample lesson plan, for instance, in which the prime aim is to foster the use of gesture and movement in expressing emotion and building character, all of the session's components are targeted toward that goal.

Creative Dramatics Sample Lesson Plan

GOALS

1. Participants will become more sensitive to the effectiveness of facial expression, movement, and gesture in expressing emotion.
2. Each individual will exhibit a more positive appreciation of body self-image.
3. Following a sequence of sensitizing warmups (isolating body parts, sculpting, group tableau), each participant will have built up a framework from which to develop a characterization.
4. Participants will achieve a level of confidence allowing them to cooperatively plan group skits.
5. Individuals will understand how leisure education themes can be integrated into dramatic activities.

I. *Narrative motivation* (standing in circle): "People can express what they feel inside by never speaking a word. What are you feeling now? How do you think your body is showing this? (Can think to themselves or share with the group.) Our emotions can be communicated through gesture, movements, and facial expressions.

"Look at someone else in the group. What does that person seem to be expressing through his or her body? Share your impressions with that person to see if your impressions were correct.

"We often don't take the time to think about how expressive each part of our body can be. Let's have some fun and focus on how these body parts speak for us."

Warm-Up Activity (in circle):
 Say "Why?" with your head.
 Say "I'm happy" with your toes.
 Say "I'm the best" with your fingers.
 Say "I feel lazy" with your legs.
 Say "I'm surprised at you" with your jaw.
 Say "How dare you say that!" with your back.
 Say "I'm not sure" with your shoulders.
 Say "I don't understand" with your eyes.
 Say "These shoes are too tight" with your toes.
 Say "I'm the best dancer" with your legs.
 Say "I can't stand it" with your head.

II. *Narrative motivation* (standing in circle): "Now that you've explored how expressive every part of the body is, imagine what skill it takes to carve these out of stone. Imagine that you are a sculptor. You are about to sculpt a statue which depicts someone engaged in a leisure activity you have always wanted to do. Picture the individual in action. What is the person doing? What is the expression of the body?"

Activity. "Each of you take turns being the sculptor with the other person the clay."

Sidecoaching. "This exercise takes concentration on the part of both sculptor and clay. Use all spatial levels in arranging your statue."

Narrative discussion. "Which did you enjoy the most; being the sculptor or the clay being molded? Was it clearly evident to you what leisure activity you were being sculpted into?'

Activity. "Let's go around the room now, counting off in 6's. Each person remember the leisure activity you were sculpted into. When I call your number, find the rest of your group and immediately freeze into a group sculpture (group tableau) in the middle of the circle."

Narrative discussion. "Let's sit down in a circle. What moods did you see reflected in people's bodies? in their faces?"

Narrative motivation. "Each of these group pictures suggested interesting situations if only those characters could be brought to life to tell their stories. Who are these characters? What type of character would do the leisure activity you depicted? How old are you? What do you look like? How do you walk and talk? Take time to think about who you are. Where do you live? What do you do for a living? What are your educational, financial, and family backgrounds?"

Activity. "Now I'd like you to move in character to your group. As a group, develop a situation around what happens when you bring your group tableau to life. Remember to stay in character. As a group now, decide on your relationship to each other in the group and the main theme or conflict surrounding this interaction. Decide where the action is taking place. After agreeing on these guidelines, your group wll assume its former group tableau. At the sound of the drum beat, you will bring the scene to life, bringing out your relationships and conflicts through dialogue, gesture, and movement. Retain your leisure activity as part of your characterization. Within 3 to 5 minutes, bring the scene to its resolution and end in a new group tableau."

Narrative discussion. "What interesting situations developed when your characters came to life? What did the characters you interacted with say or do that helped project their personalities?

"In terms of leisure education, did you find yourself identifying with any of the leisure activities your partners demonstrated? Why? Why not? Could you relate certain personality characteristics to certain leisure pursuits?

"Today we've looked at how people express themselves through the way they move and play. In your own lives, take a good look at how you yourself are celebrating your body, your spirit."

It should be acknowledged that players will often respond with interpretations and actions that do not correlate with the intended sequence of the lesson plan. The creative dramatics leader must learn how to adapt to such developments and not become a slave to the lesson plan. Often one of the best outcomes of a session is that players became so involved in the activities that the lesson plan was never completely covered. Since spontaneity of expression is the goal of creative dramatics, the leader must learn to work with responses that don't coincide with those anticipated.

LEADERSHIP GUIDELINES

In designing a creative dramatics lesson plan, the leader must build in a framework of narrative cues and structural arrangements that ensure smooth, controlled development of the drama. The sample lesson plan will be used as an illustration.

It should be noted, for instance, that the group was usually arranged in a circle, a key component in the flow of this lesson plan. The circle is appropriate for unison playing; it puts no focus on any one individual as illustrated by the warmup in the group circle. The circle was also useful in the sculpting activity; individuals needed only turn to the person next to them to find a partner. The circle also establishes a group sense by putting players in close proximity to each other and encourages eye contact. At points throughout the session, the players were also gathered in the circle to share reactions to the prior activity. Sharing impressions of the overall session in the final circle allowed all participants to integrate their impressions of the entire session. It also gave the leader the opportunity to bring all elements of the session to a close and to make any thematic references to upcoming sessions. The final circle formation facilitates the essential "winding down period," in which the players ease out of the dramatic world to their own worlds of reality. It is the leader's responsibility to see that the players do not leave the session in such a high-strung state that they are unable to easily assume their normal duties.

It is essential to have a means of capturing attention and guiding the flow of the creative dramatics sessons. This may take any number of forms, including the use of a clap, a drumbeat, or the use of the freeze. In the sample lesson plan, the freeze was used to provide less threatening structure for the beginning player than free movement. The drumbeat served to signal when to break the freeze. Leaders should come to use one technique fairly exclusively so that it can be clearly identified as the signal for attention and transition.

The narrative cues linking one activity to another should be carefully planned to facilitate smooth transition to the next phase. For instance, the group tableaux were formed by counting off numbers. In this way, the groupings created themselves without need for embarrassing, mood-breaking gaps while people sought groups. Since creative dramatics is concerned with making drama a successful experience for all participants, the sensitive leader will utilize such arrangements as counting off numbers to prevent cliques and ostracism. Likewise, the drama activities themselves should be arranged so that they gradually escalate in their physical, emotional, and social requirements. In the sample lesson plan, for instance, the players started out by expressing themselves through isolated body parts and graduated to expressing total characterizations; similarly, individual playing expanded to include group playing.

The lesson-plan activities themselves were linked in such a way that there was a natural continuity in character development. For instance, after mentally exploring their characters, each individual had the opportunity to move in character to a group formation, rather than abruptly joining a group as if beginning a new isolated exercise. Similarly, the group tableau was a spontaneous, unintimidating method of moving toward the group cooperation that would later be required for the skit. The tableaux formed in the middle of the circle are brief and nonthreatening, but if there is any self-consciousness involved in going into the middle of the circle, the players should form tableaux in spots around the room and in unison group playing. In keeping with the philosophy that creative dramatics is designed for process and not product, at no point was the group asked to perform its skits before the rest of the players. Any group that wishes to do so, however, should be encouraged.

In the discussion periods throughout a creative dramatics session, it is advisable that the players and leader take time to evaluate the truth and sincerity of their work. Concern should be with the level of commitment and cooperation being brought to the work, not the level of talent. Feedback regarding individual players should be directed to the characters they played and not the individuals themselves. For instance, rather than saying, "John, you moved too quickly and distracted the others," you can say, "Cowboy Joshua Miller, your horse seemed out of control. Why don't we bring it back to the stable and get a tamer one?" It is absolutely essential that the player not be critiqued about "performance"; since personal growth *is* the purpose of creative dramatics, any questions that follow scenes should deal with what the players learned about themselves and others in the process.

USE OF QUESTIONS IN CREATIVE DRAMATICS

The role of questions in the creative dramatics leadership process has been advanced to an art form through the work of Dorothy Heathcote, renowned British creative dramatist. Ms. Heathcote delineates the multiple aims of these questions according to the following criteria: Questions that:

1. Assess group interest in the topic to be dramatized. (Example: "Is this space journey something that we all are ready and willing to handle?")
2. Stimulate research (Example: "What are the textures of the various planets? We have to know the surfaces in order to construct our landing gear.")
3. Supply information. (Example: "Did you know that Saturn is encircled by rings thought to be composed of icy particles?")
4. Set standard of play. (Example: "It's important that we listen to each other, right?")
5. Require a group decision. (Example: "Should this be a long or short journey?")
6. Control the class. (Example: "How can we move quietly so that no extraterrestrial beings will discover us?")
7. Establish belief. (Example: "Do you all see that rosy glow above the horizon?")

8. Establish mood or feeling. (Example: "Listen to the vast silence of space. Does it make you feel more dependent on your fellow crew members?")
9. Deepen insight. (Example: "Do you think you joined this expedition out of a desire for adventure? for public acclaim?")
10. Request approval to go back to a scene. (Example: "We may have left some important moon particles back there. Should we take another moon walk?")
11. Relate dramatic experience to personal experience. (Example: "In your own lives have you ever felt any of the emotions you experienced on our space journey?")[1]

Ms. Heathcote often plays the "devil's advocate" in order to get the group unified in its commitment to the drama; she also feigns ignorance in order to encourage active research and questioning on their part. In her questions or narrative cues she will often introduce a difficult vocabulary word so that players will have to ask the meaning.

There are times when the leader will decide that sidecoaching is too limited a form of involvement in the creative dramatics process and will choose to enter the drama as a character in a scene. Heathcote has defined some reasons for the leader to enter a scene in character:

1. To demand a response that has been missing
2. To introduce an element of surprise
3. To define a conflict between characters
4. To introduce a new conflict
5. To limit the space, time, and/or equipment if too unwieldy to work with
6. To extend the period of dramatic tension so that a true dramatic situation is experienced.

Ms. Heathcote feels that the players often need to be prevented from rushing through a scene and missing the whole essence of the conflict. And by becoming a character at points throughout a session, the leader is better able to establish the "we" relationship that should exist between leader and players.

SETTING BEHAVIOR BOUNDARIES

Dorothy Heathcote makes the very important point that prior to any creative dramatics leadership, the leader must determine the most personally desirable group structure. This determination includes setting limits on level of acceptable noise, workable group size, amount of group decision-making allowed, and a comfortable physical distance between leader and group. All too often, leaders neglect to define for themselves their parameters of acceptable player behavior; therefore, the sessions tend to have a

1. Betty Jane Wagner. *Dorothy Heathcote: Drama as a Learning Medium* (Wash, D.C.; National Education Assoc. of the U.S.), p. 61.

disturbing, unfocused quality. For instance, perhaps a leader neglects to inform the group that keeping a low volume is a prerequisite for any session. This means that when voices do rise, the leader will perceive the high volume as "noise" instead of as the active, creative involvement it is. For another creative dramatics leader, controlling volume may not be significant but controlling group size or proximity is. Each creative dramatics leader has a distinct personality, which creates unique dynamics in combination with the group character and individual identities of the players. Therefore, to ensure the success of the creative dramatics experience, it is natural and right that the leader establish behavioral boundaries for the players which are agreeable to his or her leadership style.

DRAMA THERAPY

Drama therapy is of particular relevance to recreation therapists. Drama therapy has emerged as a significant field, as illustrated by the establishment of the National Association of Drama Therapy that currently is establishing educational and certification criteria. The drama therapy curriculum incorporates drama and psychology with electives in one's area of specialization (e.g., special education, gerontology, psychiatry).

When we speak of drama therapy we mean all the ways in which the creative, humanistic art of drama provides the participant with catharsis, stimulation, recreation, or a diversion from self-absorption. This includes such diverse activities as creative movement, role playing, acting for formal drama, viewing a performance, psychodrama, sociodrama, and other related activities, and the drama therapist is involved in facilitating these therapeutic experiences. However, since for the most part drama therapy involves more informal, process-oriented approaches, drama therapy is associated with creative dramatics.

Drama therapy does not presume to guarantee the cure of a person's deeply rooted problem. Nevertheless, the drama therapy may very well relieve anxieties, raise new insights, and trigger a new direction toward rehabilitation. Drama therapy need not take place in a deeply analytical one-to-one session; it can take many forms.

Drama therapy includes a technique called "guidance drama" in which a play is chosen expressly for its potential to shed light on the specific group's problem. For instance, if a group of young prison inmates is experiencing anxiety over their upcoming reentry into society, their drama therapist might choose the play "Getting Out," which deals with this subject. An informal reading of this play would, no doubt, trigger more open discussion than would counselor-initiated questions. Theater troupes like Theater for the Forgotten, The Family, and Theater Without Bars have provided performances and workshops in prison settings. A testimony to their impact is the fact that many inmates have been inspired to initiate their own workshops when the troupes leave. Among drama therapy's benefits for these inmates may be improvement in self-image, better communication skills, concentration, and self-discipline, as well as greater willingness to accept delayed gratification while working toward the goal of the workshop or performance.

In drama therapy, the participants can evolve their own dramatization, not only from a given script, but by acting out personal thoughts and experiences. A group of street gangs channeled their fears over initiation into a revealing dramatization of the initiation rite. With the same drama therapist, local tenants experiencing conflicts with their landlords developed "The Tenant Play," which served to spark organized housing activity. Here, drama served a dual therapeutic role by helping tenants release frustration through drama while they also used it as a form of effective social protest.

In his book *Theater in My Head,* Dan Cheifetz describes his work with 8- to 11-year-olds living in a children's home. He relates how the series of creative movements, pantomimes, skits, and role plays revealed new aspects of the children's personalities, to themselves and to others. For instance, when dramatizing a marriage scene, a girl named Joyce portrayed a very sad bride. Cheifetz later learned that Joyce's father had left the home, which explained Joyce's tragic view of the marriage vow. Parents of children in these workshops said that the activities had positively affected their children's school progress and home life.

The therapeutic benefits of drama are equally important for older adults. In fact, since old age involves more adaptation to physical, psychological, and social changes than at any other period in one's life, the need for drama as a creative outlet is more vital than ever. The sociologist, Gordon Streib, has stated that the "expressive role," which includes drama, is one of the most important roles in retirement.

Sensory exploration exercises have been a particularly effective drama approach with the institutionalized geriatric population (a group that comprises approximately 5 percent of this nation's older adult population). With these residents, sensory stimulation through sounds, smells, tastes, and textures may reawaken associations with the past that can evoke dramatic narratives. Butler and Lewis in *Aging and Mental Health* describe the significance of sensory stimulation for the elderly in this way:[2]

> While the middle-aged begin to be concerned with the number of years they have left to live, older persons tend to experience a sense of immediacy, of here and now, of living in the moment. This could be called a sense of "presentness" or "elementality." The elemental things of life—children, plants, nature, human touching, physically and emotionally, color, shape—assume greater singificance as people sort out the more important from the less important. Old age can be a time of emotional and sensory awareness and enjoyment.

2. Reproduced by permission from Robert N. Butler and Myra I. Lewis, *Aging and Mental Health: Positive Psychosocial Approaches,* 3rd ed., (St. Louis: C. V. Mosby, Co., 1982), p. 37.

Butler has also promoted the Life Review concept, a process by which the elderly review their pasts in order to better understand the present. While the Life Review is usually spoken or written, it is ideally suited to recreation through drama, with actual scrapbooks, old letters, and heirlooms used in the dramatization. Such an approach provides senior participants with a sense of continuity in their lives, aids memory, and promotes feelings of security and satisfaction, all benefits of particular significance to older adults.

Life Review involves identification with pivotal experiences in one's life. Such identification became the exciting subject of a "total environment" dramatics experience in a nursing home. It grew from the residents' strong identification with their Jewish heritage and resulted in the celebration of the twenty-fifth anniversary of Israel's founding. With the cooperation of the civic community, the auditorium was converted into the environment of a jet on its way to Israel. TWA donated the flight bags, TV personalities were on hand as the plane's hosts, and the local print shop made the tickets. While the flight was simulated by engine sound effects, a historical narrative on Israel was read as the residents sang and danced. The therapeutic impact on all who participated in this vibrant event is described in the following:[3]

> When they landed, the staff, young and old, joined hands and went into dancing the Hora. Four hundred residents, plus many community visitors and staff members were all as one, and felt as if they had participated in the establishment of the state of Israel."

All drama therapy activities should be tailored to the specific needs of the population. For instance, the nursing home population is often disappointed at always being on the receiving end of goods and services, with no opportunity to be a giver. At a time in their lives when these residents resent having to depend on others, they are nevertheless forced to depend on the Social Security check, outside transportation, the nurse, medication, and so on. In the drama experience, however, they are able to extend themselves and feel a control over their environment that the nursing home reality doesn't allow. Participation in drama can be a definite asset in the mental health of the institutionalized or disabled elderly, for as individuals increasingly experience that sense of achievement, they will be less harsh on themselves for any waning physical or mental abilities.

In working with blind people, Sue Jennings, British drama therapist and author of *Remedial Drama*, allows the participants to do floor and simple paired movements to develop security. She often narrates action involving a relaxed mood, such as preparing for bed. Her themes are often ones in which sightlessness is an advantage for the reality of the dramatiza-

3. Isaiah Ginsberg, Hank Ginsberg, and Marilyn Karsen, "Motivating the Aged Through Identification," *Therapeutic Recreation Journal*, Fourth Quarter 1974, vol. 8, no. l4, p. 190.

tion, as in the case of exploring a dark underwater cavern. In working with the physically disabled, Jennings has also helped them feel that their disability can make a special contribution. For instance, wheelchair patients converted their wheelchairs into trick cars and became clowns in a circus march; others chose to narrate the action from their wheelchairs. Another time, teen girls, inhibited by their physical disabilities, draped their wheelchairs with flowing material and suddenly became graceful princesses on a magic carpet ride; the costumes helped them forget their self-consciousness. Patients with crutches came up with ingenious transformations such as boat rudders and oars.

The drama therapist can help a mentally retarded person connect concepts through movement and drama. For instance, a retarded girl was having difficulty learning to weave; she finally understood the concept as soon as she was led through the "weaving" in the game "Go In and Out the Window." Since mentally retarded individuals are often led to feel they have nothing to contribute of value, Dorothy Heathcote has designed creative dramatics sessions in which they have the opportunity to feel useful. For instance, she assumed the role of a forlorn character who elicited the aid and concern of the sympathetic players.

The deaf individual can be involved in creative dramatics. The deaf can experience moving to the rhythm of percussive vibrations and evolving these movements into a characterization. If unable to speak, the individual can mime or pantomime ideas. A theme for dramatization could be underwater exploration for buried treasure, where the ability to hear is not necessary. With resources such as the National Theater for the Deaf, the deaf are now more able to appreciate a staged performance. Theater groups like the National Theater for the Deaf communicate through multimedia, sign language, exaggerated body movements, spoken words, and written programs accompanying the action.

In a drama therapy session conducted by Dr. Eleanor Irwin of the Pittsburgh Child Guidance Center, cleft-palate children were able to safely reveal aggressive behavior in relationship to their anxieties about hospitalization. Having experienced the frustration of being poked and prodded by doctors, they relished the opportunity to become the aggressors against the imaginary doctors. Repeatedly in their session, the children chose to play large crocodilelike animals with gaping mouths. Apparently, their physical handicaps had led them to be obsessed with the ideas of oral aggression and fear of bodily injury. While playing an ambulance driver, one boy refused to give the patient an oxygen mask. Exploring this strange behavior, Irwin discovered that the boy had once had a frightful experience with an ether mask during an operation.

Irwin, Expressive Arts Therapist and Assistant Professor of Child Psychiatry at the University of Pittsburgh, states:[4]

4. Eleanor Irwin, "Facilitating Children's Language Development Through Play," *The Speech Teacher*, vol. 24, January 1975, pp. 15–23.

Since participation in fantasy play seems to foster the growth of verbal competence and ego strengths, such drama activities might be of particular help to impulsive, "acting out" children to help promote positive affective experiences.

Irwin's work with the cleft-palate children attests to this observation. After 4 months she noted that they exhibited more verbal interaction and were more willing to explore their fantasies and fears through drama. She also discovered a higher level of language competency than they had ever demonstrated before.

Ms. Irwin has also used the tableau as a means for helping participants express their innermost concerns. The tableau, as we have seen, is a dramatics exercise in which the group "freezes" like a picture. At the Family Therapy Clinic of Western Psychiatric Institute, the tableau has been adapted to the family sculpture format, whereby each family member takes turns arranging the others in a tableau. The way the individual allies certain family members, isolates others, and places them in physical attitudes all reveal the person's concept of the family relationships. The different perceptions of individuals spur interesting discussion. Any issues or conflicts raised here would, of course, be clarified in individual interviews.

Psychodrama, a specific discipline included under the title of drama therapy, is an integration of role playing and psychoanalysis in the treatment of personal problems. The subject of the psychodrama selects fellow group members who most clearly represent the people of his or her life to constitute the psychodrama. Since the dramatized situations are complex and deep-seated, only an individual trained in psychodrama from an established program (e.g., Moreno Institute in Beacon, NY) is equipped to conduct psychodrama.

While the drama therapist need not be a psychodramatist, some of the latter's techniques can be adapted and used in improvisation. One such technique is "doubling," in which someone plays the internal double of another and speaks as that person's unconscious. In the "empty chair" technique, the individual directs communication to an empty chair as if a person were seated there. This removes the threat of having the real person there and is often used in a psychodrama where the subject must relive a painful confrontation with someone. In improvisation, the empty chair technique can also be used for rehearsing an anticipated interaction with someone. This allows a person to prepare for this confrontation within a protective dramatic framework.

A basic component of drama therapy is, of course, role playing. The role-playing situation might come from the participants' suggestions or from an idea, story, or scene suggested by the leader. Role reversal, another psychodramatic technique, allows the individual to exchange roles with his or her partner in order to personally experience the motivations of another person. For instance, those found lacking in social skills can be involved in simulated job interviews where they have the opportunity to also reverse roles and perceive themselves as an employer would. A videotape of these interviews provides a means of evaluation, after which the role playing can be repeated. The ability to assume different roles has been associated with an individual's level of emotional maturity. For example, a group of highly egocentric boys could not relate what was occurring in a picture from the viewpoint of a character just entering the scene, but instead constantly related every story from their own perspectives. To remove this self-centeredness, a ten-week program was developed in which the boys improvised scenes and used role reversal to get out of their self-preoccupation. Videotaping was used to point out areas that needed improvement.

Sociodrama

Unlike psychodrama, which focuses on individual problems, sociodrama consists of role playing dealing with group social problems and decision making. Examples of subjects for sociodrama would be tenant-landlord relationships or staff-volunteer rapport. The key steps in sociodrama are:

1. Discuss the problem (e.g., tenant-landlord relationships).
2. Identify the roles (e.g., determining who will be the tenants and landlords).
3. Role play (dramatize the source of the conflict; e.g., a debate over rent increase).
4. Discuss the role playing (the audience discusses the positive and negative aspects of the role play—not the level of acting but the group dynamics evidenced and the decisions made).
5. Explore alternative interpretations (audience members discuss how the scene could have been handled differently. Suggestions might range to include more assertiveness on the tenants' part, the use of actual violence, the withholding of rent, etc.).
6. Role play the alternatives (either the same players or new ones role play the alternatives they devised, and again follow up each scene with discussion).

In both psychodrama and sociodrama, it is very important to have the audience members reflect back to the players their perceptions of the drama—to be a mirror of alternate possibilities. The presence of the group provides an opportunity for the players to see how their actions and motivations are perceived by others. The feedback from the group also provides the players with reassurance that they are not the only ones to have experienced this problem.

As indicated earlier in this chapter, any dramatic activity can take on the characteristics of informal or formal drama depending on the approach taken by the leader. The areas of pageantry, choral speaking/drama, and readers theater are cases in point. Were these activities to be conducted solely for the players themselves as a source of fun and learning, they would be viewed as informal dramatics. However, since these activities have inherent presentational qualities and most often involve rehearsal for performance, they are classified as formal dramatics and will therefore be covered under that classification.

FORMAL DRAMATICS/THEATER

Pageant

A pageant is a spectacular show used to illustrate a theme. Types of pageants include:

1. historical pageant—a historical event is depicted in dramatic episodes through dialogue, action or pantomime;
2. processional pageant—a procession of floats, each depicting a tableau;
3. masque—a short allegorical play in which the principal characters are a personification of ideas (requires less spectacle and performers because it deals with a single idea rather than an evolutionary one);
4. pastoral—a delicate type of lyric drama; the plot is more or less a vehicle for music, dance, and dignified groupings;
5. spectaculars—no play involved, sheer spectacle (such as the Sound and Light Show, Tournament of Roses parade);
6. ceremonials based on holidays;
7. pageants based on mythological or legendary material;
8. festivals and ceremonies revolving around local color and events.

The pageant integrates the arts of music, dance, drama, and visual arts. In terms of visual art, the imagery is extremely important as one is usually dealing with a large space. Since the pageant focuses on movement rather than narration, the visual picture must move the theme along. Broad symbols should be used to represent the themes (such as cross, sword). Colors should be used symbolically; for instance purple can signify passion, royalty, or sadness. Since the pageant is usually performed outdoors, the natural backdrops of the surroundings should be utilized artistically. For instance, a stream or river in the background could provide the basis for creating a castle moat. Lighting accentuates color, costuming, setting, and kinetic and static tableaux. The visual movement of the pageant is achieved through gestures, acting, groupings, and dance. Dance can consist of: (1) plot dance in which the movements advance the story line (such as a choreographed journey); (2) illustrative dance, which serves to demonstrate the cultural customs of the people; (3) symbolic dance in which the movements represent the theme of the scene (such as joy, aggression).

When staged outdoors, the pageant has particularly exciting possibilities for dramatic effect. From far distances can come processionals or groups of actors whose specific dialogue need not be heard. On an even broader scale, teams of horses, floats, or other vehicles can enter from the far horizon. Entrances and exits from a distance make an impressive sight.

The foreground area, on the other hand, should be used for solo dances, character scenes, and dialogues, as it is necessary to have the expository scenes within the visual and aural range of the audience.

In any pageant, the spectacle is more important than dialogue. Since it is usually staged outdoors and involves large numbers of people, the plot should be kept simple. The script is usually narrative, whereby a story is told while players broadly interpret the narration. The episodes are usually chronologically arranged to make the story line clearer. Since it is difficult to show subtle characterization, dialogue is deemphasized and instead the plot and theme are accentuated. Pageants are particularly appropriate for a camp program, because of location and numbers of people involved. Since large-scale planning is involved in arranging the pageant, it provides the ideal opportunity for community involvement and interagency cooperation.

Choral speaking

Choral speaking is the interpretation of literature through the arrangement of group voices. To create the appropriate aural effects to accompany the oral reading, the group's voices are divided into three ranges consisting of:

1. Light voices—having a delicate quality and higher pitch, suitable for light, happy mood
2. Dark voices—having a heavier quality, appropriate for robust, somber parts
3. Middle voices—having a wide range; can go with either light soft tones communicating gay, spirited moods or dark, louder tones communicating solemn, mysterious moods.

In interpreting the literary piece, variety may be given to a voice by a change in tempo (speed), volume (intensity), and pitch (tone of voice). As an appropriate warmup prior to the session, the group could experiment with how different tones of voice correspond to different moods (such as anger, fear, joy). From the outset, the group should decide on the interpretation of the piece and select the tempo, phrasing, and intonation to achieve this interpretation. The meaning and pronunciation of words should be stressed. To get the idea of the rhythm, the group first might be trained with jingles or nonsense verse accompanied by the rhythm of clapped hands or drum beats. The drama leader, who is basically serving as a conductor of voices rather than instruments, must work toward the achievement of one collective voice rather than many disparate voices. With hand movements, the leader can direct the group in inflections (the changes of pitch on syllable that alter meaning). For instance, falling inflection denotes finality or the end of a thought. An upward inflection denotes question, surprise, or incompleteness. The circumflex inflection rises and falls, denoting such emotions as fear, sarcasm, and excitement.

Choral speaking material should include that which has dramatic appeal, universality of theme, variety of moods, and multiple characters and ideas. Examples would include poems and prose that express group feeling, poems with sound effects, ballads, nursery rhymes, Bible passages, songs, epic poems, and humorous verse.

In working with a literary piece, the leader can use any or all of the following arrangements in the course of the interpretation:

1. Refrain—certain portions are spoken by a single voice or varied voices and the rest by a chorus
2. Dialogue—two-part or antiphonal; can change solo to one chorus, refrain to another chorus; good for poems with two definite stanzas—one chorus answers another
3. Cumulative—voices are gradually added on to build intensity
4. Unison—all speak together
5. Sequential—lines are given out per person or per chorus section; this allows for greater responsibility on the part of the individual, gives greater variety of interpretation
6. Choral drama—part of the group interprets the choral speaking through movement with the possible addition of lighting, costumes, and sound effects.

Readers Theater

Readers theater is the presentation of a literary script with the oral readers using their voices, bodies, and faces to suggest the intellectual, emotional, and sensory qualities of the piece. Readers theater differs from choral speaking in that the latter requires only oral interpretation while the former also requires physicalizing and dramatically staging the emotions and relationships described in the literary material. The staging is intentionally stark and symbolic so as to actively involve the audience in visualizing the drama.

The stage is usually a platform with few properties or costumes. However, the props and costumes can be merely suggested in order to draw more on the imaginations of the audience. The actors can be placed on different platform levels in fluctuating pyramidal and ladder arrangements suggesting the changing emotional content and interrelationships between characters. Or the script can be read in concert style with lecterns, giving a presentational effect. This technique reinforces the fact that this is a literary text being dramatized.

The material can be memorized; it should be noted, however, that the allowance of a script makes the readers theater format particularly appealing to novices and those who doubt their memorization ability.

The material chosen for readers theater should be compelling in its theme, language, action, and characterization. Possibilities include poetry, narratives, letters, diaries, biographies, plays, novels, histories, travel books, essays, and documents. An original script can also be created around a single theme or author, combining any of the written material described above. If essays are used, characterization and different points of view should be added so that the material is not abstract and uninteresting. A radio play would be suited to readers theater since the setting is already defined in the dialogue and both require considerable visualizing by the audience. Dialogue poetry in which there is conversation between two or more characters is particularly adaptable to readers theater.

Staging is the key component in the ultimate effectiveness of readers theater. It is possible to have a narrator who links scenes together, entering throughout the presentation. The narrator role can be assumed by different actors as they move in and out of characterizations. In addition to playing many roles, it is also possible for all to play each character at the same time in order to show differing personality dimensions in the role. In staging readers theater, any new idea or mood should be illustrated by a change in tempo, pitch, and physical stance and location on stage. Depending on the effect intended, onstage focus, offstage focus, or a combination of both should be used. In onstage focus, the actors relate directly to each other, maintaining eye contact and appropriate positioning. Onstage focus specifically locates the dramatic action between these one or more characters. Offstage focus, on the other hand, aims to universalize the experience by directing the words to the audience members as if they are characters in the dramatic action. Depending on the sophistication of staging desired, the readers theater presentation can be enhanced by lighting, music, sound effects, creative movement, and multimedia.

Theater Production

As described earlier in this chapter, theater or formal drama involves the presentation of drama before an audience and requires rehearsal to achieve the performance goal. The process of auditioning, casting, directing, and producing is one requiring much more study than is intended here. However, for the purpose of familiarizing the recreation leader with this area of drama leadership, basic theater terminology will be defined.

In conducting an audition or "try out" for a play, the director can use a number of techniques including requiring the actor to read the given part "cold" (without prior rehearsal) or to improvise the dramatic situation in the script.

In rehearsal, the director analyzes the script, breaking it down into its changing subplots, tempos, and climaxes. At the same time, the actors make notes on the play's subtext (the emotions and ideas that they want to project from the script). When the director begins blocking (staging the movement) of the play, the actors make the appropriate notations in their scripts. Figure 5–1 illustrates the stage positions in theater:

Upstage Right	Upstage Center	Upstage Left
Right	Center	Left
Downstage Right	Downstage Center	Downstage Left

FIGURE 5–1: Parts of the Stage

In *Let's Improvise,* Milton Polsky illustrates the importance of appropriate staging, indicating that: "Down right is best for direct narration. Down center is best for high points. Down left is good for tension. Up right is good for intrigue and eavesdropping, up center good for scenes of royalty, authority, and dignity."[5]

How the actor moves on the stage is significant to the correct projection of the play's themes and ideas. The placement of the actor in relation to the other actors and audience at various points throughout the play is indicative of the emotional subtext being portrayed. The following terms refer to stage movement:

Cross—move to another actor

Cross above—move upstage of actor

Cross downstage—move downstage of actor

Open up—turn to audience

Turn out—turn sideways, giving only part of full front to audience

Full position—face out

Profile position—turn completely sideways

¾ position—turn nearly full back so that side of head and shoulder are toward audience

Focus—look at another actor

Upstage—stand in front of another actor

Take the stage—move into a more desirable position

Give the stage—give space to another actor

Stage business—character's mannerisms (actions of hands and body and use of props)

Dress the stage—keep stage picture in balance.

Stage balance refers to appropriate visual symbolic compositions on stage. The stage groupings should tell a story, actors being arranged in ascending levels and triangular groupings that suggest the most prominent character at any one time. The characters also need to be balanced in relationship to the props and scenery on stage. To avoid a static, dull appearance, actors should avoid standing in a straight line or semi-circle; they should not be equidistant apart and should avoid bunching.

Other terms to be familiar with in theater are:

Projection—voice volume and articulation

Stage directions—instructions in the script indicating all movements and groupings on stage; they can be provided by both playwright and director

Fourth wall—name given to the imaginary side of the room facing the audience

Pit—orchestra pit

Curtain line—last line spoken before the curtain goes down

Ad lib—extemporize, make up on the spot

5. Milton Polsky, *Let's Improvise: Becoming Creative, Expressive and Spontaneous Through Drama* (Englewood Cliffs, NJ: Prentice-Hall, 1980), p. 276.

Apron—part of the stage projecting in front of the curtain

Backdrop—curtain at the back of scene

Cue—signal provided by last words of the preceding speech

Grips—stage hands

Strike the set—tear the set down

Amphitheater—a large, oval, circular, or semicircular outdoor theater with rising tiers of seats around an open playing area

Arena—a type of stage that is surrounded by the audience on all four sides, also known as theater in the round

Offstage—the areas of the stage, usually in the wings, that are not in view of the audience

Proscenium—the arch or frame surrounding the stage opening in a box or picture stage

Set—the scenery, taken as whole, for a scene or an entire play.

One of the values of theater is that it can involve people in a great number of capacities other than acting. Theater is, therefore, very well suited to recreation that aims to make creative opportunities available to all. In theater, as in recreation, every talent and interest is welcome whether it be designing sets, making costumes, selling tickets, working lights etc. Figure 5–2 illustrates how each of these talents contributes to the collective whole of a theater production.

Children's Theater

Children's theater is theater performed for children by children, adults, or both. The standards of performance should be equal to that of adult theater, but unfortunately the capabilities of the young audience are often underestimated. Because these children have grown up with the fast paced stimuli of television, they are especially capable of absorbing the introduction of new ideas and characters and multiple subplots. In fact, it is through their own dramatic play that children have evidenced their ability to sustain involvement in fantasy.

In their dramatic play, children assume roles and transform objects to simulate real life situations. In her book, *Dramatic Play in Childhood: Rehearsal for Life,* Virginia G. Koste cites the example of the children, who transforming a mud puddle into an ocean and pea pods into boats, then created their own storm effects by blowing and splashing. According to Koste, dramatic play provides the secure framework from which to master the reality of a storm—to control an event that in "real life" would be too overwhelming to absorb. Koste advises that the most effective theater, whether for children or adults, is that which appeals to everyone's need to master reality through personal involvement in the transformation. For instance, instead of a representational style of performance, in which the play is presented as reality, it would be preferable to use the presentational format in which the children are informed that they will have to cooperate in imaginatively creating this reality. For instance, by coming out from back-

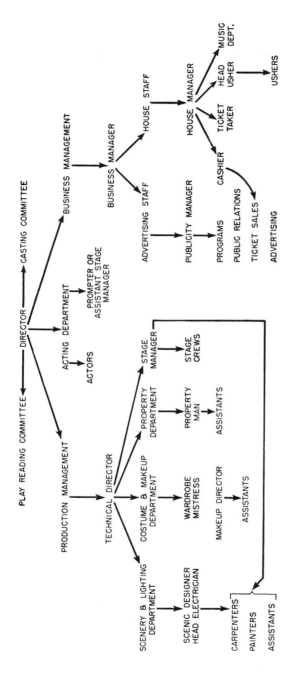

FIGURE 5–2: Organizational Chart for Theater Production

Source: Dorothy W. Lynds, "Dramatics in Recreation," in *Recreation Leadership* by H. Dan Corbin, 3rd. ed. (Englewood Cliffs, NJ: Prentice-Hall, 1970), p. 207.

stage prior to the play, holding their masks and costumes, a cast makes a collective statement to the children that says: "Join us in this 'dress up' game of pretend called theater." The presentational style of story theater holds appeal for children because the actors visibly assume various roles in much the same way that the children themselves do in play. It is often best to have natural sets and imaginative props so that the children can mentally transform the objects the way they do in their own dramatic play.

Arena staging is more similar to children's play space than is the boxed proscenium, and it invites more participation. To help elicit the involvement characteristic of children's dramatic play, the concept of participation theater has been developed. In participation theater, the playwright or actors and director add approaches in the script that will draw the children more actively into the play. This may consist of a response to a rhetorical question, the repetition of sounds, the warning or cheering of the protagonist, or the repetition of actions. In some cases, the children are asked to determine the outcome of the scene; for instance, in response to the actor's question "How will we save Christmas Day?" the children may decide to become factory workers making toys. It is evident that participation theater provides a valuable link with creative dramatics as the children are given the freedom to create at their own levels. If participation theater is undertaken, it must be done with sincerity, because children willl perceive if there is no real intent to follow up on their suggestions.

Participation theater is not restricted to children's theater; certain adult theater productions such as melodrama utilize the audience participation techniques of participation theater. Since participation theater requires great flexibility and confidence on the part of the actors, it is advisable that it not be used with fledgling performers. There need to be cut offs in space, time, and group size so that the audience's involvement does not get out of control. Choice of dramatic material is significant as it may be artificial to impose participation theater on a conventional script. In participation theater, as with any form of drama, concern for a collective response should not overshadow respect for individual differences.

Adaptations

The theater program sponsored under recreation auspices has the responsibility to ensure that all people have access to participation. In recreational theater, there is no such thing as "star billing" or "casting the box office favorite." Provisions should be made for anyone who wishes to perform, regardless of limitations. Where visual problems may exist, much help can be gained through the use of scripts with large print, colored print, or braille if necessary, as well as individual coaching. If hearing problems exist, then big cue cards, microphones, and individual coaching can serve as aids in rehearsal. For those with mobility problems, the format of readers theater might be considered since it focuses on verbal interpretation in a stylized physical arrangement requiring little movement. For those unsure of their memorization ability, it is possble to have a narrator read in the background while they respond with related actions or movements. In summary then, the play can be adapted to meet the unique needs of each individual.

SUGGESTED READINGS

KOSTE, VIRGINIA G. *Dramatic Play in Childhood: Rehearsal for Life*. New Orleans: Anchorage Press, 1978.

LEASE, RUTH AND SIKS, GERALDINE. *Creative Dramatics in Home, School and Community*. New York: Harper and Row, 1952.

McCASLIN, NELLIE. *Children and Drama*. New York: David McKay, 1975.

PIERINI, MARY PAUL FRANCIS. *Creative Dramatics: A Guide for Educators*. New York: Seabury Press, 1971.

POLSKY, MILTON. *Let's Improvise: Becoming Creative, Expressive and Spontaneous through Drama*. Englewood Cliffs, NJ: Prentice-Hall, 1980.

SCHATTNER, GERTRUD AND COURTNEY, RICHARD (EDS.). *Drama in Therapy—Volume One: Children*. New York: Drama Book Specialists, 1981.

SCHATTNER, GERTRUD AND COURTNEY, RICHARD (EDS.). *Drama in Therapy—Volume Two: Adults*. New York: Drama Book Specialists, 1981.

SHAFTEL, FANNIE AND SHAFTEL, GEORGE. *Role Playing for Social Values: Decision Making in the Social Studies Classroom*. Englewood Cliffs, NJ: Prentice-Hall, 1967.

SPOLIN, VIOLA. *Improvisation for the Theater*. Evanston, IL: Northwestern University Press, 1963.

WAGNER, BETTY JANE. *Dorothy Heathcote: Drama as a Learning Medium*. Washington, DC: National Education Association, 1976.

WARD, WINIFRED. *Creative Dramatics for the Upper Grades and Junior High School*. New York: D. Appleton and Co, 1930.

WAY, BRIAN. *Development Through Drama*. New York: Humanities Press, 1968.

6

Arts and Crafts

Arts and crafts are widely programmed as recreation activities. But since many arts and crafts programs in leisure settings are limited to pre-packaged kits and simplified crafts projects, many people have a narrow view of what constitutes arts and crafts. This chapter illustrates the broad programming possibilities in the arts and crafts area; under the direction of a skilled leader, such programs can be individualized to participants' skills and interests.

TRAINING

The abilities and training needed to teach arts and crafts in the recreational setting have been underestimated. All too often recreation leaders are assumed to be skilled in arts and crafts as a part of their general work. The field of arts and crafts, however—like drama, dance, or music—requires trained personnel. College recreation departments are forging more links with arts departments, resulting in interrelated course work on a required or elective basis. By concentrating on the visual arts, a recreation major can become an art specialist in recreation leadership; similarly, an art major can minor in recreation. Visual artists can be employed as instructors in arts and crafts classes for which recreation professionals have insufficient background. Visual artists often enjoy teaching in leisure-services settings, since they encounter highly motivated individuals who approach the leisure activity of art enthusiastically, not begrudgingly as an educational requirement. It is critical to the success of arts and crafts programs in recreation settings that a qualified administrator determine the level of art training required of the professional staff to provide quality visual arts instruction.

PROGRAMMING

Visual arts have gained increasing importance in the leisure lifestyle of the general public. Attending art museums and exhibits has grown concurrently with the public demand for more accessible arts experiences. To encourage this trend, arts institutions have made a number of changes designed to broaden their appeal and make them more accessible; these include:

> Promoting intensive use of outreach programs so that thousands of people are given an introduction to, or fresh perspective on, the field of fine arts; for instance, the National Gallery of Art in Washington, D.C., annually sends touring art shows to 4,000 communities as part of its extension services.
>
> Remodeling to produce a less formal atmosphere; most art museums now contain cafes, gift shops, and comfortable areas in which to sit and relax.
>
> Creating dynamic exhibits that make art collections more meaningful and interesting to the nonscholar; many art museums are installing electronic guide-and-lecture devices, and some have introduced motion stations that use color film, videotapes, and sound recordings to provide information concerning works of art and their creators.
>
> Adopting more aggressive promotion tactics; newspaper articles and television programs on major art shows have proven particularly effective in increasing public interest in art in general as well as in specific exhibitions.
>
> Presenting spectacular touring shows such as the Tutankhamen exhibition on loan from Egypt, which drew 8 million visitors to art museums in eight American and Canadian cities between 1976–1979.[1]

The visual arts have joined with alternate youth programs by involving young graffiti offenders in making murals as community beautification projects. Arts and crafts classes are found in every leisure setting from playgrounds to resorts, to camps, to nursing homes. Arts and crafts lend themselves to both short-term or long-term classes, thus providing attractive programming flexibility. In addition, participants also have flexibility in choosing the program format most conducive to their goals and most agreeable to their lifestyle: For example, the individual wishing to study ceramics can choose from a class, a workshop, or a drop-in center. The class gives instruction in a group setting, the workshop provides in-

1. Michael Chubb and Holly R. Chubb, *One Third of Our Time? An Introduction to Recreation Behavior and Resources* (New York: John Wiley and Sons, 1981), pp. 593–594.

struction and reinforcement of self-paced work, and the drop-in center provides a facility for self-directed activity rather than instruction.

The recreation programmer finds in arts and crafts rich sources for blending with other recreation areas. In music, participants can design their own instruments. In dance, an artwork can become the basis for creative movement. In theater, art is involved in the design and construction of sets and costumes. In literature, an art form can inspire writing or can illustrate it. In outdoor recreation, nature crafts can utilize natural outdoor materials for artistic expression: mobiles, figures, jewelry, sculptures, collages, and wall decorations can be made from such materials as nuts, driftwood, sticks, beans, shells, rocks, feathers, seeds, pine cones, berries, and moss; terrariums can be made from dried flowers, sand, and charcoal; shells and rocks make good wind chimes. Arts and crafts can integrate with social recreation in the design and construction of environmental effects such as centerpieces and decorations.

TERMINOLOGY

The terms "arts" and "crafts" are used rather loosely with little regard for the distinction between them. "Arts" refers to those activities in which the focus is self-expression ("art for art's sake"), such as painting, sculpture, and photography. "Crafts," on the other hand, refers to those activities with a utilitarian motivation: The resulting project will be put to some use. Examples include jewelry making, basketry, bookbinding, and so forth. It should be noted, however, that arts and crafts are not mutually exclusive; there is a frequent overlapping of intent behind a single activity. For example, members of a quilting group may be motivated by the quilt's functionality, thus viewing it as a craft, and by the expressive value of the quilt's designs, thus also viewing it as a form of art.

VALUE OF ARTS AND CRAFTS

(1) Arts and crafts foster the development of mental and physical skills as participants link their intellectual planning of an art project with their manual ability to carry it out. (2) Arts and crafts provide a means of self-expression and creativity. (3) Upon completion of the work, a feeling of personal satisfaction and accomplishment is experienced. (4) Individuals motivated by a need for recognition and approval can find opportunity to display their work. (5) With art forms that involve long-range work and skill development, participants derive the character-building benefit of self-discipline and perseverance. (6) In coming to a wider appreciation of craftsmanship, participants also develop cultural appreciation. (7) Arts and crafts have appeal to the individual seeking multiple stimuli: certain arts and crafts activities can be done while listening to music or a lecture, or

while watching TV or a sports match. (8) Individuals may be drawn to a craft because of its money-saving appeal, as in the case of home sewing or carpentry. (9) In an age of technology and commercialism, more and more people are being attracted to self-help projects that take them back to a simpler place and time. The Foxfire Project, in which older craftspeople teach folk arts to young people, is an illustration of this trend. (10) Arts and crafts make good hobbies because they are individually paced activities that can last a lifetime, and hobbies can be pursued for their emotional and/or monetary rewards; the proliferation of crafts fairs attests to the widespread interest in making crafts a source of income.

ART THERAPY

Working with one's hands has great therapeutic benefits. Through manipulation of arts and crafts materials, people exercise a mastery over the environment that they may not feel in real life; this feeling of control helps reduce tension and frustration. Through tactile experiences, people can release any tension or aggression into the materials being manipulated. The field of art therapy, an adjunct to recreation therapy, is concerned with the use of art in the treatment of mental, emotional, and physical disorders. Art therapy is valuable not only for the many benefits it provides the client, but also for the psychological clues that it can reveal to professional staff working with that client. Therapists often discover more about the background and psychological condition of clients from their spontaneous, nonverbal art expressions than they would from the customary verbal techniques. The psyches of clients may be more visible in the artistic symbols they make than in the thoughts they consciously weigh before speaking.

NEED SATISFACTION

The *Program Book for Recreation Professionals* by Albert Tillman gives further illustration of how crafts can be classified by the personal needs they meet. This approach is important because it avoids the customary classification of arts and crafts by material; instead, Tillman puts the emphasis on matching individual needs to the components of the craft:[2]

1. *Expressive crafts:* the appeal is the opportunity to express feelings through the work. Emphasis is on aesthetics (e.g., painting, flower arranging).
2. *Image crafts:* these often overlap with expressive crafts; image crafts center on presenting one's self-image through the work (e.g., photo collage, jewelry).
3. *Kinetic crafts:* the attraction is the tactile, sensual experience of working materials through the hands (e.g., sculpting, ceramics).

2. Albert Tillman, *The Program Book for Recreation Professionals* (Palo Alto, CA: Mayfield Pub. Co., 1973), pp. 157–160.

4. *Segment crafts:* interest revolves around making items that are part of a larger project (e.g., set for a play, illustrations for a literary magazine).

5. *Instrumental crafts:* the instrumental craft is constructed as a needed aid for another often artistic, recreation activity. The prime motivation is realization of the purpose to which the craft will be put (e.g., puppets for puppet show, instruments for rhythm band).

6. *Utilitarian crafts:* unlike instrumental crafts, utilitarian crafts are designed for practical, functional usage (e.g., memo holder, leather belt). The money-saving factor is an appeal.

7. *Decorative crafts:* these are ornamental crafts, temporary in nature, used to beautify the surroundings (e.g., candles, centerpiece).

8. *Gift crafts:* motivation is to have a completed gift for one's friend or family. A gift craft can be any craft as long as the motivation is gift-giving.

9. *Sales crafts:* profit-making from sale of the crafts is the motivation. Any craft sold for money is a sales craft.

10. *Learning crafts:* prime aim is to prompt learning (of geography, the environment, other cultures, etc.). For example, to learn about tribal customs, participants may construct masks or build instruments reflective of the culture.

11. *Time-filling crafts:* these crafts are approached merely with the idea of "staying busy." They can be any crafts where the motivation is "keeping occupied" rather than aesthetic expression.

The above classifications are helpful in looking at participant needs in relationship to arts and crafts participation. However, care should be taken not to view this as a rating scale, for none of the classifications listed above is more worthy than another.

OTHER CLASSIFICATIONS

The scope of arts and crafts activities is vast, and numerous classifications have been made by authors in an attempt to document this variety. The following two classification systems—the first by Farrell and Lundegren, and the second by Shivers—reflect the breadth of the arts and crafts field:

GROUPING OF ARTS ACTIVITIES BY MATERIALS[3]

Graphics
poster design, murals, cards, etc.
paper models
flags, banners

Painting
oil on wood, canvas, other fabric
watercolor
gouache
acrylic
finger paint mixes

Photography
still, black and white, color
motion, 8 mm, 16 mm, 35 mm

Printing
woodcarving blocks
linoleum blocks
silk screening
stencils
miscellaneous materials, carrots, potatoes

3. Patricia Farrell and Herbeta M. Lundegren, *The Process of Recreation Programming: Theory and Technique* (New York: John Wiley and Sons, 1978), pp. 144–152.

Sketching
pencil
etching on metals and scrimshaw
charcoal
pastel

Sculpture/Welding
wood: walnut, oak, driftwood, etc.
stone
clay
sand
metal
plastic
glass

Ceramics
pottery
mosaics
plaster of Paris

Homemaking
needlepoint, crewel
sewing and millinery
candlemaking
quilting
canning, cooking, baking
gourmet cooking

Home repair
furniture and carpentry
electricity, heat, water, paint
lawn and garden

Jewelry
copper, silver, gold
baubles, bangles, beads
shells, stones, etc.

Leathercraft

Paper
Papier-maché
collage
airplanes, kites, origami

Scrap craft
use of any scrap material from wood,
    styrofoam, eggs, milk and meat,
    cartons, etc.

Weaving
card, loom
macrame
hooking, braiding, knitting

Woodmaking

TYPES OF ARTS AND CRAFTS[4]

Graphic Art
oil painting
watercolor painting
wash drawing
pen and ink drawing
finger painting
charcoal sketching
pastel drawing
photography
dry point etching
silk screen painting
crayon drawing

Animal
leather craft
shell craft
bone carving
horn carving
taxidermy

Plastic Art
stone sculpture
metal sculpture
clay sculpture
glass etching
ivory carving
wood carving
precious metal smithing
lapidary
tapestry making
mosaic tile making
glass blowing
mobiles

Marine Crafts
knot tying
rope making
sail making
boat repairing
surfboard shaping

4. Jay Shivers, *Essentials in Recreation Services* (Philadelphia: Lea and Febiger, 1978), pp. 234–236.

Vegetable
weaving
sewing
crocheting
needlepoint
embroidery
basketry
block printing
knitting
paper sculpture
raffia work
appliqueing
cardboard sculpture
wood carving
crepe paper craft
papier-maché craft
dyeing
woodworking
candle making
whittling
hooking
braiding

Mineral
metal craft
clay modeling
glass making
bead craft
ceramics
plastic lacing
plaster of paris
jewelry making
pottery making
sand sculpture
stone craft
soap carving
chemical crafts
snow sculpture
ice sculpture
coral craft

Industrial Crafts
electrical shop
masonry

smithing
mechanical arts
plumbing
cabinet making
tool and dye making
furniture refinishing
fur coat remodeling
hat designing
dress designing
gift wrapping
tinkering
bookbinding
woodworking
clock making
glass grinding
printing/book making

Automotive Crafts
building automobiles
repairing automobiles
motor tuning
boat designing
plane constructing
bicycle making
model making
glider making
motorcycle repairs

Nature Crafts
fly tying
lashing
canoe repairing
shelter building
fire making
implement making
net making
cooking
specimen mounting
driftwood craft
stenciling
spatter painting
vegetable printing
potato puppetry
Indian craft

AN ARTS AND CRAFTS "HOW TO" SAMPLER

Since this book is not intended as an arts and crafts training manual, it is not feasible to include "how to" directions for each of the art media listed above. Readers who are interested in a particular activity should consult pertinent arts and crafts textbooks in the library. However, a sampling of arts and crafts will be given detailed illustration in this chapter to familiarize readers with the "how to" format to be found in other references. (The following section of this chapter, with the exception of minor additional footnotes, was written by the late Edna Bottorf, professor emeritus and chairperson of the Art Department of Lock Haven State University.)

The recreation leader has many arts and crafts ideas to choose from. Some require more tools than others; some have a wider range of application; while still others may be carried out by practically all ages. The following are easily handled and taught, have a wide appeal, and are inexpensive and practical. Under each craft described below are given the materials and tools, the possible objects to be made, and the directions for carrying out the activity. Where necessary, illustrations are furnished to explain a procedure or usage of equipment and supplies. In all crafts, the designs and procedures are determined by the qualities inherent in the material. The worker should always keep this in mind and not attempt to use a material in a manner inconsistent with its nature.

Clay Modeling

The materials of clay modeling are clay, water, and plaster of paris. The necessary equipment includes a knife, a sharp stick or modeling tools, plastic bags, cloths, newspapers, containers, a board or oilcloth to work on, a rolling pin or length of broom handle, sandpaper, a sponge, a kidney rubber, brushes, glazes, and a kiln. Pottery, dishes, boxes, tiles, jewelry, figurines, and beads may be modeled from clay.

Preparation of the material. Clay can be secured from local deposits or purchased from a supply house. The native clay must sometimes be refined if firing is desired. Purchased clay comes wet or dry (flour) and in a variety of colors. Add water to clay flour and knead well the resulting mass. If it is sticky, add more flour or spread the mass out and knead it until it comes freely from the hands. If objects are to be fired or turned on the wheel, pound the clay well until all air bubbles are removed and the clay is consistent throughout. After preparing the clay, allow it to "ripen" in an air-tight container for at least a day. Clay is soft and pliable when wet, but hardens when dried and baked.

Thumb, coil, and slab methods. A ball of clay can be pushed into a desired shape by manipulation of the fingers (thumb method). It can be rolled into evenly shaped coils or cut into strips. Objects can be built up by placing such coils or strips on top of each other, the shape being determined by the placing of the coils (coil method). Objects may also be made by rolling the clay with a rolling pin into sheets, cutting sections from the sheets and fastening these together (slab method).

To fasten clay pieces together securely, score (mark with lines) the parts that touch, moisten with clay slip, and firmly rub together. Clay slip is made by mixing water and clay powder to the consistency of cream.

Wheel method.   In making objects on the wheel, center the clay mass first. Keep the hands wet while working so that the object will not stick to them and be pulled loose. Shape the object by pressure of one hand on the outside and the other hand on the inside.

Figure modeling.   Animals or figures can be built up with coils or fashioned with the fingers, orange sticks, knives, or bits of wire. Pull out parts from the original mass or fasten on with slip. Hollow solid objects to facilitate drying without cracking. Flowers and other forms make interesting costume jewelry if pins are glued to their backs.

Mold method.   Objects may also be made by casting in a plaster of paris mold. One-piece molds can be made from clay or other objects that have no undercutting. Objects must be coated with glycerin, vaseline, or clay slip to keep from sticking to the plaster of paris. Place the coated object open side down in a cardboard box that is at least two inches larger on all sides than the object. Slowly sift plaster of paris over a quantity of water (large enough to fill the box) until dry powder rests on the top. Slowly stir mixture with the fingers until it is creamy throughout. Carefully pour this over the object to fill the box. Tap the box lightly on the side to dislodge air bubbles. When the plaster of paris has heated and become firm, tear the box free and carefully remove the object.

After being dried thoroughly, the mold is ready for use. Pour clay slip into it, filling it completely. As the mold absorbs the water, note the thickness of the model and add more slip until the desired thickness is secured. Pour off the surplus slip. As it dries, the clay form shrinks and separates from the mold. If it adheres at any point, gently loosen it with a knife to prevent warping or cracking. Reverse the mold to remove the form and dry throughly before using again.

Drying.   The clay shrinks when drying and, especially in the case of thick pieces, should be kept from drafts or heat until thoroughly dry. Quick drying and shrinking of the exterior may cause the object to crack. Dry forms are called "green" ware.

Finishing.   Surfaces of dried pieces can be smoothed with a wet sponge, finger, kidney rubber, knife, or fine sandpaper.

Decorating.   While still moist or after drying, objects can be decorated with colored underglaze paints or crayons or with colored clay slips (engobes). Designs may be scratched into the surface or through the dried colored slip (sgraffito decoration).

Firing.   Stack green ware in the kiln quite compactly for firing. Air should be able to circulate fairly well. Do not place heavy pieces on thin ones. Directions for firing are furnished with the kilns. Fired pieces are called "biscuit" ware.

Glazing. To withstand water, biscuit pieces must be glazed. Glazes come in powder form and a variety of colors. The powder is mixed with water to the consistency of cream and applied to the object by dipping, pouring, spraying, or patting on with a brush. Protect the surfaces of the kiln or shelves with a coating of kiln wash (a powder mixed with water to the consistency of cream and brushed on). Place the glazed objects on small stilts. Do not let them touch each other or the kiln. Follow the kiln directions for firing.

Experimentation in modeling objects, mixing glazes, or decorating should be encouraged.

Notes. In cold weather, dryness can be checked by holding object against a window. If moisture gathers, it is not dry.

When considered dry, the object may be placed on top of the kiln after it is heated to insure thorough drying.

Do not use the same brush, even if washed, in different colored glazes or engobes.

Protect working surfaces with paper or oilcloth. Roll out the clay in slab ware on the cloth side of oilcloth. Pull the cloth from the clay and not the clay from the cloth to prevent distortion of the shape.

If no kiln is available, an "Indian kiln" might be tried whereby the objects are buried under stones and covered with wood that is then fired and kept hot for some hours. If this is not practical, objects can be painted with tempera paints and varnished or shellacked. Tempera paint and pencil marks will burn off in firing.

Stenciling

The materials used in stenciling are stencil paper, paint (tempera or textile), wax crayons, and cloth or paper. The equipment necessary includes a sharp knife, scissors or a razor blade, turpentine, and stencil brushes. For silk-screen painting, one needs a wooden frame, silk or organdy, silk-screen stencil paper, adhering and block-out liquid, and a squeegee. The stencil process produces such items as greeting cards, posters, bookplates, bookmarks, wrapping papers, wall hangings, articles of clothing, and colored prints.

Stenciling is one method of repeating a design numerous times. The procedure involves brushing color onto the desired surface through openings cut into an oiled paper.

Planning the design. In making a design, avoid long narrow areas or much twisting or curving unless the space is broken at intervals, especially at turnings. Secure areas lying within other areas to an outer edge unless they are to be made in more than one color, in which case a separate stencil should be made for each color. Trace the design on the stencil paper. With a sharp tool, cut out the areas to be removed following on the outside of the line so that the opening will actually be larger than the desired shape.

Procedure. Place the cut stencil on the material to be stenciled. Load a brush with color but brush out thoroughly on a cardboard or dish so that the brush looks comparatively dry. Too much paint clogs the openings and gets under the stencil. Direct the brush briskly from the edge to the center of the opening (Figure 6–1). If necessary, repeat the stroke in order, especially with cloth, to insure that the paint will get into the material and not just on the nap. Remove the stencil. When the color is dry, apply the second color through the second stencil. Before using a stencil a second time, check the back and wipe off any paint that may have run under the edges. In stenciling with textile paint on cloth, a second color may be added immediately after the first, but allow twenty four hours for complete drying. In stenciling on cloth with either textile paint or wax crayons, set the color by ironing over the reversed cloth using a pressing cloth, dampened with white vinegar, and a hot iron.

Stippling. Paint may be stippled on paper by dipping a toothbrush in tempera paint and brushing a stick or comb over the upturned bristles from the end toward the handle. A spray of fine drops is thus created and can be directed on the stencil. Be sure all surfaces not to be painted are well covered in this process.

If used in textile paint, brushes must be cleaned in turpentine and washed with soap and warm water.

Silk-screen printing. Silk-screen printing is a form of stenciling. It is used by artists in printing serigraphs or in industry for commercial work. It can be used for the same purposes as other stencils.

For amateur workers, the following method is best. Stretch a fine and even-meshed silk or organdy tightly over a wooden frame. Cut a stencil from special silk-screen stencil paper and fasten it to the outside of the material according to the directions furnished with the stencil paper (there are several kinds). Seal the corners and edges on the inside of the frame with brown adhesive paper so that paint cannot get through. Put a quantity of thick paint in one end of the frame. Place the frame over the area to be stenciled. Insert a squeegee at the end where the paint has been placed and firmly draw it over the stencil to the opposite side pushing the paint ahead of it. Although one brushing is often sufficient, to insure a solid color, re-

STENCILING

FIGURE 6–1 Stenciling

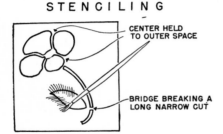

CENTER HELD
TO OUTER SPACE

BRIDGE BREAKING A
LONG NARROW CUT

verse the squeegee and put it back in the opposite direction. More than one color can be applied by preparing a separate frame for each color.

The stencil can be removed and the frame used again, but the process is rather tedious. Directions for this come with the stencil paper used.

Notes. When using more than one stencil for a design, be sure the stencils match perfectly.

When using textile paints, prepare the paints and material according to the directions furnished with the paints.

Material must be tightly stretched during stenciling.

For a different and effective result, brush in from the edge without filling the opening completely; also brush a deeper tone or color in from the edge of an opening already filled with color.

Rough edges are the result of too much or too runny a paint on the brush.

Block Printing

Block printing is another method of reproducing a design an indefinite number of times. Its basic materials are linoleum blocks (mounted or unmounted) or wood blocks, paper or cloth on which the design is printed, oil or tempera paint or printer's ink, a potato, inner tube, sticks of wood shaped with a knife or file, or a soap eraser. The necessary equipment is a slab of glass, rubber brayer, palette knife, hammer, spoon, or washing-machine wringer, and a knife, razor blade, or cutting tools. Block printing illustrations can be designed for such items as calendars, publications, invitations, wall plaques, and book ends.

Making the design. Scrap linoleum is much cheaper and more easily secured than mounted linoleum (mounted for use in a printing machine). Since linoleum is quite soft and chips fairly easily, designs should consist of large printed areas broken perhaps by small areas or lines of white rather than of thin printed lines.

Fine-grained wood blocks can also be used, the cuts usually being made on the end grain. Since wood is stronger than linoleum and finer lines can be cut and still be strong, the design usually puts less emphasis on mass than is the case with linoleum blocks.

Cutting the block. Paint the linoleum with a thin coat of light-colored tempera paint so that the transferred design can be easily seen. Since the design will appear reversed when printed, reverse it before transferring it to the linoleum. Outline the areas to be printed with a sharp knife, gouge, or razor blade with the tool slanting away from these areas or lines. This leaves areas that widen toward the bottom and are therefore stronger. With the knife or wider gouge, remove the areas not to be printed. The larger the area, the deeper should be the cut; fine lines may be quite shallow (Figure 6–2).

SLANTING   DEEP CUT   SHALLOW CUT

FIGURE 6–2 Cutting the block

Printing the block.   Put a drop of printer's ink on a slab of glass. Run a rubber brayer over this in different directions until the brayer is evenly coated with a fairly thin coat of ink. Run the brayer over the linoleum until all uncut surfaces are evenly covered. Place the material to be printed on a pad or paper or felt. Turn the linoleum over and place it on the spot to be printed. The design can be transferred to the material through hand pressure to the back of the block if unmounted linoleum is used, or several sharp blows with a hammer on the back of mounted blocks. Unmounted blocks placed on paper may be run through a wringer for printing. Ink the block again for each new printing. Clean the block, brayer, and glass slab with turpentine and wash the glass with soap and water.

Fasten a hook on the back of a cut linoleum block and hang it on the wall for a decoration. Parts may be colored if desired. A small piece of wood fastened on the front of a block transforms it into one of a pair of book ends.

Printing with sticks.   Block printing can also be done by using sticks of varying shapes (match ends, pencils, wood scraps). Vary edges by chipping or filing. Press the ends on an inked pad or piece of felt on which paint has been spread thinly. Designs can be created by printing together sticks of varying sizes or shapes (Figure 6–3). Designs can be cut into a raw potato or on a soap eraser and painted as in stick painting; color may be brushed on.

Beadwork

Beads (wooden, tile, or seed) can be woven or strung to make belts, bags, tiles, bracelets, purses, and headbands, using only the beads themselves and an extremely thin, wirelike needle, thread, and a loom.

Seed-bead weaving.   Designs are worked on a cross-section paper, each block representing one bead. If planned with colored pencils or crayons, the finished effect can be determined.

FIGURE 6–3 Printing from sticks

Warp threads are strung on a bead loom. The space between threads is the width of a bead. The number of threads used, therefore, determines the width of the finished object.

String a needle with strong thread and tie the thread to an outside warp thread. Following the pattern, string all of the beads of the first row on the thread, bring them up on the underside of the loom, each bead in its proper place (Figure 6–4 a–b). Pass the needle back through the beads but this time on the top of the warp threads ending at the starting place (Figure 6–4b). Pull thread tight. Put the succeeding rows of beads on in the same manner.

Wooden and tile beads. Wooden and tile beads are used to make purses and tiles. Designs are made by using different colored beads. Beads on one row alternate between beads on the row above and below it. This method of stringing the beads together is shown in Figure 6–4.

Leather Work

Leather work can produce such items as book covers, book ends, purses, billfolds, key cases, picture frames, belts, and desk sets. Generally, modeling tools or a nutpick, a sharp knife, a punch, stamps or dies, and a hammer are the only tools required. Designs can be applied to leather by tooling, stamping, or carving.

Tooling. Designs for tooling by the beginner should avoid narrow raised areas, straight lines, or curves that are to be perfect arcs or circles; these require more skill. It is easy to go out of bounds and not easy to correct such errors. Always allow a one-fourth-inch border for lacing. Cut the leather with a sharp knife to the size needed. Wet it with a sponge or under running water. If held under a spigot, let the water hit the under side. When it begins to show through on the right side, it is wet enough. If water appears when the leather is pressed, it is too wet and should be allowed to dry somewhat before using. Trace the design on the right side of the leather with a rather sharp metal tool, a knitting needle, or a nutpick. Be careful to keep the pattern flat (do not thumbtack it on the leather); do not cut through the paper. Remove the paper and go over the lines impressed on the leather.

B E A D W O R K

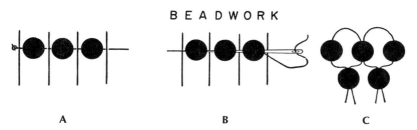

A	B	C

FIGURE 6–4 (a–b) Seed beads (c) Tile or wood beads

To get a raised design, use a modeling tool or the back of the nutpick point. Work on a smooth firm surface so that no creases will show through on the leather. Although a hard wood slab or piece of glass is recommended, a pad of paper absorbs extra moisture and raises the design higher. Press with a rotary stroke over the areas to be lowered. Outline the design again when finished.

A stippled effect is also interesting. Press the background area with a sharp pointed tool, distributing the dots evenly but not mechanically.

If the design is not high enough, turn the leather over and use a rounded tool to press from the wrong side. Be sure to outline the design on the right side again. Be careful to keep the leather in shape. It stretches while wet and can get out of shape easily.

Stamping.   Stamps can be made from a linoleum block. In this case, cut out the part to be raised and cut to an even depth. Metal dies or stamps can be purchased or made from nails or firm wood blocks or sticks. File edges for variety.

Plan a design first on a blotter with the dies or stamps. Group them together to form larger patterns or to form borders.

Wet the leather and stamp the design where desired. Use hand pressure on the stamps.

Carving.   Keep the design simple. Do not use narrow spaces. Use a carving leather such as cowhide. Cut the desired pieces. Soak for five minutes. Roll, grain side out, and place in an airtight container overnight.

Trace the design as for tooling leather. Using a sharp, straightedged knife, cut around the design with a vertical cut, piercing halfway through the leather. With a modeling tool, press the cut edges slightly to remove the sharp, raw-looking edge, Using a background stamp, press down the area around the design using sharp, strong blows on the stamp from a hammer so that the background will be pressed lower than the design. There are other stamps that can be used on the raised areas for variety and detail.

Lacing.   Holes for lacing are punched about one eighth of an inch in from the edge. A spacing tool may be used to space the holes evenly or they may be gauged by eye. If two edges are to be laced together, it is better to punch one side and mark the holes on the second from the first so that the holes will match perfectly.

The easiest lacing is to bring the lace through two matching holes from the back to the front. Do not let the lace twist or turn. Pull the lace through. Come through the next two matching holes. Pull the lace taut. Proceed around the piece. The ends can be drawn through the inside and glued down or caught between the two pieces between the edge and the holes.

A more elaborate lacing can be secured by pushing the lace through the hole from the front to the back (Figure 6–5). Repeat in the second hole.

FIGURE 6–5 Lacing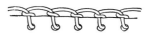

Do not pull tight. This leaves a loop on top. Bring the lace to the front but push it back through the loop. Now take up the loop by pulling it tight after which pull the end of the lace tight. Keep the lace flat; do not let it turn or twist.

Push the lace through the next hole. Again, do not pull tight but leave a loop and proceed as before. Work always from the front of the object.

There are also other lacings possible.

Laces can be joined together by splicing the ends and cementing them together with rubber cement.

Finishing. Leather can be left in its natural color or colored with leather dyes, enamels, acids, or waterproof colored inks. Ink is somewhat easier to handle. Be careful to apply it evenly to avoid spots.

Leather can be cleaned with a lather from saddle soap. It can be darkened in several ways, one being by applying neat's-foot oil. Apply it evenly and not too heavily. Leather can also be finished by applying a liquid wax with a cloth. Rub well.

Blueprinting

Blueprinting paper must be kept wrapped and in a dark place when not in use. One must work quickly in a semidark room.

Cut paper to the desired size and lay on a board, colored side up. Place fine-lined plants or other objects on the paper in an interesting arrangement. Place the sheet of glass on top. Expose to the sunlight from one and a half to two minutes. Remove glass and plants and immerse in water until a blue color and white areas appear. Dry between blotters.

Candle Making

Dipped candles. Heat pieces of old candles until they are liquid in form. Cut a piece of cord to the desired length of candle plus six inches or so for handling. Tie this piece of cord to the center of a stick for convenience in drying. Dip the string into the wax mixture that should be deeper than the desired candle length. Remove and allow to cool. Dip again and cool. Continue until the candle reaches the desired thickness. To cool, the stick can be laid over two supports with the candles suspended between them.

Molded candles. Any metal mold can be used, including original ones made from tin cans. Fasten the cord to a small piece of metal to weight it while pouring. Place it in the mold with the weight at the bottom of the mold. Hold the string upright by the left hand. Carefully pour a little of the melted mixture in the mold. Allow it to cool in order to keep the cord in place. Holding the cord upright again with the left hand (or tied over the center of a stick placed across the center of the mold), fill the mold by carefully pouring the mixture. When cool, remove from the mold by dipping the mold into very warm water. The heat will melt the wax next to the mold, and the candle can then be turned out easily.

Paper Craft—Beads

Cylindrical beads. Cut strips of fairly heavy paper, such as wallpaper, art paper, or wrapping paper, as long and as wide as desired. The width of the bead is determined by the width of the paper strips; the thickness by the weight of the paper and length of the strips. Cover one side or back with paste. Beginning at one end of the strip of paper, wind it over a thin dowel or wire, keeping the edges even and the sides smooth. Remove it from the wire to dry.

Round beads. Cut the strip into the desired width of bead at one end and taper it to a point at the center of the other end. Begin at the wide end to roll on the dowel.

Decoration. These beads may be painted with tempera paint and varnished. If so desired, simple designs of dots or bands, wavy or straight, maybe applied before varnishing. The beads may be strung together or with other beads.

Felt

For figures such as toys, hollow forms are made by putting together pieces of felt, either new or salvaged from old hats, or by rolling the felt into tubular shapes and sewing or pasting. Except for very small figures, a stuffing of old cloth can be added for strength.

Forms such as flowers may be made by cutting the pieces and sewing them together. Decorations, either raised or flat, may be made in a similar way but sewed to a background such as a belt or purse. Flat pieces may be appliquéd. Embroidery can be applied to such pieces for additional decorative value.

Yarn Figures

Animal or doll figures can easily be made of yarn and thread. Cut pieces of cardboard of varying lengths to the proportion of heads, arms, legs, and body. If desired, head and body, both arms, or both legs may be measured together. Wrap the yarn around the length of the cardboard. Slip a piece of yarn under each end and tie the strands of yarn together securely before removing from the cardboard. The tied ends are kept at the ends of the sections. With another piece of yarn, tie around the neck, waist, elbow, and so forth. Tie arms and legs in their proper positions. Mark the eyes by sewing dark knots or beads in the proper places.

A young lady doll without legs can be made by cutting yarn at the bottom of the "body" so that the yarn will spread out to form a skirt. A Dutch-trousered man can be made by tying at the waist while dividing the rest of the body into two sections for trousers and tying just above the ends to form the ends of the trousers and short feet.

Fluffy animal bodies can be made by wrapping yarn around the length of a cardboard strip made as long and as wide as the desired body. Hold a wire down the center and sew the wire to the wool catching all threads (on both sides) securely. Cut along the edges of the cardboard. The body fluffs out. Other parts of the body can be made in the same way and then fastened together.

Paper Sculpture

Figures, masks, maps, Christmas-tree decorations, and other artistic items can be sculpted from paper. Paper sculpture secures a three-dimensional effect created by folding back pieces of sections, by cutting strips and curling over a pencil or scissor edge, and by bending and pasting parts. Objects may be freestanding or pasted to a background.

For instance, a mask (Figure 6–6) might be made from a triangular piece of paper folded down the center. The upper edge can be cut into strips and curled forward to represent hair. Strips treated in the same way can be pasted on the chin for a beard and openings cut for eyes. For an eyebrow, a strip of paper can be pasted above the eye, projecting from the surface in the center and curled on the end. For a nose, another triangular piece folded down the center can be pasted projecting out from the first fold. Other strips like the eyebrows are to be added for a mustache. A little practice and experimentation will result in many other forms and ideas. Yarns or other material may be added also, if desired.

FIGURE 6–6: Paper Sculpture   **PAPER SCULPTURE**

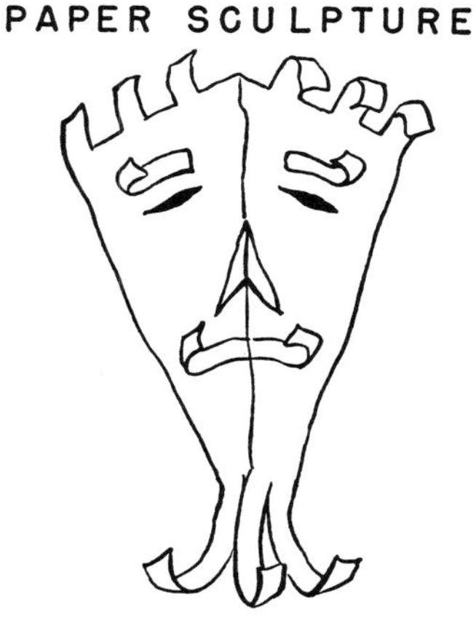

Pyrography

Wooden objects such as plaques, bookends, and boxes can be decorated with a woodburning pencil.

The pencil is allowed to get hot. Press the point along a line, drawing the blade over the wood. The blade burns the wood to a brown color. Be careful not to burn the wood too deeply. The design may be outlined only. If a strippled background is desired, the point can be touched to the surface at more or less equal intervals. A little practice will develop skill.

Pyrography can be applied to leather surfaces as well as wood.

Finger Painting

Finger painting may be used to decorate such items as book covers or linings, wrapping and other decorative papers, box tops, wooden bowls, and bookends. On wooden surfaces, the addition of shellac or varnish will give permanency to the design, if applied quickly so as not to disturb the paint.

Dip paper in water and lay it on a flat surface (a desk top, drawing board, or even the floor), smoothing out all wrinkles. Place a good teaspoonful of finger paint on the wet surface. Spread it over the surface, using the hands. Designs are secured by wiping off the color down to the white paper by using the fingers, fingernails, palm, fist, or even the side of the arm. Cardboard strips with nicks cut on the side, combs and lids can also be used. Designs can also be made by patting with the finger tips, palms, and so forth.

Other colors can be introduced by wiping out areas of the first color and adding the new in its place.

As the paper curls when it dries, thumbtack it to a smooth surface for drying.

Although almost any paper may be used, the more absorbent papers do not permit much manipulation or experimentation. A cheaper substitute for finger paint can be made by adding powdered paint or tempera to boiled starch (after cooling). This can be made softer by adding soap flakes. This substitute, like substitute papers, restricts manipulation and experimentation because it dries more quickly.

Crayon, Ink, and Watercolor

Crayonex.   For decoration, wax crayon designs can be made on such items as household articles, clothing, and wooden objects such as boxes or screens.

Cloth.   Draw a design and transfer it to the material. Stretch and fasten the material to a drawing board. Fill in the areas with wax crayons, stroking in one direction and pressing firmly. Brush off any excess wax that comes off on the material.

Place a blotter on a board; put the waxed cloth, face down, on the blotter. Press with a hot iron. The blotter absorbs the melting wax. If blotters are not available, place the cloth between two sheets of clean paper to press.

Wood. Rub the wax crayon into desired areas. Brush off the excess. Wiping the object with a cloth dipped in turpentine gives it a nice finish. Also, brushing over the colored design with india ink gives it an interesting effect as the wax resists the ink that spreads into tiny spaces between the strokes.

Crayon etching. Cover paper with crayon colors. Cover this with black crayon or black tempera paint with soap added to make it adhere to the crayon. Design is made by scratching through the black surface with finger or a sharp instrument.[5]

Crayon resist. After drawing with crayon, paint over it with india ink or dark tempera color to make exciting images.[6]

Oriental scrolls (soda-straw painting). Put drop of india ink in center of manila paper. Blow drop around paper through a straw. After it dries, outline the resulting figures with crayon.[7]

Water color blend. Paint with watercolor on a piece of wet paper; the colors will blend into interesting images.

Nature Crafts

The following nature crafts were submitted by the Recreation Leadership and Supervision class at Ithaca College (instructor, Elizabeth Ann Griffin).

Rock art. (Materials needed are glue, paint, brushes, wire, and rocks.) Rocks can be made into rock pets; with wire they can become sculptures; with cutouts they can be decoupaged; and with paint they can become paperweights. The flat rocks are best. Rocks should be cleaned before use. Example: To make a turtle, you need a flat rock for the base, a large round one for the shell, a smaller one for the head, and four small narrow rocks for the limbs.

Leaf mats. Collect leaves, choose the ones you like, and arrange them between two sheets of waxed paper. Then place newspaper over the waxed paper and iron the two sheets together.

5. Howard G. Danford, *Creative Leadership in Recreation* (Boston: Allyn and Bacon, 1964), p. 301.
6. Ibid., p. 301.
7. Ibid., p. 304.

Terrarium.   Fill a jar with dirt. Plant seeds or small plants in the jars. Add little dried flowers or plastic animals. Decorate the outside of the container.

Mobile.   Make a frame from coat hangers or driftwood. Put holes in the nature objects you collect and string them from the frame.

Walnut animals.   (Supplies include halves of walnut shells, marbles, felt, straw, glue.) Halves of walnut shells are used for the bodies, with bits of felt attached for the eyes, head, feet, and tail. The whiskers are straw from an old broom. Put each animal on top of a marble.

Driftwood plant holder.   Carve out a spot from a piece of driftwood. In that spot put a potted plant, or plant directly into the hole. Decorate the wood with paint or materials.

Other Ideas

The following arts and crafts ideas are credited to the text *Methods and Materials of Recreation Leadership* by Maryhelen Vannier:[8]

Jig-saw puzzles.   Make your own jigsaw puzzle. Paint or paste a picture on a large piece of thin wood and cut into jigsaw pieces.

Cork jewelry.   Cut bottle cork in half and decorate with a face (for example, put tacks, yarn, or clips as earrings). Fasten a safety pin on the back for a pin.

Simple toy making.   Cut windows into milk cartons. Use bottle caps for wheels. Paint each carton a different color and join together with wire or string to form a caravan or train.

Wire sculpture.   Shape thin wire with metal cutters or pliers. Attach to a wooden base. Add construction paper, cloth, yarn, and other materials for color and effect.

Old sock dolls.   Split sock front and sew up each half to make legs. Stuff with old rags or cotton. Tie a ribbon around the tip for a head. Add face and costume.

Papier-Maché

Papier-maché, made from old newspapers and commercial paste (or a paste made of flour and water), can be used to make masks, marionette

---

8. Maryhelen Vannier, *Methods and Materials of Recreation Leadership* (Philadelphia: Lea and Febiger, 1977), pp. 134–137.

heads, bowls, trays, relief maps, and other items. There are two procedures in making papier-maché objects. One reduces the paper to a pulp; the other uses torn strips.

Pulp method. Tear (do not cut) newspaper, paper towels, or tissues into small pieces about one-fourth inch in size. Cover these with water (hot water hastens the process) and allow to soak for a day or so. Knead the paper thoroughly until mushy. Remove surplus water since just enough is needed for the mass to hold together. Add flour and knead again. Grease the object to be used as a mold so that the pulp will not stick to it, or spread cheesecloth over it by pressing it into the crevices (for masks on a clay base). Press a ball of the pulp over the surface, smoothing it out to an even depth. Add more pulp as needed, smoothing edges together securely. Allow to stand until dry. Remove thick pieces from the mold as soon as they are dry enough to handle so that drying will be more even.

Torn strips. Prepare the mold as for pulp. Tear (do not cut) the paper into strips or small pieces. Dip the strip into a flour paste (cold or cooked). Apply it to the surface of the mold, fitting it into crevices. For larger surfaces and objects, larger or longer strips can be used. For smaller objects or parts, smaller strips or pieces should be torn. After the form has been completely covered—with the strips or pieces overlapping—add a second layer. To be sure only one layer at a time is being applied, printed news sections can be alternated with colored comic sections. Do not add too many layers at a time. Allow to dry thoroughly and remove from the mold. More layers can then be added if desired.

If an unusually large form is to be made, it can be built over a chicken-wire frame, a mass of crushed paper, or a rolled paper or wooden frame. Children can cavort on animals made of papier-maché designed over a wooden frame.

Masks can be made over a silk stocking pulled over another person's head. Use gummed paper tape for the first layer. When this layer is complete, cut the stocking up the back of the head, inserting the left hand between the stocking and hair so that no hair will be cut. Pull off the mask with a swift movement. Place crushed paper inside the mask and allow it to dry thoroughly before proceeding with more layers of paper. Wads of paper or cloth can be secured to the mask with paper strips in order to build up features, especially if grotesque ones are desired.

When enough layers have been added, sandpaper the form. Sandpapering can be done between layers for neater work. Paint the object with tempera paints and shellac or varnish. Remember that these finishes will change the colors.

Masks can be finished with such items as yarns, rope, and fur used for hair. A papier-maché mask can also be made around a balloon that is a bit larger than the head of the mask wearer. After the papier-maché has been molded around the balloon, the balloon is popped by puncturing it with a pin, thus leaving the mask intact.

Puppetry

Puppetry, as described in Chapter 5, is an excellent artistic vehicle for integrating drama with arts and crafts. There are puppet designs to meet every skill level and interest. Depending on the level of sophistication desired, a puppet can be created in one session or designed and refined over an extended period. This section outlines some methods of puppet making.

The following illustrations are provided by Maryhelen Vannier in *Methods and Materials of Recreation Leadership*:[9]

Paper-bag puppet.   Paint a face on a paper bag and attach yarn and additional materials for facial parts. Blow up the bag and secure at base with an elastic that holds a stick used for control of the puppet.

Sock puppet.   Decorate sock like a face and insert hand for control.

Ball puppet.   Cut two finger holes in a ball and cover puppeteer arm with material to represent a costume.

Lightbulb puppet.   Paint a face on a lightbulb and cover puppeteer arm with material to represent a costume.

Box puppet.   Paint a face on a round ice cream carton or square half-pint milk carton. Insert hand in the open end of the box. Cover puppeteer arm with material to represent a costume.

Spoon puppet.   Paint a face on a wooden or metal spoon. Make hair or beard from yarn, cellophane, wood shavings, or thread.

Marionettes

A marionette head can be made of clay, papier-mâché, or even a dried apple. A cardboard tube or wooden dowel may be used for the neck.

A hand marionette requires only the hollow head and a dress with two sleeves fastened to it. The figure is manipulated by the index finger in the head, and the thumb and middle finger in the sleeves.

A string marionette can be quite simple or very complex. A simple one requires a body made of sticks or stuffed cloth with free-moving joints tied together with strings or leather thongs, or with cloth bodies stitched at the joints. To these, attach the head, hands, and feet. After dressing, fasten

9. Maryhelen Vannier, *Methods and Materials of Recreation Leadership* (Philadelphia: Lea and Febiger, 1977), pp. 115–117.

strings to the head, hands, and knees. For convenience in manipulation, fasten the strings to sticks, the hand strings on one stick and the knee strings on another. With a little practice, the figures can be moved quite realistically. For more complicated movements attach strings to the feet, elbows, and other joints.

Should the puppeteers wish to have some form of puppet stage, this can be improvised in a number of ingenious ways. For a small puppet stage, a facial-tissue or shoe box with one end cut can be used. A larger puppet stage can be achieved by cutting out a refrigerator-sized box, or by simply draping a cloth over a table so as to hide the puppeteers below.

PHYSICAL RESOURCES

For the best arts and crafts program a suitable room should be found where equipment and materials may be conveniently kept and supervised, where an adequate working space is provided, and competent supervision or teaching offered. Such a room need not be large or elaborate. A simple arrangement permits more ease in working and in supervision. Tools and equipment should be sturdy to survive constant wear.

Only basic tools are to be provided so that less time of the supervisor need be given to their care; more ingenuity can be developed among the workers to create or improvise additional tools. Likewise, although common or locally available materials should be supplied or pointed out, participants should be encouraged to be on the lookout for other possible materials, especially among waste products. Thus, an inquiring and critical attitude as well as respect for materials will be developed.

INSTRUCTIONAL GUIDELINES

The activities or crafts provided should take into consideration the age and abilities of the participants. There should be enough difficulty to create a feeling of satisfaction in having attained achievement over challenge, but not so much difficulty that poor results will give a feeling of failure or frustration. Every project should bring a feeling of satisfactory achievement; there should be fun in the doing.

Since people entering a class in arts and crafts usually do so with the desire of actually making some particular object they have in mind and can use, they do not care to spend time on preliminary exercises or projects. It takes careful handling to persuade beginners to attempt a simpler project if they have originally chosen one beyond a beginner's abilities.

At the beginning of a project, time spent on theory, history, or research related to this project may destroy interest and enthusiasm. It is often only as the individual progresses on the project that curiosity about such information may be aroused. For instance, someone wishing to learn to weave may have some definite final product in mind and wish to begin on that immediately. While weaving, the person may become interested in how the yarns are made and dyed, how rugs have been woven in the past by other people, and so on. However, in this case, the interest in further factual information has grown out of work on the project by the participant rather than by the instructor's presentation.

AIMS AND STANDARDS

From the very beginning, originality and experimentation with techniques, tools, materials, methods, and designs should be encouraged—but not to the extent that the participant becomes discouraged or confused. Initial challenges should be mainly concerned with the mastery of essential skills and the materials to be used. The term "recreational art" should never mean anything less than seeking the highest quality in one's expressive ability.

SUGGESTED READINGS

BROOKS, W. E. AND BARKLY, K. *Design Your Own Craftwork*. Levittown, NY: Transatlantic Arts, 1970.
BUTLER, ANNE AND GREEN, DAVID. *Pattern and Embroidery*. Newton Center, MA: Charles T. Branford, 1970.
CAPUA, SARAJEAN. *Jewelry Anyone Can Make*. Hollywood, FL: Dukane Press, 1971.
CUTLER, KATHERINE N. *Creative Shellcraft*. New York: Lothrop, Lee and Shepard, 1971.
KAMPMAN, LOTHAR. *Creating With Clay*. New York: Van Nostrand Reinhold, 1971.
LASKIN, J. *Arts and Crafts Activities Desk Book*. Englewood Cliffs, NJ: Prentice-Hall, 1971.
MATTIL, EDWARD L. *Meaning in Crafts*. Englewood Cliffs, NJ: Prentice-Hall, 1971.
MELL, HOWARD AND FISHER, ERIC. *Modelling, Building and Carving*. New York: Drake Publishers, 1971.
SHIVERS, JAY S. AND CALDER, CLARENCE, R. *Recreational Crafts*. New York: McGraw-Hill, 1974.
WILCOX, DONALD. *Modern Leather Design*. New York: Ballantine Books, 1971.

7

Dance

INTRODUCTION

Dance, one of the oldest means of nonverbal communication, can be viewed as a celebration of life. In so much as dance is a means of self-expression, it reflects the spirit of people and of the time and place in which they live. Dance provides the spectator with pleasure; the participant gains physical skill, agility, and a sense of self-esteem.

Dance may be recognized as an art and as a recreational activity. Dance becomes theatrical dance when the individual exercises hard work and training to achieve mastery over the dance form, be it ballet, modern dance, jazz, ethnic dance, or any other. The goal of such dance forms, however, does not have to be performance. The value of dance as recreation is high, whether the goal is formal presentation or informal enjoyment. In terms of informal dance participation, folk dance, square dance, and social dance are particularly appropriate since they welcome variable skill levels.

Recently dance has enjoyed widespread popularity due to television and motion picture exposure. The image of the dance has become a symbol of inspiration for many people. Active, strong, and attractive, the dancer's physical excellence has aroused new respect for the condition of the body. Society's growing concern for health and physical fitness has prompted the origination of new exercise programs that combine the principles of dance with calisthenics. Among these new programs are jazzercise and aerobic dance. Done to music, these body-conditioning approaches appeal to all age groups, providing both physiological benefits and amusement.

Due to the popularity of dance, recreational organizations are finding it necessary to accommodate this growing interest. These organizations should provide individuals with the opportunity to experience and explore dance in its various forms, thereby fostering an educated appreciation for the aesthetic and physical qualities of the activity.

A brief explanation of a few of the current dance forms will be presented in this chapter. Also provided is a chart that delineates the elements of movement. Included within this chapter is a detailed presentation of creative dance for children. A bibliography is also furnished to aid leaders in their search for resource material.

FOLK DANCE

Folk dance is one of the most basic forms of dance. Simple dance steps, easily executed by adults and children of all ages, originated in the traditional, daily activities of the common peoples of the world. This recreational dance idiom celebrates the cultural traditions of various ethnic groups, depicting their customs, rituals, and occupations. As a means of socialization, folk dance provides participants with an opportunity to mix and to make new acquaintances. It also develops an appreciation and respect for the ethnic heritage of others.

Typically, most folk dances rely on some of the same dance forms, including (1) the circle dance, done without partners—for example, Kolos, Horas; (2) the round dance, done in a double circle of couples, moving counterclockwise; (3) contra dance, consisting of two opposing lines—for example, reels, longway sets; (4) the square dance, during which cues are given by a caller; and (5) mixers, incorporating partner exchange.

The leader should begin by introducing simple folk dances, those comprised of walking, running, skipping, sliding, and of the step-hop, shuffle, and grape-vine steps. Mixers generally fit into this category and are an ideal way of breaking the ice, giving individuals a chance to circulate and informally meet other participants. These dances, easily mastered, provide the participants with a feeling of success and security that will encourage them to attempt more difficult folk dances.

All folk dances contain the following basic folk steps. Those steps performed in double meter are: (1) the Schottische, (2) the two step, (3) and the polka. Basic folk dance steps performed in triple meter are: (1) the waltz, and (2) the mazurka.

To facilitate learning, the leader should (1) demonstrate the step by standing with back to the participants, (2) have the participants clap the rhythm, (3) break down the step, (4) allow time to practice the step with the music and in the manner in which it is to be performed (forward, backward, turning; with or without partners), and finally (5) structure the folk dance in which the step is to be applied.

The suggested readings at the end of this chapter include references that provide a more extensive presentation of folk dance (specific dances, formations, dance positions, cultural background, record information).

TAP DANCE

America's tap dance is a unique blend of the Irish jig, the English Lancashire clog dance, and the syncopated beat of the African tribal dance. This happy-go-lucky dance has been performed by minstrels, vaudevillians, and by screen and stage entertainers. Tap dance is purely entertainment, and it is the heart of the American musical.

Tap dance participants take delight in making music with their feet. Some of the essential foot movements in tap dance are: step, stomp, brush, shuffle, flop, toe taps and digs, and heel scuff. Simple enough to be performed by anyone, these movements may be elaborated upon to create advanced rhythmical patterns. Combining rhythm, timing, syncopation, form, and interpretation, tap dance is an attention-commanding performance.

The five elements of rhythm, timing, syncopation, form, and interpretation are present within all dance forms and are very apparent in tap dance. Modification of these elements produces dynamic changes that may affect the overall characteristics of a given form. Rhythm lends to tap the underlying beat during which a consistent relationship between time, movement, and distance is established. Timing divides the rhythm, by means of accents, into consistent groupings, such as 3/4 or 4/4 meter. Adding interest and variety to rhythmical patterns is the element of syncopation, which divides rhythm into inconsistent groupings by shifting the regular rhythmic accent. Form provides shaping, shading, and structure to spacial design and body contour. And finally interpretation brings life, personality, and significance to the performance.

JAZZ DANCE

Jazz dance finds its history rooted in the African culture where dance was considered a celebration of all aspects of life. This form of dance has survived and undergone cultural, economical, and geographical changes, and it will continue to parallel and exemplify the current music trends. Theatrical jazz dance is closely associated with the social dance of a particular decade. The dance of the American black culture has been and continues to be its primary source of inspiration. What was initially the street dance of the black slave evolved into the American stage dance of the minstrel, vaudeville, musical review, and motion picture screen.

Owing to the fact that jazz dance is performed to current rock and jazz music, it enjoys immense popularity among the younger set. Jazz dance in the recreational setting may expose the participant to a variety of basic social dance steps that have been stylistically altered to keep up with the latest trends. Although jazz dance has endured innumerable changes, the essential features still remain: (1) the use of body isolations; (2) syncopated rhythm; (3) polyrhythm; (4) rapid transference of weight; and (5) the use of bent knees, which gives it an earthy appearance.

BALLET

Classical ballet, considered one of the most esthetic forms of dance, evolved from the court dances performed by the French and Italian nobility of the sixteenth and seventeenth centuries. Courtiers during these lavish celebrations exhibited elegance and ease in their dance movements. These refined qualities of movement have endured for centuries and are reflected in the current form of ballet.

The application of the principles of classical ballet allows the ballet dancer to glide, leap, turn, and even balance on toe with feather light agility. Proper body alignment (achieved by dropping the tailbone, lifting abdominals, relaxing shoulders and distributing weight over the feet) must be maintained while executing both the simplest and the most complex ballet actions. These principles apply to all dance forms.

Coupled with body alignment is the principle of "turn out." Initiated from the hip sockets, this outward rotation of the hips, ranging from 45 to 180 degrees (from the opposing leg), accentuates the aesthetic line of the dancer and provides greater freedom for sideward motion. Furthermore, the five positions of the feet serve as the body's foundation for all ballet movements.

The leader of a ballet class should be concerned with the physical well-being of the participants. Because ballet makes enormous demands on the body, physical abuse to the joints, muscles, ligaments, and tendons must be avoided. Great care taken in the preparation of ballet progressions will in most cases prevent long-term physical damage. Participants should have the muscular strength and flexibility required for each ballet movement.

MODERN DANCE

Modern dance is a compilation of all types of movement and their modification to fit particular expressive purposes. It acknowledges complete freedom and exploration of movement derived from one's own need for expression. Modern dance allows the emotional needs of the individual to dictate and invent movement, in contrast to that movement which takes its shape from a predetermined dance vocabulary.

Many major innovators have influenced the evolutionary course of modern dance, and their successors continue to rejuvenate the spirit of this dance form. A few of the most influential modern dance figures and their contributions to this art form will be discussed.

Isadora Duncan, considered the mother of modern dance, met with much opposition. Her approach to dance was regarded as unconventional, impulsive, and a shock to the dance audience. Duncan felt, however, that in order to convey and evoke emotion, one had to work with feelings rather than form. She relied a great deal on improvisation, which allowed her inner spirit to be the guiding force behind her dance. Inspired by nature, Duncan's dances depicted nature, emotion, softness, simplicity, and beauty. She is responsible for planting the artistic seeds from which creative choreographic expression would grow.

Doris Humphrey, on the opposite end of the continuum, was not so concerned with emotions directing movement as she was with the method of dance construction—of giving her dances structure. She maintained that impulsive emotion could only be depicted through the conscious ordering of time and space. Her exploration of balance and imbalance led to the formalization of her technique known as "fall and recovery." Because of her development and understanding of the choreographic tools, Doris Humphrey is regarded by many as the most proficient choreographer of her time.

Martha Graham, a renowned dancer and choreographer of this century, is known for her theatrical dance drama. Borrowing from literature, her dances depict the psychological makeup of individual characters. Her movements (sharp, percussive, and angular) are indicative of human conflict and its resolution.

The Graham dance technique is a highly stylized form of modern dance, based upon the breath cycles of the body which cause contraction and release. This specialized technique is as complex as its forerunner, ballet. The technique evolved from the choreographer's need to outwardly express internal emotions. With each new choreographic endeavor, the technique developed further toward the codified Graham method.

Modern dance in the recreational setting may concern itself with dance technique involving body alignment, axial and locomotor movements, and dance terminology. Through movement exploration, participants realize their movement capabilities, and may discover their own movement preferences. Modern dance may serve as a primary source of self-expression.

AEROBIC DANCE

Aerobic dance has enjoyed growing popularity since its inception in 1971. Originated by Jacki Sorensen, this exercise program provides physical fitness and fun. People of all ages and backgrounds are taking advantage of this challenging new exercise that trains and improves the cardiovascular system, tones skeletal muscles, and relieves mental and emotional stress.

Dancing to popular music, participants walk, run, jump, skip, swing, and stretch continuously for 30 to 40 minutes. Nonstop dance routines are choreographed so that they may be performed at rates corresponding to walking, running, or jogging, thus allowing individual participants to select a pace most appropriate to their own physical condition.

The aerobic dance workout contains a warmup, a peak work, and a cool-down phase. Five to 10 minutes are devoted to the warmup, during which slow stretch exercises prepare the muscles, ligaments, and tendons for more strenuous activity. A thorough and slow warmup is an essential part of all dance activities. It reduces the chances of injury and should never be overlooked.

The peak phase of aerobic dancing lasts anywhere from 15 to 30 minutes, making the greatest demands on the participant. Designed to condition the heart and lungs and burn calories, this vigorous phase puts participants' endurance to the test. At no time should participants stop the bouncing action incorporated in the dance steps.

Finally, the cool-down phase, most frequently overlooked during physical activities, returns the heart rate to an acceptable recovery level. Slow gentle stretching movements allow the muscles to relax, thus reducing aches and pains as well as restoring blood to the brain, preventing dizziness.

Aerobic dance may serve as a very convenient form of physical fitness. Done only three times a week for 40 minutes, it can keep weight down, improve circulation and endurance, and give the participant a feeling of accomplishment.

DANCE THERAPY

Dance or movement therapy, an adjunct to therapeutic recreation, provides the client with a physical outlet for self-expression that is less threatening than verbal communication. Through training in psychology and dance, the dance therapist develops the skills to nurture movement that produces therapeutic benefits for the client. In addition to the personal benefits derived by the client, the dance therapist also values dance therapy as a means of diagnosing client mood and behavior. Contrary to what the term "dance" suggests, there is no attempt to choreograph specific movement. Rather, the aim is to encourage clients to fully explore their own bodies and spirits. The goals of dance therapy vary in relationship to the different disabilities being treated. For instance, creative movement with wheelchair clients will assume dynamics and objectives different from those of psychiatric clients.

CREATIVE DANCE FOR CHILDREN

In creative dance, children discover how body, mind, and spirit can combine in the outward expression of the self through movement. Creative dance is not rigid. Through creative problem solving, children are allowed to discover movement for themselves and fine-tune their instrument (the body) without the fear of failure. A creative dance class liberates itself from competition, enabling the children to concentrate on their own rate of motor development. Once the children are comfortable with knowing and understanding themselves through movement, they are more clearly able to communicate their feelings to those around them.

In a creative dance class there are no wrong answers, simply different approaches. No disappointment is shown nor discouragement spoken. Everyone's contributions should be regarded as extremely important. The leader should take time to give every child equal attention by acknowledging each one's presence verbally, and by giving each a reassuring hug.

It is important for creative dance leaders to be open, honest, and genuine in their approach to children. The children sensitive to these characteristics, will grow to trust a leader with their own feelings, which will later be translated into movement. Through this process, children will develop their imaginations, thus giving them the capabilities to visualize and assimilate situations that are different from their everyday experiences.

FIGURE 7–1 Elements of Dance

BODY
Body Parts: external and internal
Shapes: angular and curved
Axial Movements: bending, twisting, stretching, shaking, turning, pulsing, pulling
Locomotor Movements: walk, run, skip, jump, leap, slide, gallop, roll, crawl

FORCE
Strong and Light
Tension and Relaxation
Sharp and Smooth

SPACE
Direct and Indirect Approaches: up, down, over, under, around, through, forward, backward, sideways
Dimension/Range/Size: big, small, tall, wide, narrow
Levels: high, medium, low

TIME
Tempo: fast, slow, moderate
Rhythm: underlying pulse, metric, or nonmetric
Accent: stressed

The leaders will serve as the children's guides, taking them on a journey toward the discovery of the elements of dance defined as *body, space, force,* and *time.* Through the application of these elements, children will discover their kinesthetic sense and will begin to understand their spacial relationship to other objects.

IDEAS FOR CREATIVE DANCE EXPLORATION
WITH CHILDREN

Body Parts, External and Internal

Begin simply by having the children explore different ways in which they can move their heads, shoulders, backs, arms, hands, trunks, hips, legs, and feet. Example: head, head; shoulder, shoulder; hip, hip; knee, knee; collapse.

These body parts may move independently of one another, or emphasis may be placed on two or more body parts working simultaneously. Example: hip and head; knee and elbow; foot and hand; back and arm.

After the children feel comfortable with simple body isolations, more complex patterns may be introduced by altering time and space elements. Example: Slow arm; slow arm; fast knee; shoulder front, back; repeat. Any combination of isolations may also be done as the children change the direction their bodies face.

Bones and joints.   Discuss the human skeleton and its supportive and protective properties. Explain how the bones give us our different shape and form. Demonstrate how the body's joints, along with its bones, allow for a wide range of movement. Invite the children to discover the various ways in which bones, in cooperation with their joints, work to accomplish various tasks, and how with each task their bodies take on new shapes. Example: "Bend over, touch your toes, freeze; look at your shape . . . bend your knees, sit on your chair, freeze . . . look at your shape."

Muscles.   Describe to the children how the muscles expand and contract, and how both strength and flexibility are required to accomplish all movement. Using bands of elastic 4 feet in circumference, have each child step inside the elastic form and experiment with movement involving different body parts. Emphasis should be placed on the tension and relaxation of different muscle groups as they push, pull, bend, and stretch. This activity may also be done in groups of two or more.

Lungs.   Explain to the children how their breathing pattern triggers the inflation and deflation of the lungs, and inform them that during inhalation oxygen is transported from the lungs to the muscles, helping to prevent muscle fatigue. Breath, an essential part of all action, influences the force of movement.

Give each child a paper bag to blow up. Have each child pay particular attention to the inflation and deflation of the bags. Next, have the children experiment with short fast breaths and long slow breaths, then see how the different breathing patterns affect movement. Example: "Now let's pretend you're the paper bag. Inhale, blow yourself up, exhale, melt down to the floor, take one long deep breath that makes you float up to standing. Pop! The air escapes. Collapse to the floor."

Heart. The heart produces the natural underlying rhythmical pulse of the body. Ask the children to place their hands over their hearts to feel them beating. Next, clap the heart's rhythm and then have them transfer the rhythm to another body part. Use this basic rhythm in conjunction with fundamental locomotor movements. It may be helpful for the children to verbalize the pulse, which will aid rhythmical consistency. Example: "Put your hand on your heart. Can you catch that beat? Take it now right into your feet, clap your hands and shake your head. Bend down around, and bounce to the beat."

Shapes

Make a mobile containing various three-dimensional shapes (for example, square, circle, rectangle, diamond). Ask the children to identify and make these shapes with their bodies, individually, in pairs, and as a group. After completing this activity, ask them to look around the room, find a new shape, and duplicate it with their bodies. Next, have them change shapes on every fourth count, on every second count, and then on every count. At first, children will imitate one other, but after a while they will delight in discovering their very own shapes. Shaping is something that can be used often. It is a good way to structure an activity, giving it a beginning and an end.

Axial and Locomotor Movements

Differentiate between axial movements (those which occur around the center axis of the body) and locomotor movements (those which move through and cover space). Discuss with the children how these basic movements may be influenced by their inner attitudes and environmental conditions. Present numerous hypothetical situations that will stimulate the children's imaginations, enabling them to discover different forms of axial and locomotor movements. Example: "Walk as if you are in a hurry. Walk as if you have all day. Along the way you meet a friend and you run along to play."

Another approach to axial and locomotor movements is the application of movement sequencing. For example: run, run; walk, walk; twist, bend, jump, swing. There are numerous movement combination possibilities. Allow the children time to invent their own.

Space

Direction. Using locomotor movements, have the children experiment with change of direction, emphasizing the use of all available space. Example: "Run forward, run backward, run sideward, run around yourself, run to the center, run to the corner." Change locomotor movement and rate of speed.

Using paper airplanes to illustrate pathways in space (straight, curved, angular), have the children trace these patterns. Emphasize shape of body takeoff, flight, and landing.

Provide children with an opportunity to design their own pathways by drawing crayon designs on paper; these will serve as visual aids for the reconstruction of spatial designs. For fun, have them trade designs with one another.

Dimension/Range/Size. Exploration of dimension, range, and size of movement may be introduced to the children by discussing proportional size and its spatial relationship.

Using an everyday gesture such as waving or nodding, allow the children to increase the size of these movements, making them larger than life and then reversing the process. Or have the children walk across the floor using twenty small steps, then cover the same amount of space using big steps.

Levels. With levels we explore that aspect of space which deals with the height of movement in relationship to the floor and ceiling. Levels can be explored by the use of axial and locomotor movements, body parts, and shapes. Children find this element exciting as it permits them to explore jumping, collapsing, and rolling movements within the context of one lesson. Example: "Take a high level shape—hold; move to a low-level shape—hold; move to a middle-level shape. Move across the floor at high level, come back across the floor at a middle level, come to the center moving at a low level."

Time

Fast/Slow. Experiment with locomotor and axial movements, altering the rate of speed at which they are done. Have the children move as slowly as they possibly can and then, on cue, as fast as they can. Emphasize the use of levels, directional changes, and body parts. Repeat this exercise until precise rhythmical changes have been accomplished.

Accent. Demonstrate the use of accent by having the children clap as they walk, giving each step equal emphasis. Next, vary the accents on different steps. Example: *1* 2 3 4, 1 *2* 3 4, 1 2 *3* 4, 1 2 3 *4*. Reverse the process. Additional contrast may be achieved through varying body, space, and force elements.

Force

Explain to the children how the element of force may influence the appearance of movement. Force is determined by the amount of strength exerted to perform a particular task. For example, the amount of energy required to lift a lead ball is much greater than that for lifting a ping-pong ball. Obviously, the weight of the ball determines the outward appearance and dynamic quality of the movement.

There are numerous activities in which the children can experience the element of force. The leader may find it helpful to utilize props to illustrate the varying degrees. Using balloons, have the children gently toss them around the room. Next, have the children stand in pairs a few feet apart and hit the balloon back and forth. Finally, have the children go to opposite ends of the room and try to send the balloons to their partners. Each of these activities requires a varying amount of muscular exertion ranging from light to strong.

For self-exploration, have the children experiment with varying degrees of muscular energy required to: (1) push open a heavy door, (2) pull it closed; (3) fling a frisbee; (4) throw a heavy ball; (5) glide as if floating in air; and (6) relax all muscular tension, falling to the floor. Repeat the movements above in a consecutive order to form a movement phrase.

As can be seen, there are numerous possibilities for exploration of the elements of dance. What has been presented here are just a few examples. The leader should feel free to experiment and build upon the given framework. Any movement idea can be effective as long as the objective of the lesson is presented in a clear and concise manner.

CONSTRUCTING A CHILDREN'S LESSON PLAN FOR CREATIVE DANCE

At the beginning of every dance class it is very important to get the children moving. Allow them the freedom to experiment with natural body movements (stretching, swaying, swinging, walking, running, bending, twisting, collapsing).

The development of the lesson is basic: Theme, Method of Exploration, Structure. Establish what theme is to be explored and determine what elements will be used to support the main theme. For example, if the purpose of the lesson is to explore locomotor movements, perhaps time and space will be appropriate element helpers. Next, ask questions directly pertaining to the theme, and make movement and exploration suggestions that will motivate the children to start moving and exploring. Such a lesson plan might be expressed in the following way:

THEME—EXPLORING BODY PARTS

Questions
> *How* many different ways can you move your arm?

Can you swing, shake, bend, or stretch your arm?

What happens when you relax the muscles in your arm?

Where does the body go when you fling your arm?

Structure

Standing in place, experiment with swinging, shaking, bending, stretching, and flinging your arm. Allow the weight of the arm to move the body. As you fling your arm does it spin you around? As you stretch your arm does it pull you up onto your toes? As you circle your arm does it make you hop? When you circle both arms together does it make you jump?

Repeat, using other body parts. Help the children become aware of directional changes and range of motion as they explore. After a period of time, the children will feel very comfortable with this class structure and they will begin to understand and express through movement the abstract concepts presented.

LEADER

An effective dance leader (1) strives for self-improvement; (2) is receptive to group needs; and (3) assumes responsibility for participants' success. While textbooks and instructional manuals may provide the leader with important information (dance techniques, concepts, steps, combinations), they should be supplemented with formal dance training. This primary source of information will supply the leader with an opportunity to experience the physical and mental demands involved in the execution of dance movement. Dance fundamentals can then be realized and communicated in an accurate manner. Continual training will develop movement vocabulary that can be applied and stylistically adapted to a variety of dance forms.

Dance training is no longer confined to a class of elitists. More recently, recreational organizations and universities and their affiliates have made dance accessible to people regardless of age, sex, and economic backgrounds. This diversification requires a leader who is receptive to group needs and who remains open to suggestions and new approaches in teaching.

When preparing the dance activity, the leader should: consider the physical and mental capabilities of the group; prepare material in a manner that will be appealing and appropriate to the specific group; and utilize teaching methods that will be beneficial to all those involved.

The leader should first demonstrate the entire dance combination at the tempo it is to be performed, before breaking it down for the class. Since music and rhythm play such an intricate role in dance, the use of consistent counts is required. Counts serve as a type of mental landmark that assist our powers of recall. When learning a step with a difficult rhythm, it is helpful for the class to clap to the rhythm before attempting the step.

One phrase should be taught at a time, and counts and cue words should be called out with the dynamic quality that matches the movement. This type of prompting subconsciously suggests to the student the amount of energy each step deserves. Imagery may also help with unexperienced dancers when working in the area of theatrical dance.

Dance material should be taught with a logical progression. Warmup and succeeding exercises should prepare the individual for the culminating phase of the class. The attitude and teaching approach leaders adopt will determine the overall success of a group. An exuberant instructor who presents material with enthusiasm will motivate the group and create an enjoyable learning atmosphere.

THE DANCE SPACE

One can make the best of any assigned space to be used for recreational dancing by taking into consideration the safety factors and physical comforts of the given locale. A thorough examination of these conditions will promote learning and enjoyment. A variety of spaces is encountered, ranging in size from classrooms to gymnasiums. Regardless of the size, the area should be cleared of all obstructions, thus allowing the participant to enjoy the freedom of movement.

Particular attention should be given to the space's floor. It should be clean and checked frequently for nails, tacks, or other protrusions that may cause injury. On a tiled floor, the leader must keep in mind that this nonresilient surface may induce muscle fatigue and can cause such injuries as shin splints; jumping, therefore, should be kept to a minimum. The same holds true for carpeted areas; sliding and rolling movements are also discouraged because they may be the source of rug burns. The ideal dance setting requires a wooden floor. A floating or sprung floor is most desirable; however, a common hardwood floor is sufficient. Although a highly varnished or newly waxed floor may have an attractive appearance, it will be slippery and hinder secure footing while dancing. Floors should be stripped of all varnish and wax, and cleaned with water only.

The ideal setting should be adequate for the size of the class. An area no smaller than 20 by 30 feet is recommended. Overcrowded rooms restrict participants from enjoying dance movement to its fullest potential. Participants who are physically comfortable will be more responsive and eager to learn. Their concentration will be focused on the dance activity, not be distracted by otherwise avoidable physical discomforts. Therefore, the setting should be equipped with proper ventilation and temperature control. Adequate lighting, both natural and artificial if possible, will also facilitate learning and encourage a positive attitude.

Essential equipment for the dance setting is a cassette tape recorder or a record player. The latter, equipped with a variable speed control, is preferable. This feature allows the participant to practice specific dance steps or exercises at a slower rate until they have been mastered. Permanent or portable *barres* are also useful and are considered an essential feature of the ballet class. These long, horizontal metal or wooden handrails should be approximately 3 feet 6 inches from the floor. Lower railings are, of course, necessary for children's classes. Constructed in a sturdy manner, *barres* will provide the participants with a sense of security while they strive to develop muscular strength and balance.

The dance idiom should determine the type of dance setting. Social- and folk-dance classes can easily be accommodated in any large open area, aerobic dance works well in a gymnasium, and ballet and modern dance require the privacy of a dance studio.

SUGGESTED READINGS

Dance History

KIRSTEIN, LINCOLN. *Dance: A Short History of Classical Theatrical Dancing.* New York: G. P. Putnam's Sons, 1935; Brooklyn: Dance Horizons, 1974.
KRAUS, RICHARD. *History of the Dance.* Englewood Cliffs, NJ: Prentice-Hall, 1969.
MEERLOO, JOOST A. *The Dance from Ritual to Rock and Roll—Ballet to Ballroom.* Philadelphia and New York: Chilton Company, 1960.
SACHS, CURT. *World History of the Dance.* Trans. Bessie Schonberg. New York: W. W. Norton, 1937.
SORELL, WALTER. *The Dance Through the Ages.* New York: Grossett and Dunlap, 1967.

Teaching of Dance

CAYOU, DOLORES. *Modern Jazz Dance.* Palo Alto, CA: National Press Books, 1972.
GIORDANO, GUS (ED.). *Anthology of American Jazz Dance.* Evanston, IL: Orion Publishing House, 1975.
HAMMOND, SANDRA. *Ballet Basics.* Palo Alto, CA: National Press Books, 1974.
HAYES, ELIZABETH. *An Introduction to the Teaching of Dance.* New York; The Ronald Press Co., 1963.
LOCKHART, AILEENE AND PEASE, ESTHER E. *Modern Dance: Building and Teaching Lessons.* Dubuque, IA: Wm. C. Brown Company Publishers, 1977.
PENROD, JAMES AND PLASTINO, JANICE GUDDS. *The Dancer Prepares.* Palo Alto, CA: The National Press, 1970.

Folk and Social Dance

HARRIS, JANE A., PITTMAN, ANN, AND WALLER, MARLYS S. *Dance a While.* Minneapolis, MN: Burgess Publishing Company, 1968.
HALL, J. TILLMAN. *Dance! A Complete Guide to Social, Folk and Square Dancing.* Belmont, CA: Wadsworth Publishing Company, 1963.
KRAUS, RICHARD. *Folk Dance.* New York: MacMillan, 1962.
LIDSTER, MIRIAM D. AND TAMBURINI, DOROTHY H. *Folk Dance Progressions.* Belmont, CA: Wadsworth Publishing Company, 1965.
WHITE, BETTY. *Ballroom Dancebook for Teachers.* New York: David McKay Company, 1962.

Creative Dance for Children

BOORMAN, JOYCE. *Creative Dance in the First Three Grades.* New York: David McKay, 1969.
JOYCE, MARY. *First Steps in Teaching Creative Dance to Children.* Palo Alto, CA: Mayfield Publishing Company, 1980.
METTLER, BARBARA. *Materials of Dance as a Creative Art Activity.* Tuscon, Arizona: Mettler Studios, 1960.

8

Music

As a form of creative expression, music is at the base of much of our leisure satisfaction. Music in our lives is multifaceted and rich . . . singing around the campfire, diversional humming at work, practicing an instrument, attending a concert, roller skating to the beat of piped-in music, collecting and playing records . . . and much more.

Jay Shivers defines music as[1]

> any activity that produces vocal or instrumental tonal or atonal sounds having some form of syncopation or tempo. Music may be thought of as being either vocally or instrumentally produced, a combination of these forms, the act of creating music, and an appreciation of performance."

TYPES OF MUSIC ACTIVITIES

The following list graphically illustrates the scope of leisure opportunities available in music:

1. Jay Shivers, *Essentials in Recreation Services*. (Philadelphia: Lea and Febiger, 1978), p. 243.

VOCAL

Community singing

Barbershop quartets

Solos

A cappella choirs (without accompaniment)

Madrigal groups (two- or three-part singing originating in Elizabethan England and usually unaccompanied)

Glee clubs

Choruses (men's, women's, and mixed)

Ensembles

Voice classes

Folk-singing clubs

Informal singing groups

Christmas carolling

INSTRUMENTAL

Instrument instruction

Chamber music (music suitable for performance in a small space, e.g., trios, quartets, quintets)

Wind ensemble (group consisting of brass wind instruments, e.g., trumpets, trombones, horns, tubas, and woodwinds, e.g., flute, oboe, bassoon, clarinet)

String ensemble (group consisting of stringed instruments in the violin family)

Percussion band (group consisting of drums)

Bands

Orchestras

Bell choirs

Fife and drum corps

Marching bands

Rhythm bands

Musical-instrument lending library

Drum and bugle corps

Solo/duet/trio/small-ensemble performances

LISTENING/MUSIC APPRECIATION

Tape or record listening library for library use or home loan

Music appreciation class

Radio

Television

Background music

Music collections (sheet music, instruments, records)

Study groups

Live concerts

Organ recitals

Record playing

Musicology (history of music)

MUSIC COMPOSITION

Lyric composition
Score composition
Original song contest
Music composition classes
Music composition clubs

MUSIC PROGRAM INTEGRATION (Music incorporated into other activities, e.g., dance, drama, art, literary, outdoor)

Instrument making
Music camps
Musical theater
Concerts in the park
Music therapy
Circuses
Pageants
Talent or variety shows
Background music (e.g., for art class, ice-skating tournament)
Mental quizzes on music
Operas
Operetta (a short, comical musical play)
Oratorio (a lengthy, dramatic musical composition usually dealing with a religious theme; presented with musical accompaniment but no stage action, costumes, or sets)
Music festival
Creative movement activities
Interpretive singing games
Party games (e.g., musical chairs)
Folk dances
Parades

FORMAL/INFORMAL MUSIC

Within the above classifications are activities that require some formal musical knowledge and rehearsal (formal music activities) and activities that necessitate little or no training or rehearsal (informal music activities.) Formal music activities may require music theory and sightsinging (the ability to read music), the ability to play an instrument, and the commitment to practice. Pursuit of a formal music activity is usually accompanied by a desire to achieve excellence, both for individual satisfaction and for performance. Examples of formal music activities include instrumental training and performing, music composition, and performing in musical plays.

Informal music activities do not involve formal study of music or extended rehearsal. They consist of a variety of both impromptu and long-range musical pursuits. If there is performance, it does not require the level of preparation that accompanies formal music. Examples of informal music activities include talent shows, rhythm bands, action songs and games, music listening, informal singing groups, and music appreciation groups.

MUSIC LEADERSHIP TRAINING

It is clear that the recreation leader who directs formal music activities must have considerable music background. If the recreation leader does not have this experience, then the services of a musician, music teacher, retired music professor, or music specialist in recreation may be sought. Informal music activities, on the other hand, can often be conducted by a recreation leader with only some moderate training, since informal music activities do not require extensive music knowledge. To help equip recreation leaders, more and more college recreation departments are including music leadership classes as required or elective courses in their curricula. Figure 8–1, an outline for a course entitled "Music for Recreation Majors," indicates the skills expected of a recreation leader engaged in music leadership.[2]

LEADING GROUP SINGING

Since group singing is most common in recreation programs, this chapter will provide a more detailed consideration of this fundamental music activity. As a point of historical information, the churches can be credited with the inauguration of group singing in the forms of hymns and spirituals, although, as far back as ancient Greek drama, choruses already existed. Greek choruses consisted of a number of people on the stage who either explained the action of the play or commented in song on the events portrayed. In modern times, group singing has been influenced in a number of ways. During World War I many Americans sang doughboy songs such as "Johnny Get Your Gun" and "Over There." Public and religious schools, settlement houses, community centers, camps, and playgrounds have promoted group singing. The influence of the family piano also deserves note as the inspiration for many makeshift harmony groups. Group singing was also fostered by movie theater organists who asked audiences to "follow the bouncing ball" above the lyrics on the movie screen. It is important to note that, community singing today often fails to include contemporary songs in its programs. Excluding songs that the majority of people are purchasing and singing on their own only retards the progress of community singing.

2. From The School of Music, Ithaca College, Ithaca, New York.

FIGURE 8–1   Music for Recreation Majors

COURSE OUTLINE: Planning and implementing musical experiences in recreational programs. Required for Recreation Majors.

RATIONALE: This course is designed to provide those in recreational leadership with the methods and materials necessary for planning and implementing musical experiences in community or industrial recreational programs. This course will be molded specifically for the recreation major, in order to meet the practical needs of those in charge of recreation activities.

COURSE OBJECTIVES:

1. To develop a sound philosophy of the role of music in a recreational setting.
2. To understand the attitudes, goals, and skills for the varied groupings to be found in recreational programs.
3. To gain skill in planning and implementing musical experiences for those varied groups.
4. To develop the skills and understandings necessary to carry on a viable recreational music program.

PROPOSED CONTENT

A. MAJOR AREAS OF RECREATIONAL MUSIC
   I. Recreational Singing
      a. Introductory experience with typical recreational songs. (1 week)
      b. Necessary study of elements of music, as needed. (1 week)
         1. pitch
         2. rhythm
         3. scales (major/minor)
         4. meter/tempo
         5. notation
      c. Song leading—conducting (2 weeks)
         1. basic conducting patterns for different meters and styles
         2. phrasing, dynamics
         3. organization, planning, and preparation of the singing experience
         4. unaccompanied singing
   II. Accompaniments
      a. Pitched accompaniments (3 weeks)
         1. formation of primary chords for use in accompaniment
         2. use of voices for accompaniment
         3. instrumental skills for use in accompaniment
            a. guitar (minimal skill needed)
            b. piano (minimal skill needed)
            c. working knowledge of other common instruments (autoharp, ukelele, recorder, etc.)
            d. stylistic application to the singing situation
      b. Rhythm accompaniments (1 week)
         1. working knowledge of basic rhythm/percussion instruments (formal and informal—tambourine, drums, hand-clapping, body movement, etc.)
         2. use of more complex rhythmic setting—divided or group rhythmic effects
         3. stylistic application to the singing situation
      c. Combination of pitched and rhythmic accompaniments (1 week)
      d. Use of available resources
   III. Movement Activities
      a. Use of the following, as appropriate, for various age groups (2 weeks)
         1. singing games—action games
         2. circle, square, folk dancing
         3. free movement
         4. movement stories

B. RESOURCES
    I.   Available recordings for use in recreational music.
    II.   Available books and periodicals for use in recreational music.
C. PROJECTS: Application of A and B above to specific situations. (3 weeks)
    I.   General: The more commonly encountered situations and age groups.
    II.   Special styles or problems
        a.   very young
        b.   very old
        c.   barbershop, all men, all women
        d.   handicapped (music as therapy)
    III.   Making up songs and rhythmic activities to meet specific situations and resources.
D. TEXTS
    R. Phyllis Galineau: *Songs in Action*
    Batcheller and Monsouri: *Music in Recreation and Leisure*
    Snyder and Higgins: *Comprehensive Guitar Method*
    To be purchased: Aulos Recorder and *Funway Preband Method Book*
Special Projects:
    Direct experiences in actual recreational situations:
       Conducting recreational singing/movement at shelter-care homes.
    Laboratory Sessions: Functional Guitar and Recorder

Group singing eliminates the self-consciousness of singing on one's own, thus encouraging many people to enjoy the singing experience who would otherwise be reluctant. Community singing also tends to permeate the group with a congenial and binding spirit. It is not far-fetched to believe that the ability to sing harmoniously in a group can contribute to an attitude of general harmonious living. In addition to being suitable as a program in itself, group singing can be employed as an opening feature at assemblies, rallies, town meetings, and similar events. In such situations singing acts as a socializing and integrating element, "warming up" the group for the activities to follow.

In selecting the program of songs to be sung, it is essential that the leader determine the interests, ages, experiences, and musical literacy of the group. If the group gathers regularly, the leader will have had ample opportunity to learn its musical tastes. In performance, it is wise to allow some request numbers from the audience. When a request is made and there are no printed lyrics available, the leader can suggest that audience members who are unfamiliar with the words simply hum the tune. Alternate slow with vigorous tunes so as to avoid possible boredom. An overdose of slow tunes may lead to lethargy, while an excess of fast tunes may be exhausting. Another trick is to select a better-than-average singer to sing solo parts while others join the song at the choruses. A variation on this is to use a soloist while the rest hum. Sentimental tunes like "Carry Me Back to Old Virginny" and "Beautiful Dreamer" are best suited to this humming technique.

Leading group singing need not involve massive groups; the setting and number of participants can be as small and low-key as desired. For instance, novelty songs adapt themselves to many recreational settings such as camps, daycare programs, playgrounds, adult party mixers, and so on.

Songs can be divided into rounds, as with the song, "Row, Row, Row Your Boat." The group is divided into three sections that sing the lyric lines in staggered overlapping harmonies. Other songs suitable for renditions in round include "I'd Like to Teach the World to Sing," "Three Blind Mice," and "Are You Sleeping, Brother John?"

Part songs also allow for variations in group singing. In the part song, one group sings a verse asking a question and the other group answers, or different sets of words or melodies are sung against each other simultaneously.

The inclusion of songs that entail body movement are very popular. The song "Down By the Old Mill Stream" will serve as an illustration of how the recreation leader can pantomime movement cues that the group follows in conjunction with its singing.

"Down by the Old Mill Stream"

Down by the old (*stroke beard*) mill (*circular motion with hands*) stream (*sweeping motion of arms while giving ripple effect with fingers*),
Where I (*motion to self*) first met (*shake hands with self*) you (*point at neighbor*).
With your (*point at neighbor*) eyes (*point at own eyes*) so blue (*point at sky*),
Dressed (*sweep over clothing*) in gingham too (*display two fingers*).
It was there (*point away from self*) I (*point to self*) knew (*point at brain*),
That you (*point at neighbor*) loved (*embrace self*) me (*point to self*) true.
You (*point at neighbor*) were sixteen (*display both open hands—ten, then open one hand—five, then display one finger to total sixteen*).
My (*point at self*) village queen (*circular motion over own head to signify a crown*),
Down by the old mill stream (*motions as above*).

The group, of course need not follow the leader's motions in regimented fashion; rather, the leader should encourage group members to be creative in their interpretation of the song through movement. If done with a large audience, action songs provide a release for the audience's energy and also develop further camaraderie.

A group's interest in singing is often increased when they are divided by some classification (for example, male/female or tall/short) with each subgroup having the chance to sing alone. The two groups join together for a final chorus, indicating that, while each group sang well individually, they sound best when contributing to a unified whole. This leadership approach helps safeguard against an unhealthy emphasis on competition. Harry Robert Wilson suggests some creative grouping ideas in *Lead a Song:*[3]

> Divisions can be made in the following ways, many of which offer some jovial good fun: married/single, everyone over 35 years of age/everyone under 35 years of age, everyone who is happy/everyone who is unhappy, everyone who

---

3. Harry Robert Wilson, *Lead a Song* (Chicago: Hall and McCreary Company), p. 90.

went to church last Sunday/everyone who did not go to church last Sunday, Democrats/Republicans, sopranos/altos, tenors/basses, freshmen/sophomores/juniors/seniors (in schools), students who expect to get their diploma or degree/students who never expect to get their diploma or degree, everyone in the balcony/everyone on the main floor, all those who help their mothers wash the dishes/all those who do not help their mothers wash the dishes.

Song leaders should be versed in the methods of instructing a song by rote, as there is no telling when song sheets or books will be unavailable. Consequently, the song should be one that is simple and learned readily. The group will be more motivated if given an explanation of the song's background, including the circumstances and time of its creation, and the customs of the period. The following steps in teaching a song are suggested:

1. The group should hear the words and music sung by the leader.
2. Then the song is divided into phrases, with the group repeating each phrase after it is sung by the leader.
3. This procedure is followed until the entire song is covered.
4. It is then sung in its entirety by the leader.
5. The group should sing it through on its own, thereby completing the technique.

Futhermore, recorded music can be used as an audio aid for song teaching.

In interpreting the song, the less experienced leader may not be certain of the tempo intended by the composer. Be guided therefore by the principle that it is better to err by being too rapid in tempo than by being too slow; a tune that drags becomes almost intolerable. And become familiar with the Italian musical terms pertaining to tempo, for they are used more frequently than English designations.

GLOSSARY OF MUSICAL TERMS

Adagio—slowly, leisurely
Allegro—quick, cheerful
Andante—slow, a walking tempo
Animato—spirited, with animation
Cantabile—flowing, in a singing style
Common time—4/4
Crescendo—gradually louder
Cut time—2/2
Diminuendo—gradually softer

Dolce—sweet
Forte—loud
Largo—very slow, broad
Mezzo forte—moderately loud
Moderato—in moderate tempo
Piano—soft
Pianissimo—very soft
Valse—a waltz
Vivace—lively, quick

Of basic importance in community singing, as in all other recreational activities, is leadership. It is essential that the leader should possess an elementary knowledge of music. The leader should be familiar with the accepted hand movements that are used to lead songs written in the various tempi. In addition, ability to sing well enough to lead the group will prove helpful.

The following are the more common tempi and the simplified methods of leading them:

A.   Two-four time (2/4)   —Two beat

B.   Three-four time (3/4)   —Three beat

> *Note:* Music written in 3/8 time can be led as though the music were written in 3/4 or waltz time.

C.   Four-four time (4/4)   —Four beat

> *Note:* Many songs written in 4/4 time, especially those in the more popular vein, are played and sung in "cut time" or 2/4 time. Even though some songs may be written in cut time (C2/2) they may be beat out in 4/4 time if of a slow tempo. Experiment beforehand to see which is most advisable.

D.   Six-eight time (6/8)   —Six beat

> *Note:* When leading marches in 6/8 time, the two-beat method should be used.[4]

In leading, the movements of the leader should be clear-cut so as to indicate precisely what is meant. The movements of the right hand usually designate the tempo, whereas those of the left hand signify increase in volume with the palm upward, or decrease in volume with the palm downward. An abrupt and angular motion can be used to denote a snappy, majestic beat, whereas a curved beat indicates a melodious song.

Some song leaders secure the desired effect by motioning downward while emphasizing each syllable. This also spares the song leader the need to distinguish whether a song should start with the downbeat or upbeat.

Progressive leadership steps.   As a supplement, let us consider how to organize and conduct a large-scale community sing in progressive steps:

1.   Secure adequate publicity through the newspapers, bulletins, posters and the like.
2.   If there is to be a large audience, it will be of advantage to use an amplifier or public address system.

4. Wilson, *Lead a Song*, p. 74.

3. It is essential that each member of the audience be given a copy of the words to each song. Do not take for granted that the lyrics are known, since the least bit of uncertainty as to the exact wording will definitely cause a decrease in volume.

4. When the program is conducted during the evening or in an enclosed area where the procuring of adequate light is a problem, it is advisable to use a projector to cast the words on a screen. An opaque projector is a great aid for this purpose.

5. The leader should stand in a position so that movements can be easily seen by everyone.

6. As a variation with some groups, it may be advisable for the leader to walk among the members of the audience while leading them. This method will often improve the leader-audience relationship and increase the response.

7. All participants in the community sing, whether seated or standing, should be close together as a unit. This will make possible a better blending of voices and facilitate the spreading of enthusiasm. It will also assist the group in keeping time with the music.

8. Musical accompaniment is an essential aid. A piano, accordion, organ, or a similarly appropriate musical instrument can be used.

9. The playing of a few bars of each song prior to its singing is recommended so that the group will hear a sample of the key and tempo of each song. It will also serve to refresh the memory of those who may not be very familiar with the tune.

10. Impress the audience with the fact that community singing differs from other forms of audience entertainment in that each singer contributes toward the enjoyment of the others; the best results are secured when all sing in unison. Seek their wholehearted cooperation and participation on this basis.

11. The leader and accompanist should select a key suited to the majority of the group. Use a pitch pipe if a piano is not at hand.

12. To add variety to the singing, have the group whistle and hum designated portions of songs.

13. Interject phrases of encouragement such as "That was great!" and "Let's try to make it perfect!" When a song is sung poorly, it is usually desirable to repeat it, while at the same time pointing out the shortcomings in a good-natured manner.

14. Should the program be scheduled to last an hour or more, one must guard against tiring the singers' voices. An intermission is suggested during which some form of entertainment might be provided. This can take such forms as amateur singing, harmonica playing and instrumental recitals. An intermission program of this sort will serve the dual purpose of entertaining the audience, while at the same time enabling its members to rest their voices.

15. Just as the public speaker finds it invaluable to practice speeches before a mirror, so can the song leader benefit by seeing how he or she appears to the audience.

16. Another means of improving the performance is to have someone take notes of the song session as an impartial observer and make a list of the obvious faults: then the leader should take every opportunity to make the needed corrections.

17. Sincere enthusiasm and naturalness in speech on the part of the leader will improve his or her standing with the audience. Opportunities to employ humor will often arise. One can use these to good advantage providing they are not overdone.

These suggestions are intended to help prevent the common problems associated with community singing. Nevertheless, all the advice in the world cannot substitute for experience.

LEADING RHYTHM ACTIVITIES

The recreation leader should also be able to conduct rhythm activities. The basis of all music is rhythm that finds an outlet through the body. Rhythm must be felt inwardly before it can be reflected in the individual's behavior. The development of a person's rhythmic sense should be started as early in life as possible, preferably in early childhood. Children should be exposed to the following simple rhythmic motions accompanied by appropriate music: walking, galloping, hand-clapping, tapping with hands or feet, head swaying, total body swaying, jumping, skipping, and marching. Children may respond to a single beat in a measure or a group of beats. Thus the child develops the ability to coordinate body reactions via rhythmic and emotional responses. Some children lack the ability to react with suitable rhythmic responses: this shortcoming can usually be overcome through frequent rhythm exercises. But guard against employing the same musical numbers for an extended period since the learned responses may then revolve around the songs rather than the rhythms themselves.

Rhythm Opportunities for All Ages

Rhythm activities should be a conscious part of recreation programs for all age groups. Rhythm activities have been narrowly associated with children because of their importance to motor development; however, creative rhythm and movement are equally important to older people. For instance, bamboo pole movement done to a set rhythm is a fun party activity for adults as well as an excellent test of agility and rhythm for youth. In this activity, two bamboo poles are held at ends by partners. The poles, just inches from the ground, are clapped together twice in the middle, then twice away from one another about two feet apart. A third participant attempts to step into the gap made while the poles are apart. It takes good rhythmic sense in order to sidestep the poles without getting trapped.

Music can stimulate free-form expression that exercises all parts of the body or motivates specific pantomime activity. Objects can be used to accompany any creative rhythms to music (bouncing balls, hoops, scarves). Other musical sounds may suggest a certain mood and elicit a corresponding movement (swift, soft, light flute notes suggest a movement of quick steps like falling raindrops). Games can be built around rhythmic activity as illustrated by the rhythm game "Chickie Boom Boom" from Jane Harris' File of Fun:[5]

5. Jane A. Harris, *File O' Fun—Card File for Social Recreation* (Minneapolis: Burgess Publishing Company, 1970), p. 105.

CHICKIE BOOM BOOM   6 years and up
Creative Action Game   Any number

EQUIPMENT: None
FORMATION: The players sit in a circle. They take turns being the leader.
RHYTHM: The words are said by the players over and over.
"Chickie chickie boom boom. Chickie boom boom."
   1   2   3   4   5   6   7
(pause) It is an eight-count rhythm. The last beat is a pause before starting over. The last word count, 7, is accented.
ACTION: This game is played like singing a song in round form with the leader starting it, and the next player picking it up the following time through. Each child around the circle picks it up from the person before him. In addition to the rhythm, the leader starts a different action each time, and these actions pass right around the circle too. The action may be made with the hands, feet, head, or body, and it changes each time through the rhyme.
EXAMPLE: First time—Leader says the rhyme and claps his hands to the rhythm.

          Second time—Leader repeats rhyme and touches fingertips together to the rhythm. The second player in line begins the leader's first action.

          Third time—Leader repeats rhyme and snaps fingers to rhythm. The second player picks up the second action and the third player starts the first action.

Any time the leader wishes to end the game he merely stops the rhythm and the action, and it will carry on around the circle and end with the last person.
LEADERSHIP SUGGESTIONS: It is best not to permit the same leader to go on too long as all will want a chance to imitate the actions. This is a good family game.

Rhythm Band

A particularly effective way to foster rhythmic expression is through the rhythm band. The rhythm band uses easily played, often homemade, instruments to create rhythms. The percussion instruments are to be viewed as extensions of tapping toes, clapping hands, and snapping fingers. Thus the rhythm band offers a learning progression for those who have advanced from body rhythms and provides a basic exposure to instrumental music. Since children must confine their responses to a designated beat, the rhythm band serves as a significant motor development activity. While it is true that rhythm bands have been popularized as a means of developing children's motor coordination and body image, the rhythm band is a music activity equally enjoyable for adults. The recreation leader should disregard any references associating rhythm bands solely with preschool programming. The success of rhythm bands with adults is dependent on the level of leadership and the music selected.

Most rhythm bands use some of the following common instruments:

Triangles	Ocarinas
Tambourines	Marimbas
Drums	Maracas
Rhythm Sticks	Bird Whistles
Sleigh bells	Shepherd's Pipes
Rhythm-Tone Gourds	Bazookas
Cymbals	Kazoos
Wood blocks	Jungle Clogs
Sand blocks	Castanets

While there are standard instruments, rhythm bands often derive more appeal when the instruments are homemade. Rhythm band members consider the making of their instruments a major part of the enjoyment of the rhythm band experience.

Glass objects are simple, fruitful sources of sound. For example, glasses or soda bottles of varying sizes may be used; shading of tone is achieved by adding water until the desired note is secured. Colored water added to each glass container results in distinguishable colors that simplify the identification of each note. In a similar vein, each container can be numbered; tunes are then played simply by following numbers instead of notes. Suitable for a drum effect are gourds, butter tubs, hollow stumps, and kegs (covered with aviator's linen coated with shellac for a drum skin). A tambourine can be made by stretching wet sheepskin across a rim with thumbtacks to hold it in place and tiny bells attached to the rim. Other rhythmical instruments can be made by using horseshoes or railroad spikes for triangles, round cereal boxes for drums, and combs with tissue paper to carry melodies hummed on them. A xylophone can be made with strips of wood of varying lengths; suspended from a rope, the strips of wood produce different notes.

In her book *Recreation Leadership,* Maryhelen Vannier demonstrates how to create a number of rhythm instruments:[6]

Tambourine—Sew two paper plates front to front with yarn. Tie tiny bells around the sewed edge.

Wooden Sticks—Saw a broom or mop handle into 6-inch lengths.

Washboard—Paint a metal washboard with bright colors and play with the fingers, a brush, or thimbles on the fingers

Ukelele box—Cut notches in the end of a candy box parallel to the long sides. Fit rubber bands into each notch and strum.

Sand blocks—Cover two wooden blocks of blackboard-eraser size with emery or sandpiper and rub together.

Roofing disks—Loosely nail one or two roofing disks to two tongue depressors glued together. Strike against palms of the hand.

6. Maryhelen Vannier, *Methods and Materials of Recreation Leadership* (Philadelphia: Lea and Febiger, 1977), pp. 101–102.

Wooden shaker or rattle—Partly fill a large can with rice, popcorn, or tiny rocks. Cut a hole in one end and insert stick handle.

In a rhythm band, the participants can make sound effects, improvise and create original rhythms, or give their interpretations of a given song. If an improvisation is the format, participants are encouraged to be inventive in exploring rhythmic expression as a group. If song interpretation is the goal, familiar recorded or piano music should be played through at least once; thereupon, the band is to play, with each person interpreting the music in his or her own fashion. The guiding hand of the leader should be felt, but not at the expense of spontaneity and enjoyment. Everyone should be encouraged to lead the band, aiding acquisition of leadership skills, better insight into the importance of cooperation, and the enhancement of musical ability. The reading of rhythmic symbols can be taught, with emphasis on the shading of tone, proper phrasing, and rhythm.

At the outset of a rhythm band session, each instrument should be introduced with its origin explained. Each participant should have the opportunity to explore the other instruments. All instruments of one type should be kept in a distinct section to facilitate appropriate musical choices. Once the participants become more familiar with music, they should feel free to suggest the instruments most suitable for each phase of the music.

MUSIC INSTRUCTION

Recreation agencies have been criticized for not providing more variety in music programs. This criticism is not totally invalid, for many agency music programs are limited solely to occasional special events and elementary music classes. For a music program to be good it must offer a balance of performance and instruction. To maintain a high level of interest, instruction should be provided according to skill levels for all ages (beginning, intermediate, and advanced). Interagency cooperation could help facilitate this progression. For instance, the municipal recreation department could develop a fine introductory program, with referrals to a private music school or adult education program better equipped to handle advanced classes. To help offset participant cost for instruments, there should be some community lend-lease system for obtaining instruments.

MUSICAL PERFORMANCE

A recreation agency's music program may also consist of supplying the space or the money for a class or performance. For instance, a health spa may include live band performances in its adjoining nightclub to attract more people to the fitness facility. Concerts are scheduled in the park to make the arts more accessible to all. The municipal recreation department may purchase a mobile wagon to transport performances into neighbor-hoods normally isolated from such art experiences.

To insure the availability of live musical performances to the general public, the Music Performance Trust Fund (MPTF) provides presentations in cosponsorship with leisure service agencies. Funded by the recording industry under agreement with the American Federation of Musicians, MPTF is the largest sponsor of live music in the world. In the early 1940s, professional musicians found that records posed a threat to the existence of live music. To counteract this trend, MPTF was created as a separate, inde-pendent trust to receive and disburse for the public welfare a portion of the revenues derived from record sales. MPTF has taken its performances to VA hospitals, nursing homes, parks, schools, malls, and any number of other settings. For a performance site to be approved, the performance must be free to the public and cannot be used to assist a political, fundraising, religious, social, ethnic, veteran, commercial, labor, or indus-trial organization where the purpose is to promote a particular group. Cosponsor funds are based on the agency's ability to pay and are used to subsidize publicity and performance costs. Since its inception, MPTF has spent over $160 million for nearly one million American and Canadian performances.

The accessibility of live musical performances has educated the public to a greater appreciation of music. According to Michael and Holly Chubb in *One Third of Our Time,* "Opera attendance rose from 2 million in 1950 to more than 10 million in 1979.[7] The popularity of music as a leisure activity is also evidenced by the fact that "the recording industry was a 3 billion dollar industry in 1978."[8]

THE INTEGRATION OF MUSIC WITH OTHER RECREATION PROGRAM ACTIVITY AREAS

A popular recreational program for music is the music camp, which allows for a short but intensive exposure to music instruction in a leisure setting conducive to learning. The mornings are usually spent in formal music study (harmony, theory, conducting, instrument study, chorus) and after-noons are devoted to recreation, with maximum use of the outdoor setting.

The music camp is an example of how music can be integrated with other program areas, in this case outdoor recreation. Music is also a compo-nent of dance, as it forms the basis for movement. Music is also incorpora-ted into drama, where it enhances the theme of the presentation. Music can be correlated with arts and crafts in any number of ways. It can be used to provide background music to inspire artistic creation; the art medium itself may be the basis for the creation of musical instruments or for the design-

7. Michael Chubb and Holly R. Chubb, *One Third of Our Time? An Introduction to Recrea-tion Behavior and Resources* (New York: John Wiley and Sons, 1981), p. 575.
8. Ibid., p. 581.

ing of stage sets for musical theater. Music also combines with social recreation to provide singing and dancing mixers that encourage socialization. For instance, in the activity Vocal Duets Extraordinary, each individual is presented with half of a song sheet. The person who has the other half becomes that individual duet partner to sing the song for the rest of the group. Many games, such as "London Bridge," require musical accompaniment. Similarly, music is often a background to sports activities (skating, gymnastics, roller skating), where it serves as an energizing motivator for the participants. Music can be incorporated into literary activities, for example, when music questions are part of mental quizzes as in the following exercises:

CAN YOU ANSWER THIS ONE?[9]

Each one-word answer is also a common musical term.
>What do you open a lock with? *A key*
>How does the photographer tell you to look? *Sharp*
>What tragedy can happen to your car tire? *Flat*
>What does your tailor take, first of all? *Measure*
>If as an Army captain, you get a promotion, what is your new rank? *Major*

In practically every concerto, at one point (usually toward the end of the first movement) the orchestra leaves off and the solo instrument plays an extended passage in free style, soloist and orchestra presently coming together to bring the movement to a close. What is such a passage called? *Cadenza*

Genius has had its handicaps and penalties; composers have gone deaf, blind or mad. Can you name two in each category?

Blind	*Mad*
Delius	Smetana
Bach	Hugo Wolf
Handel	Schumann

In what opera does a mechanical doll sing? *"Tales of Hoffman"*

What orchestra instrument gives the others the pitch? *Oboe*

What have the following in common: Minuet, sarabande, bourree, courante, galliard? *Dances*

Everybody knows that Beethoven's "Sixth Symphony" is nicknamed Pastoral. Can you recall two other works each of which is also called Pastoral Symphony? The oratorio, *The Messiah*, by Handel; *The Second Symphony*, by Vaughan Williams.

Reginald DeKoven has composed a song that has become practically the national anthem of the bridal service itself. What is its title and for what operetta was it written? "Oh Promise Me," *Robin Hood*.

Which composers wrote the two most popular wedding marches? *Mendelssohn, Wagner*

To which of these does the bride march up the aisle to be married? Wagner's "Bridal Chorus" from *Lohengrin*

9. Ted Cott, *Victor Book of Musical Fun* (New York: Simon and Schuster, 1945), p. 45.

To which one does she come down the aisle with her husband? Mendelssohn's "Wedding March.'

MATCHING MUSICAL TERMS

1.	A slang term applied to "the four hundred"	*Swells*
2.	The prohibition law did away with them	*Bars*
3.	A derogatory term applied to lawyers	*Sharp*
4.	Terms related to our national game	*Base and Run*
5.	A part of a fish	*Scale*
6.	Something used by a shepherd	*Staff*
7.	That which betrays one's birthplace	*Accent*
8.	Something related to railroads	*Lines and Ties*
9.	Something to take when tired	*Rests*
10.	The name of a girl	*Grace*
11.	Two parts of a dollar	*Quarters and Halves*
12.	A portion of a sentence	*Phrase*
13.	An unaffected person	*Natural*
14.	A reflection upon character	*Slur*
15.	A plant for seasoning	*Time (thyme)*
16.	Obtainable from a bank	*Notes*
17.	Found on a check	*Signature*
18.	It is free at gas stations	*Air*
19.	Used for bundling	*Cord (chord)*
20.	Something used by a seamstress	*Measure*
21.	A telegraph operator uses it constantly	*Key*
22.	An important officer	*Major*
23.	Belated to a policeman	*Beat*

MUSIC THERAPY

Music therapy is an important adjunct to therapeutic recreation. Music therapists use music and psychological interventions in the treatment of emotional and physical disorders. They work with recreation therapists in providing their clients with new perspectives and skills. Goals and objectives are individualized to the unique needs of each client within each special population and include such aims as increasing self-esteem, stimulating motor activity, and providing outlets for emotional expression.

RECREATIONAL VALUE

In summary, music activities in recreation programs serve basic human needs. Music is a vehicle for self-expression and personal creativity. It provides emotional release and relaxation. In addition, music is a major socializing agent that unifies its participants. Music celebrates the human spirit and fosters cultural identity. Music provides many opportunities for skill development and the accompanying discipline to achieve performance standards.

SUGGESTED READINGS

ALVIN, JULIETTE. *Music Therapy.* New York: Basic Books, 1975.

BAIRD, FORREST J. *Music Skills for Recreation Leaders.* Dubuque, IA: William C. Brown, 1963.

BATCHELLER, JOHN AND MONSOUR, SALLY. *Music in Recreation and Leisure.* Dubuque, IA: William C. Brown, 1972.

BERNSTEIN, MARTIN AND PICKER, MARTIN. *An Introduction to Music.* Englewood Cliffs, NJ: Prentice-Hall, 1972.

CHUBB, MICHAEL AND CHUBB, HOLLY R. *One Third of Our Time? An Introduction to Recreation Behavior and Resources.* New York: John Wiley and Sons, 1981.

COTT, TED. *Victor Book of Musical Fun.* New York: Simon and Schuster, 1945.

HOOD, MARGUERITE. *Teaching Rhythm and Using Classroom Instruments.* Englewood Cliffs, NJ: Prentice-Hall, 1970.

MUSSELMAN, JOSEPH A. *The Uses of Music.* Englewood Cliffs, NJ: Prentice-Hall, 1972.

NYE, ROBERT ET AL. *Singing with Children.* Belmont, CA: Wadsworth Publishing, 1970.

SHIVERS, JAY. *Essentials in Recreation Services.* Philadelphia: Lea and Febiger, 1978.

9

Mental/Linguistic Recreation

The fact that recreation leadership training originated in schools of physical education has led to the widespread misconception that recreation is synonymous solely with physical activity and sport. Due to this limited perspective, recreation leaders have not adequately explored the many nonphysical pursuits that constitute "re-creation" of mind and spirit. One such area is that of mental recreation (mental quizzes and games, foreign language study, literary activities). This chapter is designed to acquaint the recreation leader with the wide diversity of activities within this subject area, their values to the participant, and their broad application to the variety of recreation settings.

PROGRAM AREA DEFINED

Mental activities refer to those which rely primarily on intellectual reasoning. Programs such as educational classes, public forums, current events classes, lectures, discussion groups, and travelogues (films and speakers on travel) are all included within this recreational category.

Mental Exercises and Games

The current popularity of adult school classes for self-enrichment attests to the attraction of mental activity as a leisure choice. The proliferation of computer games in homes and commercial establishments suggests that mental activity may be the recreation of the future. More and more recreation agencies are installing video games in their facilities, recognizing that their presence contributes greatly to a facility's appeal.

Despite the widespread popularity of video games, mental games derived from the written text still continue to absorb the minds of many. These activities include brain teasers, crossword puzzles, jigsaw puzzles, guessing games and word games (anagrams, word searches, etc.), samples of which are included at the end of this chapter. Such activities serve as good icebreaker and mixer materials.

Mental quizzes and games can be designed with the intent of bringing members together for group problem solving and socializing. For instance, individuals may be given clues to a party game in which they must collaborate with others in order to succeed (for example, a treasure hunt, matching question-answer pairs).

Magic, another popular mental activity, serves as a stimulating individual hobby that can also be performed before a group.

As an exercise of strategy and reasoning, card games and board games such as canasta, Scrabble, and chess continue to occupy considerable leisure time. The availability of a lounge or activity room for playing such games contributes to the natural leisure environment that a recreation agency hopes to create. Such mental exercise also insures a good balance with the usual predominance of physical activity offered.

Literary Activities

Literary activities cover a broad spectrum, for they encompass activities involving reading, writing, and/or communication. They include:

Book clubs.   Club members meet periodically to discuss their literary selections. Book clubs can be devoted to general selections or specialized subjects such as a science-fiction club or classics club.

Reading classes.   Individuals elect to use their leisure time for the improvement of their reading rate and comprehension.

Reading clubs.   The club serves as an incentive to read more as there is usually some form of recognition of progress, be it material reward (for example, certificate) or group approval.

Book review clubs.   The group meets to discuss book reviews, usually of books that all members have read.

Playreading groups.　　The group assumes roles in selected plays for the purpose of informal enjoyment or with the intent of ultimate performance.

Poetry readings.　　Participants read their own or others' poetry for the purpose of informal enjoyment or with the intent of ultimate performance. In the presentation of poetry before an audience, should a more dramatic impact be sought, readers' theater can be staged. (For further information on readers' theater, see the chapter on drama.)

(*Note:* People who wish to present literature, their own or others, before an audience can do so even if they can't attend due to illness or institutionalization. They can tape the literary pieces for circulation or presentation over a public address system. For instance, in a convalescent home, one patient's inspirational writings reached her fellow patients via cassette tape, building an audience of admirers not seen by her but always felt. Likewise, in a nursing home, those unable to physically dramatize their creative ideas for their fellow residents taped them as a radio show that filtered throughout the home on the public address system.)

Writing groups.　　A writing group appeals to a wide spectrum of interests, be it self-enrichment, skill development, or even the prestige of publication. It should be noted that any participant interested in submitting written work for commercial publication should consult *The Writer's Digest*, which lists markets in all literary areas, including poetry, short-story, novel, play, and greeting-card writing. Writing groups include:

short story group

poetry club

technical writing club—Often affiliated with industry or community recreation programs; concerned with developing proficiency in the writing of technical and organizational material (e.g., business memos, professional speeches)

playwriting club

letter writing club—Letter writing projects are a particularly significant recreational outlet for homebound individuals seeking to reach beyond their confined environment. For those unable to read or write due to educational or physical limitations, cassette tapes can be mailed in lieu of written correspondence. Letter writing can also serve as a creative introduction to a program (e.g., a pen-pal program between senior citizens and youth prior to their meeting in a mutual recreation activity).

journal writing class—A popular program in both therapeutic and community programs, journal writing involves recording personal experiences and insights in a diary. The process is considered therapeutic in that the writer experiences a catharsis by documenting feelings that are often barely conscious. The individual's review of past entries serves as a valuable means of self-growth, as the writing reveals personal evolution over time.

journalism club—The club studies and writes journalistic articles, perhaps for publication in a newsletter of its creation. Members are taught the format for news articles, features, editorials, advertisements, and headlines. The journalism club can be an extension of the recreation agency's public relations work.

genealogy club—Participants research their family backgrounds to construct their genealogies. They build the base for the continuation of their heritage by recording the life stories of the present older generation. Oral history (the writing and/or tape recording of life histories) is an enriching experience for interviewer and interviewee alike, particularly when the young are asking questions of the elderly. Many oral history programs house their manuscripts and tapes in libraries in recognition of their value as an historical treasure. The Foxfire Program in Appalachia illustrates an intergenerational oral history program in action. In oral history programs, the interests and capabilities of the interviewees determine whether the life stories are written by interviewees themselves, are transcribed, or are taped by an interviewer. Books and articles of oral history guideline questions are available (e.g., *An Oral History Primer* by Gary L. Shumway and William G. Hartley, copyright 1973 by the authors, Box 11894, Salt Lake City, Utah 84147).

Folklore club. In the folklore club, the study of the literature and oral history of various peoples is integrated with appreciation of their other forms of artistic expression (dance, music, art, cooking). Often, this culminates in an ethnic festival, a special event that celebrates these unique cultural contributions.

Forensic clubs. Also known as debating clubs, members research topics in preparation for public debate and argumentation. Forensic clubs, like the choral speaking and public speaking described below, combine elements of communication and performance with the literary word.

Public speaking class. Participants are taught effective styles of delivery for the presentation of their own or others' written ideas. Such classes are particularly popular in businesses that require workers to creatively translate ideas from the drawing board into convincing oral communication.

Choral speaking groups. The choral speaking group is arranged by voice in much the same way as the choral singing group, with the exception that they collectively present the written word rather than song. Voices are directed in a variety of solo and unison arrangements best suited to dramatize the literary material. More information on choral speaking is to be found in the drama chapter.

Book collecting. As a personal self-directed activity, book collecting is an enjoyable lifetime leisure pursuit. Should book collectors wish to find a group that shares their interest, book collectors' clubs are available.

Bibliotherapy. Bibliotherapy, derived from the root words *biblio* (book) and *therapeuein* (cure), refers to the use of literature as a form of therapeutic recreation. The bibliotherapist, trained in library science and psychology, recommends reading selections that will produce an identification and catharsis in the client. Selections are chosen on the basis of their approximation to the client's own life stories. For instance, in the Philadelphia juvenile court and probation office, the library placed books with content common to the experiences of youthful offenders. Seeing one's own problems mirrored in a text is a nonthreatening way of beginning to come to terms with oneself. The page provides a safe distance from which to view the problem and is a much more appealing modality than an initial question-answer counseling period. The book is discussed individually with the bibliotherapist or in a discussion group organized by the bibliotherapist. Since bibliotherapy involves counseling skills as well as a broad knowledge of literature, specialized training is necessary. St. Elizabeth's Hospital in Washington, DC, offers such a program, but more are needed.

Poetry therapy. Poetry therapy falls under the category of bibliotherapy and requires the same skills. The distinction between poetry therapy and bibliotherapy is that the succinct, emotional quality of poetry allows for a more immediate response as opposed to awaiting the completion of a novel or short story. Each poetry therapy session can therefore be complete in and of itself. Poetry therapy is more likely to spark individual creative writing than is bibliotherapy; in reflecting upon the poetry, the participants are often asked to write their own poems on the theme. St. Elizabeth's Hospital trains poetry therapists. Courses in poetry therapy can be found in progressive educational programs such as the New School for Social Research in New York City. Books are available on the subject; these include two books written by Dr. Jack Leedy (published by Harper and Row) titled *Poetry the Healer* and *Poetry Therapy—The Use of Poetry in the Treatment of Emotional Disorders.* Bibliotherapy and poetry therapy continue to grow in visibility as part of the expansion of the entire arts-in-therapy field (drama therapy, music therapy, dance therapy, and art therapy)

Library programs. The library offers a wide variety of services on its site as well as in the community. In addition to book clubs, reading clubs, and speakers, the library's creative programming includes films, puppetry, music listening, storytelling, and other services. Bookmobiles make literary resources available to industry, schools, institutions, and the general community. The library can set up a book collection in any community agency requesting it (senior citizens center, hospital, industry) and return periodically to replenish the supply. Films, records, and tapes are loaned out as well. In addition to the large print books available in most libraries for use by the visually handicapped, affiliate libraries of the Library for the Blind and Physically Handicapped offer many other services including (1) braille books and magazines; (2) talking books—printed material recorded on flexible discs at a special speed; (3) cassette books; (4) cassette machines, talking machines, and record players; (5) free mailing privileges to receive all library materials. The bibliography at the end of this book contains a list of references pertinent to the literary interests of the visually handicapped.

As a leisure choice, individuals may volunteer to work in the library as reference aides, cataloguers, shelf stockers, and so forth. They may also learn to assist visually handicapped readers by converting texts into braille or taping stories.

The library is no longer the stereotyped fortress of books where mandatory quiet is the rule; it is an agency whose literary offerings are the hub from which many innovative programs are designed. In their book *One Third of Our Time?*, Michael and Holly Chubb cite a number of developments in library services that reflect the library's expansion to a leisure environment. These developments include:[1]

> Rooms that may be used by members of the community for meetings and special events.
>
> Comfortably furnished lounge areas suitable for casual reading, quiet conversation, or informal group discussion.
>
> Play areas for children.
>
> Activity rooms for young people that can be used on an informal basis or as the location for workshops, demonstrations, discussion groups, parties and club meetings.
>
> Parklike grounds for public use and enjoyment, including for people who are not regular library users.
>
> Display cases and wall space that can accommodate special exhibits.

The Chubbs also cite the library's sophisticated use of the media as a large factor in its growing appeal as a leisure choice. For example, they refer to the Washington, DC library's Dial-A-Story program in which children call in over the phone to hear taped stories.

STORYTELLING

Storytelling is an art applicable to many leisure settings, be it a resort party, around a campfire, or in the playground. Storytelling preserves the cultural heritage and builds literary judgment in the listener. By becoming absorbed in the life stories presented in literature, the listener develops sensitivity to the many poignant human dramas of daily life. Since storytelling has such universal application as a recreational activity, the following section is devoted completely to storytelling techniques. This section has been provided by Spencer G. Shaw, Professor of Librarianship, Graduate School of Library and Information Science, University of Washington, Seattle.

1. Michael Chubb and Holly R. Chubb. *One Third of Our Time? An Introduction to Recreation Behavior and Resources* (New York: John Wiley and Sons, 1981), pp. 510–511.

I. PREPARING FOR STORYTELLING

A. THE STORYTELLER:

1. *Personal Attributes*:

Sense of artistry and dignity	Interpretative ability
Creative imagination	Rich literary background
Contagious enthusiasm	Positive response to a story and to an audience

2. *Essentials for Learning Stories:*

Be familiar with material—read silently and aloud several times
Analyze story—make a mental or written outline
Memorize ideas
Retain language and style
Engage in repeated oral practice and refinement in retelling
Insert appropriate gestures and expressions

3. *Effective Storytelling Qualities*:

Delivery:	*Body Movements*:
Proper speed; Excellent diction; Clarity; pitch; Full voice; Use of pause; Proper breath control; Good tonal qualities	Proper eye contact; Limited use of gestures; Good posture standing or sitting; Responsive facial expressions

4. *Negative Qualities to Avoid in Storytelling*:

Overdramatic	Moralizing
Talking down to audience	Stumbling, repeating
Use of indirect discourse	Going off on tangents
Frequent explanations	Interrupting or being interrupted with questions

5. *Negative Qualities to Avoid in Reading Stories Aloud*:

Eye span limited to page	Monotone
Improper position of book	Stumbling
Leafing pages unconsciously	Rapid reading
Improper projection of voice	

B. THE STORY: Types of stories are relative, and the selections included under a particular category may be listed under others.

1. *Type of Story*:

Adventure	Parables	Holiday stories
Animal	Legends, hero tales	Humorous tales
Religious	Realistic stories	Proverbs
Epic (episodes)	Traditional folk tales	Tall tales
Fables	Myths	
Modern fanciful tales		

2. *Story Structure*: Uncover the external structure of each story using a suggested written or mental outline to determine the component parts and their interrelationship one with another.

a. *Theme*:   Strong, understandable, well-defined.
b. *Introduction*:   Indicates time, setting, characters, problem to be solved, or hope to be fulfilled.
c. *Plot*:   Logical development, economy of incidents, some elements of suspense, series of crises.
d. *Climax*:   Answers the curiosity or anticipation aroused in introduction; resolves the problem or fulfills the hope.
e. *Conclusion*:   Follows climax quickly, finishes story, avoids stated moral (except in a fable).
f. *Style*:   Fluid, direct; recognizes peculiarities of author's expressions and indicated story flavor.
g. *Characters*:   Appealing, believable, contrasting, natural, and appropriately suited for every role.
h. *Vocabulary*:   Simple, expressive; devoid of slang, stereotyped dialect, or colloquialisms.

II. *PLANNING FOR STORYTELLING*: Use some of the essentials related to good program planning.

  A. *THE AUDIENCE*: Develop a sensitive response to audience interests and potentials in story selections and presentations. Secure as much information as possible about the audience before planning the program. Following are essentials: Age range; backgrounds and experiences; personality traits; physical and emotional status of participants; any particular or special pressures that may be present in the group; intellectual and educational level of the group; language limitations—non-English speaking, bilingual; general interest and attention span.

    1. *Composition*: Mixed groups, homogeneous or heterogeneous in terms of age, cultural, national, ethnic, and religious backgrounds.

  B. *THE SITUATION:* Answer the questions—who, what, where, when, how?

    1. *Agency: Suggested Situations for Planned Storytelling in Different Agencies*

Library
Browsing periods
Class visits to library
Holiday observances
Special programs (Book Week, National Library Week, author's birthday)
Regular story time
Club meetings
Operation Headstart
Adult education classes

Community Centers, Camps, Parks
Club groups
Inclement weather
Holiday observances
Indoor fireside entertainment
Special programs (birthdays, anniversaries)
Stay-at-home camps
Playground activity, outdoor story time
Regular story time
Correlated with crafts, trips, etc.
Operation Headstart

School
Assembly programs
Library periods
Holiday observances
With units of study

Religious Institutions
Holiday observances (Easter, Christmas, Purim, Hanukkah)
Part of worship service

During inclement weather
After rest or lunch periods
After tests or study periods
Individualized reading programs
Homebound children
Operation Headstart

Special programs—clubs, game or stunt nights
Visits to shut-ins
Junior religious service
Units of study
Related to religious music, symbols, windows, etc.
Day camps, summer vacation Bible school

Institutions
Library periods
Classroom visits
Special programs
Ward visits
Bedside visitation
Holiday observances
Units of study

Radio and Television
Holiday observances
Book Week, National Library Week
Weekly series
Education programs
Library programs
Radio and/or television "specials"

2. *Type of Storytelling Programs*: Preschool and picture book story time; story time with older audiences (learned stories); read-aloud story time; family story time; outdoor story time; poetry and storytelling festivals.
3. *Schedule*: Weekly, Monthly, Seasonal, Special.
4. *Length*: Determined by age, interest and attention span, size of audience.
5. *Publicity*: Use of all possible media to advertise program—bulletin boards, brochures, posters, announcements, news release, direct mail, radio, television.

C. *THE PROGRAM ARRANGEMENT*: Develop programs with unity, balance, coherence.

Theme for storytelling program
Number of stories
Balanced story selections

Poetry
Order of telling
Finger plays (younger audiences)

D. *THE LOCATION FOR STORYTELLING*: Frame the storytelling with a proper setting and an atmosphere conducive to listening.

1. *Essentials to Consider in the Selection of Location*:
   Absence of distractions
   Size suitable for number in audience
   Area large enough to accommodate wheelchairs, walkers, ambulatory individuals

   Good acoustics
   Clean, orderly, attractive

2. *Appearance of the Location*:
   Indoors
   Orderly furniture arrangement
   Informal, semicircular seating plan
   Well-lighted and ventilated
   Table, bookcases artistically decorated
   Comfortable seating

   Outdoors
   Shady location, grassy
   Avoidance of natural obstacles—sunlight, damp ground, rocks, tall grass, tree roots
   Orderly arrangement of benches, chairs, stools

III. *PRESENTING STORYTELLING AS AN ART*: Bring together all of the elements into an artistic pattern—a story, listeners, and a storyteller.

   A. *Assembling the group for storytelling program*
   B. *Presenting program*:
      1. Methods to begin program
      2. Introducing and telling each story
      3. Conducting allied supplemental activity (Finger plays—younger listeners; poetry reading—older listeners)
      4. Concluding program
         a. Summary of titles and sources used
         b. Quoted reference to books and/or readings
   C. *Dismissing audience*
   D. *Postprogram activity*:
      Browsing
      Creative drama
      Discussion period
      Art
      Creative writing

A SUGGESTED GUIDE TO STORY SELECTION

CHARACTERISTICS OF STORIES SUITABLE FOR USE WITH CHILDREN[2]

Appeal to the Imagination
Sendak, Maurice, *Where The Wild Things Are*
Geisel, T. S., *If I Ran the Zoo*

Embody Universal Truths
Pyle, Howard, *Apple of Contentment*
Sawyer, Ruth, *The Way of the Storyteller*

Encourage Kinship With Animals
Clark, Wila, "Indian Legends of the Pacific Northwest" in *How Beaver Stole the Fire*
Andersen, Hans C., "The Ugly Duckling"

Illustrate Common Sense and Resourcefulness
Fillmore, Parker, "The Shepherd's Nosegay" in *Clever Manka*
Jacobs, Joseph, "English Fairy Tales" in *Molly Whuppie*

Include Drama
King Arthur and His Sword
Icarus and Daedalus
Alden, Raymond, "Why the Chimes Rang" in *The Hunt for the Beautiful*
Shulevitz, Uri, *Dawn*

Make for Wonder and Laughter
Zion, Gene, *Harry the Dirty Dog*
Wadsworth, Wallace, *Paul Bunyan and His Great Blue Ox*

Offer Action and Excitement
Lang, Andrew, "The Blue Fairy Book" in *Aladdin and the Wonderful Lamp*

2. Marie L. Shedlock, "Elements to Avoid in the Selection of Material," Chapter 4 in *The Art of the Storyteller* (New York: Dover Publications, 1951), pp. 43–64.

Hatch, Mary C., "13 Danish Tales" in *The Talking Pot*
  Promote Democratic Ideals
Yashima, Taro, pseud. (Jun Iwamatsu), *Crow Boy*
Schauffler, Robert, *The Days We Celebrate*, Vol. 3
Malcolmson, Anne, "Song of Robin Hood" in *Robin Hood Rescuing Will Stutly*
  Reflect Child's Own Experience
Clark, Ann Nolan, *In My Mother's House*
McCloskey, Robert, *Time of Wonder*

CHARACTERISTICS OF STORIES UNSUITABLE FOR USE

Appeal to fear (e.g., ghost stories)
Exaggerated and coarse fun
Extreme emotionalism
Lack of respect for other races, creeds, cultures
Matters beyond the realm of child's interest or understanding
Obvious moral to story (sermonizing)

Overabundance of humor
Profanity
Sadism, gruesomeness
Sarcasm and ridicule
Sensationalism
Sentimentality
Subjective analysis of motive or feeling

Developing the Storytelling Craft

Learning a story embodies several essentials. At all times remember one important principle: memorize ideas, do not memorize words. Learn the story as a whole, keeping as close as possible to the author's wording and phrasing. If these impede the listener's understanding, the teller may alter them if that can be done without destroying the mood or style. The storyteller memorizes the *sequence* of events and the *ideas* contained in each.

The storyteller reproduces the content of the story as if actually seeing or experiencing it personally. Where there is dialogue, the storyteller should work it over until it sounds natural and spontaneous, giving each character its own unique "personality."

Once having completed these tasks, the storyteller should relate the story aloud to him or herself. Stilted expressions, worried gropings for words, and halting phrases gradually disappear as constant practice brings improvement. Having fit parts of the pattern into their respective places, the storyteller begins to strive for oral expression and proper body movements.

Oral expression for the storyteller is the principal means of conveying the ideas of the printed word to the audience. Supplemented at times by body and facial gestures, it depends upon a complete utilization of several effective voice qualities: speed, pitch, pause, and clarity. Speed has to be carefully controlled. Hearing the tale, the group must first grasp the words mentally and then form the pictures that the teller is describing. A varied rapidity of words, accompanied by an altered change of pitch, adds force to the telling. Furthermore, it enables the listeners to discern the introduction of a new situation or a change of events. It is especially useful to denote different characters speaking. Pauses set the stage for contrast; they indicate a suspenseful moment, provide a perfect setting for the introduction of a story character, and give the teller time to assume the different tones of the story characters as they engage in conversation. Clarity of expression is attained when the storyteller develops sensitivity to the choice of words in the story. Superfluous description and confused patterns of conversation become controlled with an economy of words. Clarity also depends upon clear articulation and enunciation. The running together of syllables, phrases, and sentences will rob the listeners of much of the beauty contained in the author's expressions. Proper body movements and facial expressions are vital to the success of the storytelling art.

PROGRAMMING IDEAS FOR MENTAL RECREATION

Mental recreation satisfies many needs and motivations. The need for relaxation is achieved through mental absorption. Communication skills are improved as a result of written and oral exercises. The intellectual activity provides a release from boredom in favor of mental stimulation. And in cases where the activity is shared with others, as with book-reading clubs, the benefits of socialization occurs. The remainder of this chapter is devoted to descriptions of many creative programming ideas available to the recreation leader.

Language Arts Activities

1. Adapt the format of various TV game shows to a story you like. For instance, play "Password" with all of the passwords referring to characters or events in the story. Present a character's life history through a game based on "This Is Your Life." Play "Family Feud," "Hollywood Squares," or "Jeopardy" with the categories of questions derived from topics in the story. Role play a story character in a "To Tell the Truth" panel.
2. Create a collaborative poem or story, whereby each person creates a line of a group narration as it evolves. The content need not make sense, as it is spontaneity of expression rather than continuity of thought that is encouraged. If the participants do not feel comfortable with free-form contributing, the leader may use a ball of yarn, whereby circle members pass the ball to each other as a cue to continue the story line.
3. Write a "fractured fairy tale" (a parody or comic treatment of the original tale). For example, the seven dwarfs might become members of a neighborhood gang.
4. After listening to a number of sound effects, integrate all of them into a story.
5. Listen to music and imagine the mood, people, and places it suggests to you. Write a story or poem about your images.
6. Create a business card describing yourself and what you have to offer.
7. Write metaphors or comparisons to describe yourself. ("I am a river, bending gracefully in life's turning roads.")
8. Make up your own comic strip.
9. Write original lyrics to existing tunes.
10. Compile a scrapbook of poems, pictures, and stories dealing with one theme.

11. Practice writing lines in which you use words that sound like their meaning (e.g., slimy, slithering, crunchy).

12. Obtain four containers. Fill the first with time settings written on cards (seasons, days), the second with characters (clown, plumber, teacher), the third with locations (camp, seashores, prison), and the fourth with actions (jumping, baking, skating). After picking a card from each container, combine the four elements into a story.

13. Write a story using personification (making an inanimate object take on the characteristics of a person)—for example, the alarm clock complains about severe daily headaches due to being pounded every morning.

14. Pick a character in a story you are reading. Write "letters" you believe that character would write regarding situations occurring in the story.

15. Group members write anonymous "Dear Abby" letters and exchange them amongst themselves for written responses.

16. Create a word collage describing yourself.

17. Rewrite a story from the viewpoint of a character other than the one that is central in a short story.

18. Design your own greeting cards, remembering that for sentiment to be poetry it need not rhyme.

19. Tape music, make slides, design mobiles, or draw pictures to match the mood of a favorite story.

20. Create bumper stickers illustrating the theme of a given story.

21. Create advertisements that are plays on words (e.g., "7-Up—Cure for the Common Cola").

22. Complete unfinished sentences. ("In my wildest dream I _____. In my fantasy place I _____.) Unfinished sentences provide a reassuring format to the novice writer who appreciates having a given structure on which to build ideas.

23. Write a limerick, a light or humorous poem of five lines, as in this example:

There was a young girl from Ho-ho-kus
Who thought that a rose was a crocus
It wasn't that she
Knew no botany
Her glasses were just out of focus.

Since a book such as Martin's *Sprint's and Distances* integrates the subject of sports into poetry, it is an ideal springboard to introduce sports enthusiasts to literary activity. It builds on the main interest of sport, from which literary appreciation may evolve. For instance, a poem such as "The Base Stealer" offers discussion material both in terms of baseball and its literary style.

"The Base Stealer"[3] by Robert Francis
Poised between going on and back,
Poised both ways taut like a tightrope walker
Fingertips pointing the opposites.
Now bouncing tiptoe like a dropped ball
Or a kid skipping rope, come on, come on.

3. "The Base Stealer," Copyright © 1948 by Robert Francis. Reprinted from *The Orb Weaver* by permission of Wesleyan University Press.

Running, a scattering of steps sidewise
How he teeters, skeeters, tingles, teases
Taunts them, hovers like an ecstatic bird
He's only flirting, crowd him, crowd him,
Delicate, delicate, delicate, delicate—now!

As illustrated here, any subject matter, including sports, can be integrated into literary activity. Through concrete poetry, the poet can arrange the ideas into a visual design that graphically represents their meaning. If the poet had decided to write the above poem as a concrete poem, he might have arranged the words in the form of a baseball diamond or in a circle like a baseball. Blending art and writing in such a way helps break down artificial barriers between recreational programs.

Animal, vegetable, or mineral.[4]   In this game, one person goes out of the room while the others think of some real or fictional person, object, place, or thing. After returning, the person who is "It" is given the clue that the group has thought of something that is either animal, vegetable, or mineral (or possibly a combination of these). A person, an animal, or anything made of animal substance would be classified as animal, for example. An automobile might be classified as all three, in that it might include animal (leather seat covers), vegetable (rubber floor mat), and mineral (steel body).

"It" asks as many questions as necessary to identify the thing they have in mind. The first questions should establish major categories and make clear whether or not it is a real or fictional person or thing, a single object or a class of objects, in the past or present, and so forth. Since this game may drag on if the choice is a very difficult one, it may be wise to set a time limit.

Twenty questions.   This is very much like the preceding game, except that one player is chosen to think of a person or object that is also familiar to the other players. The entire group tries to guess it, asking questions one at a time that must be answered by only "Yes," "No," or "Sometimes." They are allowed twenty questions to do this, and should begin by establishing broad categories (human, alive or dead, male or female). When this has been done, they can try to guess the actual answer. If the subject is named within the twenty-question limit, the person who guessed it begins a new game by thinking of another subject.

Advertising slogans.   Have one or two people help in compiling a list of well-known advertising phrases or slogans, taking them from television commercials or magazines. These may include such phrases as: "I'd rather fight than switch." "Wouldn't you rather buy a _____," or "_____ tastes good, like a cigarette should." The group is divided into two teams. The

4. From *Recreation Today: Program Planning and Leadership* by Richard G. Kraus, pp. 356–359. Copyright © 1977 by Scott, Foresman and Company. Reprinted by permission. (Extract includes all material through "Words on foot.")

leader calls out a slogan, and the first player to call back the name of the correct product wins and the first player to call back the name of the correct product wins a point for her team. Or the game may be played with the first player of one team given the chance to answer (if he cannot, his opponent may), and then the first player of the opposing team given a turn, and so on down the line.

Surprise portraits.   Here's an amusing drawing game. Each player writes his or her name on a small slip of paper; these are put into a hat or container that is passed around. They are mixed up, and then all players must draw a name (not their own) from the hat. Sitting in a circle, with drawing paper and crayon, each person must draw a likeness of the person whose name he or she drew. After 10 minutes, players hold up the pictures drawn, and all try to find themselves. When every portrait has been identified, the group may then vote on which two or three pictures most resemble their subjects.

Picture charades.   Players divide into teams of at least five or six each. Each team is given a pencil and a pad of paper. It selects an "artist." The artist from each team goes up to the leader (who has prepared a list of titles, famous names, or proverbs). The leader shows them all the first title or other phrase. They hurry back to their groups without saying a word (although they may shake their heads or nod, to indicate "hot" or "cold"), then draw a picture to get the idea across. The group members keep guessing until they have the solution. The first team to get it has its "artist" run up, and the leader gives that team one point. The game is continued several times, until each player has been an "artist."

Hidden proverbs.   One player leaves the room while the others agree on a well-known proverb or popular saying. The player comes back and tries to guess the proverb by asking the other players in turn a series of questions. In their responses, they must each use a word of the proverb. The answer to the first question must contain in it the first word of the proverb. The answer to the next must contain the second word of the proverb, and so on. Although the players try to conceal these words as cleverly as possible, the player who went out is given three chances to guess the proverb—and usually can do it! Then, the player who gave the last clue becomes "It" and the game starts again.

Words on foot.   Players are divided into teams of eight or ten. Each group is given the same set of letter cards; let us say they include the letters: *r, o, a, b, s, t, m, l, e, c.* Each group, standing by itself, faces a spelling line. The leader, on the side, calls out a word using the letters that were given. At once, the players with the correct letter cards run forward, stand on the spelling line facing their teams in the correct order, and hold up their cards. The first team to spell the word correctly wins a point. They return to their groups, and the game is repeated again and again until the first team with ten points wins.

Typical words for the above list of letters would be:

cost	cast	male	race	lest	boast
beast	steal	meal	cart	lame	clear

The following mental games appear in the collection *Why Does the Elephant Eat Mothballs?: Riddles, Rhymes, 'Rithmetic* by Jane Spencer:

Historical Events: With what incidents are the following connected?

1. "Nearer my God, to Thee." (*Sinking of the Titanic*)
2. "Remember the Alamo!" (*War with Mexico*)
3. "One if by land, two if by sea." (*Paul Revere's ride*)
4. "Seward's folly." (*Purchase of Alaska*)
5. "Remember the Maine!" (*Spanish-American War*)

Objects: What persons or characters are associated with the following?
1. A coat of many colors—*Joseph*
2. A cotton gin—*Eli Whitney*
3. A pound of flesh—*Shylock*
4. A silver lamp—*Aladdin*
5. A steamboat—*Robert Fulton*

Famous Persons:
1. I'm the scientist who was the proponent of the theory of evolution. (*Charles Darwin*)
2. I'm the man who tried to jump across the Grand Canyon on a motorcycle. (*Evel Knievel*)
3. I'm the monk who was well known for my love of nature. (*St. Francis of Assisi*)
4. I'm the author who wrote a large number of books whose setting was always in the West. (*Zane Grey*)
5. I'm the radio character whose closet was always in a mess. (*Fibber McGee*)

Proverbs: (Fill in the blank.)
1. One man's _____is another man's poison. (*meat*)
2. A little _____is a dangerous thing. (*knowledge*)
3. _____ speak louder than words. (*Actions*)
4. It is better to be _____than sorry. (*safe*)
5. It takes two to make a _____. (*bargain*)

Crimes and Criminals: What name do you think of in connection with the following?
1. An island penal institution, now closed—*Alcatraz*
2. Organizer of juvenile thieves in "Oliver Twist"—*Fagin*
3. Famous cartoon detective—*Dick Tracy*
4. Famous train robber—*Jesse James*
5. He stole some tarts—The Knave of Hearts

FIGURE 9-1 Which Way Words

Starting with the correspondingly numbered circle, fit the answer to each clue into the connected circles, one letter in each. When completed, the five lines with the heavily outlined circles reading across will contain related 9-letter words.

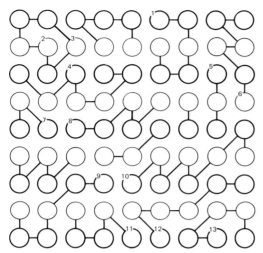

1. _____ grits
2. Nebula
3. Wed secretly
4. Emperor
5. Chorus
6. Aquatic
7. Leases
8. Rusted
9. Swamp
10. Rifle
11. Pivots
12. Heroic

WHICH WAY WORDS
1. Hominy, 2. Galaxy, 3. Elope, 4. Monarch, 5. Choir, 6. Marine, 7. Charters, 8. Corroded, 9. Morass, 10. Browning, 11. Proxy, 12. Hinges, 13. Noble. Nine-letter entries: Xylophone, Harmonica, Accordion, Trombones, Saxophone.

Source: Louise Barth, (ed.), *Approved Crossword Puzzles* (Stamford, CT: Penny Press, 1983), p. 55.

Who Said It?

1. "The buck stops here." (*Harry S. Truman*)
2. "We shall overcome." (*Martin Luther King*, Jr.)
3. "Some men see things as they are and say 'Why?' I dream things that never were and say, 'Why not?' " (*Robert Kennedy*)
4. "Watson, come here." (*Alexander Graham Bell*)
5. "Leaping lizards!" (*Orphan Annie*)

Sport Quiz:

1. Who was the "Brown Bomber"? (*Joe Louis*)
2. Where is baseball's Hall of Fame? (*Cooperstown, NY*)
3. In what sport do you win by pinning your opponent? (*wrestling*)
4. Who are the two most famous archers in history and legend? (*William Tell and Robin Hood*)
5. What famous football player was known as the "Galloping Ghost"? (*Red Grange*)

Questions can be added to each of these games by the players themselves.[5]

5. Jane Spencer. *Why Does the Elephant Eat Mothballs?: Riddles, Rhymes, 'Rithmetic* (Buffalo, NY: Potentials Development for Health and Aging Services, 1980).

FIGURE 9–2 Unscramblers
Rearrange the pairs of letters given in the left-hand column to form the names of eight well-known people. Then match them to their occupations which are given in the right-hand columns.

MYSTERY NAMES							OCCUPATIONS
1. ED	OM	ON	TH	IS	AS		a. Boxer
2. NO	YC	RS	MM	ON	JI		b. Actor
3. VI	JU	ER	LI	NG	US		c. Composer
4. CH	SB	NS	AR	RO	ON	LE	d. Tennis player
5. TE	DB	ON	ER	LE	AR	NS	IN	e. General
6. OP	AS	PA	SO	BL	IC		f. Basketball player
7. EF	ER	ZI	JO	RA			g. Artist
8. MS	WI	RM	LL	HE	IA	AN	h. Inventor

7-a: Joe Frazier, 8-e: William Sherman.
5-c: Leonard Bernstein, 6-g: Pablo Picasso
3-f: Julius Erving, 4-b: Charles Bronson,
1-h: Thomas Edison, 2-d: Jimmy Connors,
UNSCRAMBLERS

Source: Louise Barth, (ed.), *Approved Crossword Puzzles* (Stamford, CT: Penny Press, 1983), p. 55.

SUGGESTED READINGS[6]

ARBUTHNOT, MARY HILL. *The Arbuthnot Anthology of Children's Literature.* 4th ed. Rev. by Zina Sutherland. Chicago: Scott, Foresman, 1976.

ASSOCIATION FOR LIBRARY SERVICE TO CHILDREN. *Let's Read Together: Books for Family Enjoyment.* 4th ed. Chicago: American Library Association, 1981.

*ASSOCIATION FOR LIBRARY SERVICE TO CHILDREN. *Opening Doors for Pre-School Children and Their Parents.* 2nd ed. Chicago: American Library Association, 1981, pamphlet.

BAKER, AUGUSTA AND GREENE, ELLEN. *A Story-telling Manual.* New York: R. R. Bowker and Co., 1977.

*BAUER, CAROLINE FELLER. *Handbook for Storytellers.* Chicago: American Library Association, 1977.

BETTELHEIM, BRUNO. *The Uses of Enchantment: The Meaning and Importance of Fairy Tales.* New York: Alfred A. Knopf, 1976.

*BRYANT, SARA CONE. *How to Tell Stories to Children.* Reprint of 1924 ed. Detroit: Gale Research, 1973.

CAMPBELL, JOSEPH. *"Folkloristic Commentary" in Grimm's Fairy Tales.* Complete edition. New York: Pantheon Books, 1944, pp. 833–863.

*CARLSON, BERNICE W. *Listen! and Help Tell the Story.* Nashville, TN: Abingdon Press, 1965.

*CATHER, LAURA E., HAUSHALTER, MARION, RUSSELL, VIRGINIA A. *Stories to Tell to Children: A Selected List.* 8th ed. Pittsburgh: University of Pittsburgh Press for Carnegie Library of Pittsburgh Children's Services, 1974.

*CHILD STUDY ASSOCIATION OF AMERICA. *Reading with Your Child Through Age Five.* With 1976 Supplement. New York: Child Study Association of America, 1972.

CLARKSON, ATELIA AND CROSS, GILBERT B. *World Folktales: A Scribner Resource Collection.* New York: Charles Scribner's Sons, 1980.

COOK, ELIZABETH. *The Ordinary and the Fabulous: An Introduction to Myths, Legends, and Fairy Tales for Teachers and Storytellers.* Cambridge, England: Cambridge University Press, 1969.

6. These suggested *reference* and *resource* aids are recommended for your professional and artistic enrichment. It is essential in selecting and presenting your stories and your programs (1) *to know your audience,* (2) *to know your resources,* and (3) *to know your techniques.* The entries with an asterisk (*) include materials suitable for storytelling with younger listeners.

COUGHLAN, MARGARET N., COMPILER. *Folklore from Africa to the United States: An Annotated Bibliography*. Washington, DC: Children's Book Section, Library of Congress, 1977.

*FOSTER, JOANNA, COMPILER. *How to Conduct Effective Picture Book Programs: A Handbook*. New York: Westchester Library System, 1967.

*GRAYSON, MARION. *Let's Do Fingerplays*. Washington, DC: Robert B. Luci, 1962.

GRIMM, JAKOB L. K. *Grimm's Fairy Tales, Complete Edition*. New York: Pantheon Books, 1944.

HOLLOWELL, LILLIAN, (ED.). *A Book of Children's Literature*. New York: Holt, Rinehart and Winston, 1977.

Horn Book Magazine. "Storytelling Issue," June 1983. Boston: The Horn Book, Inc.

HUCK, CHARLOTTE AND YOUNG, DORIS. *Children's Literature in the Elementary School*. 3rd ed. New York: Holt, Rinehart and Winston, 1976; chap. 3, "Picture Books," pp. 92–156; chap. 4, "Traditional Literature: Folk Tales, Fables, Myths, Epic Literature; chap. 5, "The Bible as Literature," pp. 158–246; chap. 6, "Poetry," pp. 308–391.

IRELAND, NORMA A. *Index to Fairy Tales, 1949 to 1972, Including Folklore, Legends and Myths in Collections*. Westwood, MA: F. W. Faxon, 1973.

*JOHNSON, FIRNE, (ED.). *Start Early for an Early Start: You and the Young Child*. Chicago: Children's Services Division, American Library Association, 1976.

KIMMEL, MARGARET M. AND SEGEL, ELIZABETH. *For Reading Out Loud! A Guide to Sharing Books with Children*. New York: Delacorte Press, 1983.

*LIMA, CAROLYN W. *A to Zoo: Subject Access to Children's Picture Books*. New York: R. R. Bowker, 1982.

MACDONALD, MARGARET READ. *The Storyteller's Sourcebook: A Subject, Title, and Motif Index to Folklore Collections for Children*. Detroit: Neal-Schuman Publishers/Gale Research, 1981.

*MOORE, VARDINE. *Pre-School Story Hour*. 2nd ed. Metuchen, NJ: Scarecrow Press, 1972.

*NEW YORK LIBRARY ASSN. *Once Upon a Time*. Rev. ed. by the Picture Book Committee, Children's and Young Adult Section, New York Library Association. New York: The New York Public Library.

SAWYER, RUTH. *The Way of the Storyteller*. Rev. ed. New York: The Viking Press, 1962.

TASHJIAN, VIRGINIA. *Juba This and Juba That: Story Hour Stretches for Large and Small Groups*. Boston: Little, Brown, 1969.

ULLOM, JUDITH, COMPILER. *Folklore of the North American Indians: An Annotated Bibliography*. Washington, DC: Library of Congress, 1959.

WILSON, JANE. *The Story Experience*. Metuchen, NJ: The Scarecrow Press, 1979.

YOLEN, JANE. *Touch Magic: Fantasy, Fairie and Folklore in the Literature of Childhood*. New York: Philomel Books, 1981.

ZEIGLER, ELSIE B., COMPILER. *Folklore: An Annotated Bibliography and Index to Single Editions*. Westwood, MA: F. W. Faxon, 1973.

10

Outdoor Recreation

FEDERAL GOVERNMENT SUPPORT OF OUTDOOR RECREATION

The federal government's interest in outdoor recreation was first evidenced in 1864 when, by congressional act, Yosemite Valley and the Mariposa Big Tree Grove were given to California for recreation purposes. In 1872 President Grant affixed his signature to the bill that created Yellowstone National Park. As early as 1868, the Commissioner of the Office of Education recognized in a first report that a relationship existed between education and recreation.

The Bureau of Fisheries was created in 1871 and later became the Fish and Wildlife Service. Congress authorized the use of national forest areas for recreation in 1897, thereby providing for picnic areas, camp sites, and the like for outdoor recreation, including fishing, hunting, camping, and picnicking.

The federal government's interest in recreation gained real impetus at the turn of this century. Increased efforts were exerted for the use of federal land and water areas for recreational purposes. By 1906, authorization was given the president to establish national monuments. The Children's Bureau came into existence in 1912 and soon became cognizant of the recreation problems and needs of children and youth; by 1915 it had made a study of the play facilities for children in the District of Columbia. In 1914 the Extension Service of the Department of Agriculture came into being under the Smith-Lever Act, whereby impetus was given to recreation in rural areas. In 1916 the National Park Service was organized to administer the national monuments, parks, and reservations associated with military recreation in World War I. (Not until 1933 did those sites shift over from the military to the National Park Service.) The depression years marked a period of intense recreational construction; thousands of trails were built throughout the United States by the Civilian Conservation Corps. In 1944, Congress designated that the Department of the Army, through its Corps of Engineers, provide for the recreational use of reservoirs.

The federal government, as mandated by the Outdoor Recreation Resources Commission Report, has established the Land and Water Conservation Fund that provides funding to the states via the Department of the Interior. Under its administration, the Urban Park and Recreation Recovery Act of 1978 provides funding for physical rehabilitation and revitalization of urban park and recreation systems.

Consistently, the federal government has expanded the scope and emphasis it has placed on parks and recreation. This increased emphasis has exerted a domino effect on the states and their municipalities. Expanded leisure time and population pressures have led to a more concerted effort to enlarge the allocation of space in and around urban centers.

This focus of federal policy has been brought to the forefront by way of transfer of title of federally owned land and by financial support. In 1985, the Housing and Urban Development Act amended the Open Space Land Program so as to increase aid for acquiring and advancing urban open-space lands: small parks in crowded sectors were also constructed. As in the Land and Water Conservation Fund, the federal government provided 50 percent of the cost. Though not always implemented, the Housing and Urban Development Act also recognized the vital role trained leadership can play in maximizing the value of recreation at these sites. The Wild and Scenic Rivers Act of 1968 initially set aside eight river areas where waters are protected from pollution and sport. Also in 1968, the National Trails System Act set up a national system of trails and protected rivers.

CAMPING

Value of Camping

Camping is a popular form of outdoor recreation. It can be practiced alone as well as with mixed groups and families, and it is not costly. Camping provides an opportunity for adventure, challenges the imagination, and builds self-reliance and independent thinking. Camping can be the perfect setting for learning to get along with others and practicing the give and take of communal living. And it provides a welcome respite from the tension and congestion of urban living. Specialized camps—such as tennis, computer, or drama camps—attract many participants, for outdoor living often offers a setting more conducive to the learning process. Camping encourages an appreciation of the simpler things in life; it emphasizes active participation rather than mere spectating, the living of adventure rather than the yearning for it.

The organization that has fostered camping more than perhaps any other is the ACA or American Camping Association. Its nationwide membership receives the ACA publication *Camping Magazine* and, since the ACA investigates and approves camps for inclusion in its directory, its endorsement is a positive promotion for any camp. (A prospective camper should review a camp's health and safety factors against ACA standards.)

Types of Camps

Institutional camps are usually non-profit and are largely run by such organizations as Girl Scouts, Boys Clubs, 4-H Clubs, settlement houses, "Y's," and church camps. They serve a unique purpose: making camp available for many who could not otherwise attend more costly private camps. In addition, there are health camps conducted by service clubs and charitable groups, sports camps, and camps for such special populations as the blind or physically disabled. Some school systems acknowledge camping as an important adjunct of their curricula and own their own campsites offering camping opportunities on a year-round basis. Also, a number of colleges have helped spearhead school camping; they conduct demonstrations, workshops, and seminars and issue descriptive literature. In conservation camps, field trips and lectures impart understanding of such issues as stream pollution, reforestation, farm fish ponds, forest game, land restoration, and erosion of our natural resources.

Public camps are run by city, state, and federal agencies. For instance, a community camp program can be administered through the city recreation department. In this case, a camp commission representing youth and civic organizations, clubs, fraternal organizations, and churches is appointed by the mayor to serve as an advisory board. In view of expanded free time, longer paid vacations, the renewed importance of the family, and the growing interest in outdoor living, family camping warrants a more vital position in recreation programs.

The day camp offers the camp experience without the requirement of overnight sleeping. Participants are bussed daily to camp from a recreation program, such as a YWCA/YMCA, school, senior citizen center, or settlement house.

An "outpost camp" is a laboratory for the application of skills taught at day camp. In the outpost camp, campers practice such skills as axemanship, cooking, nature lore, camp making, outfitting, mapping, and first aid. The duration of an outpost hike may extend from half-day or 1-day trial trips to 3-day undertakings. Needless to say, in any camping situation a minimum of gear should be carried. The following items are suggested for an outpost hike to supply a group of ten:

1 axe
5 small tents
1 water bucket
1 folding shovel
1 camp cook kit
10 sleeping bags
10 ponchos
1 first aid kit

Other suggested items are: a lantern, inflatable mattresses, water bag, kerosene stove, messkits, wash basin, all-purpose jackknife, and a tent (9 by 12 feet) for headquarters.

Fire Building

Safety measures. In building a fire, it is advisable to select a spot that is clear of underbrush and overhanging branches and is removed from tree trunks. Leaf mold should be removed, since the fire can burn for days and can travel quite far; the danger of starting a forest fire is to be considered at all times. The practice of surrounding the fire area with rocks, sand, and soil is a wise precautionary measure.

Preparatory hints. Cooking over a high flame is not advisable; it is apt to heat the food unevenly and char the cooking utensils as well. Soaping the pots prior to cooking will keep them from turning black. The use of aluminum foil as a food wrap to be placed on hot coals is highly recommended, with a double thickness to be used if the foil is of light weight.

The wood needed for the fire should be gathered in advance so that the camper will not have to leave the fire once it is lighted. Separate piles of tinder, kindling, and hardwood should be made to facilitate feeding the fire. In starting a fire, place a forked stick about 6 inches in length in the ground at about a 45-degree angle. Keep the forked end out and place a handful of tinder on it so that it is kept off the ground to permit air to infiltrate. Broken, dry, plant stalks in a vertical position are suggested to start the fire. The type of fire that is desired can then be built above this.

Altar fire. An altar fire is particularly suited for a campfire meeting for it gives off a steady light with a minimal use of fuel. Logs about three inches in diameter and three feet long should be placed parallel on the ground two feet apart. Next, others should be crisscrossed above them in a square shape. Kindling wood can then be placed on top.

Reflector fire.   This type of fire is desirable for reflecting warmth into a tent or for baking. The reflector is made by forcing two small logs about one and a half feet apart into the ground at a short angle away from the fire. Logs are then placed one on top of the other to comprise a wall which reflects the heat from a small tepee fire.

Tepee fire.   This simple type of fire provides a quick-burning fire since there is a good draft. Furthermore, it can be used as the foundation for other types of fires. Kindling wood plus some hardwood is stacked as a teepee. A few whittled shavings from the end of each twig should be lit, as this causes the fire to spread more readily to the other portions.

Extinguishing the fire.   To assure fire safety, campers should be trained to kill glowing coals with water and cover the fire area with soil.

Camp Program Planning

The camping program should be varied, flexible, and comprehensive. Activities that lend themselves to the camp's natural setting should be emphasized. This is not meant to preclude the use of sports, games, and physical education activities; however, the unique atmosphere of camp warrants the stressing of such activities as nature lore, campfire activities, hiking, trail-blazing, nature crafts, pageants, ceremonials, and Indian lore. At the outset of the camp have a general orientation meeting in which the campers are introduced to camp personnel and camp policies and programs. A preprepared camp schedule will serve as a guide to the staff and help them chart their agendas. But rainy weather programs should be worked out in advance so that worthwhile and meaningful programs can be provided. Campers can be informed of any alterations in the schedule during the morning assembly, which follows the flag raising, warmup exercises, and cleanup period.

Special Events

The Program Planning chapter outlines in detail the components of program-planning for special events. This section will highlight those special events particularly appropriate to the camp setting. It is understood that the imaginations of camp leaders will create other events that are especially suited to their situations and more in keeping with the interests of their groups.

Splash parties	Fly tying
Socials and parties	Bait-casting exhibitions
Storytelling	Marksmanship
Quiz shows	Nature expeditions
Forums	Water pageants
Barbecues	Treasure and scavenger hunts
Tournaments	Field trips (farms, canneries)

Hikes (short or overnight)	Canoe trips
Explorations	Campfire programs:
Fishing trips	camp sings
Trail laying	first-night campfire
Axemanship	candlelight ceremonials
Knot tying	campfire dramatization of a hero/
	heroine of the region
	closing and awards ceremonials

Camp Administration

Camps are best run democratically, and many camps operate with the assistance of a committee of campers under the sponsorship of an adult leader. The committee is chosen by a duly conducted election. This "camp council," as it is called, can be of inestimable assistance to the camp director. The group works out any plans or problems pertaining to the camp program. A camper's infractions against the rules can also be handled by this council.

The camp director is the responsible head of the camp program and the leaders who conduct the activities. It is the director's duty to interview and to hire the members of the staff, to consult with them in the organization of the camp program, to channel and direct their efforts, to conduct round table meetings, and to impart needed information. For instance, staff should be duly informed of terms of employment including duties, salary, hours, and vacation or sick time. The business side of camp direction may include the purchasing of equipment, food and menu planning, kitchen management, the overseeing of the refreshment stand and trading post, and the supervision of a postal service for campers.

If the camp is of sufficient size, an assistant director may be employed, responsible for many of the duties that would normally belong to the director. In addition, the assistant director may be given some special leadership assignment or added supervisory duties. Next in order comes the specialist who supervises a specific activity area (music, arts and crafts, waterfront). Many camps operate on the ratio of one counselor for every eight to ten campers.

Trial camp weekends are advertised to attract potential campers. In a children's camp, it is desirable for a representative of the camp to have direct contact with the parents of each camper. The use of camp reunions— father-and-son, and mother-and-daughter parties—is also beneficial. In addition, pamphlets, letters, camp newspapers and magazines, demonstrations, exhibitions, movies, slides, and photographs will keep parents informed.

At least one full-time nurse should be available to authorize the medical examinations of applicants and handle day-to-day medical needs. All camp staff should have completed an American Red Cross First Aid course in order to handle any emergency that arises. All should have certification in CPR (cardiopulmonary resuscitation).

Emergencies and Precautions

It is necessary that camp staff be informed of likely emergencies and what to do in response to them. The danger of fire should be recognized in view of the fact that the camp is surrounded by easily ignited trees and log structures. Fire fighting equipment should be periodically checked. If tents are used, care should be taken that they are fire retardant. A fire patrol should be organized consisting of staff and campers from each section of the camp. Periodic fire drills should be required to help familiarize the fire patrol and the campers with the procedures to be followed should a fire arise.

Beyond fire safety, there are a number of other safety measures to be observed. Adequate first aid equipment must be assured. Certified lifeguards should be equipped with catamarans and life buoys and should have clear visibility of the swimming area, unblocked by trees or cabins. The telephone numbers of forest rangers, physicians, and hospitals should be posted at all telephones. To insure complete accessibility for these service personnel, it is essential that there be clearly visible maps indicating the region in which the camp is situated and the area occupied by the camp, with its roads and paths prominently marked.

Missing Camper

To prevent campers from being lost, have each counselor or leader be responsible for a designated number of campers and make a periodic check of these campers. Should any group of campers leave the camp for a hike or an overnight trip, the names of each camper making the trip should be filed at the camp office. Not only should periodic checks be made of the number on the trip, but a responsible person should be placed at the head of the group and another at the rear. At any waterfront area or pool, safeguards should include the use of the "buddy" system and the presence of an approved lifeguard.

HIKING

Hiking is a form of outdoor recreation that can be fitted to the participant's interests and abilities. It can be strenuous or moderate; it can be solo or in a group, and hiking is inexpensive. Hiking as an exercise reduces obesity and the likelihood of illness. Also, activities associated with hiking (backpacking, wood chopping) improve muscle strength and toning. The opportunity for variety is built into the hiking experience, for there are a myriad number of hiking destinations: historical spots, lookouts, state parks, forests, lakes, caves. Self-reliance is encouraged through a number of activities associated with hiking, such as map reading, cooking, fire building, and coping with adverse weather conditions.

Outward Bound

Nowhere are the self-reliance and character-building aspects of outdoor recreation more evident than in Outward Bound experiences. Outward Bound programs incorporate challenging nature adventures that are designed to force participants back upon their own resources; these include the "Burma Bridge," rope courses, tree stump jumps, mountain climbing, and stretcher rescues. All participants experience the "solo," where for two days and nights individuals are on their own with only periodic interruptions by supervisors. Participants learn a great deal about themselves through Outward Bound—their strengths, their weaknesses, their ability to work as a team, to persist in light of hardship, etc. While Outward Bound is popular with people of all ages and backgrounds, it is often specifically prescribed as rehabilitation for young criminal offenders; accustomed to hiding behind a facade of harshness and game playing, they are forced to come to terms with their own vulnerability and dependence on others while on an Outward Bound experience. Though costs range from $250 to $1200, Outward Bound offers considerable financial aid for those in need on a first-come, first-serve basis. It offers 4- to 26-day courses and is international in scope, including trips in Africa, Asia, Europe, Australia, and the Pacific. For further information, contact Outward Bound at 1-800-243-8520 or write 384 Field Point Road, Greenwich, CT 06830.

Types of Hikes

Interest in hiking can be increased by giving the hike a special destination and purpose. Collectors' hikes afford an opportunity to collect butterflies, insects, leaves, birds' eggs, and so on. Nature hikes can be used to investigate insects, animals, flowers, nests, and trees. Exploring hikes are conducted to search for the "unknown." Get-together hikes are undertaken by at least two groups who plan a common rendezvous after starting from different points. "Visit" hikes afford the opportunity for an exchange of visits between organized camps. Trail-blazing hikes are made over a new trail with a campsite laid out at the other end. Hiking enthusiasts are often attracted to cross-country skiing and the access to wide open spaces and exploration. Cave exploration, or spelunking, is an adventurous form of hiking; there are an estimated 30,000 caves in the United States.

Outfitting the Hiker

Simplicity and compactness of gear are to be given primary consideration when outfitting for hiking. Since the shoulders can support weight most efficiently, the use of a knapsack is effective. The importance of properly fitting shoes should be emphasized; use a high-top shoe that provides ample room for the toes while giving a snug fit at the heel and the hollow part of the longitudinal arch of the foot. Woolen socks are preferred, since they absorb perspiration best and ease irritation. For those whose feet blister readily, cotton hose can be worn underneath woolen ones. The clothing to be worn while hiking should be suitable to the season; ample comfort should result without overheating or chilling. Wherever possible, the use of dehydrated foods is recommended; not only are they less weight to carry, they also add variety to the meals. A first-aid kit should contain the usual items, plus talcum powder for irritations, a snake-bite kit (if the region is known for poisonous snakes), a metal coat hanger to be used for splinting, and a triangular bandage that serves multiple purposes in first aid.

Hiking Etiquette

If private property is used on a portion of the hike, permission should be secured from the owner. No attempt should be made to destroy branches or in general any flora or fauna. It is usually preferable to hike cross-country rather than to use highways. If it should be necessary to use highways, walk the left side of the road and in single file. Wear light-colored clothing if hiking in dusk or at night; use a flashlight to warn on-coming motorists. Clothes with reflector markings should be worn in the darkness. Whenever possible, the hiking plan should be to reach the destination before dusk. Needless to say, hitchhiking is illegal and dangerous, so stay on foot.

Organizing a Hiking Group

When there are enough candidates, added interest can be achieved by setting up organized hiking groups. The characteristics to consider in designing a successful hiking group are:

Congeniality and informality
Varied occupations and interests among the hikers to promote more social stimulation
Diverse leaders with expertise in different aspects of hiking
Variety of trips to sustain interest (e.g., weekend trips, joint trips with other hiking groups)
Adherence to scheduling

Spring and fall are usually the most suitable seasons for hiking, since the weather is neither too warm nor too cold. Still, the summer and winter months must not be entirely discounted, for they are often periods when highly interesting hiking trips may be taken.

Hiking Activities

Orienteering.   Activities that can be conducted on hikes are unlimited. One such activity is orienteering. In orienteering hikers follow a battery of instructions—natural landmarks and distances to be traveled—with the use of a compass and map to find an undisclosed location. Competition is often introduced between individuals or teams to complete the assignment first within a given time. The scouting movement and the military have contributed to the interest in orienteering.

When fixing one's location in orienteering, the map should be turned so that magnetic north lines up with the compass needle. One should bear in mind that true north and magnetic north differ in many sectors. Should a compass not be available, it is possible to spot north with the aid of a watch and the sun. By holding the watch so that the direction of the hour hand points toward the sun, south will be found by cutting in half the space between the hour hand and twelve; this will hold true for the morning and afternoon. During the noon hour, south will be in line with the shadow cast by holding a matchstick at the hour hand. An allowance should be made for the one-hour advance in daylight savings.

Fitness trails. Fitness trails, a natural addition to hiking trails, have added a new appeal to the hiking experience. The fitness trail—or "par course" as it is otherwise called—entails anywhere from twelve to twenty-four stopping points that serve as exercise stations. At each exercise station, a sign tells the exercise to be done and the number of repetitions. Obstacles can be included in the par course by incorporating barriers to be climbed over or crawled under. Par courses can be improvised or purchased commercially from a number of suppliers. The par course is a lifetime leisure skill because it is self-directed and can be adapted to any fitness level. With the continued rising interest in fitness, par courses have become increasingly popular. Parks and recreation departments and industrial recreation programs have provided par courses; industrial par courses allow workers to pursue a self-paced fitness program in the context of their workday and other obligations.

Nature-lore Hiking

Since nature study is so integral to the significance of a hiking experience, the following section is devoted exclusively to the description of naturalist activities on hikes. Extensive information is provided on how recreation leaders can integrate the qualities and techniques of the naturalist into their leadership styles.

The nature hike. Nature lore is essentially an outdoor activity, and most of the instruction can be effected in connection with organized hikes. These hikes should be conducted through "wildernesses," areas that are as primitive as possible. Such areas are usually to be found in the vicinity of summer camps, rural, and even suburban communities. In the larger towns, there may be parks, set aside long ago, which still retain many of the characteristics of the virgin woods. In many urban settings, there are also tiny nooks and corners, often close to industrial areas, where neglect has allowed them to "go back to nature" and which are sometimes surprisingly interesting. The capable naturalist makes use of whatever resources he or she can find.

Hikes are planned and conducted, as far as possible, in the spirit of adventurous exploration. They are motivated by a purpose that is determined by the desires of the participants and announced beforehand by the naturalist.

The naturalist gives the hike a sense of purpose by first stating clearly a definite objective and leading the participants into an area where that objective is most easily reached. (The naturalist might say, "Today we will go to the east side of Sugar Loaf Mountain and look for ginseng. There are other choice plants to be found there as well.") Whatever may be the primary objective of the hike, it is very likely that something else may well be more vividly remembered. Possibly these unexpected developments are the most significant features of any hike.

Related outcomes. The objectives of a hike vary with the seasons, but there is no time when nature is not interesting. Consecutive hikes are directed into different and contrasting areas. One day will be spent wandering in the shade of an upland forest, another day will witness a journey through a swamp.

The naturalist takes it for granted that the beginner sees the woods as a strange place; even, indeed, as a forbidding one. In the minds of many there lurk tales of fierce animals, poisonous plants and reptiles, and vast, gloomy spaces from whence the lost never return. Therefore, the first lessons are aimed at developing a confidence in the woods. There are bound to be apprehensive questions that should be met honestly.

Conducting a hike. For much of the time on the trail, only the voice of the naturalist is required to keep the group together. At every step are interesting things to talk about, and the naturalist speaks in tones low enough so that participants must stay close enough to hear. Now and then, the naturalist directs the group to travel for a distance in complete silence.

A "headquarters" is established at a conspicuous object, such as a big tree or rock; and the group scatters in all directions while the naturalist remains at the headquarters. After about 10 minutes the naturalist blows a whistle, summoning the hikers back with whatever specimens they have found. The naturalist calls the roll, the specimens are examined and commented upon, and the journey is resumed. At the end of the hike, the naturalist summarizes briefly what they have seen, mentions by name those who have achieved outstanding observation, and thanks the group for their participation.

In conducting a hike with children, the naturalist should be attentive to the fact that unless their energy is directed, the hike can take on the characteristics of a steeplechase. To prevent this, it is suggested that for the first 10 or 15 minutes, the group march briskly in a double line with the naturalist leading the way. No effort is made to do any studying of nature at this time, and not until the objective is reached or the place of departure is far behind is the discipline relaxed. By this time, the desire to run has largely been dissipated, the group will stay together, and the naturalist can then begin the teaching of nature lore.

The explorers are led to the places where wild berries grow. They learn to collect the succulent pot herbs such as purslane or redroot pigweed, and cook them over an open fire in a tin pail. They learn how to make tea from the hemlock or sassafras. They learn to recognize the nut-bearing trees. It begins to appear that the forest is not such a dreadful place after all, but one filled with a variety of good foods.

But mere identification of a plant or rock is far from enough to be of use to the hikers unless they are able to relate it to something familiar. A strangely colored pebble may be just a piece of rock, but it has much greater significance if the naturalist can say something like "Here is a piece of sedimentary rock that has been rolled around on the bottom of the lake for a long time."

From this beginning, the formation of rocks can be discussed, the action of the water on formations, and so forth. Perhaps the specimen has a mineral content: "This is iron, see this rusty streak?" As nearly everyone is familiar with some phase of the vast steel industry, all the naturalist has to do is to fill in the gaps in the story. It is brought out that this iron, exposed under certain conditions to other materials found in nature, coal and limestone, becomes the well-known substance that has given its name to the steel industry.

Night hikes.   At night, nature takes on a different aspect. The wood, familiar enough in the light of day, becomes a gloomy, mysterious place upon nightfall. At most seasons of the year, it is filled with strange sounds and invisible beings. A hike in the darkness is an unforgettable experience. The usual reason for a night hike is for star study. A treeless hilltop is the best place to study the stars, a spot somewhat remote and apart, from which the entire heavens can be viewed. A good telescope is a useful adjunct to star study, but is not necessary unless the group expects to delve more deeply into the wonders of astronomy than the average naturalist is able to go. There is much of interest to be seen with the naked eye, and the naturalist points out the various constellations with the aid of a strong flashlight that sends a bright, narrow beam far into the sky.

There are legends that may be related at this time (for the mood is usually very receptive for the storyteller), legends that have come to us from two distinct sources: the deserts of Asia Minor and the plains and woodlands of America. Those of the desert nomads are the legends that have given the names to the constellations.

In addition to identifying some of the outstanding groups of stars, together with a discussion about how to tell directions at night, the hikers should learn something of the immense distances and sizes that exist in the regions beyond us. They should be made to see how the Earth, impressive though it may be, is only one tiny speck in a vast universe. Certain hikers who show more than the usual interest in star study may wish to undertake a special project. The ceiling of the clubroom or nature lodge is a suggested place upon which to reproduce the sky at night. The project is more effective if the stars can be powdered with luminous paint.

Bird walks. Bird walks are usually taken in the early morning, because the birds are most active at that time of day; but there is no point in going before it is light enough to distinguish bird colors. An isolated tree or group of trees in an open field makes an ideal spot to see birds, and it is only necessary to sit motionless nearby while the birds come and go. Occasionally, one of the hikers can be sent to investigate a strange song ringing out of a nearby thicket.

"Go see what is making that noise," says the naturalist to one of the group. "I'm not sure what it is, but I suspect it is one of the rarer warblers. Get a good look at it, note the size and the coloration, and we'll look it up."

The assignment of "individual missions" provides added incentive to the explorers who become eager to share their unique findings with the group upon their return. Bird walks are apt to be short affairs, because it is necessary to get the group back in time for breakfast. In the average locality, twenty species seen in one morning is a good number, and it is not unusual to see fifty, sixty, or more, during the season.

Insect study. Insect study is included in some nature programs and offers a tremendous field of activity. Equipped with nets and jars, the insect study group sweeps across the fields and through thickets, around and across the swamps and swales. The forenoon and late afternoon are good times to study insects. As with other forms of nature lore, interest centers on great numbers of specimens of different kinds. The research necessary in insect study is probably greater and more precise than any other field. Each specimen should be carefully examined, for even the commonest butterflies occur in rare and various forms. A specialty such as insect study may lead some to make it a lifelong hobby.

Mammals. It is virtually impossible to observe many wild animals on the average nature hike since the group is apt to make so much noise that the creatures go into hiding at their approach, and because many of them are nocturnal and are asleep at the time when hikes usually take place. There are more animals around than the casual passerby can even be aware of. Almost every brushy hillside supports a family of rabbits; woodchucks live in or near the grassy meadows; mink and muskrats inhabit the sluggish streams that are not polluted by waste; and the skunks make a living wherever they happen to be. Nut-bearing trees attract the squirrels, while deer are known to live within sight of metropolitan areas. Mice, several species of them, are fairly abundant everywhere; and tiny shrews are much more common than is generally thought. The raccoon, the opossum, and the wily fox are not rare. But, in the course of a hike with the average group, few of these creatures are ever seen. Often, however, their tracks are abundant, their dens easily found, and their presence easily established.

Trees. The ages and experience of the study group will determine just how precise they will be in identifying trees. Those of the age group found in primary grades may find it enough of a challenge to distinguish a maple from an oak. Older students will wish to know more; they will expect to learn the differences between varieties of the same species. It is easier to begin the study of trees while they are in leaf, because the shape and colors of the leaves are often the best means of identification; the lesson is only half taught, however, if there is no effort made to identify them in the winter.

Axes and hatchets have little place on hikes of this sort, largely because there is always the temptation to hack and wound the trees. Examples of the results of this practice are found in all woodlands frequented by irresponsible hikers; the scarred and decayed trunks can serve as object lessons.

The trees will likely be the oldest things that nature students will encounter. It is not impossible to find oaks, elms, and pines that have endured since the early days of this country.

Plant life. Very likely, the greatest interest in plant life will be in those that have the brightest blossoms. Many such plants are abundant enough so that they can be collected without any danger of extinction, but some of them are rare enough to prohibit picking altogether. There are many settings where the collecting of plant life of all kinds is strictly forbidden. In the average rural area, there will be no enforced restrictions except those which the naturalist imposes.

It has been suggested previously that many wild plants can be cooked as food. There are a few that are unwholesome as food while possessing value as sources of medicine. Certain mushrooms are excellent foods. Unless the naturalist is especially competent, it is wise to leave all of them alone, since some are highly poisonous.

Nature handicraft. Nature lore lends itself easily to various forms of handicraft. Animal and bird tracks found in the mud can be cast in plaster of paris and incorporated into unusual book ends or paperweights. Interesting colorful plaques can be made of leafcasts. There are transparent plastic materials in which can be imbedded showy insects and blossoms to form the basis for attractive costume jewelry. Materials for basketry, such as grasses, reeds, and the like, are easily found in nature. The ingenious incorporation of nature with arts and crafts can constitute a worthwhile and productive portion of an integrated recreation program. Due to the scenic beauty involved in nature lore, photography is a popular adjunct activity to hiking. These pictures can, in turn, be framed by nature's materials, such as bark or reeds.

Museums.   One of the outgrowths of the nature lore program is frequently a museum. Specimens of all sorts are bound to accumulate wherever a group of nature students gather and the development of the museum is largely a matter of mounting, classifying, and arranging the material at hand. However competent the student curators may prove to be, the naturalist should take an active interest in the proceedings, making certain that all labels are accurate and that the entire display reflects neatness and order. The size, arrangement, and scope of the museum necessarily should follow the dictates of the available space. Often, a camp will dedicate an entire building as a nature lodge; a club may be able to set aside a small room for the purpose, while a school may have to be content with using a nature display to brighten an obscure corner. A very large space is not especially recommended because it will require so much material to make a good showing.

Specimens can be of many sorts: butterflies, moths, and other insects; different kinds of woods, showing both the bark and a section of the heartwood; samples of rocks; and pressed leaves and flowering plants mounted on sheets of cardboard. Charts for display can be drawn up tracing the stages from the raw materials to their finished products. Space can be devoted to Indian relics if any of the group are inclined in that direction, for archeology is a part of nature lore.

The walls of the museum are good places to display lists such as these: "Birds Seen This Year," "Trees and Shrubs," "Plants," "Insects Found."

These lists may be hand-printed, with good black ink, on long sheets of white cardboard; include the name of the species, when found, and by whom. In connection with the name of the finder, it is well to add some designation, like an address, or group number. Here are a couple of samples:

Cardinal: July 8. John Welton, Troop 27, Silver Lake.
Black Cohosh: August 12. Jane Phillips, Bumblebee Cabin.

These lists are started from scratch every season. They become actively growing entities and keep their appeal to the very end, as every student strives to discover new and strange items to record upon them. The specimens of the museum remain the properties of the donors. Because some of the materials that are displayed will eventually be taken home as souvenirs, there will be more or less constant replacement.

The nature trail.   Under certain situations, the development of a nature trail makes an excellent project. It is especially adaptable to summer camping, although it should be effective in any place where signs and labels can be posted. Briefly, a nature trail is simply a well-marked path winding its way through a woodland alongside which are signs that identify and explain the many things that occur there. It might be described, in effect, as a sort of outdoor museum. The labels should be neatly prepared and small enough to be relatively inconspicuous so that they remain modestly in the background. An ideal location for such a trail would be a smooth well-drained path that meanders its way in an irregular circle over gently rolling terrain terminating at the place of beginning. In its course, it should skirt a grassy glade, a small section of marsh or swale, cross a small brook over a substantial bridge, and touch the shore of a crystal clear pond. It should be 200 or 300 yards in length.

Signs should not be nailed to the trees, but displayed from posts set as close as possible to wherever the attention is directed. Small objects may be more precisely located by wires or strings stretched between them and the signs that relate to them. The labels can be typewritten or printed on small file cards. They are tacked to thin, soft wood, such as orange-crate material. There is nothing wrong in having a signboard large enough to contain three or four labels or even more if they can be hidden slightly by bushes. Great care should be taken that the labels do not mar the natural effect. The cards may be waterproofed after they are printed by dipping them in melted paraffin. If so treated, they should last for two seasons.

THE NATURALIST

Nature is so vast that it is often taken for granted or overlooked altogether. It is for this reason that a naturalist is needed to help the layperson appreciate nature's many facets. The naturalist may be a teacher, a hobbyist in a club, counselor in a camp, or a professional scientist.

The naturalist referred to in these pages is of semiprofessional standing and views nature in its entirety, rather than one who limits his or her studies to a specific field.

Training and Role of the Naturalist

To become a naturalist able to instruct nature lore, it is well to have a background of biology equivalent to that taught in the average high school. Coupled with this should be some field experience, such as exploring the woods and fields, seeing what there is to see, and developing one's observation. Beginning naturalists should permit their minds to ask all kinds of questions since, later on, their students will be doing that very thing. "What is this plant? What is this insect? Why is it found here? What is it doing?"

At first, of course, many questions will go unanswered. Possibly, too, there will be a tendency to jump to incorrect conclusions that will have to be corrected as one's knowledge and experience develops. Every good public library has reference books that the naturalist can refer to while assembling a personal library. Talking with other naturalists often clears up puzzling problems. The merit-badge programs of both Boy and Girl Scouts are invaluable in getting a start as a naturalist. Gradually, a proficiency in recognizing some of the plants, trees, birds, and insects is developed: and the neophyte naturalist is ready to begin teaching.

The questions raised by participants are the best form of education for the naturalist. It is often quite possible, when leading the same group on successive hikes, to enlist the participants themselves in the research process. This process is especially useful since it has the added value of giving the participants a responsible part in the program.

Approaches to nature lore. Because Americans are traditionally an outdoor people, a general knowledge of what the outdoors holds has become a part of the national culture. Hunting, fishing, hiking, skiing, and camping are sports that take one to the primitive environment of the wilderness, the enjoyment of which is greatly enhanced if one has learned how fully to appreciate it.

Since much of our literature is filled with references to objects found in nature, nature lore has great potential for integration with literary arts programs. A spruce thicket, for example, may mean merely a grove of trees to some; but those who have fought their way through a tangled mass of resistant branches armed with sharp, fragrant needles, know exactly what an author attempts to convey. It can be said that nature lore has an important cultural approach.

There is a second approach, which we will call the esthetic. Nature is filled with that which we call beauty. It is found in the sunrise, the sunset, the rainbow, in the bright colors of the flowers, the birds, and the insects. Closely akin to beauty is the majesty that is found in a noble old tree, a river, or a mountain. Nature has many moods, ranging from the cool tranquility of the moonlit night to the terrible anger of the storm.

The third approach of nature lore appeals to the practical. After the students have gone about with the naturalist on several hikes, and have observed and examined all of the more conspicuous features of the landscape, it will begin to occur to them that most of the things they have seen bear direct influence on man's very existence. "Why is this land so barren?" "Because improper agricultural methods have depleted the soil." "Why are there no fish or any other aquatic life in this stream?" "Because the waste products of industrial plants have poisoned it." It is at this point that the phrase "The Conservation of Natural Resources" begins to take on significance. These trees, these many plants, these rocks that contain important minerals, this fertile soil, this pure water—all are resources, all are important.

HOSTELING

The term "hosteling" stems from the word "hostel," an inn or lodge for overnight guests. Hosteling is a form of travel that stresses informality, affordability, and camaraderie. Hostels are a series of shelters along the traveler's road, the major intent of which is to create an atmosphere where people can easily meet and learn about each other.

American Youth Hostels, Inc. (AYH) provides youth hostels in this country and assists in the development of new ones in the United States, worldwide. There are approximately 4500 hostels in 61 countries and more than 200 in the United States. Most states also have AYH chartered councils. In addition, AYH assists its members in their travels abroad by planning sponsored trips and by encouraging individual hosteling. These culturally enriching travel opportunities are made available at minimal costs. AYH is affiliated with the International Youth Hostel Federation, which recognizes all AYH youth and adult passes worldwide.

Hostels are modest accommodations, usually situated in farm structures, barns, cabins, or lodges specially constructed for this purpose. In addition, garages, grange halls, YWCAs and YMCAs, college dormitories, and community halls are also used as hostels. Hosteling is sponsored by public-spirited citizens—representing schools, service clubs, churches, and civic and recreational organizations—who recognize the great value of this wholesome activity. Those who have the facilities and leadership necessary to start a hostel and are interested in doing so, should contact AYH. The preferable distance is 15 miles between camps, with the hostel itself on a secondary road removed from auto and pedestrian congestion. The hostel site should have a pure water supply and possess desirable scenic and recreational features. Contact can be made with AYH at National Headquarters, 132 Spring Street, New York, NY, 10012. AYH issues a calendar of events and its *Handbook* to all passholders.

Hostels are not only for students; travelers by car can also stop at hostels for the informal sociability they provide. The Elderhostel program has been designed so that older adults can travel between hostels, each of which offers a uniquely different educational program. Since simplicity and ease of travel are basic to hosteling, travelers keep baggage to a minimum: typical items include the hostel pass, eating utensils, change of clothes, and a towel.

The hostel recreation program should be as diverse and balanced as any other recreation program. The following is a list recommended for the hostel recreation program:

First aid instruction
Make first aid kit
Care of bicycle
Handicrafts (activities in repairing hostel; making equipment)
Meal planning
    Nutrition
    Mathematics (planning quantities, prices)
    Use of dehydrated foods
Camp cooking
    Fire making
    Use of axe
    Aluminum foil cooking

Trip planning
    Secure maps from Department of Conservation, National Park Service, or U.S. Geological Survey
    Topography
    Geography (map out bicycling and hiking trails)
    Mathematics (calculate distance to be covered)
    Trail blazing
    Reading accounts of similar trips
    Correspondence with AYH Headquarters or Chartered Council
Nature lore
Science
    Astronomy—how to find way by stars; how to find north with a watch and the sun
    Botany—flora en route
    Zoology—animal world en route
    Hygiene—how to care for overworked feet and legs: how to relax
    Body mechanics—how to carry knapsack with a minimum of strain
National and international relations
Language study
Recreational activities at hostels:
    Folk dancing
    Square dancing
    Social dancing
    Social recreation
    Group singing
    Arts and crafts
    Storytelling
    Group discussions
Photography (picture record of trip)

ROWING, CANOEING, AND SAILING

Boating activities have become increasingly popular leisure pursuits. As an introduction for the recreation professional, this section outlines the key fundamentals in boating. However, it should be understood from the outset that safe operation of any boat requires "hands on" instruction from skilled boat operators. For sailing in particular, instruction by a competent teacher is highly important. Free U.S. Power Squadron classes are offered primarily in the coastal areas in the safe handling of motorboats and sailboats.

Rowing

While not a very difficult skill to acquire, rowing can be learned more readily if broken down into fundamentals and learned progressively. These instructions are but preliminary to their practical application on the water.

Fundamentals. Whenever feasible, one should enter a rowboat from the side with both hands on the gunwales. The first step should be somewhat equidistant between the gunwales to help keep the boat on an even keel. This holds true also when entering from the bow or stern.

In determining the length of the oar, measure the width of the oarsman's thwart from gunwale to gunwhale plus the freeboard distance from the water line to the gunwale. Ash or spruce oars are most commonly used. The grip on the oar should be firm enough to keep it from turning.

Rowing calls for a rhythmical coordination of the entire body. The parts of the body that are used most prominently are the hands, wrists, arms, legs, feet, and back. The back is especially important since its pull can ease the strain on the other parts. The legs should be braced.

The fundamentals of rowing can be conveniently divided into four phases:

Canoeing

Canoe size and care. Canoes come in varied sizes, ranging from 11 to 35 feet. As a utility canoe for juniors, the 16-foot craft is highly recom-

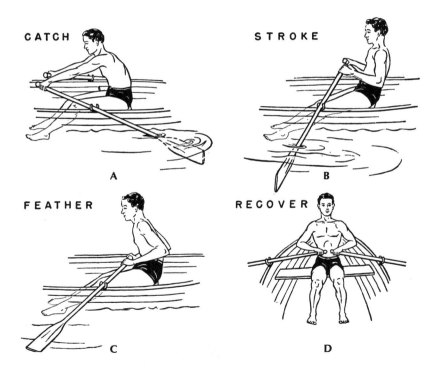

FIGURE 10–1 (a) Catch—when the blades strike the water at right angles with the arms fully extended and the legs bent. (b) Stroke—the motion started under catch is continued with greater vigor as the blades are pulled through the water in a vertical position until they surface; the legs are extended as the back exerts a backward pull. (c) Feather—upon clearing the water, the oars are feathered by flexing the wrists backward so that the blades are parallel to the water's surface; as a result, the wind or waves will exert minimal influence on the blades. (d) Recover—the feathered oars are pulled to a position of momentary recovery with the grip positions of the oars almost touching each other

mended, while the 15-foot canoe is preferred for solo canoe mastery. The larger war canoe is useful for crew or group canoeing, competitive canoeing, or cruising.

The 16-foot canoe can be used to accommodate up to three paddlers so long as there is no equipment to be carted. Mass training opportunities are afforded by the war canoe with its 35-foot length. The 17-foot or 18-foot canoe is often used for adult groups, while the 16-foot size is usually best for youths.

On land, the canoe should be kept from contact with sand, mud, gravel, or rocks. When afloat, canoeists must look out for submerged rocks and tree stumps. If damage occurs, canvas-covered canoes possess the advantage that they can be repaired and patched easily. Wooden canoes are somewhat more rugged. Canoes of aluminum or sheet metal can take even more rough usage. On the other hand, they are noisy in rough water.

When refinishing the canoe, remove the old paint with sandpaper or paint and varnish remover. The addition of paint or varnish to previous coats will add weight to the craft. Finishes with linseed oil are not recommended for canvas canoes since oil tends to weaken the cotton fibers in the canvas.

Canoes should be stored on racks in the upside-down position. A shed or covering will shield the canoes while they are stored from the sun. If the canoe is used in salt water, hosing down with fresh water will help to protect the finish against the salt-water action.

Paddle selection. It is commonly recommended that the size of a single-blade paddle should be 6 inches shorter than the paddler. Another way to measure is to have the grip reach the eye level as the blade is turned downward. Paddles can be purchased in stock sizes from 4 to 6 feet in length at intervals of 6 inches.

Spruce paddles are light in weight, with the wood highly suitable for a camp paddle construction program. Ash makes a heavier paddle with its characteristic strength. Maple is similar to ash in strength but has a tendency toward warping unless given special care.

The double-blade paddle provides a readily learned and efficient means of handling a canoe. It is particularly suitable for newcomers to canoeing since they can make more rapid progress with this type of paddle.

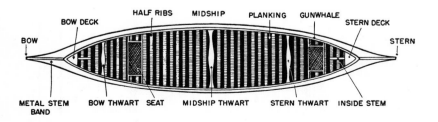

FIGURE 10–2 The canoe

The double-blade paddle length should be determined by the width of the canoe; the usual lengths vary from 8 to 9 ½ feet.

Canoeing strokes. The basic strokes are considered in the order of difficulty for the learner. They will be treated briefly here in view of the vast variety of subjects to be covered. More detailed information can be secured from any of the books listed as source material at the end of this chapter.

1. Bow stroke and back water stroke. The bow stroke is used by the paddler up front when there are two handling the canoe. For the right-handed person, the top of the paddle should be held shoulder high in the left hand as the right hand grasps the shaft and extends forward as far as possible. The stroke should be straight backward and close to the gunwale.

The back water stroke is the reverse of the bow stroke. With the blade as far back as possible, the right arm presses downward until the starting position of the bow stroke is reached. Both the bow stroke and back water stroke are completed as they reach the vertical position alongside the body.

2. Pull-to. In the pull-to, the starting position is the same as for the bow stroke except the blade is parallel to the gunwale. Reach out sidewards with the paddle and pull the canoe toward the paddle. Force should be exerted by both arms. Repeated stroking can be achieved best by turning the blade so that it is perpendicular to the gunwale as it is pushed and pulled until the paddle returns to the starting position. This stroke pulls the canoe closer to the side where the stroking is executed.

3. Pushover stroke. The pushover stroke is carried out in reverse fashion of the pull-to. It moves the canoe away from the paddle.

4. Sweep stroke and reverse. The sweep stroke is begun in similar fashion to the bow stroke with the sweep executed by reaching out close to the bow and making an arc. The size of the arc can be determined by the distance that the bow is to be turned away from the paddler's position without loss of momentum; the reverse is achieved by stroking the very opposite of the "sweep."

5. "J" stroke. The "J" stroke is a stern stroke employing the starting position of the bow stroke. Since the stroke up to this point causes the bow to turn away from the side of the paddler, the rounding out of the stroke to simulate a "J" causes the canoe to straighten its course. At the completion of the bow stroke, the right hand is near the side of the body with the left arm extended over the water. The "J" portion is executed by turning the blade counterclockwise with the left hand and by pushing away with the right hand as the left hand pulls toward the left.

Sailing

Tacking. Perhaps the most intriguing part of sailing to the landlubber is the problem of how a boat can sail in a southerly direction when the wind is coming from the south. This brings up the question of tacking,

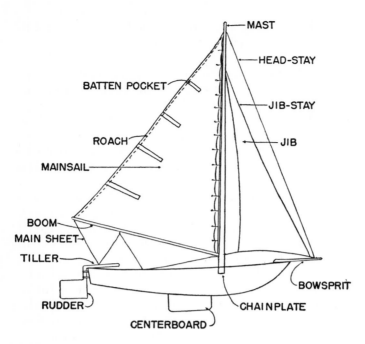

FIGURE 10-3 The sailboat

which refers to a zigzag course to be taken in order to reach the southerly destination. Obviously, a boat cannot sail directly against the wind. On the other hand, by tacking or trying to sail close-hauled (with the sail pulled in close to the boat), the boat can sail fairly close to the wind. Through a series of tacks with the wind directing its force first on one side of the sail and then on the other, the boat will gradually approach its destination.

When sailing in water where there is no current, tacks of equal length are usually taken. In the event the boat encounters a current, then the length of the tacks should vary. If the current is flowing in the general direction one is sailing, then the longer tack would be the one that can take fuller advantage of this aid toward one's goal. Should the current flow against the boat's destination, then the short tack would be the one that meets the greater strength of the current; meeting the force of a current at an angle will set a craft back less than if head on. Maneuvering the boat so that its direction is changed when heading into the wind is referred to as "coming about." A jib takes place when the sail shifts from one side to the other while the wind is blowing from the stern or rear of the boat. Jibing calls for skillful handling, or else the force of the jibe may cause damage to the rigging.

Sail pull. Another question that is often raised is "Why is a boat able to move when its sails are in a close-hauled position?" The answer lies in a combination of forces. As the wind strikes the sail at an angle, it also creates a vacuum pull on the other side of the sail. The two combine to give the boat a forward pulling force. The fastest sailing point is attained when the wind strikes the sail at a right angle or 90° angle. Resistance to lateral sway is provided by the centerboard or keel, which contributes thereby toward the boat's forward motion.

Adjusting sail to the wind. Some sailboat people recommend that the boom (pole at bottom of the sail) should be in line with the wind pennant at the top of the mast. While more advanced sailboat enthusiasts will want to develop their feel of the boat and make adjustments accordingly, this piece of advice will prove of some assistance. This hint is more accurate and useful when the boat is close-hauled while sailing close to the wind. It becomes less so as the wind approaches from the side (abeam) or slightly to the rear (abaft the beam).

There are varied rigs among sailboats. A boat with a cat rig has one sail with one line or sheet to control it; a sloop has two sails, a mainsail or larger sail and a jib or small triangular sail before the mast. If the mainsail is three-sided, it is a marconi rig. If it is foursided, it is gaff-rigged.

Figures 10–4 through 10–6 will serve to show how to adjust the sail in keeping with differing wind directions.

The helm. The helm is that portion of the sailboat where the tiller or steering device of the craft is situated. Varying the resistance of the rudder against the water causes the boat to turn. A turn of the tiller toward the left will cause the bow of the boat to head toward the right. Conversely, forcing the tiller toward the right will steer the boat toward the left. Facility at handling the tiller and familiarity with these maneuverings will come readily through practice.

Everything on board ship should be shipshape and properly stored. Moreover, the lines and gear throughout the craft and particularly at the helm should be free of encumbrances. A knock-down breeze may come along without any warning; inability to respond immediately by letting out the sail and heading over with the rudder may mean a swamped boat. Needless to say, the line attached to the mainsail should never be tied down.

FIGURE 10–4 Close-hauled—with the wind coming almost directly ahead, the boat is close-hauled with the main and jib sheets pulled in close to the boat. The boat can then be steered close to the wind.

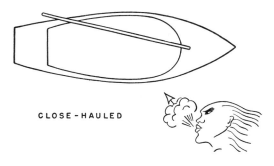

CLOSE-HAULED

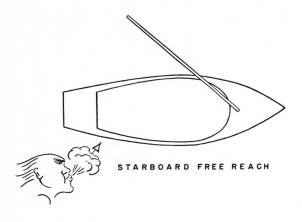

STARBOARD FREE REACH

FIGURE 10–5 Starboard free reach—when the direction is considerably away from the wind, we have a starboard free reach.

RUNNING BEFORE THE WIND

FIGURE 10–6 Running before the wind—should the wind's direction be from the rear or near it, we have running before the wind.

Safety and First Aid

Boat safety. The rapid growth in popularity of boating and sailing has exceeded the expectations of most enthusiasts. There is little doubt that if handled in a sane manner, boating and sailing can be safely conducted. On the debit side we note that hundreds of lives are lost in water transport accidents. It is a fact that a great proportion of these deaths occurred in the handling of small craft.

The ability to swim is highly desirable for anyone who handles a boat, and particularly so in handling canoes or sailboats. The navigator should be aware of how to handle the boat under all conditions and know the maximum number of occupants the boat can hold. The boat should be checked for defects and leaks, and an approved boat cushion that doubles as a life preserver or a vest-type of life preserver should be on board for every passenger. Should it have a motor, added precautions are necessary; it should be checked thoroughly before one starts out. Maritime regulations require a fire extinguisher on boats that are motor-driven.

Suggestions for Safety[1]

1. Do not overload. Maintain adequate freeboard at all times; consider the sea conditions, the duration of the trip, the predicted weather, and the experience of the operator.

2. Be especially careful when operating in any area where swimmers might be. They are often difficult to see.

3. Watch your wake. It might capsize a small craft; it can damage boats or property along the shore. You are responsible. Pass through anchorages only at minimum speed.

4. Keep firefighting and lifesaving equipment in good condition and readily available at all times.

5. Consider what action you would take under various emergency conditions—man overboard, fog, fire, a stove-in plank or other bad leak, motor breakdown, bad storm, collision.

6. Have an adequate anchor and sufficient line to assure good holding in a blow (at least six times depth of water).

7. Know the various distress signals. A recognized distress signal used on small boats is to raise and lower slowly and repeatedly the arms outstretched to each side.

8. Always have up-to-date chart (or charts) of your area on board.

9. Always instruct at least one other person on board in the rudiments of boat handling in case you are disabled—or fall overboard.

10. Water ski only when you are well clear of all other boats, bathers, and obstructions and there are two persons in the boat to maintain a proper lookout.

11. Before departing on a boat trip, you should advise a responsible friend or relative about where you intend to cruise. Be sure that the person has a good description of your boat. Keep the person advised of any changes in your cruise plans. By doing these things, your friend or relative will be able to tell the Coast Guard where to search for you and what type of boat to look for if you fail to return. Be sure to advise the same person when you arrive so as to prevent any false alarms about your safety.

NAUTICAL TERMS

Aft or abaft—toward the rear or stern.

Abeam—at right angles with the craft's keel.

Amidships—toward the middle of a craft.

Astern—in the rear or behind a craft.

Awash—on a level with the water.

Beach—to drive onto a beach or strand a craft.

Beam—extreme breadth or width of a craft.

Belay—a pin or cleat around which a line is fastened.

Bow—forward part of a craft; also the prow or stem.

Calk—to drive oakum or cotton into the seams of a craft.

Capsize—to upset or overturn.

1. Excerpted from *Pleasure Craft*, U.S. Coast Guard, 1966.

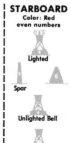

← PORT | **STARBOARD →**

Yield right-of-way to boats in your DANGER ZONE!

DANGER ZONE (Dead ahead to 2 points abaft your starboard beam)

REMEMBER THESE RULES

1. **OVERTAKING-PASSING:** Boat being passed has the right-of-way. **KEEP CLEAR.**
2. **MEETING HEAD ON:** Keep to the right.
3. **CROSSING:** Boat on right has the right-of-way. Slow down and permit him to pass.

WHISTLE SIGNALS

ONE LONG BLAST: Warning signal (Coming out of slip)
ONE SHORT BLAST: Pass on my port side
TWO SHORT BLASTS: Pass on my starboard
THREE SHORT BLASTS: Engines in reverse
FOUR OR MORE BLASTS: Danger signal

CHANNEL BUOY GUIDE
Entering port or going upstream

PORT SIDE Color: Black odd numbers	**MID-CHANNEL** Color: Black & White no numbers	**STARBOARD** Color: Red even numbers
Lighted	Lighted	Lighted
Can Spar	Can Spar Nun	Spar
	JUNCTION	
Unlighted Bell	Red and Black Lighted	Unlighted Bell
Unlighted Whistle	Can Spar Nun	Unlighted Whistle

STORM WARNINGS

RED FLAG Small craft (winds to 38 mph)	2 RED FLAGS Gale (up to 54 mph)	SQUARE RED FLAG—BLACK BOX (whole gale)	2 SQUARE RED FLAGS BLACK BOX (Hurricane)

USE COMMON SENSE AFLOAT

©1966

FIGURE 10–7 Saling rules and signals

Source: Outboard Boating Club of America, 1966.

Chop—sudden wind shift; choppy or turbulent water.

Cleats—a wedge-shaped piece of metal or wood on which to fasten ropes.

Crest—the top of a wave.

Deck—floor portion of a craft.

Deck, aft—behind the midportion of a craft.

Dock—a slip between two piers or alongside a pier.

Draft—depth of water needed to float a craft.

Ebb—flowing back of the tide.

Eddy—a whirlpool.

Even keel—a balanced craft with both sides equidistant from the water.

Fair—clear weather.

Fast—firmly fixed.

Fathom—six feet in length.

Fore—portions of a craft between amidship and bow.

Fore and aft—in general line with the length of a vessel.

Frame—one of the craft's ribs.

Freeboard—distance between the water line and the gunwale.

Gunwale—upper edge of a boat's side.

Heel—the amount of tilting of a sailboat when the wind causes it to lean away from an even keel.

Helm—portion of the craft from which its direction is controlled.

Jib—the small sail.

Keel—built-up timber or metal extending along the middle of a craft's bottom.

Knot—a speed designation of a nautical mile (6,080.20 feet) per hour.

Landlubber—one who spends his life on land or anyone who is awkward on a craft.

Leeward—opposite to the wind's source; opposite of windward.

Midship—middle of a craft's length.

Port—left side of a craft.

Prow—front end of a vessel.

Rudder—steering device for maneuvering a craft.

Sheet—line attached to a sail.

Skeg—afterpart of a craft's keel.

Sloop—a sailboat with two sails: a jib and a mainsail.

Starboard—right side of a craft.

Stem—bow frame connected to lower end of keel.

Stern—aft end of a craft.

Thwart—wooden reinforcements extending across a rowboat; a seat.

Tiller—attachment to the rudder for steering.

Topside—side of the hull above the water line.

Trim—readiness of a craft for sailing.

Tumble home—receding of a craft's beam as it nears the rail.

Underway—craft that has started to move.

Veer—turning or changing of the wind.

Wake—churned water left by a craft under way.

Boating-related Activities

Boating integrates well with other recreation activities. For instance, it offers opportunities for arts and crafts, such as boat painting; sail, oar, and paddle making; knot tying. Many sports activities are associated with boating. Competitive outlets are afforded through such activities as sculling, rowboating, canoeing, speedboating, and sailing. Other related sports include the following activities:

Skin and scuba diving. Prior to a scuba- or skin-diving course, the participant should be required to take a swim test, medical examination, and medical history interview. New divers also need to improve breathing ability; hyperventilation underwater may be followed by a blackout, and air embolisms can be caused by failure to exhale adequately during ascent. To insure safety, careful attention should be given to the cleaning, maintenance, and repair of equipment.

Water-skiing. The towboat operator during water skiing is basically responsible for the skier's safety. An observer is also required in the towboat. Before skiing, the skier should be well versed with the skier-operator signals. A lifebelt or jacket is to be worn by the skier at all times. The sport of aquaplaning operates along the same concept as water skiing in that a boat tows a rider; however, in aquaplaning the skier rides on a board rather than skis.

A boat used exclusively for skiing or aquaplaning should have removed from it any fittings that might snag the tow rope. The tow hitch should be solidly constructed. All boat operators should be fully informed of the regulations governing boating in their states. A speeding boat is a generator of great force, and of potential danger if not properly handled.

Windsurfing. At windsurfing sailing schools the teaching methods include the use of a land simulator (a sailboard mounted on a swivel with a complete rig of sail, wishbone boom, and mast). Early on, beginners need to learn how to position one's body and balance on the board. The basic technique involves tilting the mast forward to sail off the wind and tilting it aft to sail into the wind. For those in variable climates, the use of a wet suit can make it possible to have an extended season (the wet suit is also used in surfing). Winds in excess of 15 knots warrant postponement of plans to windsurf.

RECREATIONAL SWIMMING

Skill in swimming is one of the most essential abilities one can develop. Safe behavior in and about the water is of equal importance. In choosing a swimming site, make sure that the water is clean and the area patrolled by a skilled lifeguard. The use of the "buddy system" while swimming is particularly important when bathing in the surf or in very crowded swimming pools. Furthermore, instruction in life-saving techniques will do much toward making the individual a safer swimmer as well as a dependable companion for other swimmers.

In recreational swimming, emphasis is placed on the fun element as opposed to competitive swimming, wherein speed and winning are of prime importance. There are some unmistakable trends in swimming today, and in recreational swimming in particular. Some of the more important of these are:

1. Recognition of swimming as perhaps the most popular individual recreation activity. It is usually at or near the top as a preferred activity in recreational interest polls.
2. Increased participation on the part of both sexes.
3. A vast increase in the construction of swimming pools.
4. Continued emphasis on swimming by the American Red Cross, resulting in increase in the number of water-safety instructors. Also, the quality of the instruction has improved. There has been improvement in the analysis of swimming techniques and their application to individual swimmer's needs and abilities.

Special Events for Swim Programs

Special events are an important means of highlighting selected aspects of a recreation program. In that vein, special events within the swim program serve to draw attention to swimmers' accomplishments and stimulate interest in the swim program among the spectators. The following are some examples of special events for swim programs:

Carnival	Swimming contest
Diving contest or exhibition	Telegraphic meet
1890s to present swimsuit exhibition	Parents' night (father-and-son,
Learn-to swim program	mother-and-daughter)
Bathing beauty contest	Water ballet
Baby parade	A night in Venice
Lifesaving exhibition	Pet parade
	Stunt night

As a culminating project, the water pageant is perhaps unsurpassed. It suitability as a means of displaying the achievements of those who take part in the program makes it a highly regarded special event. In the water pageant, the sport of swimming becomes a collaborative, creative activity.

In staging a special event in the water, it is necessary to think of both participant and spectator. Where maneuverability is important to the participant, as in the case of water games, events should be staged in the shallow area of the water. Certainly, any event should be placed as close as possible to where the majority of people are seated. The swimming distance for any game should not strain the participant nor require so much time as to bore the spectator.

Swimming Games

The swimming games that follow are suitable as part of one of the special events listed above.

Watermelon polo. With teams in place, the game is started by placing the watermelon in the center of the pool equidistant from both goals (any part of the end line of the pool). The team that forces the watermelon to its opponents' end line or goal scores a point. The first team to score three points is designated the winner.

Push ball. The game of Push Ball is played similarly to Watermelon Polo, with a large, inflated ball. As for the scoring, that can be adjusted to the time available. The first team to score three or five points wins.

Greased-pole walk. A heavily greased pole is suspended about 9 feet over the water. The object is to walk the pole until the very end so as to qualify as the winner.

Three-legged race. The participants compete in pairs shoulder-to-shoulder, with the inner legs to comprise the third leg.

Coin fetch. Fifty or 100 pennies are scattered in the deep end. At a given signal, those competing dive to recover as many coins as possible within the time allotted (2 or 3 minutes). The winner is the one who comes up with the most pennies.

Tug o'war.   Evenly divided teams line up opposite each other. They are to tug on a line with a buoy at the center. The buoy should be equidistant between markers on the deck. The winner is the team that pulls its opponents so that the buoy reaches an imaginary line in line with the deck marker.

Comedy dives and antics.   The special event can often be enhanced by the inclusion of such comic elements as slapstick rescue attempts, diving in pairs, and clowning on the pool deck.

Beginner Swimming Games[2]

Water potato race.   The Water Potato Race is run much the same as the Land Potato Race. Five pucks for each team of five people are laid out in line with the direction in which the race is to be run. The first contestant stands about 8 feet from the first puck. At the signal the contestant goes out to the first puck, returns it to the starting point, touching the hand of the next contestant in line. This one now goes on to pick up the second puck. This is continued until the five pucks are brought in. The first team to finish is the winner.

Balloon relay.   Two teams are divided into two parts, one half going to stand at the deep end of the pool, the other standing in shallow water. The deep-end half has one balloon per person. At the signal, the first person in the deep-end section jumps into the water holding the balloon. After entering the water the contestant levels off, turns over, and does a kick glide with hands stretched out overhead, holding the balloon in the water. When the first contestant reaches the shallow end of the pool, the next teammate takes the balloon and does a kick glide on front to the deep end of the pool, placing the balloon on the edge of the pool, ready for the next person in line to jump into the water to start the procedure over again. The winning team is the first team to finish at the deep end with the balloons tucked under their arms.

The wild duck.   Three circles of rope, each one foot in diameter, are placed in the water. A rock is placed within each circle. The circles of rope should be placed about 6 feet from the edge of the pool, although the distance may be varied in the course of the game. The teams line up, either as individual contestants with three in one race, or as teams of two or three.

2. This entire games section is derived from the manual *Recreational Swimming* through the permission of the Brooklyn chapter of the American Red Cross.

Using a prone glide and holding their breaths, the "ducks" push off from the side of the pool, keeping their eyes open to look for the circle and the "food" within it. When found, it is brought back to the starting point using a kick glide. A fellow "duck" takes the "food" and, gliding back to the circle, places the rock within it. When the swimmer returns to the starting point, the next contestant goes off in search of it. Any number of cycles may be made in the game. The first team to finish is declared the winner.

Floating fiction. Any number of contestants are lined up at the starting point with their backs to the finish line. Each is given a sheet of newspaper. At the signal "Go," the contestants push off in a glide on the back, kick, and read aloud from the newspaper. The first to cross the finish line is the winner. Failure to keep the paper up, to read it aloud, or to remain in a floating position disqualifies a contestant.

Wheelbarrow race. The contestants are paired off. One lies in a prone float position with legs apart. The other grasps the first contestant's ankles, as in the wheelbarrow race on land. At the signal "Go," teams race to the other side, the floating partner paddling with his or her hands. The first team to finish is declared the winner.

Snatch game (a variation of artillery skirmish). Two teams line up facing each other and each team is numbered consecutively from one to the number of players. The instructor stands at the deep end of the pool with a water polo ball. The instructor calls a number and throws the ball into the center of the swimming area between the two teams. The contestants whose numbers are called run or swim out to retrieve the ball and return it to their teams. If tagged while carrying the ball, one point is scored for the tagging team. If home is reached safely, a point is scored for that team. The team with the highest number of points wins.

Baton race. The contestants are split into two teams and a 20-yard course is laid out in waist-deep water. The first contestant in each team is given a baton or any similar object that can be carried easily in the hand. At the signal, the contestant swims with the baton to the other end of the pool where the instructor is standing. The swimmer taps the instructor with the baton and returns on back to teammates where he or she passes the baton to the next person. If the baton is dropped, it must be recovered before progressing. The first team to finish is the winner.

Intermediate Swimming Games

Arch relay. Two teams line up in waist-deep water with their legs apart. The rear in each column swims through the arches of the legs to the front of the column. The column moves back to make room and the new rear player comes forward through the arches. The first team to restore the original order is the winner.

Water volleyball. Two equal teams are arranged on opposite sides of a rope stretched 3 feet above the head. The rules should be simple and the game played in shallow water. The object is to keep the ball going back and forth without falling into the water.

The first team to reach twenty-one points is the winner. The ball may be put into play from any position, or the rules for ordinary volleyball may be applied.

Puck snatch. Two teams, A and B, line up on opposite sides of the pool, and a puck or other easily visible object is placed in the center of the playing area. Numbers are given to each contestant and the number determines the stroke each player will use in the game: (1) front crawl of arms and legs, (2) side stroke of arms and scissors kick, (3) breast stroke of arms and legs, (4) sculling with hands and flutter kick, and (5) elementary back stroke.

The instructor calls a number and a contestant from each team goes out to retrieve the puck. If the water is deep enough, a plain front dive may be executed; if not, a running jump will serve. The object is to bring the puck to the surface and show it to the other contestants. Once a player touches the puck, it belongs to that person unless it is dropped, in which case it is again free. If touches are made simultaneously, the contestants bring it to the surface together and a point is scored for each side. The game should be played for a specified number of minutes and the team with the highest number of points at the end of that period is declared the winner.

Straw hat race. The contestants line up, each wearing a farmer's straw hat. They dive into deep water, recover the hat after completely submerging themselves and race to the other end of the pool or other finish line.

Water punch ball. The contestants are divided into two teams, of which one takes positions in the water to correspond to the field positions of Land Punch Ball, and the other sends its members to punch the ball until three outs are made. The positions are then reversed. The rules are the same as in Land Punch Ball with the following additions: When the player punches the ball, he or she makes a running jump into the water, and swims to first base under water. In going to second base, the player must use a leg stroke. To third base, the player uses an arm stroke, and may use free style to come home.

Balloon relay. The teams line up in relay position, one balloon to a team. Swimming is done on the back using a leg stroke, and the hands are used to keep the ball out of the water by light taps. If the balloon is dropped, it must be retrieved before progress can be resumed.

Kickboard relay. Two equal teams line up, half at each end of the pool. The first swimmer on each team awaits the signal by holding the board in one hand and the starting marker in the other. At the signal, the swimmer kicks across the pool, handing the board to the next teammate, who returns it, and so on. The type of kick may be varied, such as flutter kick, breast stroke kick, scissors kick, and so forth. The first team to complete a cycle wins.

Apple race. Members of two teams race to the center of the pool where fifty or so apples have been placed. Upon reaching the center, the contestants take one apple in each hand and return to the starting point doing the side stroke. They place the apples on the side and go back for more apples, continuing to do so until there are no more apples. The team retrieving the most apples wins.

Advanced Swimming Games

Water punch ball. A diamond is made by placing a rowboat at each base. The field team must tread water with the exception of the catcher, who may lean against the dock or the edge of the pool. The batter must punch the water polo ball and then swim to first base. Fielders try to tag the swimmer off base. The game is scored as in baseball.

Virginia reel. The group is divided into two teams, numbered, and placed opposite each other:

1	2	3	4	5	6	7	8	9	10
10	9	8	7	6	5	4	3	2	1

The instructor calls a number and names an advanced skill. The contestants having that number exchange places by doing what the instructor has called for. The contestant reaching the opposite side first scores a point for his or her team. The skills are not called for in progression. Use crawl, breast stroke, backstroke, and so forth.

Red Rover. The teams face each other and one contestant calls to another by name (I call so-and-so over). The one called tries to swim past the "caller" without being tagged. If the person is tagged by the caller they both "call" and endeavor to catch the next contestant. Contestants may surface dive and swim under water to avoid being caught.

Name it. The instructor names an article of the lifesaving equipment near at hand. The first person to find it scores a point for the team. However, if the person is unable to demonstrate its use, the other team scores five points. The game gives practice in taking charge of elementary rescues using towels, paddles, shepherd's crook, ring buoy, surfboard, or canoe.

Couple tag.   The group is divided into pairs who swim while holding hands. One pair is "it." The object is to tag a pair without releasing the hands. Only one of the pair has to be tagged, and releasing the partner's hands to avoid being tagged makes that couple "it."

Modified water polo.   This game is a contact game and is considered to be valuable preparation for lifesaving since it prepares a swimmer against the frantic fear that often occurs when one is grabbed in the water.

Provision is made for scoring to be easier and the rules are made as simple as possible. Periods may be adjusted to suit the group being worked with; a suggestion is made that there be two halves, each composed of two quarters not to exceed 5 minutes in length. Any area not exceeding 75 feet in length may be used. Pool ends are preferred, but ropes may be used instead. The entire end or rope length is the goal.

Play starts with the referee throwing the ball (a regulation water polo ball, if possible) into the center of the pool and blowing a whistle. At the whistle, all players of both teams dive into the water. A race is made for the ball. The team securing it tries to progress with it by swimming or clever passing to striking distance for the goal. Plays and signals may be used. If a goal is made, both teams withdraw to their own ends, and the ball is given to the team scored upon. Play is resumed immediately upon indication of the referee. (Note: It is not necessary to get out of the water.) Play is continuous except for fouls or out-of-bounds balls. Cessation of play is indicated by the referee's whistle.

When a ball goes out of bounds, it is given to the opposite team at the point where it was thrown out of bounds. In this case, the defending team cannot approach closer than 6 feet to the contestant throwing it in. "Time out" is called for all foul throws, and the ball is again thrown in the center by the referee as in the start of the game.

A touch goal made by an attacking contestant touching the ball to any part of the end counts five points; a thrown goal made by an attacking contestant throwing the ball from at least 15 feet away and striking the rope or end, before striking the water, counts three points; a foul throw made by a contestant treading water at the 15-foot mark, throwing the ball, and striking the end or rope before the ball strikes the water, counts one point.

The number of contestants playing will depend somewhat upon the size of the area and local conditions. It is recommended, in order to keep the contestants distributed and to have some teamwork in passing, that the contestants be divided into: (1) forwards—those who are fast swimmers and swim down and attempt to score; (2) backs—those who play usually in an intermediate position and either pass the ball down to the forwards or receive it from the goal tenders and and feed it to the forwards; and (3) goal tenders—those who are the poorest swimmers but who are seaworthy. Their duty is to defend the goal by intercepting thrown balls or fending off attacking players who have the ball.

Fouls are classified as follows: (1) Technical—called for unnecessary delay of the game, failure to play within 30 seconds after being instructed to do so by the referee, or holding to end or rope when in possession of the ball. One free throw is awarded. (2) Personal—roughness, slapping, kicking, tackling a player who does not have the ball, or holding a player under longer than 3 seconds. Two free throws are awarded.

Water soccer or international water polo. This game is played in the Olympics and by teams in the Middle West and on the Pacific Coast. It is a game of skill and speed rather than contact. It may be highly technical, but for recreational use in camps is not played as such. It may be played with simple rules very much like Modified Water Polo.

A simple game of water polo may be set up according to the following rules: Goals are fixed at the ends in the center made by a cross bar 10 feet wide and from 3 to 8 feet high, depending upon the depth at the end. The regular number of contestants is seven, but any number may be used depending upon the area, so long as the sides are equally divided. A suggestion is made to divide the contestants into forwards, backs, and one goal tender. A score is made by throwing the ball into the net, and each score counts one point. Fouls are penalized by awarding a free throw to the opposite team at the point where the foul occurs. Foul shots are awarded for touching the ball with both hands at the same time, interfering with an opponent in any away unless the opponent is holding the ball, holding the ball under water, unnecessary delay in playing the ball (10-second limit), and roughing any player. Violators are penalized by giving the ball to the opposing team. Official rules on the playing of Modified Water Polo and Water Soccer are available from the National Collegiate Athletic Association.

Creative Swimming Instruction

A child learns swimming skills much more readily if the instructions are not given as straight directions, but instead have some creative content. The following exercises illustrate how creative dramatics can be integrated into the teaching of specific swimming skills.

Breath holding. "How does a motor boat sound? Make the sound by taking a deep breath and letting out your breath under water."

Rhythmic breathing. "Did you ever notice ducks dive into the water for their food and then surface to eat it? Let's become ducks. Dive down to the bottom of the water for your fish and bring it to the top." (Colored stones could be placed at the bottom of the pool to represent fish.)

Prone float and back float. "You are a turtle floating on the water. Lie on your back with your arms and legs outstretched on the water."

Prone glide. "You are a canoe gliding on the water. Lie face down in the water, stretch out your arms and glide through the water."

Back glide. "Now the canoe becomes a small boat as you glide in the water with your hands behind your body."

Kick glide. "Now your small boat has been transformed into a steamboat churning down the Mississippi River. The only steam power is the force of your own kicking in the water, so let the power begin."

Arm stroke and leg stroke combined. "But a steamboat is incomplete without a paddle. Add arm and leg strokes to make the paddle."

SUGGESTED READINGS

AMERICAN NATIONAL RED CROSS. *Canoeing.* New York: Doubleday, 1976.
AMERICAN NATIONAL RED CROSS. *Swimming for the Handicapped: Instructor's Manual.* Washington, DC: American National Red Cross, 1975.
AMERICAN SCHOOL AND COMMUNITY SAFETY ASSOCIATION. *Safety in Aquatic Activities.* Reston, VA: American Alliance for Physical Education, Recreation and Dance, 1977.
AMERICAN YOUTH HOSTELS: *The Official American Youth Hostels Handbook.* Delaplane, VA: American Youth Hostels, 1983.
ARMBRUSTER, DAVID A., ET AL. *Swimming and Diving.* St. Louis, MO: C. V. Mosby, 1973.
BAIRSTOW, JEFFREY H. *Camping Year Round.* New York: Random House, 1983.
BALL, EDITH L. *Hosteling: The New Program in Community Recreation.* New York: American Youth Hostels, 1971.
DALRYMPLE, BYRON. *Survival in the Outdoors.* New York: E. P. Dutton, 1972.
DONALDSON, GEORGE AND GOERING, OSWALD. *Perspective in Outdoor Education.* Dubuque, IA: Wm. C. Brown, 1972.
FRANKEL, LILLIAN AND GODFREY. *101 Best Nature Games and Projects.* New York: Gramercy Publishing House, 1974.
GABRIELSEN, M. ALEXANDER, ET AL. *Aquatics Handbook.* Englewood Cliffs, NJ: Prentice-Hall, 1968.
HILLCOURT, WILLIAM. *New Field Book of Nature Activities and Conservation.* New York: Putnam, 1971.
JENSEN, CLAYNE R. AND THORSTENSON, CLARK T. *Issues in Outdoor Recreation.* Minneapolis, MN: Burgess Publishing, 1977.
McKENZIE, M. M. AND SPEARS, BETTY. *Beginning Swimming.* Belmont, CA: Wadsworth, 1974.
MEIER, JOEL. *Adventure Outdoor Activities.* Salt Lake City, UT: Brighton, 1980.
MITCHELL, A. VIOLA AND MEIER, JOEL F. *Leadership and Programming for the Organized Camp.* Philadelphia, PA: Saunders, 1983.
RISK, PAUL H. *Outdoor Safety and Survival.* New York: John Wiley and Sons, 1983.
U.S. COAST GUARD AUXILIARY. *Boating Skills and Seamanship.* 9th ed. Washington, DC: U.S. Coast Guard, 1984.
VAN DER SMISSEN, BETTY. *Outdoor Recreation Users and Programming.* Martinsville, IN: American Camping Association, 1982.
WINNETT, THOMAS. *Backpacking for Fun.* Berkeley, CA: Wilderness Press, 1972.

11

Social Recreation

The term "social recreation" refers to those activities that have socialization as a primary purpose. By this definition, then, all types of recreation have some potential as social recreation. The program possibilities are limitless, but some examples include a group hike (outdoor recreation), book discussion club (literary), chorus (music), square dance (dance), group pantomime (drama), New Games (sports and games), quilting group (arts and crafts), group travel, and community volunteer work.

But the term "social recreation" refers more specifically to those activities intentionally designed to bring people together. It is these organized social recreation activities and events that will be the focus of this chapter.

VALUE OF SOCIAL RECREATION

Social recreation events are many. We can include in this category parties and dances, picnics and banquets, festivals and reunions, talent programs, and a variety of other special events. The benefits to be derived from social recreation are numerous. Opportunities are afforded for: (1) participating in wholesome fun; (2) socializing; (3) developing new interests; (4) improving ability to get along with others; (5) developing poise, personality, and maturity; and (6) finding outlets for self-expression. Social recreation helps contribute toward the development of social competence. Because people benefit from sharing experiences with others, social recreation is in high regard within the field of recreation. There are no leisure services settings, from armed forces recreation to resorts to psychiatric clinics, that do not require social recreation leadership skills of their recreation personnel.

PLANNING PRINCIPLES

The planning of a social recreation program should be a cooperative venture. Committees representing those who will participate can be of inestimable value to the leader (planning, publicity, entertainment, refreshments, decorations, cleanup). This grassroots programming approach can help prevent the failures caused by choosing activities above or below the participants' interest and ability levels. Whenever possible, the activity should stem from the needs and interests of the group. And the leader should be sensitive to the unique background and demographics of the community: For instance, a Monte Carlo Casino night might be offensive to certain ethnic or religious groups.

The following serves as a checklist of guidelines to follow in planning a social recreation event:

1. Identify your guests—single or mixed ages? number? marital status? single sex or coed? any special interests or limitations? A critical factor in the planning process is knowledge of the participants' degree of familiarity with each other. For instance, the leader will program very different mixer activities for a monthly PTA group than for a cruise singles party in which the group is meeting for the first time. If possible, the leader should try to determine the degree of "recreation literacy" of the group. For instance, it would be disastrous to offer a carnival with an obstacle course beyond the coordination abilities of the participants. Above all, a social recreation event should assure contentment and sociability—conditions which will not occur if the program has built-in failure experiences for the participants.

2. What is the setting for the event? Is there sufficient space? Are the facilities suitable for the intent of the gathering? (For example, can the floor be used for dancing if so desired?) Will there be sufficient parking, rest rooms, heat and ventilation, sound system equipment? When can the set-up crew have access to the space?

3. What is the purpose of the event? A celebration for a holiday or an individual? A family gathering? Will the group come dressed for the activities being considered?

4. When is the event scheduled? (Time, date, duration.) Is there any holiday affiliation? If refreshments are included, are they well spaced throughout the event so as to not overshadow the social activities? If refreshments are served too early in the program, participants may feel less inclined to remain for the activities.

5. What is the budget? Will this restrict purchases? Can materials be donated?

Some social recreation events require that the recreation leader make the technical arrangements but do no actual leadership of activities during the event. For instance, a group renting a community center room for a class reunion may plan an informal evening of food and conversation and therefore need no social mixers or games. They may ask that the recreation leader be there as a presence rather than an activity provider.

On the other hand, there are many social recreation events in which the recreation leader is asked to be prepared with a number of activities to promote the social ambience of the gathering. Since a comfortable social atmosphere is the goal, the leader's social leadership skills should be natural and well-timed, not obtrusive or directive. A leader can instill enthusiasm in a group just by sheer energy and sincerity. It is vital that the leader possess sensitivity to the tempo of the social events because the indiscriminate introduction of a mixer or game can actually interrupt social interaction rather than enhance it.

SOCIAL RECREATION ACTIVITIES

The social recreation leader's tools are those creative activities that foster social interaction in an informal, nonthreatening manner. Jane A. Harris, author of *File O'Fun—A Card File for Social Recreation,* has broken down these activities into the categories of: preparty activities, defrosters, stunts, get-acquainted activities, mixers (musical and "no partner"), ballroom dance novelties, table and card games, tricks and puzzles, party relays, active games, inactive games, skits, and special events. These categories will be explained in the following pages and further activity ideas given at the end of the chapter. Special events is such a major program area that an entire section of this chapter is devoted to it.

Preparty activity. A preparty activity is designed for first arrivals to facilitate interaction and minimize the sense of having to wait for things to happen. As a preparty activity, first arrivals can be creatively integrated into the preparation for the party, as in the case of nametag or decoration making. However, this preparty activity should only be adopted if it enhances the theme of the gathering; in no way should it be busy work or an exploitation of available labor. The preparty activity usually lasts no more than the 15 or 20 minutes it takes for all to arrive. "Lapse of Memory" is an example of a preparty activity. Guests are asked to come to a party with something about them that indicates a lapse of memory or error. The leader gives out pencils and paper. The guest that compiles the longest list of names and corresponding errors is the winner. (Examples of errors include different-colored socks, one earring, and so forth.)[1]

1. "Lapse of Memory" contributed from Leadership and Supervision class, Ithaca College, Instructor—Elizabeth Ann Griffin, Assistant Professor.

Get-acquainted mixer.   A good get-acquainted mixer to include is a method for learning names, thus both initiating the party and eliminating the awkwardness of name introduction. In the get-acquainted mixer "How Do You Do?," have the group line up in concentric circles, evenly divided. As the music starts or as the whistle is blown, the inner circle starts marching clockwise while the outside circle moves counterclockwise. When the music stops or the whistle sounds again, the circles face each other, with introductions and conversations taking place between those opposite each other. This is continued until all have had a chance to meet.

Defroster.   Unlike the preparty activity designed as a preface to the social occasion, the defroster can be introduced at any time throughout the event. As its name suggests, it is intended to "defrost" any coolness in the social atmosphere through activity that requires interaction. Example defroster: each person is given the line of a song to hum or sing and moves throughout the group listening for any other individuals who might be assigned the same tune; when these individuals find each other, they sing their song in unison.

Stunt.   A stunt is an informal, often comical performance of a written or improvised piece. (The stunt is discussed further in the chapter on recreational drama.) In a drama stunt, the audience is urged to participate in given ways, as in the creation of sound effects, percussion, and so forth. The stunt is largely based on audience participation, and a popular stunt format is the melodrama. A stunt can also be a wild exhibition or competition, like a contest to see which team can put on the most layers of clothes in a limited time.

Musical mixer.   A musical mixer is an activity with changing dance partners. An example would be the arrangement of two circles, women on the outside, men on the inside. Both circles walk to the right until the music stops, at which time they dance with the partners opposite them. This can continue indefinitely until all have been introduced to the majority of new dance partners.

"No-partner" mixer.   The "no-partner" mixer promotes a social interaction not by changing partners, but by group dancing. For instance, folk or line dances develop a group spirit that fosters sociability.

Ballroom dance novelty.   While the musical and no-partner mixers are intended to bring people into contact with a maximum number of individuals, the ballroom dance novelty is only intended to bring about a temporary change in partners. In this situation, the dancers are usually couples who would not want to be involved in a dance mixer that would separate them from each other for a long period. An example of a ballroom dance novelty is the cut-in dance in which people change partners or "cut-in" upon a verbal signal from the leader.

Table and card games/tricks and puzzles. Table and card games, and tricks and puzzles were discussed earlier in the chapter on mental recreation activities. These games are included here because they are a form of social recreation. Table and card games, such as the Horse Race with Cards, are enjoyable sociable activities fostering small-group discussion.

Horse Race with Cards[2]

Table Game	7 years and up 4 players

EQUIPMENT: 1. 1 deck of cards—take out 32 cards; 4 aces plus seven of each suit (2, 3, 4, 5, Jack, Queen, and King).
               2. A race track sheet about 5' × 1½', marked off in 4 lanes about 20 squares long.
               3. Envelopes of beans for each player for the pay-off to the winner.

FORMATION: The target is laid out on a long table. At the starting end of the table the 4 Aces are laid out, 1 in each lane to represent the racing horses. 1 player for each horse comes up to move the horses along as the leader turns the cards, which indicate the move for the horse of that suit.

ACTION: The leader shuffles the prepared deck of cards and lays it in front of him face down. Then he begins the race by turning 1 card up, and the appropriate horse (of same suit) is moved according to rules. This continues until 1 horse wins the race.

Rule: 1. Card 2, 3, 4, 5, moves horse that many squares forward for appropriate horse.
            2. Jack means 1 move backwards.
            3. Queen means 2 moves backwards.
            4. King moves horse of its suit to the lead position, changing places with the lead horse.
            5. The winner of the race will receive as many beans from each other player as the number of squares he was behind.
            6. When the leader runs out of cards there is a new shuffle and the process begins again until one horse wins the race.

LEADERSHIP SUGGESTIONS: 1. 7 cards of each suit may be taken from 4 decks of cards. This provides more cards to turn and generally one can get through the game without shuffling again. 2. This game can be played with teams if there are more people.

Working on a trick or puzzle brings people together; by nature of the enterprise, they must cooperate with each other to solve the problem.

2. Jane A. Harris, *File O' Fun—Card File for Social Recreation* (Minneapolis: Burgess Publishing, 1970), p. 65.

Party relay. The party relay contributes to a social atmosphere by building the camaraderie that comes from teamwork. Examples of party relays are the Sack Race, Three-legged Race, Wheelbarrow Race, and Duck-walk Race. The leader, however, should assure that the participants' zest for competition does not become so all-consuming that it robs the enjoyment from the experience.

Skit. As defined in the chapter on drama, a skit is an improvisation that has a plot line; it is most often humorous, but not necessarily so. The skit is a popular form of social recreation; examples are found in the drama chapter.

ACTIVE SOCIAL GAMES

Low-organization and High-organization Games

An active game fosters socialization, as the physical exercise promotes relaxation and social ease. Games can be divided into categories of "low organization" and "high organization." In games of low organization the rules are simple, with a minimum of social interaction and cooperation required of the players. This type of play is suited to the self-centered makeup of the young child. Games of high organization are characterized by more complex rules, with a shift of emphasis away from the individual to group play. Games of high organization are more advanced than low-organization games because they require greater skill, agility, kinesthetic sense, and socialization skills.

Principles in Game Leadership

1. Select games with the age group, skills, and "game literacy" of the participants in mind.
2. Plan the program thoroughly prior to the arrival of the participants.
3. Have technical needs in place before beginning the game (e.g., equipment, marking off of courts, goal lines).
4. From the start, teach the participants to respect the sound of the whistle or whatever means of direction is used.
5. Teach the game in simple, concise language, taking the following steps:
   Name the game.
   Place the players in proper formation.
   Explain the game.
   Repeat the explanations with a demonstration.
   Ask questions to assure participant understanding.
   Start play.
6. If selecting a player to be "it" or the leader, use a competitive means, thereby avoiding any possibility of favoritism (e.g., winner of race, the most free throws).
7. Use penalties sparingly, if at all, as they reduce the sheer enjoyment of play.

8. Avoid the use of the elimination factor in games. As a model for emulation, New Games activities permit players to creatively alter the components of a game in order to prevent elimination factors. The New Games text referred to at the end of this chapter contains sixty New Games and describes how to create and referee a New Games tournament.
9. Encourage in participants such attributes as sportsmanship and playing to the best of one's ability.
10. Start your program preferably with games familiar to the group, then branch off into new ones.

INACTIVE SOCIAL GAMES

An inactive social game incorporates many of the activities already discussed in other chapters—musical rhythm games, creative drama, mental quizzes, and so on. Inactive games—like table and card games, tricks and puzzles—are offered at points in the program where sedentary small-group participation is deemed appropriate. An example of an inactive game that also incorporates musical rhythm and mental exercise is "Categories." In "Categories," the participants are seated in a circle with everyone facing the center. A rhythmic pattern is started by everybody slapping their knees twice with both hands, then raising their hands overhead and snapping their fingers twice. On the next rhythmic finger-snapping count, the leader says "categories." The next person in line must name a category on the next rhythmic count. The third person in line must name an object in this category, and every subsequent person in line must do likewise until one person misses. An example of a category might be "automobiles," followed by the naming of a Ford, a Dodge, and so forth. The penalty for missing one of the categories is to drop out of the game, or if a point system is used, the person who misses scores a point; the winner of the game is the person with the fewest points.

SOCIAL RECREATION LEADERSHIP GUIDELINES

The social recreation activities listed above, like any program tools, are only effective if used skillfully. The following are guidelines to follow in introducing social recreation activities:

1. Remember that the event should not be crammed with an excessive number of planned activities. The activities should not predominate but should supplement the atmosphere where necessary. Remember that there are other happenings at the event that occur spontaneously without need for leadership.
2. The first mixer or get-acquainted activity which all participate in should be one whose success you are fairly sure of. The mood that the activity creates establishes the tone for the event to come.

3. There should be diversity in activities offered (e.g., defrosters, active games, get-acquainted mixers). To prevent fatigue and boredom, alternate physical and sedentary activities. Also, use variety in arranging couple, small-group, and large-group activity. The transition between activities should be smooth. Change the physical position of mixers to different spots throughout the space.

4. Look for signs of disinterest in an activity: "Kill the activity before it dies." Be flexible!

5. Playing time of an event can be controlled by announcing the termination time in advance or by indicating the winning point score if applicable.

6. Despite tradition or given directions, any activity can have its competitive element removed. The elimination of "players" and references to "winners" can be omitted, and the game or mixer played for the sheer fun of it.

THEMATIC PLANNING

For maximum effectiveness, social events often incorporate a theme that is carried through every aspect of the event including invitations, decorations, and activities. In many cases, this approach consists of giving creative names to fairly common program activities.

As an illustration, we will discuss the components of a "Spring Has Sprung" party. The essentials of the program invitation (date, time, place, theme, RSVP, contribution, suitable apparel) are enhanced by the enclosure of a packet of seedlings to herald the spring theme. The setting itself is decorated with crepe paper flowers strung along the walls and tables, with windowboxes also filled with flowers. The refreshment table settings all carry the floral motif. Participants design their own floral name tags from an assortment of arts and crafts materials. Later, as a defroster activity, guests look through magazines to select a picture of a flower that best typifies their personalities and then clip the pictures to their clothing (for example, an orchid might reflect a person of passion and deep feelings). Then everyone circulates throughout the group, asking people about their choices and seeking those who might have made the same floral choice. A musical mixer can then be introduced in which teams are given a limited amount of time to think of as many songs as possible with the name of a flower in the title (The Yellow Rose of Texas, When You Wore a Tulip). Each team then sings portions of each song for the rest of the group. A party relay race entitled "Water the Garden" requires that each member of the relay team water a plant 20 feet from the home base. As a concluding activity, everyone is instructed in how to make silk flowers, which they then bring home as a reminder of their spring celebration.

SPECIAL EVENTS

In recreation programming the special event is exactly what its name implies—an activity that "stands out" in scope and quality from the regularly scheduled activities. A special event can add that extra spark which draws public attention to the sponsoring agency's leisure services program.

Value of Special Events

A special event can be a recreation program's culminating activity; for instance, a camp's summer pageant demonstrates what the campers have learned and done in their summer of crafts, nature lore, and other activities. A special event can give participants a chance to showcase accomplishments, as in the case of a team gymnastics demonstration at the local shopping mall. A special event can be designed primarily to attract the public to existing or projected programs, as in the case of a "Big Band Bash" to herald the opening of the new racquetball complex. Special events allow for the integration of various program areas around one theme. For instance, for a carnival theme, the acting class can become clowns, the art class can design the decorations, the cooking class can make refreshments. Special events are often built around holidays and special occasions that provide an excellent base for creative programming ideas. Such events encourage civic and ethnic pride by celebrating the achievements of individual races and countries. While certain traditional holidays are celebrated every year (Fourth of July, Christmas), there are many others that have unique programming potential. Recreation leaders need only exercise interest and initiative in commemorating those holidays significant to their community. Examples of near-forgotten holidays that can be "resurrected" through special events include:[3]

> Inauguration Day (January 20, the day of the President's inauguration), National Freedom Day (February 1, celebrating the Emancipation Proclamation), Alamo Day (March 6, celebrating the standoff at the Alamo by Davy Crockett's boys), Pan American Day (April 14, to foster intercontinental solidarity and cooperation among members of the Organization of American States), Patriot's Day (third Monday in April, to celebrate the American Colonies breaking free from the British), Loyalty Day (May 1, to stimulate patriotic displays in the United States to counter May Day celebrations in the Soviet Union), Cinco de Mayo (May 5, to commemorate the efforts of Mexicans to retain their national independence), Armed Forces Day (third Saturday in May, a chance for the Armed Forces to display their readiness), Bunker Hill Day (June 17, a celebration of the American colonists' victory in that famous battle), Citizenship Day (September 17, a celebration of the immigration of foreign citizens to the United States), American Indian Day (fourth Friday in September, in honor of Native Americans), United Nations Day (October 24, to honor the United Nations), Election Day (Tuesday after first Monday in November, a day for casting a vote), Bill of Rights Day (December 15, a day to reaffirm our national purpose, proclaimed by President Franklin Roosevelt in 1941), and Forefather's Day (December 21, in celebration of our founding fathers). In addition to these holidays manufacturers and special interest groups have promoted a huge number of "special" days, such as National Cheese Day or Aviation Day.

The special event can be viewed as a significant laboratory session in which to integrate all of the programming skills one has previously mas-

---

3. Michael Chubb and Holly R. Chubb, *One Third Of Our Time? An Introduction to Recreation Behavior and Resources* (New York: John Wiley and Sons, 1981), p. 152.

tered as a recreation professional; since the special event is a one-time rather than a long-term effort, the recreation leader often feels more secure in taking risks with innovative programming in this situation.

Types of Special Events

In his *Program Book for Recreation Professionals,* Albert Tillman classifies the wide spectrum of special events according to the following categories:[4]

I. *Performances*

    A. *Culminations*—Climaxing events that summarize and recognize participants' interactions (e.g., water pageant, ice-skating show). To give a comprehensive view of the programs of the agency, the culminating activity can incorporate a variety of program areas. For example, an Olympics event can include a welcome song created by the music class and sports activities from the agency's sports program. The tournament is an example of a "culmination" special event. A tournament can be arranged around any activity (e.g., shuffleboard, volleyball, chess, scrabble, drama).

    B. *Entertainments*—Dramatize participants' achievements; differ from culminations in that there is interaction with the audience, with the emphasis on entertainment (e.g., talent show, puppet show).

    C. *Skill contests*—Skill demonstrations intended to attract interest in an activity (e.g., photography contest; baking contest; "Learn to Swim Campaign" incorporating exhibits of diving, relays, and synchronized swimming). Sports and play days are examples of skill contests. In sports days, all participants are segregated into teams, with each team or group retaining its identity. The activities program can include the gamut of team games (volleyball, softball, track and field, basketball, etc.), dual games (doubles in tennis, badminton, paddle tennis), and water activities. In play days, the distinction is that groups from different agencies are combined together on teams to foster interaction. The same activities as those associated with sports days also characterize play days, with the distinction being that each is played for a relatively short period of time.

II. *Exhibits*—Materials are shown that were derived from regularly scheduled recreation programs or self-directed leisure pursuits. Knowing that their works will be displayed often gives added incentive to participants (e.g., science fair, doll show, crafts show, pet show, flower show).

III. *Social Occasions:*

    A. *Fundraisers*—The social event is built around a profit-making venture (e.g., auctions, bazaars, flea market, theater party, antique show, swap meet (including barter of personal services), trade show, Las Vegas/casino night).

    B. *Conglomerates*—multiinterest events that incorporate smaller special events (e.g., county fair, carnival, circus, Mardi Gras festival). A parade is an example of a conglomerate special event. Exact timing and delegation of responsibilities to committees will help assure the success of the parade. For point of illustration, a parade with a bonfire event will be discussed:

        1. Organization committee sets up the general plan in consultation

4. Albert Tillman, *The Program Book for Recreation Professionals* (Palo Alto, CA: Mayfield Publishing, 1973), p. 205.

with the other committees. Time of departure, broadcast on radio or TV, and firewood collection fall within its province.

2. Safety committee arranges for police escort, route to follow, roping off of the bonfire area, and firefighting equipment at the fire.

3. Publicity committee to publicize the event is essential. See program-planning chapter for promotion techniques. Mimeographed notices with the schedule of events is recommended. A broadcast of the program can be made on radio and television.

4. Program committee decides on events such as speeches, entertainment, music, and singing. In the event there are to be dancing and refreshments following the parade, then a subcommittee in these two added phases can be appointed.

C. *Indoor parties*—(e.g., ice cream social, Sadie Hawkins dance).

D. *Outdoor parties*—(e.g., block party, street fair).

E. *Celebrations*—Revolve around holidays and special occasions and incorporate elements of pageantry (e.g., banquet, awards night, ball, family night, rodeo, Harvest Festival and Dance, ethnic festival).

IV. *Amusements*—Involve little planning or skill; spontaneous.

A. *No-skill contests*—(E.g., sidewalk chalk-art contest, dress-up day, sand-sculpting contest, guessing contest).

B. *Stunts*—Judged according to level of difficulty and originality (e.g., trampoline jumping contest, high-jump contest).

V. *Instructional*—Intended to teach new skill or information (e.g., bicycle safety day, orienteering adventure).

VI. *Promotional*—Designed to promote interest in the agency (e.g., pep rallies, open house for health spa, cross-country ski demonstration, exhibition games).

VII. *Excursions*—Trips (e.g., tours, hay rides, hikes, midnight cruises).

While Tillman classifies special events by format, Edginton, Compton, and Hanson classify special events by content, as illustrated in Figure 11–1.

FIGURE 11–1 Examples of Special Events

Holidays and Special Days	Seasons
Christmas	Winter Carnival
Thanksgiving	Spring Fling
Easter	Summer Evening
Valentine's Day	Fall Frolic
St. Patrick's	First Day of Spring
Fourth of July	Midsummer's Night
Washington's Birthday	
Lincoln's Birthday	
Martin Luther King's Birthday	Special Days
Dominion Day	
Queen Victoria Day	Hobo Day
Hallowe'en	Outer Space Day
Ides of March	Wild West Day
April Fool's Day	Backward Day
May Day	Gay Nineties
Father's Day	Roaring Twenties
Mother's Day	Fifties Day
Flag Day	Circus Day
Arbor Day	Clown Parade

THE ARTS	SPECIALTIES

THE ARTS

Battle of the Bands
Fiddlers Contest
Barber Shop Singing
Sweet Adelines
Art in the Park
Hobby Show
Craft Auction
Film Festival

ETHNIC AND INTERNATIONAL

Spanish Night
French Riviera
A Night in Venice
Mexican Hat Dance
Scandinavian Vikings
Scottish Kilts
Irish Sweepstakes
British Jubilee
Flight to Tokyo
Midnight in Moscow
Canadian Sunset
Greek Islands
German Polka Day
Black Culture Day
Jewish Festival

LOCOMOTION

Tractor Pull
Soap Box Derby
Sport Car Rally
Bicycle Derby
Steam Engine Days

SPORTS AND GAMES

Punt, Pass, and Kick
Hit, Throw, and Run
Junior Olympics
Ping Pong Tournament
Gymnastic Clinic
Marble Madness

SPECIALTIES

Freckle Contest
Bubble Gum Blowing Contest
Watermelon Seed Spitting Contest
Pie-Eating Contest
Egg Throwing
Treasure Hunt
White Elephants
Scavenger Hunt

ANIMALS

Fishing Derby
Dog Show
Cat Show
Pet Show
Farm Animal Show
Horse Show
Unusual Pet Show

INSTRUCTIONALS

Workshops
Clinics
Symposia
Demonstrations
Lectures
Forums
Conventions
Conferences

PROMOTIONALS

Open House
Master Demonstrations
Exhibition Games
Sports Skills Contests
  Basketball Free Throws
  Pass, Punt, and Kick Football
  Catch, Throw, and Run Baseball
Grand Openings
Pep Rallies

Source: Christopher R. Edginton, David M. Compton, Carole J. Hanson, *Recreation and Leisure Programming: A Guide for the Professional,* Copyright © 1980 by Saunders College/Holt, Reinhart and Winston. Reprinted by permission of CBS College Publishing, p. 168.

Special Event Planning Checklist

The following checklist serves as a valuable resource in planning a special event. Not all items below are applicable to every special event, but the reference serves as a general guideline.

PRELIMINARY CONSIDERATIONS:

The event
    people to be served?
    expectations for the event?

where? when? why? enough planning time?

source of funding—general funds? admission charge?

level of community interest and involvement in planning the event?

will event impede regular programming?

PREPLANNING:

Determine date, time, facilities and equipment needed.

Select program chairperson and general program committee.

PLANNING:

Locate facility and equipment.

Locate means of transporting participants as well as equipment and supplies.

Determine personnel requirements including volunteers.

Design public relations approaches (media, distribution of novelty items, promotional event).

Establish rain date (optional).

Do safety and insurance check.

Conduct inventory of physical arrangements (microphone, decorations, podium, signs, outlets, audiovisual materials).

Finance assessment—fundraising level, fees to be charged, itemized budget for expenditure.

Establish follow-up meeting date after the event for committee reports and evaluations.

ESTABLISHMENT OF COMMITTEES AND CHAIRPEOPLE

(all of the committees outlined below will not be applicable to every special event):

Overall program committee—arranges program content including activities and speakers; schedules personnel including chaperones, judges, officials, activity leaders, and volunteers; designs written program; determines awards and method of thanking people; oversees all committees; obtains committee reports to compile final evaluation.

Finance committee—develops budget; collects funds; authorizes purchases.

Publicity committee—develops and distributes announcements for media (includes information on event's time, place, optional rain date, special features, fees if applicable, parking, reservations if applicable); works on promotional events, novelty items, tickets, and invitations if applicable; can organize a telephone calling committee to promote the event.

Equipment and supplies committee—obtains necessary materials including donations of money and goods from local establishments.

Physical arrangements committee—approves the physical layout for the event and supervises plant management during the event; makes necessary physical changes in the environment; arranges for parking guards.

Transportation committee—arranges for transportation of equipment and supplies for the event; organizes transportation routes and insures means of transportation for any interested resident.

Safety committee—obtains necessary permits; requests coverage by police and rescue squad.

Refreshments committee—arranges for provision of food and/or concessions.

Reception committee—greets guests; conducts mixers; distributes name tags; takes admission money.

Clean-up committee—returns area to its original appearance prior to the event.

As reflected in the committee breakdown above, the special event requires extensive programming beyond the normal routine of the agency. However, it is important to insure that the regularly scheduled programs do not suffer from lack of attention as a result.

RECREATION PROFESSIONAL AS FACILITATOR

Providing social recreation is not solely limited to the programming described throughout this chapter but also includes providing facilities, equipment, and consultation to individuals and groups planning their own social recreation events. Agency personnel may provide program ideas and written guidelines for social recreation activities. College recreation departments make student leaders available to the community as part of the students' education and in keeping with the school's role as community servant. Materials such as sports equipment and table games can be loaned out for parties, picnics, home entertainment, and other forms of social recreation. There can be individual creative program kits loaned for any social events (for example, Casino Night package with games of chance, New Games Day package including earth ball). It is recommended that a deposit be required before loaning out any equipment or program kit. A prearranged list of fees for objects lost and damaged should be shown to the borrower prior to the loan to avoid any later misunderstanding.

Providing a comfortable environment for socializing is a significant social recreation service in and of itself. These environments include those always available to the general community (community center lounge, drop-in center, hospital reading/television room) and those made available for specific social events (dance studio for dance, restaurant social hall for reception). In summary, the leisure services agency that makes space, equipment, and professional consultation available to the community for social recreation purposes is performing its role as leisure educator by facilitating self-directed leisure pursuits.

FURTHER ACTIVITY SUGGESTIONS FOR SOCIAL RECREATION

Preparty Activities

Who Am I? This game is played in pairs. Each contestant attempts to guess the prominent figure name pinned on his or her back by asking yes and no questions of the other players (for example, "Am I a sports figure?"

"Do I live in this century?") Participants keep a tally of the number of questions they must ask before guessing their identity. The contestant who guesses successfully with the least number of questions wins.

The following two activities were contributed by the Leadership and Supervision class at Ithaca College:

X Marks the Spot.   Place a number of Xs on the floor with tape. Do not tell the guests which X has been designated the lucky X. All the guests circulate around the room, shaking hands and exchanging names while the music is playing. When the music stops, the couple found standing on the lucky X wins.

Bag It.   Fill bags with familiar objects. Players try to guess the objects only by feeling the outside of the bag. The person who identifies the most objects is the winner. Guests submit their guesses on pieces of paper as they arrive at the event during the preparty period.

Defrosters

Completion.   Each person is given the piece of a larger picture and seeks out those who have the other pieces to complete the picture. Each person is given half of a quotation, proverb, or saying that implies a paired association (e.g., ham and cheese, Romeo and Juliet) and mingles among the group to find the person with the matching half.

Progressive Pictures.   Each player is given a sheet of paper and a pencil and begins by drawing a head at the top of the paper. The person then folds the sheet so that the head is hidden but a bit of the neck still shows. At a signal, all the players pass their folded sheets to the players to their right. Then they draw the upper part of the body down to the waist including the arms. This is folded and passed to the right. The total drawing is completed in two more stages (to the knees and then to the feet). The drawings are then unfolded and displayed. The results are visually quite humorous.[5]

I've Got Your Number.   Give each guest a number, which is pinned to a conspicuous place and worn throughout the game. Now give each person a slip of instructions containing such directions as: "Introduce number 4 to number 3," "Shake hands with number 6 and number 7," "Find out the color of number 11's eyes," "Ask number 1 to describe a favorite breakfast."

Newspaper Scavenger Hunt.   Divide the group into small teams. Provide each team with a stack of newspapers. Ask the teams to find the same

5. From *Recreation Today—Program Planning and Leadership* Richard G. Kraus, p. 358. Copyright © 1977 by Scott, Foresman and Company. Reprinted by permission.

item such as an advertisement for a coat, a news story, or picture of a famous person. The players scavenge through the newspapers, tear out the item, and bring it to a person appointed collector. The first team to find an item scores a point.

Get Acquainted Activities

Name Bingo. Each player is given a sheet of paper that is marked off in five rows of five boxes each for a total of twenty-five squares, as in a bingo card. If there are fewer than twenty-five players, it may be best to have sheets with three rows of three boxes each, for nine squares. The mixer is played like bingo, except that names substitute for numbers. Players move around the room asking others their names and printing each one (first and last) in a square until all the squares are filled. Then the game leader calls out the names of players, one by one from a complete list of names. When players hear a name called that is on their sheets, they draw a line through it. The first player to cross out an entire line of boxes horizontally, vertically, or diagonally wins and calls out "Name Bingo!"[6]

Getting to Know You. Develop a list of characteristics (e.g., likes to travel, cooks well). Circulate among the group and write the names of those whose interests correspond to each of these characteristics. After a period of time, everyone forms into a general group and discusses their findings about each other.

A Pack of Fun. In small groups devise a pack of cards in which there is a card to represent the identity of each group member. For instance, someone considered to have fine taste in clothes might be depicted as a king or queen. After the cards are designed and discussed, a standard game can be played with them (such as matching pairs in "Go Fish!").

Name-droppers. At some point during the gathering, everyone will be asked to give a one-word description of the new people they have met. The word must begin with the first letter in the person's name (e.g., "serious Steve").

Table and Card Games[7]

Old Maid (Card game, 5 years and up, two to six players).

EQUIPMENT: one deck of regular playing cards. FORMATION: The first dealer removes three Queens from the deck, leaving the Queen of Spades, then deals out all the cards. Players make pairs (two of any number) and discard pairs from hand. ACTION: The dealer draws one card from the

6. Ibid., p. 343.
7. Jane A. Harris, *File O' Fun—Card File for Social Recreation* (Minneapolis: Burgess Publishing, 1970), pp. 68–72.

person on his or her right. If dealer can make a pair, dealer will discard it from hand. Then each player in turn draws from the hand on the right. The last card will be the Queen of Spades as it has no mates. The person left with it at the end is the "old maid."

Concentration (Card game, 6 years and up, two to four players).

EQUIPMENT: one deck of regular playing cards. FORMATION: All cards are laid out, face down, in even rows, six across and eight down plus the extras. ACTION: The dealer takes the first turn. Dealer will turn up any two cards hoping to find a pair. If dealer does get a pair, dealer keeps the cards. If not, they must be turned over again. As each player attempts this in turn, players of course try to remember where the cards already turned up were in order to make pairs. The one who takes the most cards is the winner.

Hearts (Card game, 8 years and up, two to six players).

EQUIPMENT: one regular deck of cards. FORMATION: All the cards are dealt. Each player passes three cards to the player at left. ACTION: The game begins by the player to the left of the dealer putting down a card in any suit. In turn, around the table, each player must follow suit if he or she has a card in that suit or throw off from another suit. The highest card in the suit led takes the trick. There is no trump. No one may lead hearts until the first heart has been thrown off. OBJECT: Not to take any hearts or the Queen of Spades. Each heart counts one point against the player. The Queen of Spades counts thirteen against. If any one player can take all thirteen of the hearts *and* the Queen of Spades, he or she wins 26 plus points. LEADERSHIP SUGGESTIONS: (1) In dealing, if there are a few extra cards left after dealing everyone the same number, these go into the first trick taken and so may cause doubt as to number of hearts in play. (2) Players will learn to throw off high cards of another suit to avoid taking tricks.

Inactive Games

People Anagrams[8] (Inactive game, 8 years and up, ten to fifty players).

EQUIPMENT: Individual score cards, pencils, and a 3″ × 5″ card with a pin fastened on it for each person. FORMATION: Players are instructed to print on their 3″ × 5″ card a large letter—the first letter of their first or last name—and pin the card on in front where it can be seen clearly by all. LEADERSHIP SUGGESTIONS: By asking for a show of hands, the leader can find out how many vowels there will be among the group if they use the first letter of their first name. If there are none with the letter A, E, I, O, U, the leader should ask who has a last name beginning with the missing letters and tell them to use that letter. This provides the possibility of more word combinations and makes the game livelier. It may be necessary to assign some person a vowel letter. ACTION: On a signal, all players will circulate around and get together with other letters making a word. When they go up to the leader to get checked off, each will add to his or her score

8. Adapted from the game "Word Maker" in *Handbook of Coed Teen Activity,* by Edith and David Demarche (New York: Association Press)

card the word and the number of points equal to the number of letters in that word. They go off to find another word. This may continue as long as the total group seems involved in making words—perhaps 8–10 minutes. But if the words do not come fast, the leader should stop the activity sooner. LEADERSHIP SUGGESTIONS: If the group is over twenty in size, there should be different leaders assigned to different locations so people won't pile up at one spot to get their words checked out. OBJECT: For each individual to be part of as many words as possible, thereby accumulating a score as high as possible. Any legitimate word is allowed. No abbreviations are allowed, however.

Singing Charades[9] (Inactive game, 14 years and up, six to eight on a team).

EQUIPMENT: Pencils and paper. FORMATION: A large group is divided into teams. Each team is arranged about a spot where one can write and all can be close enough to see. ACTION: Each group sends one person to the center of the room where that person and other entries are given the name of a song (the leader whispers it). Players rush back to their own team with paper and pencil and draw out a picture which they think best describes the song. (No words can be written or said by the artist.) The team tries to guess what the song is and immediately sings it out when they get it. The first team to sing the correct song wins. Each team sends another entry. The game may be repeated for each team member or until the leader wishes to stop. OBJECT: To guess the song quickly and win as many times as possible. LEADERSHIP SUGGESTIONS: It is important that each group be an equal distance from the leader. Whispering is not always heard. A leader may wish to have each song title printed on a card so that all contestants may read it at the same time. The choice of songs is very important. They must be songs that everyone will know. It is wise for leaders to have several lists of songs appropriate for various ages. At Christmas, carols can be used so everybody can join in the singing once it is started. It is sufficient most times for the group to sing out only the first line or two of the song, but at Christmas it is fun to sing the whole carol.

Name That Tune. As songs are played, the guests write down what they feel to be song titles. The player with the most correct titles wins.

Sing Out. Each team is given the same topic (for example, seasons) and must list all the songs they associate with that topic ("Summertime," "Summer of '42"). At the end of a given time period, each team sings portions of all of its songs for the rest of the group.

Concentration (musical rhythm game). Each participant (up to thirty players) sits in a chair that is situated in a semicircle. Beginning with the first chair and going from left to right, the leader numbers each chair consecutively. Each player assumes the number of the chair in which he or she sits. The game is started by the number 1 player, who begins a rhythm by slapping thighs and clapping twice. While clapping hands, the player repeats his or her own seat number and the number of another player.

9. Harris, *File O' Fun*, p. 124.

Players whose numbers are called must repeat their own number and give a number of one of the other players while repeating the motions and retaining the rhythm. If players whose numbers are called cannot repeat their number in the clapping part of the rhythm, they move to the last chair of the semicircle. This leaves an empty seat, and all players move up one chair and obtain a new seat number. The object of the game is to sit in the first chair at the end of a certain period of time. The player who gets the chair will be declared the winner. Strategy: Call as often as possible the numbers of those players sitting in the first few chairs so that they will make an error and will have to move. In this way, more people assume new numbers and more confusing fun results.

Other Inactive Games.

1. Guess the number of beans, coins, marbles, cherries, and so forth, in a jar. The one who is closest to the correct amount earns 10 points while 7, 5, 3, and 1 points to those next in line can be given.
2. Toss ten playing cards into a hat from top part of a chair; 5, 3, 2, and 1 points may be given the four highest scores.
3. Guess the exact time an alarm clock, the face of which is taped, will ring. Scoring similar to 1 or 2 above may be used.
4. Drop ten clothespins into a milk bottle from the top portion of a chair. Score as in 2 above.
5. Toss ten jar rubber rings at a board on which nails are numbered one to ten in the order of difficulty. Score as in 2.
6. Toss five darts at a numbered target board (one to ten). Score as in 1.
7. Total the number of successful throws at an ash can or refuse basket 10 feet away from the target. Score as in 2.
8. Count the number of coins (slugs) that can be tossed into a small glass at the bottom of a large glass receptacle of about 2 or 3 gallons filled with water. Score as in 2.
9. Total number scored by rolling a pair of dice three times. Score as in 1.
10. Take ten tries to get a tennis ball into a wastebasket after a bounce. The table is to be waist-high with the basket removed 6 feet from the table's edge. Score as in 2.

Follow the Rhythm.[10]   Everyone sits in a circle. Choose one person to leave the room. A leader is chosen who starts and periodically changes the beat or rhythm as the person reenters and tries to guess the leader. Everyone follows the leader (for example, tapping floor, clapping hands). You win if you guess the leader.

Rain Storm.   Participants sit on the floor Indian-style in a large circle. The leader starts the rain by tapping his or her fingers on the floor. Then the second person joins in with the first, then the third, the fourth, and so on. When the light rain gets back to the leader, the leader taps harder and

10. The following two activities were submitted from the Ithaca College Leadership and Supervision class.

the cycle is repeated. The rain starts out being very light, gets louder and louder, then softer and softer, and finally stops.

Party Ideas

Zodiac Signs. To decorate the zodiac theme, make cookies and centerpieces in the shape of zodiac signs. Have people act out their signs' personalities in pantomime.

Outer Space Party. With a theme like this, almost any decorations that look crazy will suffice. Use lots of tin foil and strings for effect, have planets dangling from walls and ceiling. Everybody comes in a space costume of original design. Play "spacy" electronic music.

St. Valentine's Day Party. Decorations and refreshments include: pink streamers, cardboard hearts, posters containing proverbs on love, red jello or ice cream in heart-shaped molds, pink lemonade. Favorite love songs can be played and sung by the participants.

Active Games: Relays

Relays have proved themselves an exceedingly popular form of play. For one, they invariably sustain interest until the very end. Furthermore, they can be used to incorporate skills and stunts. Capable coaches know the value of minimizing the boredom of teaching fundamentals by employing game situations.

The simple and shuttle are the two common types of relays used in game play. In the Simple Relay, the players are placed in line and evenly divided in number. The first one in each line runs a designated distance to the wall, touches it, and returns to touch the hand of the second person who has moved up to the line; the first runner thereupon goes to the end of the line. This continues until all have competed. The team that completes the run first is called the winner. Under the Shuttle Relay plan, each line or team is divided in half with each half directly opposite the other, although a designated distance apart. The lines or teams are numbered A, B, and onward, while the halves have the odd numbers, 1, 3, 5, and so forth on one side and the even ones, 2, 4, 6, and so forth, on the other. At a given signal, the first player of line A runs to 2A and tags that person; 2A does likewise by running to tag 3A and so on; the numbers of line B do likewise. The line that finishes first is designated the winner. The shuttle principle can be extended so that the run is continued until each runner returns to his or her original position. Under the first described system, the players find themselves lined up opposite their original starting positions. Sports fundamentals such as dribbling and shooting in basketball can be taught interestingly in the shuttle or simple forms.

Wheelbarrow Relay.   This relay can be played by having two or three more columns competing against each other, or by having any number of pairs competing. The first one, A, in the column places his or her hands on the ground as the one behind A, B, grasps his or her knees while resting on each hip, thereby simulating a human wheelbarrow. Upon traversing a given distance and returning, B becomes the wheelbarrow for C. C, returning, becomes the wheelbarrow for D, and so on until all have participated. The column that finishes first wins. When competing in pairs, the couple that finishes first is designated the winner.

Leap Frog Relay.   The players on each team line up one behind the other about 4 feet removed, with their hands on their knees. The rear person leaps over each player on his or her side and stoops over at the front, whereupon the new rear player does the same. This is continued until the first player has jumped over all teammates and crossed a designated goal line.

Zigzag Relay.   Teams I and II form separate circles about 10 feet apart. Designate the leader in each circle who is to start zigzagging to the right at the command "go." After completing the circle, the leader returns to his or her original position and tags the player on the right. This is continued until all the players have run. The team that finishes first is the winner.

Overhead Relay.   Form two even parallel lines about 2 feet apart. The first person on each line passes a ball overhead until it reaches the last one. The last person runs forward, stands in front of the line and passes the ball the same as before. The line that makes the entire round first is the winner. Note: The same game may be played "underlegs," or combined as an "over and under" relay.

German Football.   Equipment: One broom or stick for each team (minimum, two brooms); chairs—enough for everybody, plus two extras to serve as goals; rag tied in knots or a stuffed sock. Two equal teams sit facing each other. Team members count off, starting at opposite ends. Each team has chair for a goal at one or both ends. The stuffed sock or rag tied in knots is placed in the middle of the two teams. The leader calls out a number, such as "number 3." Each number 3 runs to the opposite team's goal, grabs the broom or stick, and rushes to the center trying to push the object (sock or rag) to his or her own team's goal. A point is scored if the player get the object between the legs of the chair at his or her own goal. If a "stall" occurs, the leader tells the runners to lift their brooms above their heads and throws the rag or sock between them for a restart.

Indoor Track Meet

Shot Put—uses a balloon, table tennis ball, or cotton ball.

Javelin—consists of a straw or wooden applicator.

Discus—a paper plate is thrown.

Standing broad jump—players heel the starting line and jump backward.

Five-mile stretch—any number of teammates, but the same number from each team touch the line and the rest lie from toe to head in any manner; the team with the longest line wins.

Lead-up Games. The use of lead-up games, wherein fundamentals can be practiced more interestingly, is growing in popularity. As was mentioned before, relays offer numerous possibilities. That lead-up games of the nonrelay type are equally valuable may be gathered by examining the games that can be utilized for the sports of soccer, volleyball, baseball, and basketball; their fundamentals include such skills as passing, kicking, and shooting at a target (spot or player).

Soccer.

Scrimmage. The rules are similar to those of Modified Soccer, except that the players are seated and not permitted to run. They can crawl. If players stand up or rise above a crawl they are eliminated from the game until a goal is scored, whereupon they enter the game again.

Kick Ball. One team lines up at one end of the gym. The other team takes the field as follows: Two players stand on the farther end line, about 20 feet apart; the remaining players of the fielding team cover the playing area. The first player of the kicking team kicks the ball, which is resting on home plate. The ball must go past the foul line and into the playing area. The opponents, by the use of their feet only, pass-kick the ball to either of their two "linemen." The "lineman" receives the ball without using hands and kicks it back to the opponents' end of the gym. The player who kicked the ball must run from home plate to the other end of the gym and must beat the ball back to his or her wall to score a point. No outs are kept. Each player kicks in order until everyone has had one turn. The teams then change positions. Play nine innings. The players should be numbered and always kick in consecutive order.

Modified Soccer. The group is divided into two teams. Each team is to designate one half as guards and the remainder as forwards. The guards are not permitted to pass the middle line of the court, whereas the forwards are. The hands are not to be used at all. After a goal is scored, the forwards of both teams become the guards and the guards become the forwards. The opposite wall or the area between the foul-shooting area (free-throw line) against the wall may be used as the goal. If players touch the ball with their hands they are eliminated from the game until a goal is scored, whereupon they enter the game again.

Volleyball

Volley Catch Ball. A ball is thrown by each team over the net from the back of its court. The balls must be kept in the air at all times and must be caught each time, not batted with the hands. The ball so caught is passed either to a teammate or is thrown directly over the net into the other court. The balls are tossed back and forth from team to team. One point is scored against a team and given to its opponents each time a ball strikes the floor in its own court, but the ball that hits the floor should be continued in play. A net ball is in play. Use one ball at first and later advance to two or even three balls. Use a scorer or referee in each court. Twenty-one points is a game. Change courts after each game.

Keep It Up. The leader starts the contest by giving a signal, at which time one player in each group tosses the ball of that group in the air. The ball is then volleyed (batted preferably with two hands, not caught or thrown) from one player to another of the same team without any special order until it strikes the wall, ground, ceiling, or some obstacle upon which it is declared dead. Each time the ball is tapped by one of the players, his or her team calls aloud, "One two, three, etc." counting this way the number of successful volleys made. After the ball has been declared dead, a new game is started; the counting starts again at one. Each group keeps a count of its best score, the highest determining the winning team at the end of the contest. There should be a judge for each team.
Variation: Each team is to have one continuous volley in each period. The team that volleys the most gets a point, twenty-one points win.

Baseball

Hit Pin Baseball. A club is placed at each of the four bases. The pitcher rolls the air-filled ball to home plate. When batters kick a fair ball, they run around the bases and knock down the club at each base. The fielders throw the ball first to the first baseman. If by hitting the Indian club with the ball the fielder knocks down the club before a batter can do so, the batter is out. No matter where a fair ball is fielded, it must be thrown to first base. If the first baseman cannot put the runner out he or she throws the ball to the second baseman. Similarly, the second baseman who fails to knock down the club before the batter does, must throw to third, and the third baseman to home. If the runner reaches home first and kicks down the club, one point is scored for his or her team. The only way the batter can be put out is by a baseman knocking over an Indian club with the ball before the runner kicks it over.

Kick Baseball.   The rules used are similar to those of baseball except that the ball is kicked rather than batted. The ball can either be rolled in to the "batter" or kicked after placing the ball on home plate.

Roley Poley.   By a competitive means the batter is selected. The batter either throws the ball up to bat it or has someone pitch it. If the batted ball is caught on a fly, the batter is out and the catcher gets up at bat. If it is a bounced ball, then the catcher tosses the ball at the bat, and if the bat is struck without the batter catching the ball, he or she gets up at bat. If the batter catches the ball he or she remains at bat.

Bat Ball.   The first player of the batting team tosses the inflated ball up, hits it with a fist into the playing area, and attempts to reach the far wall without being hit by the ball. The fielding team, observing basketball regulations, attempts to strike the batter with the ball to put the player out; there must be no running with the ball. Hitters must run only to the far wall with their hit. They run home on the next hit ball. After runners have reached their wall or base, the ball is returned to the batting line. The second player now hits the ball and attempts to reach the far wall, while the first one, assuming he or she was safe, tries to reach the home wall without being hit. If successful, that player scores a point. The fielders may play either or both of the players. The last batter of each team must try to make a home run every inning. All players are up in each inning. A 30-foot short line is recommended.

Corner Ball.   The court is divided in the middle, with a base marked in each corner. Team A takes half of the field and stations a player in each of the two bases in B territory. These players must stay on the base and the B players must stay off. The object of the game is for each team to make as many passes from their field players to players on bases as possible. The team winning the toss gets the ball first and keeps it until their opponents intercept a pass or until they fumble the ball and let it touch the floor.

Basketball

Basket Baseball.   One team is at bat at home plate. The batter tosses a basketball in the air, strikes it with a fist, and must run around the bases and make a home run before the opponents can shoot the ball through the farther basket. The batter must reach home plate before the basket is made to score a run. If the ball goes through the basket before runners reach home, they are out and no run is scored. A foul ball is out.

3–2–1.   All players line up behind the foul-shot area and follow in rotation. During the first series, the players are allowed three tries in which to shoot the basket, then two tries, and finally one. If at any time players fail to make the basket in the allotted number of tries, they are eliminated. If all fail, more attempts are permitted until one player is successful, whereupon all those preceding in the series are eliminated and those who follow must also make the shot to continue. If not, the maker of the shot is the winner.

Clock Basketball. Twelve-hour checks are marked about the basket area. All start at the foul-shooting line and shoot in rotation. When the foul shot is made, the player starts at "one o'clock" and advances "one hour" whenever the shot is completed. After "twelve o'clock" is completed a "long" shot is selected and the first one to make it is acknowledged the winner of the game.

SUGGESTED READINGS

BALL, EDITH AND CIPRIANO, ROBERT E. *Leisure Services Preparation: A Competency-Based Approach.* Englewood Cliffs, NJ: Prentice-Hall, 1978.

CARLSON, REYNOLD, MACLEAN, JANET R., DEPPE, THEODORE, AND PETERSON, JAMES A. *Recreation and Leisure: The Changing Scene.* Belmont, CA: Wadsworth, 1979.

CORBIN, H. DAN AND TAIT, WILLIAM, J. *Education for Leisure.* Englewood Cliffs, NJ: Prentice-Hall, 1973.

EDGINTON, CHRISTOPHER R., COMPTON, DAVID M., AND HANSON, CAROLE J. *Recreation and Leisure Programming: A Guide for the Professional.* Philadelphia: Saunders College, 1980.

EISENBERG, HELEN AND LARRY. *Omnibus of Fun.* New York: Association Press, 1969.

HARRIS, JANE A. *File O' Fun—Card File for Social Recreation.* Minneapolis: Burgess Publishing, 1970.

ICKIS, MARGUERITE. *Book of Festivals and Holidays.* New York: Dodd, Mead, 1970.

JERNIGAN, SARA S. AND VENDIEN, C. LYNN. *Playtime: A World Recreation Handbook,* New York: McGraw-Hill, 1972.

KRAUS, RICHARD. *Social Recreation.* St. Louis: C. V. Mosby, 1979.

KRAUS, RICHARD. *Recreation Today: Program Planning and Leadership.* Santa Monica, CA: Goodyear Publishing, 1977.

NEW GAMES FOUNDATION. *The New Games Book.* New York: Doubleday, 1976.

Epilogue

The Present Is Prologue: A Challenge to the Profession

The delivery of leisure services operates within the larger context of the society in which we live. Social dynamics impact on the amount of free time available for leisure as well as the quality of those individual leisure experiences. To be equipped to meet this professional challenge, recreation personnel must be as knowledgeable of these social factors as they are of recreation leadership and programming principles. To develop a philosophy of leisure and recreation programming, every recreation professional must be knowledgeable in how these social dynamics impact on participant leisure satisfaction. These societal factors will be discussed within this chapter.

CHANGING LIFESTYLES

Overpopulation places demands on recreational space and programs, and it affects the quality of the leisure experience for the individual. At the present growth rates, 12 billion people are expected to populate the planet in the year 2030. Other demographic projections indicate that by the year 2000, those between 25 and 64 years of age will increase by more than 25 percent, thus constituting more than half of our population; those under

25 will comprise 36 percent, those 65 and over 18.1 percent. The "baby boom" generation of 1947–1957 has resulted today in the age 35–44 group being the fastest growing of all, and the over-85 age group has increased almost as rapidly.

Population pressures have brought vastly intensified demands on our leisure resources. For example, in the Grand Canyon National Park it is necessary to book a burro ride at least 6 months in advance. This "people congestion" is evidenced in every imaginable leisure activity: Picnic areas are overflowing by 10 A.M., there are 5-hour waiting periods prior to teeing off at the golf course; municipal swimming pools at best often allow only wading due to wall-to-wall people. Most of our population lives in urban settings within a limited space. The resulting atmosphere of anonymity has replaced the neighborliness once characteristic of our communities. Where people once spontaneously came together for recreation, apartment complexes now hire recreation directors to introduce next-door "strangers" to each other. The rise of mobility in this country has negative consequences when it results in transiency, lack of roots, disruption of families, and loss of identity. This rise in social alienation has led many to turn to recreation agencies to meet their social needs. Senior citizen centers, singles organizations, street youth programs, and others all attract people who acknowledge that loneliness has led them to seek out agencies that might connect them with other people.

Changes in societal lifestyles influence leisure services. Since the nuclear family is no longer truly representative of most households, recreation personnel must reexamine their concept of family recreation, the type of programs they provide, and the schedules they offer. For example, we can no longer consider Sunday the standard day for programming family recreation in a society where people in households have additional jobs and varied obligations. The leisure services profession as a whole must be more inventive in its programming philosophy, content, and scheduling to meet the needs of diversified living units, including widowed and divorced parents, ethnically mixed couples, unmarried mothers, unwed living partners, single parents (male or female), homosexual couples, mixed families through remarriage, and so forth. The number of divorced couples and children of divorced parents has risen. The percentage of American women in the labor force by the year 2000 will be 75 percent. The number of children in nursery schools has doubled since 1970. The oft-heard term "latchkey child" highlights the concern over the numbers of children returning after school to homes where parents are absent due to work, separation, or divorce. Without available after-school programs, parents advise latchkey children to lock themselves in the home until a guardian arrives. More and more industries are providing child-care programs to serve the needs of their employees. Afterschool recreation programs have also emerged in response to this demonstrated need for child supervision.

In their book *Toward a Typology of Juvenile Offenders*, Sheldon and

Eleanor Glueck indicate that several factors contribute to youthful criminal activity: lack of family cohesiveness, absence of family-shared recreation, and insufficient home-based recreation materials conducive to family-shared recreation. These findings point to the pressing need for recreation agencies to provide families with resource information and materials for home-based recreation. But this is a role that recreation professionals have been slow to fill, due to the misconception that they are solely responsible for attracting "numbers" to attend agency programs. Time, money, and interest factors lead many households to avoid organized programs in favor of self-initiated ones, however, and recreation professionals should be available with this guidance.

The high level of consumer interest in home-based, self-directed leisure pursuits is reflected in the rising popularity of board games. In the "Trends" section of the October 1984 issue of *Forbes Magazine,* a report entitled "Back to the Parlor" predicted a chronic shortage of Trivial Pursuit games despite a production speed of one per second and a sale of 22 million games in 1984. The report indicated that the entire board game industry earned $300 million in wholesale profits in 1983. Even many of the original board games that have been on the market for years have shown an increase in sales; for instance, the game Scrabble increased its sales by 35 percent in 1983.

MEDIA

The impact of media on individual and family leisure lifestyles has been enormous. There has been a steady rise in television viewing over a 20-year period, from an estimated four and one-half hours of daily viewing in 1950 to more than seven hours in 1983.

Drawbacks

While many children's programs are educational and beneficial, there is a danger of letting television take the place of families playing together. For example, there are now round-the-clock children's cable television networks that can become substitutes for play experiences if viewed in excess.

Television has become a major focus of many people's leisure lifestyles. Many have purchased video cassette recorders in order to tape TV programs while away from home or to view popular movies through the rental or purchase of videotapes.

Questions arise as to the desirability of watching TV excessively at the expense of other edifying and diversified leisure pursuits. Individuals homebound due to disability or emotional or physical illness have acknowledged that they keep the television on as "background voice," as this is the closest approximation to company they receive. This phenomenon only accentuates the need for recreation outreach workers to bring recreation materials (crafts, plants, and so forth) to those isolated from community resources and socialization.

Aside from its negative influence, it should be noted that television offers a wide variety of stimulating, educational programs that can enhance one's leisure if chosen with discrimination. Media technology can be harnessed for its positive benefits in order to enrich leisure services delivery. For instance, videotapes of recreational activities are made available to community residents for self-instructional purposes. Local hobbyists can make informative tapes on the details and advantages of their hobbies. The availability of such videotapes to the institutionalized and homebound makes the agency's leisure education efforts a truly community-wide effort. Media also permit individuals to communicate via cassette or videotape, should writing be a physical hardship or simply not of interest.

Television's strengths as a communications medium have been adapted to serve the diverse interests within each community. Special program networks such as the Spanish International Network present programs relevant to their respective constituents. Independent stations provide attractive, educational programs such as "novels for TV." TV broadcasters such as the Public Broadcasting System meet their subscribers' demands for more quality programming in ways the commercial networks do not. Recreation programs can be publicized freely on cable TV through community access, and through cable stations the viewers can exercise more decision-making regarding their viewing interests.

Library media resources (films, tapes, recordings of books, aids for the visually handicapped) are available for use in the library or on a home-loan basis. In every leisure services agency the application of media programs is limitless ("slide show under the stars" at camp, daily film on the cruise ship, filmmaking class at the community center).

But recreation leaders should be forewarned, because the media explosion has also led to a jaded consumer of leisure services. Recreation agencies find that what was once viewed as a novel program (travelogues, a slide show) now attracts little interest due to the fact that the same content is available within the comforts of one's own home on the TV or VCR. Similarly, the abundance of movie malls presenting multiple films simultaneously is likely to overshadow the classic film series being offered at the local recreation center. Consider the dominating impact of a media event in this illustration: "The San Francisco Ballet's appearance on the 'Dance in America' TV series reached an audience that would take thirty-four years to equal if the group performed to capacity houses every single day."[1]

In light of media popularity, the recreation leader may be tempted to inject an "entertainment type quality" into programming to attract participants. Recreation directors may observe with concern that their constituents are moving compulsively from one activity to another in much the

1. Michael and Holly R. Chubb, *One Third of Our Time? An Introduction to Recreation Behavior and Resources* (New York: John Wiley and Sons, 1981), p. 585.

same way they have been accustomed to move from channel to channel; participants can become conditioned to expect recreation, like media, to switch quickly from one "high" to another. Now, youth not only play high-tech, fast-paced video games, but they actually become figures in the video game itself. In the live electronic game Photon, players move through an extraterrestrial maze and gain (or lose) points by "shooting" (or being shot by) members of the opposing team. In this age of multiple stimuli, recreation activity has come to mean just another background diversion, an attitude that frustrates recreation leaders expecting more concentration and commitment.

MATERIAL CONSUMPTION

The compulsive search for new forms of stimulation reflects society's craze for material consumption. People convince themselves that the void in their lives can be filled by buying the latest ski outfit or the most talked-about furniture and later wonder why, as their rooms crowd with purchases, their lives seem to diminish in quality. The 1980s will be remembered as the age of parents trampling each other to purchase Cabbage Patch dolls, only to find children often more interested in creating some plaything from a neutral object (ball of yarn, a pot, a cardboard box).

While inflation has reduced some people's ability to buy the recreational materials or pursue the recreational activities they would wish, many have retained sufficient discretionary income to pursue the leisure activities of their choice. It is true that the inability to meet the challenge of discretionary income has led to empty materialism. People mistakenly believe that leisure satisfaction must be bought and that those without adequate financial means are denied it. Ascribing to this belief, for example, would be someone who identifies leisure as an expensive yearly vacation. Yet people actually enjoy a great number of simple daily pleasures: reading, gardening, talking to a friend, star-gazing. It is sad that some will never view these as leisure because they are informal and free! Recreation leaders have a responsibility to teach the rewards of such simple leisure opportunities; no one should come to the end of their days feeling that they have not known leisure because they have not known sufficient money!

EXPANDED FREE TIME

In general, the availability of discretionary time (free time devoid of work or other obligations) is occurring more and more throughout the lifespan prior to retirement. People are receiving more discretionary time due to labor and time-saving devices; shorter work weeks; more vacation time; provision of sabbaticals; and early retirement. Through an arrangement known as flex time, workers have some choice as to the time frame in which they will work, thus gaining the ability to create blocks of free time in the sequence they wish. This has helped parents comfortably adjust their work schedules to permit sharing in child care. Similarly, the concept of job sharing allows two or more people to perform the same job on a part-time basis, thus increasing free time. In arranging work and discretionary time periods, individuals should examine those time frames that seem most conducive to their leisure needs. One person may prefer a longer weekend, another individual a series of midweek afternoon breaks.

However, free time does not insure a leisure experience unless individuals enter into those open hours with some concept of their values and interests. Leisure education offers ways to approach discretionary time with assurance rather than dread. Oftentimes, individuals seek out a second job, not to fill a financial need but to fill the empty hours. It is unfortunate that people often let the predominant work ethic circumvent the possibility of new experiences in recreation. Challengers of the linear lifestyle pattern (school–job–retirement) feel that the prescribed roles associated with specific ages have limited the development of a natural, evolutionary response to leisure and living.

ENVIRONMENTAL POLLUTION

The use of limited resources by a burgeoning population has contributed to environmental pollution. This condition mars the quality of leisure experiences in endless ways: garbage floating down the river detracts from the pleasure of a picnic; broken glass on an asphalt basketball court is an eyesore as well as a safety hazard; billboards lining the byways minimize the esthetics of a travel vacation; smoke-filled factory towns make outdoor recreation experiences sensory aversions rather than sensory pleasures. Our leisure choices themselves are often restricted by the existence of such pollution factors. For instance, critical levels of air pollution can result in a citywide shutdown of many outdoor recreation programs. Similarly, water recreation (fishing, swimming, and so forth) can be canceled when water pollution is at health-hazard levels.

TECHNOLOGY

The rise in mechanization has led to some worker dissatisfaction with the quality of the work experience. While work can be a source of pride and self-esteem, for many it is analogous to being an insignificant cog in a technological machine. As computers replace many tasks normally done by humans, it is especially important to preserve the human element in the workplace. The need to ensure the harmonious blending of human and machine has led to the creation of an actual science to monitor their coexistence. The science of biotechnology, or the interaction of human and machine, will take on new dimensions in the twenty-first century as computers assume a bigger role in labor.

By enriching jobs and redesigning tasks so that some autonomy, skill development, and variety are provided, industry may increase worker satisfaction. Overall life satisfaction is achieved when the individual is helped to see a sense of purpose in both work and leisure lifestyles. Industrial recreation is responsible for the building of employee morale through company sponsorship of leisure counseling and recreational programs. Just as vocational counselors are trained to help individuals assess how to identify and achieve career goals, avocational or leisure counselors are conducting the same assessments of leisure choices.

Using the New Leisure Time

Technology has created more discretionary time for leisure through the creation of time- and labor-saving devices. This trend is perhaps no more graphically evident than in the current interest in robots as human servants. Harvard University has instituted an undergraduate course in robotics to train students in the design and installation of robots. The Robotics Experimenters Amateur League (REAL) has a nationwide membership of 175 individuals who have chosen robot building as a form of recreation. Hubotics, Inc. of Carlsbad, California has introduced a $3495 "Hubot," a robot with a 12-inch TV set, stereo cassette player, videogame set, digital clock, personal computer, and synthesized voice with a 1200-word vocabulary, (options include a drink tray, burglar alarm, fire alarm, and vacuum cleaner). People tend to frantically purchase such time-saving devices as robots in order to expand their free time—time to be used for they know not what! The creation of increased discretionary time must be accompanied by an understanding of how to find leisure in that time, for unless there is some sense of fulfillment in the additional free time, it becomes a source of frustration and boredom.

To offset this development, as mentioned earlier, leisure education is critically important to help people come to terms with their own leisure values and interests.

Rise of Computer Use

The growth of computerization has had a major impact on perceptions of work and leisure. The lines between work and nonwork hours and between workplace and home become indistinguishable when a home computer permits one to process data and transmit instant reports to the office without leaving one's easy chair. In the future this process, "telecommuting," will require individuals to be even more diligent in protecting leisure needs, or they will inadvertently be swept into round-the-clock work at home. Approximately 200 firms are experimenting with telecommuting.

The computer occupies a major part of many work lives, and as a recreational choice also meets many diversified needs:

People use them to play games, prepare tax returns, monitor investments, write resumes and trace their family trees. Increasingly, owners of home computers are tapping large data banks to call up news reports and stock quotes, to order goods and scan airline schedules. People also use such services to send messages to other subscribers over phone lines, a medium that has already produced electronic romances.[2]

The idea of the computer as a means of socialization is a surprising testimony, since the computer would suggest visions of isolated individuals embracing their machines instead of each other. (Computers can come to take the place of people, as evidenced by "Eliza," a computer counselor with programmed therapy questions.) While one would expect the interest in the computer to overshadow social contact, in the New York Personal Computer Club the very attraction to the computer becomes the basis for attraction to like-minded individuals of the opposite sex. A member of the club states,

> Now a peer is someone who shares my love of computers. The computer gives you the feeling you're still in touch with what's going on out there. You turn on the computer and you have instant intimacy.[3]

As with any leisure activity taken to excess, use of computers can become a maladaptive or destructive form of leisure. For instance, computer users have crossed the threshold of harmless play to illegal activity by tapping savings accounts, tampering with military and hospital records, violating copyrights, and transmitting pornographic illustrations or stories. The fact that 7- to 14-year olds frequent a popular New York City video arcade and charge hundreds of dollars worth of computer game play on their parents' credit cards is also a form of destructive leisure.

Unfortunately, the decision to purchase a computer for home use is not so clearly a matter of personal choice as it is submission to societal pressure. For instance, through promotional campaigns parents are made to feel that they would be negligent as guardians of their children's welfare were they not to buy them home computers. These high-pressure advertising tactics are illustrated in the following excerpts from an article entitled "Computer Worship":

> In a catchy ad by Program Design, Inc. for Baby's First Software, for example, a confident toddler stares out at the reader and his future. "Your child becomes part of the action while acquiring new skills," the ad proclaims.
>
> Also, Children's Television Workshop of Sesame Street is now pushing ENTER, a new computer magazine for 10–16 year olds. "The computer is as basic to your child's life and lifestyle as paper was to yours and mine," states a letter to parents. "And learning computer skills is (not will be) as fundamental

2. Special Report, "Ten Forces Reshaping America." Excerpted from U.S. News & World Report, issue of March 19, 1984, p. 43. Copyright 1984, U.S. News & World Report, Inc.
3. Patricia Morrisroe, "Living with the Computer," *New York*, Jan. 9, 1984, vol. 17, no. 2, p. 29.

as learning was to you and me. . . . You can consider these to be overstate-ments, but only at your youngster's peril."[4]

While there is evidence that the computer aids learning, there is con-cern as to how much its impact may be exaggerated. The Educational Prod-ucts Information Exchange, a nonprofit organization affiliated with Co-lumbia University Teachers College and Consumers Union, gives only 25 percent of the instructional software evaluated a high rating. A child's pre-occupation with an educational computer is not necessarily synonymous with learning; it may be attraction to the computer's flashy video arcade techniques.

Parents are concerned that they will be unable to communicate with their children unless they learn the computer terminology their children are learning in school and computer camp. The child, in effect, has become teacher to the parent. In light of this anticipated communication gap, more adults are seeking courses in computers. The child who has been exposed to computerized tutoring is at a distinct advantage to the novice parent!

The computer camp is described in a November 1984 issue of *Parks and Recreation*. The computer camp integrates traditional camp activities with the primary function of training the child in computer use. On a daily basis, children are exposed to beginner, intermediate, and advanced com-puter instruction, as well as computer games and computer literacy tests.

The computer has become an important component of other recrea-tion settings beside the computer camp. For instance, museums offer "hands-on" computer projects for children. Computers assist leisure coun-selors in matching client avocational interests with recommended leisure pursuits. Recreation professionals also utilize computers to assist in client assessments and the establishment of behavioral objectives. Recreation therapists also have found computers to be helpful in teaching concepts to mentally retarded clients. Another project, pertaining to therapeutic recre-ation, is the work of Playing To Win, a nonprofit organization that pro-motes computer use to teach academic skills to the educationally and so-cially disadvantaged in schools and correctional centers.

TRANSPORTATION

Much publicity has been given to the poor condition of our mass transit systems and the inadequate transportation services for disabled individu-als. People will not attend even the most attractive recreation program if it is inaccessible, particularly if it is located in a crime-ridden area. Safe and affordable transportation to the recreation site is imperative. Recreation leaders should be in the forefront in advocating improved transportation services.

4. Joseph A. Menosky, "Computer Worship," *Science*, May 1984, vol. 5, no. 4, pp. 41–42.

CRIME

The proliferation of crime has also created an environmental barrier to leisure satisfaction. Due to fear of street assault or burglary, many people become virtual prisoners in their own homes. For those who do "brave the streets" for a recreational activity, one can question how truly "at leisure" such people can be while their minds are absorbed by fears of attack or theft. Increasingly, leisure services agencies are incorporating crime prevention and self-defense classes into their programs with the understanding that self-actualization through recreation is more likely if the basic need for safety is assured. Volunteering as a neighborhood crime watcher or court monitor has become an increasingly popular leisure time activity.

PASSIVE LIFESTYLE

As a people, we are much too sedentary for our own good. While there are exceptions to this pattern, the fact remains that we are too cozy in our easy chairs, cocktail lounges, and automobiles. This state of affairs contributes to obesity, hypertension, and a host of other negative health conditions. An ABC News—Harris Survey of 1442 adults revealed the prevalence of poor eating habits and inactivity in the American population. This study found that, passive leisure activities predominated, and, when coupled with the overeating, increased prospects of poor fitness and health. Cardio-vascular, gastro-intestinal, and respiratory problems are more apt to affect this sector of our society.

LONGEVITY

People today are living much longer, a phenomenon that means expanded leisure time is available in one's later years. This extended life expectancy is attributable to outstanding medical advancements and the improved nutritional and fitness habits of each succeeding cohort of older adults. These habits have improved largely because recreation agencies have offered increasingly more visible, appealing programs that have attracted more participants. Direct correlation can be made between increased longevity and participation in stimulating recreational activities that have sustained positive physical, mental, and emotional conditioning. Having added time in their later years, older adults are viewing this expanded free time as an exciting leisure challenge. There is a tendency toward early retirement. Older adults require preretirement programs that cover not only pension plans and other factual material, but also guidance on leisure education and recreational activity. Recreation agencies of all types, be they community centers, resorts, or senior citizen centers should be responsive to the need for more programs targeted to the interests and learning methods of the preretiree and retiree.

SUMMARY

The purpose of this chapter has been to expose the student to the multiple and varied societal factors influencing the leisure experience. Students' knowledge of these dynamics within the larger society forms the basis frrom which their philosophy of leisure and recreation programming emerges. This knowledge, coupled with the leadership and programming tools discussed in this text, will enable recreation professionals to approach their responsibilities with greater insight, creativity, and vision.

SUGGESTED READINGS

BUTLER, GEORGE. *Introduction to Community Recreation.* New York: McGraw-Hill, 1975.
CHUBB, MICHAEL AND CHUBB, HOLLY R. *One Third of Our Time?* New York: John Wiley and Sons, 1981.
FOUGHT, MILLARD. *More Timewealth for You.* New York: Pyramid Books, 1969.
GLUECK, SHELDON AND ELEANOR. *Toward a Typology of Juvenile Offenders.* New York: Grune and Stratton Publishers, 1970.
HAWORTH, J. T. AND SMITH, M. A. (EDS.). *Work and Leisure.* Princeton, NJ: Princeton Book Co., 1976.
JOHNSON, DOUGLAS W. *Computer Ethics: A Guide for the New Age.* Elgin, IL: Brethren Press, 1984.
MURPHY, JAMES. *Recreation and Leisure Service.* Dubuque, IA: William C. Brown, 1975.
RUTSTEIN, NAT. *"Go Watch TV!": What and How Much Should Children Really Watch.* New York: Steed and Watch, 1974.
STEIN, THOMAS A. AND SESSOMS, DOUGLAS, (EDS.). *Recreation and Special Populations.* Boston: Holbrook Press, 1975.
WEINSTEIN, ROBERT V. *Jobs for the 21st Century.* New York: Collier Books, 1983.
WEISKOFF, DONALD. *A Guide to Recreation and Leisure.* Boston: Allyn and Bacon, 1975.

Appendix A

Visual Aids in Recreation Leadership

The adage "A picture is worth a thousand words" is particularly relevant when teaching concepts and skills to recreation participants. For this reason, visual aids are recognized as valuable tools in the recreation leadership process.

Many think of motion pictures as the sole visual aid. In addition to motion pictures, however, there are opaque projection slides, filmstrips, posters, blackboards, charts, television, VTR or VCR recordings, maps, graphs, models, and specimens. Each one of these visual aids will be discussed briefly as they relate to recreation.

TYPES OF VISUAL AIDS

Motion Pictures

The motion picture is a very valuable and interesting visual aid. In the recreation field, the motion picture reproduces skills with a clarity that resembles real-life instruction. For example, the stroke in badminton can be conveyed through the motion picture better than perhaps any other medium. Films need not only teach a skill, however; they can reflect educational or entertainment content as well.

Suggested sources for films and examples for various recreational activities will be presented later in this chapter. To enjoy fully the benefits of the motion picture, the group should be prepared for the showing in advance so that learning objectives have been matched to the film. Furthermore, a thorough discussion should follow the showing in order to answer any questions that may arise. Some projectors make it possible to stop the action at any frame desired or to slow down the action to simplify the viewer's observations. Consider using these modifications of regular motion whenever possible.

Opaque Projector

One of the most versatile and simple projection devices is the opaque projector. The opaque projector is convenient: It does not require a completely darkened room—though, naturally the darker the room, the sharper the image. It can project pictures, charts, or any content from a book, magazine, or any object that will fit within the opaque projector's base, which is usually 6 × 8 inches. Some opaque projectors come with accessories that permit, in addition, the projection of slides 2 by 2 inches and 3¼ by 4 inches, as well as of 35-mm filmstrips.

Overhead Projector

The overhead projector is a device similar to the opaque projector. It differs in that it will project (on a screen or wall) any material that is written on a plastic transparency. The recreation leader can draw or write at the projector while the group views it instantaneously. Erasures can be made with a cloth and the transparency used again. It is also possible to make permanent transparencies.

Slides

Slides, like opaque projection, are effective instruction tools, in that the length of time that any one image remains on the screen is determined by the recreation leader, who is thus able to adjust the pace to the learning abilities of the viewers. Photographic slides are 2 inches square, while silhouette and etched-glass slides are 3¼ by 4 inches in size.

The easiest to construct is the etched-glass slide. The object is simply drawn on the slide's rough side; mere erasure makes the slide useful for another drawing. The silhouette slide can be made by placing a cutout of the drawing between two clear glasses of slide size.

On-the-Spot Photography

Recreation departments can benefit from self-developing cameras that reveal their finished pictures in under a minute. This permits the leader to report without delay on such activities as contest winners, crafts exhibitors, and countless other graphic portrayals. Thus, the pictures are shown readily when their newsworthiness is at its peak.

This instant photography lends itself especially to making social functions memorable. A funny, lifesize cartoon figure with a cutout head where people can insert their own faces is always a popular photo opportunity; in fact, it may be used as a fundraiser with a fee for each picture taken. Photographs snapped as the guests arrive can also be used as place cards at parties.

Filmstrips

Filmstrips possess the same advantage as slides and are much less expensive than films. Less technical skill is needed to make one's own filmstrips than is required for motion pictures. Projectors are available that can be used both for slide and filmstrip projection.

Television

Television is a medium with unlimited possibilities. Opportunities are afforded for instruction in such areas as group musical instruments, arts and crafts, drama, sports, and hobby development. The VTR (video tape recorder) or VCR (video cassette recorder) make it possible to record and play back video tapes through a conventional TV set. A video cassette camera is an essential component that can be used in conjunction with the VTR or VCR. Camera coverage of significant events can serve to provide future publicity. Furthermore, it can be employed to determine the strengths and shortcomings of a performance or event. For example, participants in dance programs or basketball leagues can view their performance on tape and work to improve the observed flaws. In addition, the instant replay capability of this camera lends itself admirably to the analysis and instruction of particular skills and activities.

Posters

If designed clearly and attractively, posters can serve as an excellent visual aid. However, a poster left up for a prolonged period of time at one site loses much of its effectiveness, viewers ceasing to pay any attention to it. Periodic changing of posters as well as shifting them from one spot to another can add to their effectiveness as a teaching device. In addition, the use of vivid colors, the illusion of raised figures and lettering, and visual action can add to their attention-getting power and message-bearing quality.

Blackboards

The use of the blackboard is so common that it is often overlooked as an easily available and valuable teaching medium. Its utility is enhanced by the easy erasure of the board, and the use of colored chalk for more vivid illustrations. Blackboard illustrations can find many uses, in dramatics (stage layout, planning of props), sports (play diagrams, golf strokes), music (lyrics, list of song selections), and arts & crafts (designs, construction plans). Whenever feasible, the material to be placed on the board should be written or drawn before the group's arrival.

Additional Visual Aids

There are numerous other visual aids at the recreation leader's disposal. Charts find uses in such activities as arts and crafts (use of tools, types of wood) and sports (basketball plays, use of an exercise machine), in outdoor recreation (planning a hosteling itinerary, studying influence of terrain on a nation's culture). Graphs are useful in sports for scoring, while models and specimens are helpful in outdoor recreation (insect collections, leaf study).

PREPARATORY STEPS

Before projecting a motion picture, filmstrips, slides, or transparencies, advance preparation is needed. It is always advisable to preview what is to be shown. This is particularly advisable before projecting a motion picture. The projector and screen should be so situated as to clear all heads and be as easily visible as conditions will permit. The seating arrangement should be checked with this in mind. No one should sit closer to the screen than twice the picture's width, nor more than 30 degrees off to the side. The sound speaker should be near the screen at about the level of the audience's ears.

A preview of a film will help iron out possible wrinkles—in other words, is the film correctly reeled and ready to go? does it need splicing (the taping of torn pieces of film)? is the takeup reel of sufficient size? After the preview test, rewind the film. Rethread it and run the film up to the title before the audience arrives.

Before ordering a film, ask the supply source for literature describing the film. Look up the description incorporated in sources such as the *Educational Film Guide*. Ascertain whether the film size available (16 mm, 35 mm, or 8 mm) fits your projector and whether it is a sound or silent film. (See the Filmography—Appendix I—that follows for a brief description of many films suitable for recreational purposes.)

Other considerations are of equal importance when viewing films. Be sure to have at hand the instructional material that comes with a film projector. Spare fuses and bulbs should be part of a repair kit. A flashlight will prove helpful for checking things while a projector is in operation. Projectors should not be left alone while in operation. Assign someone to handle the room lights. Have the sound system warmed up before lights go off, so as not to interfere with a film's continuity.

FILMOGRAPHY

The following is a list of films that can be used in the leadership of the various recreational program areas discussed in this book. The films have been categorized by their program areas. The names and addresses of film suppliers from which these films can be obtained are given at the end of the film listing. For further sources of films, contact the film companies listed at the end of the chapter. (All films listed below are 16mm unless otherwise noted.)

Arts

General

CIRCUS TOWN   49 min., color, 82590, University of Illinois (1970).

Shows how the residents of Peru, Indiana, join together to present a full-length circus every summer. Peru was once the winter quarters of six American circuses, and it is still the home of many retired circus performers who act as trainers for trapeze, high wire, tumbling, and clown acts. The performers being trained are the town's young people (ages 6 to 20) who show the dedication and talent required for a professional level performance. *Mounted on two reels.*

FIESTA   8 min., color, 04554, University of Illinois (1977).

It's fiesta time, and this film shows all the activities: parades, ceremonies, dances, fireworks, music, and costumes. No narration. Original songs by Holly Graham.

FREE TO BE . . . YOU AND ME—FRIENDSHIP & COOPERATION   18 min., color, ESC-1746, Indiana University (1974).

Presents cartoons, puppetry, and musical segments which center on the conflicts and rewards in maintaining interpersonal relationships. Covers the topics of cooperation vs. disruptive interference; demanding special privileges; the joys and trials of having brothers and sisters; and luck, friendship, and mending quarrels. Features Marlo Thomas, Mel Brooks, The New Seekers, Tom Smothers, Cicely Tyson, and The Voices of East Harlem.

RELATIONS   41 min., color, 90179, University of Illinois (1975).

This film illustrates efforts to make arts more accessible to the general community. Three episodes are examples of the kind of relationships that are being encouraged: Wilson Douglas, fiddler, and his folk music band at the Mountain Heritage Folk Festival in Carter Caves State Park, Kentucky; Ned Williams, instructor of primitive African and Haitian dance, and his students, at Gateway National Recreation Area, Brooklyn, New York; Vilem Sokol, conductor of the Seattle Youth Symphony, in rehearsal and performance at the Northwest Music Camp in Fort Flagler State Park, Washington.

THE INCREDIBLE SAN FRANCISCO ARTISTS' SOAPBOX DERBY   24 min., color, 33123, Pennsylvania State (1977).

Covers an unusual soapbox derby staged by 104 Bay Area artists who designed their gravity-operated cars in a wide variety of unconventional vehicular shapes—a pencil, a shoe, a butterfly, a dome paved with pennies. Interviews with the artists serve as narration and as insights into the creative process.

THE MAGIC OF RED CROSS   15 min., 16 mm, 321658, American Red Cross (1977).

A magic show in a circus atmosphere is used to interest young school children in Red Cross youth, health, and safety activities.

TO BE CREATIVE   17 min., color, ESC-1649, Indiana University (1977).

Considers the many aspects of creativity found in daily life. Interviews a recently handicapped woman who has turned to drawing, a telephone line repairman, a filmmaker, and others who offer suggestions about how to integrate creativity into day-to-day living. Concludes with a Don McLean song about Vincent Van Gogh. *Inner Circle series.*

Dance

AEROBIC EXERCISING   14 min., color, HSC-1152, Indiana University (1981).

Shows the difference between aerobic and non-aerobic exercises, pointing out the advantages of aerobics. Indicates that aerobic exercises can increase strength and endurance, heighten the feeling of well-being, aid in the loss of body fat, and lower blood pressure. Suggests a plan for implementing an aerobics program, cautioning about the need for readiness, warm-up, and safety.

BEING ME   13 min., bw, 53067, University of Illinois (1969).

Documents a creative dance class for nine girls, ages 8 to 13, conducted at the Pasadena Art Museum by Hilda Mullin, an artist, teacher, and therapist.

DANCERS IN SCHOOL   28 min., color, 83442, University of Illinois (1972).

As children are shown going through their paces in dancing classes, dance instructors Murray Louis, Virginia Tanner, Bella Lewitzky, and Kate Taylor comment on their methods of training. These dancers and their companies work in residence under an artists-in-schools program.

FULL OF LIFE A-DANCIN'   30 min., color, 84399, University of Illinois (1978).

The Southern Appalachian Cloggers of North Carolina are shown in rehearsal and performance, and give personal insights as to the importance of dance in their lives.

INTRODUCTION TO DANCE (Revised Edition)   17 min., color, 51072, University of Illinois (1971).

Demonstrates that all dance steps are created from the basic locomotor steps: the walk, run, jump, hop, skip, slide, gallop, and leap. Illustrates how the combinations of these basic steps were used to create the modern social, novelty, folk, and square dances. The simplicity of these basic steps is traced and related to the present day dances in the lands of Mexico, India, New Guinea, Ethiopia, South Africa, Madagascar, and the Philippine Islands.

SQUARE DANCING FUNDAMENTALS, PART 1—LEVEL 1   18 min., color, 54633, University of Illinois (1974).

Explains and illustrates the first twenty-two fundamental square dance movements, in progression. Not more than two concepts are introduced in any dance. Simple dances using the concepts taught are performed by a group of young people.

SQUARE DANCING FUNDAMENTALS, PART 2—LEVEL 1   17 min., color, 54634, University of Illinois (1974).

Thirteen level one movements are taught and called by an instructor, learned and demonstrated by a group of young people. Includes courtesy turn, lines of four, grand chain, right and left through, promenade the corner.

SURE I CAN DANCE   25 min., color, U50476, University of Iowa (1976).

Children learn how to make their faces, their elbows, hands, and knees dance; high school students discover that through dance they can conquer problems of concentration, stage movement, and group interaction, and teachers discover dance to be a useful teaching tool for creative development.

Drama

NEW ZEBRA IN TOWN (Acceptance)   12 min., color, ESC-1354, Indiana University (1974).

Uses a puppet show about discrimination to show that acceptance often grows from suspicion when one meets something or someone new or different. Focuses on Oni, Coslo, and Butch, who don't want Zaybar Zebra, a new arrival in the neighborhood, to work with them on their school project because Zaybar's stripes are different. Observes how they all learn the value of acceptance when they realize that they are all different. *Forest Town Fables series.*

PANTOMIME: THE LANGUAGE OF THE HEART   10 min., color, U20337, University of Iowa (1975).

Marcel Marceau demonstrates the art of mime and the use of the body to communicate.

THREE LOOMS WAITING   50 min., color, U65024, University of Iowa (1972).

Dorothy Heathcote, famous creative dramatist, explains her goals as she demonstrates in actual learning situations her methods of teaching improvisational drama. Shows the response by groups of young children from diverse economic backgrounds, ages, and handicaps. Also includes scenes with student teachers applying Mrs. Heathcote's techniques.

Visual Arts

ART FROM FOUND MATERIALS   15 min., color, RSC-813, Indiana University, (1971).

Demonstrates the construction of a collage and an assemblage using materials which are usually thrown away and objects from nature supplemented by paint, ink, crayon, tape, and liquid starch. Explains that one might either search and select objects because of their shape, color, form, and texture and then develop an idea or begin with an idea and then gather the appropriate materials. Provides numerous samples of completed works as well as works in progress.

KITES OF JAPAN   29 min., color, 33656, Pennsylvania State (1976).

Japanese kites, made of bamboo and handmade paper and decorated in the *ukiyo-e* print style, are not simply a form of sport but are associated with popular faiths. The film introduces and classifies more than 200 kites from various regions of Japan, considers their history, and documents several kite-flying festivals.

SIMPLY MAKING JEWELRY   18 min., color, RSC-1056, Indiana University (1977).

Demonstrates "unit construction" approach to jewelry making. Shows a variety of readily available objects and materials which can be used as unit pieces and the tools required to make and join the units into more complex designs. Characterizes the work as an exploration, with the final jewelry pieces being a record of the process.

Arts Therapy

A SONG FOR MICHAEL   22 min., bw, NY State Education Dept. (1969).

This film presents a condensation of one actual music therapy session and demonstrates how music promotes emotional and social growth as an adjunct to psychotherapy.

CRY HELP   83 min., color, NY State Education Dept. (1970).

Focuses on arts therapy with mentally disturbed teenagers. Participants are shown using such devices as self-analysis with a video tape recorder, psychodrama, body awareness, and visual art to regain their emotional stability.

DO IT   20 min., color, NY State Education Dept. (n.d.).

The development of a drama therapy workshop for mentally handicapped persons is broken down into simple steps. Each step is an exercise or game designed to lead the handicapped individual toward discoveries. Any recreation leader contemplating the use of creative dramatics can fashion a comprehensive program from this film.

JUST FOR THE FUN OF IT   18 min., color, NY State Education Dept. (1972).

This program for mentally handicapped children demonstrates various activities useful in developing perceptual motor skills as well as improving self-image in young trainable retardate children. Several instructional methods using commonplace materials such as blankets, squeaker toys, hula hoops, etc. are illustrated.

LOOKING FOR ME   29 min., bw, NY State Education Dept. (1970).

The use of dance and movement as a therapeutic tool is explained by dance therapist, Janet Adler, as she reports on a research project in which she investigated the therapeutic benefits of patterned movement in her work with four groups: normal preschoolers, emotionally disturbed children, autistic children, and adult teachers (New York University Film Library).

REACH INSIDE—LEARNING THROUGH MUSIC   30 min., color, NY State Education Dept. (1972).

This film presents music therapy methods to be used with the mentally handicapped and severely handicapped to develop communication skills, express emotions, and attitudes. Methods demonstrated show processes by which children are given opportunities to fantasize in order to be able to allow for natural expression through the art of repetitive music. Music therapy acts as a catalyst for group participation and social interaction as a means to improve learning.

REACHING OUT—THE LIBRARY AND THE EXCEPTIONAL CHILD   25 min., color, NY State Education Dept. (n.d.).

Children with various handicaps are shown responding to books and other library materials. The film concentrates on scenes of librarian contact with children in the classroom, at home, and in the hospital.

THE SHAPE OF A LEAF 26 min., color, Guidance Information Center. (n.d.)

Retarded children, kindergarten through the eighth grade, are shown working in various arts therapy activities—making perception training boxes, painting, talking about art, doing creative stitchery, weaving, working with batik, making ceramic creche figurines, and conducting a puppet show.

SHOW ME 30 min., bw, NY State Education Dept. (n.d.).

This film is designed to promote the teaching of movement and rhythms to the mentally retarded.

General

ARTIFICIAL RESPIRATION AND FIRST AID FOR CHOKING 6 min., 16 mm, 321536, American Red Cross (1980).

A shortened version of the first part of the revised Multimedia Standard First Aid film, showing techniques for giving artificial respiration and first aid for choking emergencies. Designed to encourage interest in classes and to be used in presentations. NOTE: Replaces "Techniques of Artificial Respiration."

BRIDGES 15 min., 321610, American Red Cross. (n.d.)

This award-winning film is the story of teenagers who become volunteers with the American Red Cross, building bridges of communication and caring with other people's worlds.

CARDIOPULMONARY RESUSCITATION Super 8 mm, American Red Cross. (n.d.)

Intended to be used as part of the CPR modular instructional course or as a visual aid supplement to lecture courses. These Super 8mm silent film loop cartridges for Fisher Price Montron viewers are available for purchase, but *not for loan*. Pricing information may be obtained from the General Supply Office, National Headquarters, American Red Cross, Washington, DC 20005. CPR Infants (use first half only)—stock no. 321662; CPR Chest Compression—stock no. 321663; CPR Delayed Care 1 & 2 Rescuers—stock no. 321664; Mouth-to-mouth, mouth-to-nose breathing—stock no. 321666.

DO YOUR OWN THING 13 min., color, ESC-1744, Indiana University (1972).

Presents an animated episode with Fat Albert and the Cosby Kids as they learn the importance of participating in activities that are enjoyable whether one is a boy or a girl. Shows Penny, a new girl in the neighborhood, as she excels at sports and relates that Fat Albert loves to cook. Concludes as Fat Albert wins a baking contest and the gang appreciates the fact that everyone should "do their own thing." *Learning Values with Fat Albert and the Cosby Kids series.*

FIRST AID FOR CHILDREN—"I CAN DO IT MYSELF" 11 min., color, LSC-210, Indiana University (1978).

Shows the simple first aid procedures children can use to treat minor injuries until a responsible adult can come to their assistance. Uses dramatic vignettes to show common injuries, such as abrasions, paper cuts, black eyes, blisters, and bee stings, and their treatment. Emphasizes that all accidents should be reported to an adult.

IS IT LEZHER OR LEZHER? 31 min., color, 32380, Pennsylvania State (1976).

Many types of people, shown in a variety of leisure-time pursuits, explain why they engage in them, while experts discuss the need for such activity—to combat loneliness, boredom, aimlessness; and to achieve a sense of purpose, self-fulfillment, satisfaction. The film presents leisure counseling, activities for the disabled, program funding, and "work ethic" conflicts.

JUST THE BEGINNING 15 min., American Red Cross. (n.d.)

Produced by the Portland, OR, chapter, this film demonstrates how a Red Cross youth leadership center stimulates followup local-service programming in school and community. Youth are shown involved in a variety of activities. For loan only.

KEEP FIT, STUDY WELL, WORK HARD 13 min., color, 54486, University of Illinois (1973).

Photographed at schools in Peking, Shanghai, and Sian, this film is a revealing look at the life of young students of China. Discipline pervades their lives as illustrated by scenes of hundreds of children exercising in unison to the marching beat of broadcast music. Among other activities, students in an English class practice pronunciation of the saying by Mao Tse Tung, "Keep fit, study well, work hard." Many Chinese schools have an attached factory where part of the students' time is spent working on factory products. Younger children make and assemble chess sets while older students do more difficult jobs such as wiring generators. Concludes with the staging of a pageant honoring Lei Feng, a revolutionary hero.

LEISURE   14 min., color, 21910, Pennsylvania State (1976).

Presents a witty animated "history" of leisure, beginning with the caveman's first moment of play, through the Industrial Revolution, to today's novel situation in which we are beginning to care most about having a good environment for our leisure activities. Academy Award Winner, 1977.

LEISURE 2000   28 min., 31801, Pennsylvania State (1972).

Dr. Robert Lee discusses the emergence of more leisure time in our future and the demands it will make upon us. Examines the growing trend toward sabbaticals and continuing education and leisure's impact upon husband-wife relationships.

MULTIMEDIA STANDARD FIRST AID   53 min., 16 mm, 321517, American Red Cross (1980).

Originally produced by the American Telephone and Telegraph Company, these reels are used with student workbook and instructor material as a multimedia method of teaching standard first aid. They may be ordered from the American Red Cross General Supply Office, along with additional supplies such as checklists and tests.

PLAY AND CULTURAL CONTINUITY: PART 1—APPALACHIAN CHILDREN   23 min., color, 32151, Pennsylvania State (1975).

Spontaneous play of children in a rural coal-mining community in the Appalachian Mountains. Children from infancy to school age seen in a variety of situations, including family life, kindergarten, rambling in the mountains, and fishing. Regional environmental influence on the content of their play is discernible.

PLAY AND CULTURAL CONTINUITY: PART 2—SOUTHERN BLACK CHILDREN   27 min., color, 32152, Pennsylvania State (1975).

Presents children's vivid, dramatic play in Houston and surrounding countryside. Cultural entities, such as music, dancing, and intricate hand-clapping improvisations, and traditional folk games show the easy interaction between generations.

PLAY AND CULTURAL CONTINUITY: PART 3—MEXICAN-AMERICAN CHILDREN   28 min., color, 32201, Pennsylvania State (1975).

Setting is the Rio Grande Valley near Edinburg, Texas, an area where traditional values are maintained and passed on to children. Episodes show domestic play and enactment of experiences at clinics and livestock auctions. Illustrates the culturally defined, prescribed modes of interaction between boys and girls, and the emphasis on mutual respect between generations.

PLAY AND CULTURAL CONTINUITY: PART 4—MONTANA INDIAN CHILDREN   29 min., color, 32202, Pennsylvania State (1975).

On the Flathead Indian Reservation and surrounding countryside, the play of Indian children ranges from the universal domestic activities and "monster" play themes, to those mirroring individualistic cultural elements, such as wrapping of babies, drumming, singing, and hunting.

OF TIME, WORK, AND LEISURE   29 min., bw, ES-713, Indiana University (1963).

Presents concepts set forth in Sebastian de Grazia's study by the same name. Maintains that in our work-oriented, clock-dominated society we have won "time off" but have lost the ability to appreciate true leisure.

PIONEER LIVING: EDUCATION AND RECREATION   11 min., color, 03397, University of Illinois (1970).

Shows how pioneer communities in the early 1800s planned for their educational and cultural needs. We see school being conducted in a combination church and school building, and the enjoyment of recreational activities including quilting bees, box socials, square dancing, hay rides, and a pioneer wedding followed by the traditional shivaree.

SAFE IN RECREATION   15 min., color, 54975, University of Illinois (1974).

The ABC's (Always Be Careful) of safety in recreational activities are outlined through dramatizations of typical accidents. Situations shown involve electricity, poisonous chemicals, kite flying, playground behavior, hiking in the woods and along railroad tracks, picnic fires, poisonous plants, use of sharp tools, good sense with a fishing pole, and proper methods of handling guns. Scenes of polluted recreational areas show that destroying the beauty of nature may also produce danger sources for others.

THAT'S WHAT LIVING'S ABOUT   18 min., color, GSC-1395, Indiana University (1973).

Persuades man to pause, reflect, enjoy, and express creative skills to put meaning into free time in order to find a vital balance between work and leisure. Shows various community resources to help develop useful leisure pursuits for individuals, families, friends, and groups.

THE ANCIENT GAMES 28 min., color, 82774, University of Illinois (1972).

This documentary, conceived, written, and narrated by Erich Segal, captures the spirit of historic origins and importance of the Olympic Games. Two former U.S. Olympic decathlon champions, Bill Toomey and Rafer Johnson, compete in five events (sprint, discus throw, long jump, javelin throw, wrestling) of the Greek pentathlon as they were conducted 2,500 years ago in the original stadium at Delphi, Greece. Between events, Bill and Rafer comment on the ancient games.

THE GOOD SPORT GAME 11 min., color, ESC-1884, Indiana University (1978).

Shows how a young girl whose friends think she is a poor sport learns that good sportsmanship is a lot more fun. Explores some of the reasons for good and poor sportsmanship. *Learning Responsibility series.*

THE WILL TO WIN 16 min., color, 55013, University of Illinois (1968).

Why do people engage in high-risk sports? Why do others watch? The nature of competition, the need for challenge, and the need to win are explored. Spectacular motion picture sequences reveal the elements of danger which sportspersons face, and learn to live with, in auto racing, bull fighting, sky diving, speedboat and motorcycle racing, and to a lesser degree in football, skiing, karate, and horse racing.

TIMBROMANIA 29 min., color, 32250, Pennsylvania State (1977).

Explores the realm of stamp collecting, one of the world's most popular hobbies. Hosted by actor Ernest Borgnine—himself an avid stamp collector—the program follows the story from the 1800's, when the new stamp craze was called "timbromania" by the French, through the 1930's, when it was popularized by Franklin Roosevelt and King George V, to visits with stamp artists and collectors of today.

TWO BALL GAMES 29 min., color, U57530, University of Iowa (1975).

An eloquent study of the disappearance of fun from youthful sports. Intercut sequences of a sandlot game contrast vividly with the tense competitive atmosphere of the Little League game that reflects the ill-tempered adult's attitude toward winning.

YOU'RE TOO FAT 50 min., color, 70106, University of Illinois (1974).

This study looks at some of the scientific explanations of obesity, ways of reducing (from the sensible to the extreme) and possibilities of painless diets for the future. States that obesity is a disease of an abundant and comfortable society in which over 70 million Americans are overweight. *Mounted on two reels.*

YOUTH SERVICE PROGRAMS 15 min., 16 mm, American Red Cross.

Produced jointly by the Pasadena and Greater Long Beach chapters, California, this film illustrates youth participation at a leadership center in various community activities. For loan only.

Outdoor Recreation

BICYCLING FOR PHYSICAL FITNESS, HEALTH AND RECREATION 14 min., color, 55021, University of Illinois (1974).

Defines the benefits of bicycling through practical examples and in basic physiological terms. Demonstrates the value of bicycle riding as exercise and recreation, both in terms of achieving and maintaining physical health. Shows how cycling can be incorporated efficiently into daily living.

GET TO KNOW YOUR 10-SPEED 18 min., color, 55499, University of Illinois (1976).

While illustrating the fun, action, and spirit of bike riding, this film shows how to use a ten-speed bike properly for safety, fitness, and pleasure. Demonstrates techniques for responsible and safe riding, and includes tips on selecting the appropriate bike and accessories, making adjustments, controlling brakes, shifting gears, maintaining bicycle condition, and observing traffic rules. The struggles of Simple Sam, a young man who constantly ignores proper bicycle procedures, are humorously contrasted with several safe, happy, and successful bicyclists.

PSYCHLING 25 min., color, U50865, University of Iowa (1981).

An exciting chronicle of a cross-country bicycle trip made in the record time of 12 days, 3 hours, and 41 minutes. More importantly, it is the story of John Marino, whose personal motivation and goal-setting strategies allowed him to recover from a severe back injury and build himself into a world-class athlete despite doctors' prognosis that he would never participate in sports again.

BASIC SAILING 20 min., American Red Cross (1963).

Produced by the Columbia Yacht Company for the Red Cross, this film introduces the novice sailor to some basic sailing skills. For loan only.

BLACK ICE 11 min., color, U20535, University of Iowa (1982).

The re-emerging interest in iceboat racing is illustrated in this film.

PERSONAL FLOTATION DEVICES 14 min., 321608, American Red Cross (1976).

Illustrates PFDs—personal flotation devices—what they are, the various kinds, and how they are used to ensure safety in all recreational boating situations. Shot on Chesapeake Bay.

PREPARE TO CAST OFF 17 min., 321513, American Red Cross (1978).

A film for those who, along with the Red Cross, believe that parents can teach their own children the essentials of boating safety.

SAILING, PART 1 28 min., bw, HS-861, Indiana University (1967).

Explains the principles and terminology of elementary sailing and the effect of wind upon the sail through the use of model sailboats and a fan. Illustrates the major parts of a sailboat—the mast, boom, and centerboard housing. Emphasizes that each person must know how to swim and shows the correct way to use a life preserver.

SAILING, PART 2 27 min., bw, HS-862, Indiana University (1967).

Investigates the effects of weight placement, wind, and sail adjustment to gain smooth and efficient sailing. Demonstrates the rules of navigation, using model sailboats to show which boat would have the right of way under various conditions. Compares demonstrations with live scenes of the same maneuvers using real sailboats.

FUNDAMENTAL CANOEING 11 min., color, 53428, University of Illinois (1967).

Demonstrates the fundamentals of safe canoeing: how to launch the canoe and take it from the water, and how to portage, load, and enter it safely. Explains the parts of a canoe, choice and size of paddles. Also discusses procedures to ensure safety should the canoe capsize.

WHITEWATER PRIMER 22 min., 321577, American Red Cross (1979).

A new closeup look at whitewater canoeing, its pleasures and its hazards. The first part of the three-part series on whitewater canoeing.

THE UNCALCULATED RISK 15 min., 32158, American Red Cross (1978).

Illustrates what can go wrong when inexperienced people head downriver in canoes, rafts, and kayaks. Stresses the need for instruction *first*—as the best way to prevent accidents.

MARGIN FOR ERROR 22 min., 321529, American Red Cross (1978).

This is the third in a series of three films, beginning with the film *Whitewater Primer* and continuing with *Uncalculated Risk*. It deals with preparedness and proper procedures in whitewater canoeing.

BACKPACKING 15 min., color, 55441, University of Illinois (1975).

A basic how-to-do-it film on backpacking. There is a discussion and general description of equipment including packs, tents, sleeping bags, cooking gear, clothing, and foods. Illustrates backpacking situations in many parts of the United States.

BASIC ROCK CLIMBING 22 min., color, U30533, University of Iowa (1974).

Demonstrates the skills of rock climbing and mountaineering. Expert climbers show novices techniques of climbing, use of equipment, and safety precautions during actual climbs.

B.J. AND EDDIE—OUTWARD BOUND 27 min., color, 83189, University of Illinois (1973).

The origin and philosophy of the Outward Bound program is presented. The film emphasizes the importance of challenge in preserving self-reliance and group interdependence.

BY NATURE'S RULES   28 min., color, U50340, University of Iowa (1970).

Identifies hypothermia (sub-normal body temperature) as the foremost killer of outdoor recreationists. Describes its causes and the progressive mental and physical impairment as the disorder undergoes its course. Presents self-defense methods against hypothermia.

CLIMB   22 min., color, ESC-1592, Indiana University (1974).

Follows the thoughts and actions of two friends, from initial preparation to the moment of triumph, in their attempt to climb the sheer face of El Capitain. Shows the stages of preparation for a safe climb, the equipment needed, the plan of attack, and segments of the climb.

FLY FISHING FOR TROUT   27 min., color, 32104, Pennsylvania State (1973).

Presents factors in fly fishing including proper water temperature, approaching and entering a stream, how to cover the water effectively, where to look for trout, eliminating drag, and various casts.

FROM YELLOWSTONE TO TOMORROW   59 min., color, 70416, University of Illinois (1972).

From its inception in 1872 the National Park Service has grown to include an extensive network of 38 national parks and over 200 national monuments, historical sites, and recreational areas, many of which are shown in the film. Presented by the Bell System Family Theatre and narrated by George C. Scott, this is a centennial tribute to the National Park Service. Park service functions vary widely, requiring scientists, rangers, artists and artisans, writers and lecturers. Jonathan Winters appears in a skit portraying a "worst offender" camper who does all the wrong things, while a park ranger tries to set him "right." Other guest stars include "The 5th Dimension" and folk singer Becky Reardon, who provide the music.

HIGH ON THE WIND RIVERS   32 min., color, U50226, University of Iowa (1972).

In a 35 day outdoor school, youths are shown acquiring the skills of mountaineering, survival, and stress management.

IN THE LAND WHERE PIRATES SING   25 min., color, HSC-1191, Indiana University (1980).

Focuses on a group of children from an urban environment as they experience summer camp activities. Shows the children camping out, putting on skits, writing letters home, and participating in the final activity as camp comes to an end (John Block, American Camping Association).

INTRODUCTION TO FOREST ADVENTURING   28 min., color, HSC-788, Indiana University (1965).

Demonstrates many of the more important skills needed by anyone venturing into the forest for hiking or camping. Includes techniques such as map reading, use of a compass, fire-building and care, use and sharpening of knife and axe, and disposal of refuse. Stresses safety, knowledge, and consideration for others.

JOURNEY TO THE OUTER LIMITS: PARTS 1 AND 2   50 min., color, 50523, Pennsylvania State (1974).

Documentary follows nineteen city-bred teenagers confronting themselves and nature at Colorado's Outward Bound School. Shows their struggle with rock climbing, rappeling, rope bridges, and zipwires, which culminates in a climb up the 18,715-foot Santa Rosa peak in the Peruvian Andes. Blue Ribbon winner, American Film Festival.

ON THE TRAIL: AN INTRODUCTION TO TRAIL WALKING   9 min., color, 04241, University of Illinois (1975).

Hiking groups of different types and ages are seen on trails in city, country, state parks, and on trails laid, by permission, through private land. Demonstrates map and compass reading, trail maintenance, and finding the way by blazes and markers. Emphasis is on day hikes, which require no expensive equipment, training, or great physical strength.

ORIENTEERING   10 min., color, 04069, University of Illinois (1969).

Procedures and rules which govern the sport of orienteering are shown as the camera follows participants in the first Canadian Orienteering Competition. Orienteering combines vigorous exercise with the development and use of compass and map reading skills. One hundred feet from the starting line, runners must copy a master map onto their own, select their route across unknown terrain, find their way by compass and map to a series of control points, and race down a marked trail to the finish line.

OUTDOOR PLAY: A MOTIVATING FORCE IN EDUCATION   17 min., color, U40157, University of Iowa (1972).

Presents the unique physical and intellectual development provided by outdoor activities and shows the extensive use of improvised materials.

SUMMER CAMP   14 min., color, ESC-1769, Indiana University (1972).

Presents an animated episode involving the adventures of Fat Albert and the Cosby Kids as they set out for summer camp for the first time with mixed emotions about their fellow campers of other races. Follows a series of run-ins and pranks with the camp bully to show that they can become friends with those who are different. Begins and ends with Bill Cosby's reminiscences of his summer camp days. Suggests the inaccuracy of first impressions. *Learning Values with Fat Albert and the Cosby Kids series.*

THE WILDERNESS BELOW   12 min., color, NSC-1479, Indiana University (1973).

Follows one spelunker as he explores a cavern, revealing the beauty, mystery, and solitude experienced by those who enter these underground wilderness areas. Shows the caver lowering himself into the mouth of the cave, paddling a raft on a subterranean waterway, and exploring the cave's flora and fauna.

THIS IS CAMPING   18 min., color, NSC-1270, Indiana University (1972).

Examines briefly the history of organized camping and identifies the many facilities and activities possible. Illustrates that, through their involvement with nature and each other, campers learn cooperation, conservation, and ecology. Explains that there are both general and special purpose camps and shows a special purpose camp for the handicapped.

TO LIGHT A SPARK   26 min., color, HSC-1113, Indiana University (1978).

Depicts outdoor camping for all ages in an organized environment, covering a majority of resident activities. Identifies the benefits a person can acquire through living in a working, recreational setting. Presents a philosophy for a hands-on approach to environmental education.

BASIC PACES OF THE HORSE   24 min., color, HSC-1118, Indiana University (1979).

Presents an analysis of the basic paces of the trained horse, emphasizing how the timing and sequence of footfalls vary from pace to pace. Shows several horses performing the fundamentals and variations of the basic paces: walk, trot, canter, gallop, and rein back. *Riding Training Film series.*

DRESSAGE MOVEMENTS   23 min., color, HSC-1116, Indiana University (1979).

Shows well-trained riders and horses, including a world champion, demonstrating dressage movements from Elementary up to Grand Prix. Emphasizes the horse's rhythm, tempo, outline, balance, and suppleness. *Riding Film Training series.*

THE RIDING POSITION   18 min., color, HSC-1119, Indiana University (1979).

Takes a close look at the classical riding position, emphasizing its practicality and efficiency. Covers the sitting position, posture, position of the arms and legs, and use of the hands on the reins. *Riding Film Training series.*

TRAINING THE YOUNG HORSE   27 min., color, HSC-1115, Indiana University (1979).

Shows the careful, step-by-step training of the young horse from the handling and grooming of a foal through the introduction of complete tack and rider at three to four years old. *Riding Training Film series.*

SKATEBOARDING TO SAFETY   13 min., color, LSC-193, Indiana University (1976).
Describes the thrills and safety requirements associated with skateboarding.

SKY DIVING—SPACE AGE SPORT   14 min., color, 53417, University of Illinois (1970).
Presents sky diving as a thrilling game and competitive sport enjoyed by more than 25,000 Americans. Pictures free-fall and precision work, and shows the competitive jumper being judged on skills in free-fall maneuvers (style), and control of the chute (accuracy) in the required "International Series During Free Fall."

HANG GLIDING: THE NEW FREEDOM   15 min., color, 21724, Pennsylvania State (1974).

Presents hang gliding from the raw beginnings of learning the sport to the gracefulness of advanced fliers.

THE JOY OF SOARING   16 min., color, 55190, University of Illinois (1976).

Carefree flight, the joy of soaring, is discussed and demonstrated. How does a sailplane work? What keeps it up? Is it dangerous? These questions, and similar ones, are answered. Defines three kinds of lift: thermal, ridge, and wave. Explains the kind of training required and where to get it—through soaring clubs or in special schools. Includes a brief history of gliders.

BASICS OF CROSS COUNTRY SKIING   16 min., color, U40229, University of Iowa (1975).

Provides an introduction to the equipment and techniques needed for cross-country skiing. Correct body positioning balance and control are emphasized. Begins and ends with episodes from the grueling annual Triathlon Ski Race in Reno, Nevada.

IF YOU CAN WALK   14 min., color, 55625, University of Illinois (1976).

A definitive film on cross-country skiing. Here you see the double pole technique of an international star, followed by a young skier doing the same thing. Cinematic tricks are used to great advantage, primarily "stop action" shots and the use of "split screen" images.

THE PERILOUS DESCENT   23 min., color, 32446, Pennsylvania State (1972).

Documents the preparation and success of Yiuchiro Miura in skiing down Mt. Fuji, Japan's highest mountain, at speeds of up to 110 miles per hour. Four months of physical and psychological training culminated in the actual descent of the two-mile course in ninety seconds. From the Explorers series.

TWO, THREE, FASTEN YOUR SKI   17 min., color, 55656, University of Illinois (1975).

Presents a skiing program for the rehabilitation of handicapped children. Amputees and cerebral palsy victims are shown gliding over the snow with ease, and mastering the basic techniques of skiing: walking, gliding downhill, and executing turns.

Sports/Fitness

CONDITIONING THE YOUNG ATHLETE   20 min., color, 40462, University of Iowa (1982).

Introduces the coach to the basic principles involved in training young athletes for competition. Highlights the basic principles of conditioning, the importance of "progressive warm-up and cool-down," developing a training program for the specific sport, and a season-long program.

INTRODUCTION TO COACHING KIDS   26 min., color, 51220, University of Iowa (1981).

Designed to introduce parents and coaches to the complex and diverse roles involved in coaching young athletes. Discusses the importance in having knowledge of coaching philosophy, sport psychology, needs of teaching skills, conditioning programs, and basic sports medicine.

PREVENTION AND TREATMENT OF SPORTS INJURIES   22 min., color, 40460, University of Iowa (1982).

Examines the important role of the coach as the first line of defense in the prevention and treatment of athletic injuries. Provides the basic guidelines for the prevention and treatment of injuries.

SPORTS PSYCHOLOGY FOR COACHES   20 min., color, 40461, University of Iowa (1982).

Examines the role of the coach as both a communicator and motivator.

TEACHING SPORTS SKILLS TO YOUNG ATHLETES   20 min., color, 40459, University of Iowa (1982).

Provides coaches with basic guidelines for the planning and conducting of efficient practices and how to effectively teach sport skills to the young athlete. Highlights setting goals for the season, basic principles for conducting effective practices, and the major steps in the teaching of a sport skill.

THINKING, MOVING, AND LEARNING   20 min., color, U40106, University of Iowa (1971).

Shows 26 perceptual motor activities for preschool and primary grade children. Demonstrates a comprehensive developmental program.

YOUTH SPORTS—IS WINNING EVERYTHING? 28 min., color, 51221, University of Iowa (1980).

Designed to help parents and coaches examine their role in youth sport programs: the importance of parental needs versus the needs of young athletes; negative and positive coaching styles; what "winning" means to the athlete; the effects of championship playoffs and all-star games.

ALL THE SELF THERE IS 13 min., color, HSC-976, Indiana University (1973).

Presents various forms of physical recreation from preschool to adult levels, explaining that physical activities are necessary to develop perceptual and motor skills.

A PROGRAM FOR PHYSICAL FITNESS 17 min., color, HSC-1028, Indiana University (1974).

Describes a rationale for participating in a program designed to enhance physical performance by developing upper body, arm, and abdominal muscle strength and endurance; extending heart and lung capacity; and increasing flexibility, balance, agility, coordination, and overall power and speed. Presents parts of a conversation between a physical fitness enthusiast and a reluctant exerciser whose questions provide the structure for the film.

EVERYONE'S A WINNER: A PROGRAM FOR PHYSICAL FITNESS 17 min., color, 55686, University of Illinois (1975).

Explains that a good exercise program develops muscular strength and endurance, balance, agility, flexibility, coordination, speed, and power. Describes and illustrates a balanced program of exercise designed to meet the needs of active young people. Includes jog-walk, pull-up, sit-up, chair push-up, rope jump, and long jump.

EVERYONE'S A WINNER—BALANCE, FLEXIBILITY, AND POWER 15 min., color, 55668, University of Illinois (1976).

Describes and illustrates the tests and exercises that help develop balance, agility, flexibility, leg strength and power, qualities needed in bike riding, skateboarding, soccer, football, surfing, and dancing. One test for balance and agility is the side step, and a test for strength and power is the standing long jump.

EVERYONE'S A WINNER—HEART-LUNG ENDURANCE 16 min., color, 55687, University of Illinois (1975).

A heart specialist explains why heart-lung endurance is one of the most important elements of physical performance.

EVERYONE'S A WINNER—MUSCULAR STRENGTH AND ENDURANCE 18 min., color, 55689, University of Illinois (1975).

Describes a program for developing strength and endurance of the upper body, arms, and abdominal muscles. Correct ways to exercise knee-bent sit-ups, chair push-ups, and pull-ups are shown.

EXERCISE AND PHYSICAL FITNESS 17 min., color, HSC-1016, Indiana University (1973).

Examines, using animation and demonstrations, the historical basis for the types of and the advantages of exercising. Explains that people exercise to gain strength, endurance, flexibility, and spiritual awareness. Compares the cardiorespiratory output of a weightlifter and a runner and suggests that the safest, most profitable exercise is walking.

EXERCISE FOR ANYONE, ANYWHERE, ANYTIME 16 min., color, U30674, University of Iowa (1980).

Concentrates on no-motion exercises geared primarily for sedentary workers.

NUTRITION FOR SPORTS—FACTS AND FALLACIES 20 min., color, HSC-1160, Indiana University (1981).

Presents information from leading health experts on the special nutritional needs of athletes, including the amount of protein, fats, carbohydrates, calories, and water required by an athlete. Discusses how certain diets and eating habits have been helpful in ensuring safe and optimal athletic performances.

PHYSICAL FITNESS—IT CAN SAVE YOUR LIFE 23 min., color, U50814, University of Iowa (1977).

Examines ways to break the vicious cycle of overeating, inactivity, and poor physical health through long-range alteration of eating habits and daily exercise.

SPORTS FOR LIFE   22 min., color, 55278, University of Illinois (1976).

Physically active individuals discuss the value of exercise for physical health, the opportunity to escape from everyday problems, the need for competition and a chance to release daily frustrations, and the development of self-reliance and self-discipline.

WEEKEND ATHLETES   49 min., color, 70319, University of Illinois (1976).

Cutaway models of the human body, computers, and other advanced measuring machines are used to analyze the effects of exercise on the bones, muscles, tendons, and heart, as well as to suggest some solutions to the problems. Points out that all sports demand several basic body motions: throwing, jumping, kicking, running, and walking. Includes commentaries by medical and sports authorities.

WEIGHT TRAINING FOR EVERY BODY   18 min., color, 54877, University of Illinois (1974).

Members of an exercise class give their varying reasons for participation. The instructor tells what each exercise is to accomplish, and animation of human muscle structure indicates in red which muscles are strengthened by each movement assigned. The importance of warming up and of consistency of participation are emphasized.

WINNING ISN'T EVERYTHING   13 min., color, 84341, University of Illinois (1976).

Presents views on the destructive influence of competition in sports. Opinions of parents, coaches, and players are obtained during visits to a boys club, YMCA, and high school athletic department.

AN INVITATION TO ARCHERY   9 min., color, 04839, University of Illinois (1979).

Explores archery's fascinating history, examines modern equipment, and shows exciting ways bows and arrows are used today. Includes segments on target shooting, competitive games, field archery, bowhunting, and bow-fishing.

ADVANCED BADMINTON   22 min., color, 53376, University of Illinois (1970).

Demonstrates many phases of advanced badminton; the importance of deception in one's strokes; the main objective in all doubles play; and the two basic offensive strokes in doubles. The film is based upon the book *Advanced Badminton* by Wynn Rogers.

BASEBALL TODAY   28 min., color, 82980, University of Illinois (1974).

Plays and replays test audience knowledge of intricate baseball rules: positions, signals, awarding bases, identifying illegal pitches and balks, rules governing live balls, overthrows, checked swings, running infractions, and runner interference.

YOUR TURN IN THE BOX, WITH HANK AARON   16 min., color, 55395, University of Illinois (1971).

Hank Aaron, famous major league baseball player, instructs a young ballplayer in the fundamentals and philosophy of batting. In-depth coverage includes proper bat selection, grip, stance, swing, stride, plate coverage, correct body position, hitting, and the importance of batting practice.

THE WILLIS REED BASKETBALL SERIES   color, University of Illinois (1972).

Demonstrates and teaches the fundamentals of basketball. Filmed on location at the Willis Reed Summer Basketball Camp.

The Willis Reed Basketball Series, Starring Dick Van Arsdale In Defensive Play I   12 min., 04409.

The Willis Reed Basketball Series, Starring Dick Van Arsdale In Defensive Play II   11 min., 04410.

The Willis Reed Basketball Series, Starring Jack Marin In Forward Play I   12 min., 04413.

The Willis Reed Basketball Series, Starring Jack Marin In Forward Play II   11 min., 04414.

The Willis Reed Basketball Series, Starring Jo Jo White In Offensive Guard I   10 min., 04415.

The Willis Reed Basketball Series, Starring Jo Jo White In Offensive Guard II   11 min., 04416.

The Willis Reed Basketball Series, Starring Willis Reed In Center Play I   12 min., 04411.

The Willis Reed Basketball Series, Starring Willis Reed In Center Play II   12 min., 04412.

WOMEN'S BASKETBALL—BALL HANDLING, PASSING, DRIBBLING   15 min., color, 55841, University of Illinois (1974).

Demonstrates some of the most effective methods of ball handling, dribbling, passing, shooting, and offensive techniques that will enable the coach and women athletes to produce a winning basketball team. Players are shown as they perform in practice drills, and also in game competition.

GOODNIGHT MISS ANN   29 min., color, 84298, University of Illinois (1978).

The world of small-time professional boxing is studied in a gymnasium where young boxers are working out, being coached by trainers, and sparring with each other.

JACK NICKLAUS GOLF CLINIC   18 min., color, 55540, University of Illinois (1975).

This film was produced from footage shot to document the Jack Nicklaus Golf Clinic in Japan. The Nicklaus approach to golf, his belief in careful preparation even for practice, and his adherence to a few simple and basic ideas about golf swings, are clearly and interestingly presented.

PUTTING—GOLF'S END GAME   12 min., color, 04418, University of Illinois (1975).

Demonstrates the geometric factors of putting—its demand for "exactness" which calls for the ultimate in control of direction and distance. Emphasis is placed on a steady body, a firm but sensitive grip, and a straight-back-and-through accelerating stroke. Points out the importance of establishing a routine approach.

THE SPECIAL CHALLENGE SHOTS   14 min., color, 55311, University of Illinois (1975).

An overview of the challenges that test a golfer's skill includes: learning how to predict and cope with the natural forces of weather; recovery and topography that demand adaptations of the basic swing; sand recovery techniques; set-up and swing adjustments for uphill, downhill, and sidehill lies; negotiating dog-leg fairways and natural obstacles with intentional hooks and slices. Emphasizes the importance of practice drills for each challenge.

HORIZONTAL BAR   12 min., color, HSC-939, Indiana University (n.d.).

Demonstrates, using slow-motion photography and replay techniques, basic horizontal bar skills such as grips, mounts, dismounts, front and back hip circles, and single and double knee backward and forward techniques. Proceeds to combine the elementary skills into simple routines and shows spotting techniques. Illustrates advanced routines and a championship performance.

ON THE PARALLELS   31 min., bw, 81646, University of Illinois (1966).

Uses slow-motion, stop-action, and regular photography to present a variety of moves and exercises on the bars, plus exercises for body-conditioning that emphasize strength and endurance. Includes demonstrations of the forward roll, the dismount, the backward straddle vault, the upper arm stand, the kip, the back uprise, the handstand, and spotting and assisting techniques.

TUMBLING AND FLOOR EXERCISE   13 min., color, HSC-942, Indiana University (n.d.).

Illustrates how to perform various tumbling and floor exercises from basic to intermediate skills and how to make a smooth transition from one exercise to another. Explains the importance of a spotter when learning to do the various exercises.

TUMBLING—PRIMARY SKILLS   9 min., color, HSC-1034, Indiana University (1970).

Illustrates the proper form to be used in performing basic tumbling skills and stresses the need for safety. Demonstrates the egg sit, egg roll, forward roll, backward roll, frog head stand, and head stand. Shows the proper position of the head, hands, and feet in each skill.

HANDBALL FUNDAMENTALS   11 min., color, 01508, University of Illinois (1965).

Introduces the game of handball and its rules. Uses regular, slow-motion, and stop-motion photography as two boys demonstrate the skills involved. Shows variations in number of walls used, singles and doubles games, the use of strategy, and exploitation of the opponent's weaknesses. Stresses the value of handball for enjoyment and physical fitness throughout life.

RACQUETBALL—MOVING FAST   15 min., color, 56229, University of Illinois (1978).

Played on an outdoor three-walled handball court, or indoors in one completely enclosed, the game requires more safety consciousness than many involving larger spaces. Positions for the skip ball, z-ball, pinch shot, kill, and fly kill are illustrated in discussion and play.

RACQUETBALL—OFFENSIVE AND DEFENSIVE SHOTS   13 min., color, 56403, University of Illinois (1979).

Reviews the mechanics of getting to the ball, setting up, and hitting. Details four basic shots: the kill, the pass, the ceiling, and backwall shots. As players execute these shots, a narrator discusses the merits of each, and when they can be used most effectively.

RACQUETBALL—SERVES AND RETURNS   12 min., color, 56404, University of Illinois (1979).

Focuses on the importance of strategically placing the serve in order to force the other player into a weak return. The four basic serves are appraised: drives, Z-serve, the lob, and half-lob. Advises the type of return to use against each of these serves. Slow-motion and stop-action frames help to illustrate the timing and positioning needed for the correct execution of the serves and returns.

RACQUETBALL STRATEGY—SINGLES/DOUBLES, CUT-THROAT   12 min., color, 56405, University of Illinois (1979).

Stresses the mental demands of the sport—outthinking as well as outplaying the opponent. Demonstrates court movement and positioning for playing doubles and cut-throat.

SOCCER—HANDS OFF   17 min., color, HSC-1033, Indiana University (1975).

Pointing out that soccer is the world's oldest and most popular team sport, this film discusses the rules of soccer and the objectives of the game. Illustrates the game play of people of all ages, then helps viewers to understand some of the basic moves of soccer: traps, dribbles, instep drive, passing the ball with legs and head, and techniques of goalkeeping.

SOCCER—OFFENSIVE AND DEFENSIVE PLAY   20 min., color, 56036, University of Illinois (1976).

With slow-motion techniques and voice-over narration, the skills and theories of feinting, tackling, throw-in, passing attack, and shooting are examined and demonstrated. Helpful clues for scoring are analyzed: head shot to over, curve ball, and over-the-head scissors kick.

SOCCER—THE FUNDAMENTALS   19 min., color, 56035, University of Illinois (1976).

A coaching narration provides full details on the basic fundamentals of soccer. Basic kicks, inside, outside, instep, volley and half volley, trapping (chest, foot, thigh), heading, and juggling are demonstrated with regular photography and slow-motion camera techniques.

SOCCER—THE GOALKEEPER   20 min., color, 56035, University of Illinois (1976).

Positioning and catching, diving (falling parallel), punching, tipping, clearing and throwing, and conditioning drills are the important basics of goalkeeping. All of these movements and special skills are demonstrated with slow-motion cinema, accompanied by informative narration.

BABYSWIM   13 min., color, 22745, Pennsylvania State (1979).

Features eight infants aged six to twenty-one months in pools and in the ocean, on diving boards, and among coral reefs. Stresses that water activity improves general muscular development, physical coordination, cardiovascular efficiency, and hence mental development.

DOC: THE OLDEST MAN IN THE SEA   30 min., color, HSC-1124, Indiana University (1980).

Highlights of 57-year-old James "Doc" Counsilman's record-breaking swim of the English Channel are interwoven with flashbacks showing Doc in training for the event and at work coaching his university swimming team. Comments from Doc, Indiana University swimming coach since 1958 and two-time Olympic coach, reflect upon prior attempts by others to swim the Channel, his belief in the health and recreational value of swimming for older people, and his life as a coach and researcher.

LEARNING TO DIVE   15 min., color, 54872, University of Illinois (1973).

Explains and demonstrates basic elements of diving: the approach, execution of the dive, and entry into the water. Demonstrators include beginners as well as Olympic champions. Highlights: diving competition with children as entrants; diving camps and diving coaches in action, working on a trampoline. Stresses health and safety rules.

LIFESAVING AND WATER SAFETY SERIES   American Red Cross.

Entire series of nine films can be purchased by requesting: film stock no. 321647; ¾" v/c stock no. 321592.

LIFESAVING AND WATER SAFETY SERIES   77 min., 16 mm, v/c—¾", (1975).

A series of nine films on lifesaving and water safety. Individual films may be ordered separately by title and stock number. The films, numbered, are listed in the following:

1. BOATING SAFETY AND RESCUE   10 min., 321656.

2. DEFENSES, RELEASES, AND ESCAPES   7 min., 321653.

3. NON-SWIMMING RESCUES   7 min., 321650.

4. PREVENTIVE LIFEGUARDING   9 min., 321655.

5. REMOVAL FROM THE WATER   5 min., 321654.

6. SNORKELING SKILLS AND RESCUE TECHNIQUES   12 min., 321648.

7. SPECIAL EQUIPMENT RESCUES   9 min., 321652.

8. SURVIVAL SWIMMING   7 min., 321649.

9. SWIMMING RESCUES   8 min., 321651.

SAFE IN THE WATER   17 min., color, 53919, University of Illinois (1972).

Accidents which often occur in pools, rivers, lakes, ponds, and the ocean are dramatically reenacted and the proper rescue techniques for each mishap are indicated.

SKILLED SWIMMING, PART I   13 min., 321622, American Red Cross (1971).

Slow-motion, underwater photography, split-screen, and stop-action depict swimming strokes and related skills—sidestrokes, elementary backstrokes, turns, and starts.

SKILLED SWIMMING, PART II   19 min., 321623, American Red Cross (1971).

Crawl, butterfly, turns, backcrawls, and starts are depicted including instructor training. These two films together (Part I and Part II) teach swimming movements at all levels of instruction.

SKILLED SWIMMING NO. 1—BASIC STROKES   13 min., color, U38748, University of Iowa (1970).

Designed for those who are already basic swimmers, this film emphasizes the finer points of the side, elementary, and breast strokes. Slow-motion and underwater photography is used.

WATERSAFE   17 min., 321505, American Red Cross (1979).

Designed to promote awareness of Red Cross water safety services. Narrated by Olympic swimming star Donna deVarona.

TENNIS—BASIC TACTICS FOR DOUBLES   13 min., color, 53723, University of Illinois (1968).

Differences in tactics and psychology between singles and doubles are contrasted and demonstrated: e.g., use of the lob, moving in, and control of the net.

TENNIS—BASIC TACTICS FOR SINGLES   13 min., color, 53722, University of Illinois (1968).

Players demonstrate dangers of overplaying, use of slow, high ball, directional change, and placement of shots.

TENNIS: GROUND STROKES WITH BILLIE JEAN KING   14 min., color, HSC-895, Indiana University (1969).

Demonstrates the proper execution of the forehand and backhand drive tennis strokes. Includes discussion and illustration on the theory behind the proper grip and stance of each drive.

TENNIS: THE SERVE WITH BILLIE JEAN KING   14 min., color, HSC-894, Indiana University (1969).

Discusses and illustrates the theory behind the proper grip, stance, and toss of a serve. Includes the techniques of two advanced serves, the slice serve and the twist serve.

COPING WITH LIFE ON THE RUN   27 min., color, U50791, University of Iowa (1978).

Demonstrates how thousands of men and women from high-level executives to assembly-line workers are improving health, personal outlook, and job performance through running. Tells why we should change our sedentary lifestyle, and shows how to develop a program that restores the body's tone, helps deal with stress, and can become a profound joy in itself.

MEN'S TRACK AND FIELD—FUNDAMENTALS OF RUNNING   19 min., color, 56048, University of Illinois (1976).

Demonstrations by athletes and an effective narration teach all details on sprint start, running, finishing.

MEN'S TRACK AND FIELD—THE JUMPING EVENTS   20 min., color, 56050, University of Illinois (1976).

Demonstrates the long jump, triple jump, and pole vault. The two techniques on the cross bar, straddle roll and Fosbury flop, are analyzed.

MEN'S TRACK AND FIELD—THE RUNNING EVENTS   21 min., color, 56049, University of Illinois (1976).

Hurdle and sprint relay are fully demonstrated and studied. Covers basic strategies of competitive running, hurdling, and baton-passing techniques.

MEN'S TRACK AND FIELD—THE THROWING EVENTS   21 min., color, 56051, University of Illinois (1976).

Demonstrates the traditional field events: shot put, discus, and javelin throwing. Correct form and technique are emphasized, with recommended drills and coaching points to aid the competitor.

RUN DICK, RUN JANE   21 min., color, 54777, University of Illinois (1971).

Focuses on the beneficial physiological and psychological effects of exercise on the human body. A doctor, using animated diagrams, explains the cardio-vascular values that are derived from jogging and exercise in daily living. Statements from individuals, including George Romney, and the narrator's comments trace the steps toward physical fitness. Concluding sequence shows Larry Lewis, a 103-year-old San Franciscan who runs six miles daily around Golden Gate Park.

RUNNING BROAD JUMP (TRACK AND FIELD INSTRUCTION SERIES)   13 min., bw, 50979, University of Illinois (n.d.).

Shows principles of the running broad jump. The technique is shown through the analysis of championship-type jumps, with some slow-motion scenes. Pictures an inexperienced candidate being put through the drills needed to acquire good form.

THE JOGGER   11 min., color, 04836, University of Illinois (1977).

This film makes use of jogging as a form of meditation in which emotional and intellectual stimulation is triggered by the concentrated physical activity of running.

WOMEN'S TRACK AND FIELD—FUNDAMENTALS OF RUNNING   17 min., color, 56052, University of Illinois (1976).

Demonstrates running events at all distances, hurdling, and sprint relay techniques.

WOMEN'S TRACK AND FIELD—THE JUMPING EVENTS   15 min., color, 56054, University of Illinois (1976).

An informative documentary on long jump and high jump techniques. Teaches important points: discipline, practice, concentration, horizontal velocity, takeoff, flight, and landing.

WOMEN'S TRACK AND FIELD—THE RUNNING EVENTS   20 min., color, 56053, University of Illinois (1976).

Strategies, techniques, and rules of the distance sprints, hurdles, sprint relay exchange, and distance relay exchange are demonstrated, with an explanatory narration.

WOMEN'S TRACK AND FIELD—THE THROWING EVENTS   20 min., color, 56055, University of Illinois (1976).

Basic strategies of the shot put, discus, and javelin are demonstrated and analyzed.

VOLLEYBALL TODAY   17 min., color, 54962, University of Illinois (1975).

The first film study-demonstration based on the National Federation volleyball rules code. Subjects covered are: positioning, foot faults, legal and illegal serves, overlapping, net play, restrictions on players, etc. Slow-motion and stop-action photos of an actual game illustrate the points. *Made available through the cooperation of the Illinois High School Association.*

Therapeutic Recreation

A DAY IN THE LIFE OF BONNIE CONSOLO   16-½ min., color, NY State Education Dept. (1975).

This film shows Bonnie, born without arms, doing her daily chores using her feet as hands (e.g., driving a car, writing a letter with a pen between her toes, cutting her child's hair, preparing meals, putting on makeup, answering the phone).

A DEMONSTRATION LESSON IN PHYSICAL EDUCATION   28 min., bw, NY State Education Dept. (n.d.).

Film depicts approaches, techniques, and activities included in the physical education program for children with mean IQ of 72 and mean chronological age of 13. Activities demonstrated include responding to commands, lining up and counting off, running relay races, using narrative and creative warmup activities, teaching tumbling activities, and doing partner stunts (American Association for Health).

A DREAM TO GROW ON   28 min., color, NY State Education Dept. (1969).

Highlights the 1968 Special Olympics where mentally retarded children competed in athletic events.

AIDS FOR TEACHING THE MENTALLY RETARDED   38 min., color, NY State Education Dept. (n.d.).

Phase A—MOTOR TRAINING—11 min., color: Motor training activities for the mentally retarded are demonstrated through the use of many exercises and devices (e.g., swimming table, off-center tires).

Phase B—INITIAL PERCEPTUAL TRAINING—7 min., color: Perceptual training activities for the mentally retarded are presented through the use of many exercises and devices (e.g., sound and weight boxes, matching cards).

ALL THE WAY UP THERE   27 min., color, U50842, University of Iowa (1980).

Bruce, a 24-year-old cerebral palsy victim, realizes an impossible dream—to climb a mountain with the help of one of New Zealand's best known mountaineers.

BREAKING THE BARRIERS   14 min., 321539, American Red Cross.

A story of young, disabled people, this award-winner tells how they break down the "barriers" they encounter in the attitudes of others.

CAMPING AND OUTDOOR EDUCATION FOR EMOTIONALLY DISTURBED—CAMP WILDWOOD   30 min., color, NY State Education Dept. (1976).

Covers the varied program of a summer day camp for disabled children, preschool to late teens. In addition to accepting youth with such handicapping conditions as autism, neurological impairments, mental retardation, and learning disabilities, the camp also accepts the non-handicapped siblings of the campers to facilitate mainstreaming.

CAMPING AND RECREATIONAL FACILITIES FOR THE HANDICAPPED   20 min., color, ESC-1715, Indiana University (1979).

Examines how the designers of Camp Riley, a residential camp for handicapped youths, made the out-of-doors accessible to everyone, regardless of personal mobility. Shows the camp's cabins, trails, and transportation system, and areas specifically designed for crafts, gardening, swimming, dining, and nature study.

CAMPING AND RECREATIONAL PROGRAMS FOR THE HANDICAPPED   17 min., color, ESC-1716, Indiana University (1979).

Focuses on the programming at a camp designed with the needs of handicapped youths in mind. Shows the activities one would expect to see at a summer camp—hiking, craft classes, nature study, fishing, and boating.

CAROL JOHNSTON   16 min., color, U30538, University of Iowa (1980).

Documents the private and public life of Carol Johnston, championship gymnast, who was born with one arm. Carol is shown at home, school, and in competition dealing with a knee injury which occurs on film.

CAST NO SHADOW   27 min., color, 31876, Pennsylvania State (1973).

Shows recreation activities for severely mentally retarded, physically handicapped, multihandicapped, and emotionally disturbed children, teens, and adults at the Recreation Center for the Handicapped, Inc. in San Francisco.

CROSSBAR   33 min., color, U56222, University of Iowa (1980).

Depicts the drive and courage of an athlete determined to qualify for the Olympic trials despite the loss of a leg in a car accident.

DAN HALEY   11 min., color, U20467, University of Iowa (1980).

Portrays the active life of Dan Haley, a 16-year-old whose approaching blindness has not deterred his mobility or social involvement or musical talent in the high school band.

DANNY AND NICKY   58 min., color, NY State Education Dept. (1969).

In examining the lifestyles of Danny and Nicky, two mongoloids, the film contrasts the social and recreational opportunities in their two separate environments—a special school and a public school for the mentally retarded.

EARS TO HEAR—TEACHING DEAF CHILDREN   28 min., color, NY State Educaton Dept. (1978).

Demonstrates how profoundly deaf children can be taught to speak and to "hear" the sounds of ordinary speech. The children are prepared for mainstreaming in school and full integration into society.

FOCUS ON ABILITY   22 min., film—16mm; videocasette—¾", American Red Cross (1974).

This multiaward-winner deals comprehensively with teaching swimming to all types of handicapped individuals.

GET IT TOGETHER   21 min., color, 55638, University of Illinois (1976).

Documents the achievement of a paralyzed individual who, now, as a recreation therapist, coaches patients in wheelchair basketball, tennis, and baseball.

HAP: AMERICA AT ITS BEST (HANDICAPPED ATHLETIC PROGRAM)   27 min., color, NY State Education Dept.

Documents the Handicapped Athletic Program, a community project that was formulated to help mentally and physically handicapped children experience team-oriented athletic contests such as softball, basketball, and bowling.

IMPROVISED LIFTS AND TRANSFERS   13 min., slide/sound, 321803, American Red Cross (1979).

Deals with mobility problems frequently encountered by those working with the disabled in adapted aquatic programs.

P.E.—LEVER TO LEARNING   22 min., color, U46993, University of Iowa (1969).

Demonstrates an ingenious program devised by a physical education specialist to condition retarded children while stimulating them mentally.

PLAY IN THE HOSPITAL   40 min., color, NY State Education Dept. (n.d.).

This film shows how a well-formulated play therapy program in children's wards can eliminate trauma in children who are hospitalized frequently or for long periods.

PROGRAM OF DEVELOPMENTAL MOTOR ACTIVITIES   22 min., color, NY State Education Dept. (n.d.).

Four recognized levels of development (moving legs and arms without forward movement, crawling, creeping, and walking) are demonstrated by student clinicians who are working with youngsters to promote neurological organization.

PROMISE OF PLAY   22 min., color, NY State Education Dept. (1974).

The film displays a program offering children with mild or severe orthopedic handicaps a chance to develop skills in games and physical activities.

REACHING OUT—A STORY ABOUT MAINSTREAMING   13 min., color, NY State Education Dept.

Presents the story of a ten-year-old girl, deaf and with cerebral palsy, who is ready to be mainstreamed into a fifth grade class. The film is designed to help all children understand what it means to be handicapped.

READING IS FOR US, TOO   29 min., color, NY State Education Dept. (n.d.).

This film illustrates how trainable retarded children are taught to read—in a "flying start" prereading program.

RICK, YOU'RE IN—A STORY ABOUT MAINSTREAMING   20 min., color, NY State Education Dept.

Rick, a wheelchair basketball star, presents the decision making and adjustment necessary in the transition from a special school to a public high school.

RISING EXPECTATIONS   25 min., color, NY State Education Dept.

Gives an overview of traditional and contemporary perceptions of the abilities of handicapped individuals and employment. The film presents both architectural and attitudinal barriers.

SPECIAL CHILDREN, DIFFERENT NEEDS . . . GROWING UP HANDICAPPED   22 min., color, NY State Education Dept.

This film follows selected children from the original film, "Special Children, Special Needs," and depicts these multiply handicapped children seven years later in agency and public school settings.

SPLASH   25 min., color, NY State Education Dept. (n.d.).

Water activities, educational and recreational, are presented for use with handicapped youngsters of all types.

THE MIKADO IS COMING   21 min., color, U45379, University of Iowa (1960).

Documents the activities of severely handicapped children preparing, rehearsing, and presenting their own presentation of the Mikado.

THERAPEUTIC CAMPING   28 min., color, NY State Education Dept. (n.d.).

Reflects the rationale, philosophy, activities, approaches, and values derived from a camping program for the mentally retarded.

THIS IS COURAGE   15 min., (1967).

Captured in this film is the spirit of camaraderie that helps make Camp Courage, Minnesota, a unique experience for disabled children and adults. Campers with physical disabilities as well as speech, hearing, and vision impairments are shown participating in a variety of outdoor activities such as nature hikes, water sports, canoe trips, and horseback riding.

TO CLIMB A MOUNTAIN   16 min., color, 55544, University of Illinois (1975).

A group of blind, or partially sighted, young people from the Braille Institute participate in their first mountain-climbing expedition in the Sierras.

TO LIGHTEN THE SHADOWS   20 min., bw, NY State Education Dept. (n.d.).

Shows mentally retarded children participating in camping activities such as boating, fishing, crafts, and group singing.

TO SERVE A PURPOSE   13 min., color, ESC-1678, Indiana University (n.d.).

Stresses that recreation is an essential human need and examines the therapeutic value of recreation for the handicapped. Defines therapeutic recreation and shows a variety of handicapped people of all ages enjoying an assortment of recreational activities. Provides comments by professors and practitioners in the field of therapeutic recreation.

TRAGEDY TO TRIUMPH   27 min., color, NY State Education Dept. (n.d.).

Presents the story of Jill Kinmont, who became paralyzed from the shoulders down in an Olympic training accident and overcame obstacles to become a teacher.

WHEREVER WE FIND THEM—THE HANDICAPPED ATHLETE   28 min., color, NY State Education Dept. (1979).

Presents clips from the 21st National Wheelchair competition. Emphasizes what wheelchair athletes can do in a variety of activities.

YOU HAVE SOMETHING TO OFFER   16 min., color, ESC-1768, Indiana University (1976).

Considers how to deal with a friend who has a handicap. Portrays Duane, who must wear a special shoe on one foot, and the initial awkwardness of the Cosby Kids in dealing with him. Relates several incidents which result in the children's realizing that everyone has something to offer.

Film Supplier Resource List

For films listed in filmography section

American Red Cross:

Loans:
Audio-Visual Loan Library
Frank Stanton Production Center
American Red Cross
5816 Seminary Road
Falls Church, Virginia 22041

Purchase:
General Supply Office
American Red Cross
18th and E Streets NW
Washington, DC 20006

Courage Center
3915 Golden Valley Road
Golden Valley, Minnesota 55422

Guidance Information Center
Campbell Films, Inc.
Saxtons River, Vermont 05154

Indiana University Audio-Visual Center
Bloomington, Indiana 47405

New York State Education Department
Bureau of Program Development Film Library
Media Unit 243-M Education Building
Albany, New York 12234

Penn State University Audio-Visual Services
University Park, Pennsylvania 16802

University of Illinois Film Center
1325 South Oak Street
Champaign, Illinois 61820

University of Iowa Audio-Visual Center
C-215 Seashore Hall
Iowa City, Iowa 52242

Other commercial sources of films

ACI Media, Inc.
35 West 45th Street
New York, New York 10036

Abraham Krasker Memorial Film Library
Boston University
School of Education
765 Commonwealth Avenue
Boston, Massachusetts 02215

Aims Instructional Media Services, Inc.
626 Justin Avenue
Glendale, California 91201

American Association of Health, Physical
Education, Recreation, and Dance (AAHPERD)
1201 16th Street, NW
Washington, DC 20036

American Foundation for the Blind, Inc.
15 West 16th Street
New York, New York 10011

Appleton-Century-Crofts
440 Park Avenue So.
New York, New York 10016

BFA Educational Media
2211 Michigan Avenue
P.O. Box 1795
Santa Monica, California 90406

Barr Films
P.O. Box 5667
Pasadena, California 91107

Benchmark Films, Inc.
145 Scarborough Road
Briarcliff Manor, New York 10510

Billy Budd Films
235 East 57th Street
New York, New York 10022

Bono Film Services
1042 Wisconsin Avenue, NW
Washington, DC 20007

Bradley Wright Films
309 N. Duane
San Gabriel, California 91775

CCM Films
600 Grand Avenue
Ridgefield, New Jersey 07657

CRM McGraw-Hill Films
110 Fifteenth Street
Del Mar, California 92014

California State College
Los Angeles, California 90013

California State Department of Education
721 Capitol Mall
Sacramento, California 95814

Calvin Productions, Inc.
1105 Truman Road
Kansas City, Missouri 64106

Campus Film Distributors, Corp.
14 Madison Avenue
P.O. Box 206
Valhalla, New York 10595

Canadian Broadcasting, Corp.
P.O. Box 500
Terminal A
Toronto, Ontario, Canada

Carousel Films, Inc.
1501 Broadway (Suite 1503)
New York, New York 10036

Center Films
330 West 42nd Street
New York, New York 10036

Charles Buell
4244 Heather Road
Long Beach, California 90808

Charles E. Merrill Publishing Co.
1300 Alum Creek Drive
Columbus, Ohio 43216

Columbia Forum Productions, Ltd.
10621 Fable Row
Columbia, Maryland 21043

Connecticut Film, Inc.
6 Cobble Hill Road
Westport, Connecticut 06880

Coral Gables Academy
770 Miller Road
South Miami, Florida 33143

Davidson Films
3701 Buchanan Street
San Francisco, California 94123

Developmental Language and Speech Center
60 Ransom Avenue NE (Room 202)
Grand Rapids, Michigan 49502

Documentary Film Productions
3217 Trout Gulch Road
Aptos, California 95003

Du Art Film Laboratories
245 West 55th Street
New York, New York 10019

Educational Development Center
39 Chapel Street
Newton, Massachusetts 02160

Edward Feil Productions
4614 Prospect Avenue
Cleveland, Ohio 44103

Exceptional Child
Research Program
Teaching Research
Monmouth, Oregon 97361

Film Productions of Indianapolis
128 E. 36th Street
Indianapolis, Indiana 46205

Films Incorporated
1144 Wilmette Avenue
Wilmette, Illinois 60091

Hallmark Films and Recordings, Inc.
1511 North Avenue
Baltimore, Maryland 21213

Harvest Films, Inc.
309 Fifth Avenue
New York, New York 10016

HEW
330 Independence Avenue SW
Washington, DC 20201

Henk Newenhouse, Inc.
1825 Willow Road
Northfield, Illinois 60093

Hubbard Films
P.O. Box 104
Northbrook, Illinois 60062

Instructional Media Services
128 E. Pittsburgh Street
Greensburg, Pennsylvania 15601

International Film Bureau
332 South Michigan Avenue
Chicago, Illinois 60604

International Rehabilitation Film Library
17 East 45th Street
New York, New York 10017

KETC TV Channel 9
Broadcasting Center
6996 Millbrook Boulevard
St. Louis, Missouri 63130

Kingsbury Center Lab School
2138 Bancroft Place NW
Washington, DC 20008

La Rue Films, Inc.
159 Chicago Avenue
Chicago, Illinois 60604

Lawren Productions, Inc.
P.O. Box 666
Mendicino, California 95460

McGraw Hill Films
1221 Avenue of the Americas
New York, New York 10020

Media Five Film Distributors Division
of Dave Bell Associates, Inc.
3211 Cahuenga Blvd. West
Hollywood, California 90068

Media Guild
118 South Acacia, P.O. Box 881
Solana Beach, California 92075

Metropolitan Life Insurance Co.
Health and Welfare Division
1 Madison Avenue
New York, New York 10010

Movie Lab, Inc.
619 West 54th Street
New York, New York 10010

Music Therapy Center
351 West 51st Street
New York, New York 10019

Muskegan Area Secondary Special Education
Center
2310 Marquette Avenue
Muskegan, Michigan 49440

NTID
Rochester Institute of Technology
Public Information Office
1 Lomb Memorial Drive
Rochester, New York 14623

National Audiovisual Center
General Services Administration
Washington, DC 20409

National Film Board of Canada
1251 Avenue of the Americas
New York, New York 10020

National Foundation March of Dimes
Publishing Department
1275 Mamaroneck Avenue
White Plains, New York 10605

New York State Division for Youth
Public Education Service
Albany, New York 12234

New York University Film Library
26 Washington Place
New York, New York 10003

News Films
1 West 46th Street
New York, New York 10036

Ohio State University
Department of Cinema
159 West 19th Avenue
Columbus, Ohio 43210

The Pathway School
Box 18
Audubon, Pennsylvania 19407

Peach Enterprises, Inc.
4649 Gerald
Warren, Michigan 48902

Perennial Education, Inc.
477 Roger Williams
Highland Park, Illinois 60035

Prentice-Hall Media, Inc.
Englewood Cliffs, New Jersey 07632

Psychological Cinema Register
Penn State University, 6 Willard Bldg.
University Park, Pennsylvania 16802

Pyramid Films
P.O. Box 1048
Santa Monica, California 90406

Richfield Productions
8006 Takoma Avenue
Silver Springs, Maryland 20901

Ridley School District
Administration Building
Morton Avenue
Folsom, Pennsylvania 19033

San Francisco State College
1600 Holloway Avenue
San Francisco, California 94132

Short Film Service
122 Wardow Street
London, WI England

Smith, Kline and French Labs
1500 Garden Street
Philadelphia, Pennsylvania 19101

The South Bay Mayors' Committee for Employment of the Handicapped
2409 N. Sepulveda Blvd.—Suite 202
Manhattan Beach, California 90266

Southwest Film Lab, Inc.
3024 Fort Worth Avenue
Dallas, Texas 75211

Spencer Nelson Productions
2985 East Aurora
Boulder, Colorado 80302

Stanfield House
P.O. Box 3208
Santa Monica, California 90403

Sterling Educational Films
241 East 34th Street
New York, New York 10016

Stuart Finley, Inc.
3428 Mansfield Road
Falls Church, Virginia 22041

Total Communication Laboratory
Western Maryland College
Westminster, Maryland 21157

Universal Education and Visual Arts
Division of Universal City Studios, Inc.
100 Universal City Plaza
Universal City, California 91608

University Council for Educational Administrators
29 West Woodruff Avenue
Columbus, Ohio 43210

University of California Extension
Media Center
2223 Fulton Street
Berkeley, California 94720

University of Kansas Audio-Visual Service
Film Rental Service
746 Massachusetts Street
Lawrence, Kansas 66044

University of Minnesota
Audio Visual Library Service
Continuing Education & Extension
3300 University Avenue SE
Minneapolis, Minnesota 55414

University of Southwestern Louisiana
Lafayette, Louisiana 70501

University of Wisconsin
Bureau of Audio-Visual Instruction
1327 University Avenue
P.O. Box 2093
Madison, Wisconsin 53701

Visucom Productions
P.O. Box 5472
Redwood City, California 94063

W. A. Palmer Films, Inc.
611 Howard Street
San Francisco, California 94015

Wayne State University
Film Library
77 W. Canfield Avenue
Detroit, Michigan 48202

Appendix B

Recreation Resources

THERAPEUTIC RECREATION RESOURCES

Academy of Dentistry for the Handicapped
1240 East Main Street
Springfield, OH 45503

Administration on Aging
330 C Street SW
Washington, DC 20201

Allergy Foundation of America
801 2nd Avenue
New York, NY 10017

American Alliance for Health, Physical Education, and Recreation
Unit on Programs for the Handicapped
1201 16th Street NW
Washington, DC 20036

American Association for Rehabilitation Therapy
Box 4093
North Little Rock, AR 72216

American Association of Retired Persons
1909 K St. NW
Washington, DC 20049

American Association on Mental Deficiency
5201 Connecticut Avenue NW
Washington, DC 20015

American Blind Bowling Association
3701 Connecticut Ave. NW
Washington, DC 20008

American Camping Association
Bradford Woods
Martinsville, IN 46151

American Cancer Society, Inc.
219 East 42nd Street
New York, NY 10017

American Coalition of Citizens with Disabilities
1346 Connecticut Avenue NW, Room 817
Washington, DC 20036

American Correctional Association
4321 Hartwick Road
College Park, MD 20740

American Corrective Therapy Association
4015 Broadway, No. 21
Houston, TX 77017

American Council on Alcohol Problems, Inc.
119 Constitution Avenue NW
Washington, DC 20001

American Diabetes Association
18 East 48th Street
New York, NY 10017

American Federation of the Physically
Handicapped, Inc.
1376 National Press Building
Washington, DC 20004

American Foundation for the Blind
15 West 16th Street
New York, NY 10011

American Heart Association
44 East 23rd Street
New York, NY 10010

American Hospital Association
840 North Shore Drive
Chicago, IL 60611

American Lung Association
1740 Broadway
New York, NY 10019

American National Red Cross
17th and D Streets NW
Washington, DC 20006

American Nurses Association
10 Columbus Circle
New York, NY 10019

American Nursing Home Association
2420 Pershing Road
Kansas City, MO 64108

American Occupational Therapy Association
1383 Piccard Drive
Rockville, MD 20852

American Orthotics and Prosthetics Association
1440 N. Street NW
Washington, DC 20005

American Physical Therapy Association
1111 N Fairfax Street
Alexandria, VA 22314

American Psychiatric Association
1400 K Street NW
Washington, DC 20000

American Speech, Language and Hearing Association
10801 Rockville Pike
Rockville, MD 28852

American Wheelchair Bowling Association
2635 NE 19th Street
Pompano Beach, FL 33062

Arthritis and Rheumatism Foundation
10 Columbus Circle
New York, NY 10019

Association for Children with Learning Disabilities
4156 Library Road
Pittsburgh, PA 15234

Association for the Aid of Crippled Children
345 East 46th Street
New York, NY 10017

Boy Scouts of America
Scouting for the Handicapped
North Brunswick, NJ 08902

Bureau of Education for the Handicapped
U.S. Office of Education
400 Maryland Avenue SW
Washington, DC 20202

Children's Bureau, Office of Child Development
300 Independence Avenue SW
Washington, DC 20201

Committee on Recreation and Leisure
President's Committee on Employment of the
Handicapped
Washington, DC 20210

Committee for the Handicapped, People to People
Program
The Committee, Suite 610
LaSalle Building,
Connecticut Ave. and L Street NW
Washington, DC 20036

Council for Exceptional Children
1411 South Jefferson Davis Highway, Suite 900
Jefferson Plaza, Arlington, VA 22202

Epilepsy Foundation of America
733 15th Street NW
Washington, DC 20005

The 52 Association, Inc. (Veterans)
147 East 50th Street
New York, NY 10022

Girl Scouts of the USA
Scouting for the Handicapped
830 Third Avenue
New York, NY 10022

International Council for Exceptional Children
1201 16th Street, NW
Washington, DC 20036

International Society for Rehabilitation of the
Disabled
219 East 44th Street
New York, NY 10017

Joseph P. Kennedy, Jr., Foundation
1411 K Street NW
Washington, DC 20005

Muscular Dystrophy Association of America
1790 Broadway
New York, NY 10019

National Amputation Foundation
12–45 150th Street
Whitestone, NY 11357

National Association for Mental Health
1800 North Kent Street
Arlington, VA 22209

National Association for Retarded Citizens
2709 Avenue E East
Arlington, TX 78011

National Association of Activity Therapy and
Rehabilitation Program Directors
Box 111
Independence, IA 50644

National Association of the Deaf
814 Thayer Avenue
Silver Spring, MD 20910

National Association of the Physically Handicapped
76 Elm Street
London, OH 43140

National Congress of Organizations for the
Physically Handicapped
1627 Deborah Avenue
Rockford, IL 61103

National Correctional Recreation Association
Box 7
Moberly, MO 65270

National Council on Rehabilitation
1790 Broadway
New York, NY 10019

National Council on the Aging
1828 L Street Northwest
Washington, DC 20036

National Cystic Fibrosis Research Foundation
521 5th Avenue
New York, NY 10017

National Easter Seal Society for Crippled Children
and Adults
2023 West Ogden Avenue
Chicago, IL 60612

National Epilepsy League
203 North Wabash Avenue
Chicago, IL 60601

The National Foundation
800 2nd Avenue
New York, NY 10017

National Foundation for Neuromuscular Diseases
250 West 57th Street
New York, NY 10019

National Hemophilia Foundation
25 West 39th Street
New York, NY 10018

National Institute for Advanced Study in Teaching
Disadvantaged Youth
Room 112, 1126 16th Street NW
Washington, DC 20036

National Institutes of Health
9000 Rockville Pike
Bethesda, MD 20010

National Kidney Disease Foundation
342 Madison Avenue
New York, NY 10017

National Multiple Sclerosis Society
257 Park Avenue South
New York, NY 10010

National Paraplegia Foundation
333 North Michigan Avenue
Chicago, IL 60601

National Rehabilitation Association
1522 K Street NW
Washington, DC 20005

National Society for the Prevention of Blindness
79 Madison Avenue
New York, NY 10016

Pope Foundation
197 South West Avenue
Kankakee, IL 60901

President's Committee on Mental Retardation
U.S. Department of Health, Education,
and Welfare
Washington, DC 20201

Rehabilitation Service Administration
330 C Street SW
Washington, DC 20201

Special Olympics, Inc.
1701 K Street NW
Washington, DC 20006

United Cerebral Palsy Association
66 East 34th Street
New York, NY 10036

RECREATION AND COMPETITIVE SPORT ORGANIZATIONS SERVING SPECIAL POPULATIONS

American Athletic Association for the Deaf
3916 Lantern Drive
Silver Spring, MD 20902

American Blind Bowling Association
5338 Queensbridge Road
Madison, WI 53714

American Junior Bowling Association
Route 2, Box 750
Lutz, FL 33549

Blind Outdoor Leisure Development
533 East Main Street
Aspen, CO 81611

Indoor Sports Club
1145 Highland Street
Napoleon, OH 43545

National Amputation Foundation (Golf)
12–45 150th Street
Whitestone, NY 11357

National Amputee Skiing Association
3738 Walnut Avenue
Carmichael, CA 95608

National Foundation for Happy Horsemanship for
the Handicapped
Box 462
Malvern, PA 19355

National Handicapped Sports and Recreation
Association
4105 East Florida Avenue
Denver, CO 80222

National Inconvenienced Sportsmen's Association
3738 Walnut Avenue
Carmel, CA 96508

National Track and Field Committee for the
Visually Impaired
4244 Heather Road
Long Beach, CA 90808

National Wheelchair Athletic Association
40–24 62nd Street
Woodside, NY 11377

National Wheelchair Basketball Association
101 Seaton Building, University of Kentucky
Lexington, KY 40506

National Wheelchair Bowling Association
2635 Northeast 19th Street
Pompano Beach, FL 33062

National Wheelchair Softball Association
P.O. Box 737
Sioux Falls, SD 57101

Special Olympics, Inc.
1701 K Street NW, Suite 205
Washington, DC 20006

U.S. Deaf Skiers Association
159 Davis Avenue
Hackensack, NJ 07601

The following listing of professional associations was provided by the National Educational Council of Creative Therapies, Inc.

National Educational Council of Creative
Therapies, Inc.
20 Rip Road
Hanover, NH 03755

National Association for Drama Therapy
19 Edwards St.
New Haven, CT 06511

American Art Therapy Association, Inc.
11800 Sunrise Valley Drive
Reston, VA 22091

National Council for Therapy & Rehabilitation
Through Horticulture
9041 Comprint Court, Suite 103
Gaithersburg, MD 20877

American Association for Music Therapy
211 East 43rd St., Suite 1601
New York, NY 10017

International Phototherapy Association, Inc.
3260 Euclid Heights Blvd.
Cleveland Heights, OH 44118

National Association for Poetry Therapy
799 Broadway, Suite 629
New York, NY 10003

American Dance Therapy Association
2000 Century Plaza, Suite 230
Columbia, MD 21044

National Association for Music Therapy, Inc.
P.O. Box 610
Lawrence, KS 66044

American Society of Group Psychotherapy
& Psychodrama
259 Wolcott Ave.
Beacon, NY 12508

Other

National Recreation and Park Association/
National Therapeutic Recreation Society
3101 Park Center Drive
Alexandria, VA 22302

National Association of Social Workers, Inc.
7981 Eastern Avenue
Silver Spring, MD 20910

American Orthopsychiatric Association
19 W 44th Street
New York, NY 10036

Family Practice Center
2153 Newport Place NW
Washington, DC 20037

American Association for Counseling and
Development
5999 Stevenson Ave.
Alexandria, VA 22304

National Arts and Handicapped Information
Service
ARTS Box 2040, Grand Central Station
New York, NY 10017

The National Committee, Arts for the
Handicapped
1701 K Street, NW, Suite 801
Washington, DC 20006

International

INTERLINK
358 Strand
London WC2R OHS
United Kingdom
(01) 836-5819

British Assoc. of Art Therapists, Ltd.
13c Northwood Road
London, N6 5TL
United Kingdom

British Assoc. for Dramatherapists
7 Hatfield Road
St. Albans, Herts
United Kingdom

PERIODICALS RELATED TO THERAPEUTIC RECREATION

Aging
American Archives of Rehabilitation
 Therapy
American Corrective Therapy Journal
American Journal of Art Therapy
American Journal of Corrections
American Journal of Mental Deficiency
American Journal of Nursing
American Journal of Occupational
 Therapy
American Journal of Orthopsychiatry
American Journal of Psychiatry
American Journal of Psychology
American Journal of Public Health
American Journal of Sociology
Camping Magazine
Challenge: Recreation and Fitness for the
 Mentally Retarded
Children Today
Community Mental Health Journal
Exceptional Children
Federal Probation
Geriatrics
Hospital and Community Psychiatry
Hospitals
International Rehabilitation Review
Journal of Applied Rehabilitation
 Counseling
Journal of Counseling Psychology

Journal of Criminal Law, Criminology and
 Police Science
Journal of Gerontology
Journal of Health and Social Behavior
Journal of Health, Physical Education,
 and Recreation
Journal of Learning Disabilities
Journal of Leisure Research
Journal of Rehabilitation
Leisurability
Leisure Today
Mental Hygiene
Mental Retardation Abstracts
Mental Retardation News
MR/Mental Retardation
New Outlook for the Blind
Nursing Outlook
Parks and Recreation
Performance
Physical Therapy
Prison Journal
Programs for the Handicapped
Psychological Abstracts
Rehabilitation Literature
Rehabilitation Record
Social Work
Therapeutic Recreation Journal
Today's Child
Today's Health

OTHER THERAPEUTIC RECREATION RESOURCES

V.A. Hospitals
Chief, Recreation Therapy
Rehabilitation Medicine Service
V.A. Central Office
810 Vermont Avenue NW
Washington, DC 20420

Corrections
U.S. Department of Prisons
Department of Justice
HOLC Building
101 Indiana Avenue NW
Washington, DC 20001

Psychiatric Centers
Community Mental Health Centers
Developmental Centers
State Departments of Mental Health

Nursing Homes
State Departments of Health

Mentally Retarded
American Association on
Mental Deficiency
5201 Connecticut Avenue NW
Washington, DC 20015

COMPUTER RESOURCES IN RECREATION

COMPUTER RESOURCES LIST

Following is a listing of articles and papers on computers. This list is broken down into three categories: general knowledge, applications, and resources. (Computer references were compiled in the November 1984 issue of *Parks and Recreation*—vol. 19, no. 11, pp. 46–47.)

General Knowledge

BENNETT, WM. BRAD, ET AL., "Progressive Recreation: A Computer in Your Future," *Process and Concepts in Recreational Sports*, NIRSA, Corvallis, Oregon, 1983.

HENDERSON, KARLA AND M. DEBORAH BIALESCHKI, "Computer Consciousness and Leisure Services," *Computer Perspectives in Recreation*, Brigham Young University, March 1983.

Applications

"A Recreation Center that 'Pulls the Campus Together' ", *Athletic Purchasing and Facilities*, November 1982, Volume 6, Number 11.

ASBURY, GREG, "Computer-Based System Aids Locker Maintenance," *Athletics Purchasing and Facilities*, April 1983, Volume 7, Number 4.

AVANT, JIM, ET AL. "Use of Computers for Intramural and Recreation Programming," *Proceeding 13th NIRSA Convention*, Corvallis, Oregon, 1979.

BLEYER, WILLIAM C., "A Computerized Entry System to Control Access in Your Recreation Facility," *NIRSA Journal*, Spring 1982, Volume 6, Number 3.

CATHERALL, THOMAS S., "Taking Computers into the Field or How Long is Your Extension Cord?" *Computer Perspectives in Recreation*, Brigham Young University, March 1983.

CHEEK, DON L., "Visitor Surveys: A Snap With Computer," *Parks and Recreation*, April 1982, Volume 17, Number 4.

CHRISTIAN, JOHN W., "Enhancing the Hennepin County Park Reserve District's Financial Accountability: A Review of Several Cost Tracking Systems," *National Workshop on Computers in Recreation and Parks Proceedings*, 1981, Alexandria, VA: NRPA, 1982, pp. 38–61.

CICCIARELLA, CHARLES F., "Enter—the Microcomputer," *JOHPERD*, June 1981, pp. 60–61.

DUKE, RICHARD CHRIS, "Computerized Team Sports Scheduling," *Computer Perspectives in Recreation*, Brigham Young University, March 1983.

EWERT, ALAN, "Computer Applications in a Therapeutical Outdoor Recreation Setting," *Computer Perspectives in Recreation*, Brigham Young University, March 1983.

GUSHIKEN, THOMAS T. AND JOEL B. WORRA, "Computerized Meet Scheduling Utilizing Three Variables," *Computer Perspectives in Recreation*, Brigham Young University, March 1983.

HADERLIE, BRIAN M., "Computerized Instant Scheduling: Having Your Cake and Eating it too," *Computer Perspectives in Recreation*, March 1983.

HADERLIE, BRIAN M. AND WM. BRAD BENNETT, "Expanding Computer Use in Therapeutic Recreation," *T.W.U. RECap*, Texas Women's University, Fall Issue, 1983.

HOLLEY, BRUCE, "Automated Intramurals," *Proceeding 13th Annual NIRSA*, Corvallis, Oregon, 1979.

HOWE, CHRISTINE Z., "Let Your Computer Do the Calculating," *Parks & Recreation*, January 1982, pp. 70–72.

HOWE, CHRISTINE Z., "Microcomputer Applications for the Manager of the Future," *Computer Perspectives in Recreation*, Brigham Young University, March 1983.

MAAS, GERALD M., "Intramural Sports Scheduling: The Computer vs 'Instant Scheduling,' " *NIRSA Journal*, October 1981, Volume 6, Number 1.

SHIRLEY, DENNIS, "The Computer, A Space Age Management Tool, Arrives," *Parks and Recreation*, March 1980, Volume 13, Number 3.

STUYT, JEFF A., "Software in the Eighties: Information Exchange and Clearinghouse Applications," *Computer Perspectives in Recreation*, Brigham Young University, March 1983.

STUYT, JEFF A., "National Distribution," *Computer Update*, H.P.E.R. Texas Tech University, Lubbock, Texas, Spring 1984.

SHARPLESS, DANIEL R., "Computers: A Research Aid," *Parks and Recreation*, October 1979, Volume 2, Number 10.

SHARPLESS, DANIEL R., "Trends in Computer Use in Parks and Recreation," *National Workshop on Computers in Recreation and Parks Proceedings*, 1981, Alexandria, VA: NRPA, 1982, pp. 111–116.

STUYT, JEFF A., "Computer Update," *Michigan Leisure*, Winter 1983, pp. 18, 21.

WATTS, ROBERT T., "Computers in Parks and Recreation: Preparation for the Future," *National Workshop on Computers in Recreation and Parks Proceedings*, 1981, Alexandria, VA: NRPA, 1982, pp 37–44.

WATTS, ROBERT T., "RDECIS: A Recreation Management Decision Simulation," *Computer Perspectives in Recreation*, Brigham Young University, March 1983.

Resources

BAMMELL, GENE, AND L. BAMMELL, *Leisure and Human Behavior*, Dubuque, Iowa: Wm. C. Brown, 1982.

BRACEY, GERALD W., "Computers in Education—What the Research Shows," *Electronic Learning*, November/December 1982.

EVANS, CHRISTOPHER, *The Micro Millenium*, New York: Viking Press, 1980, p. 76.

FAZIO, JAMES R., AND DOUGLAS L. GILBERT, *Public Relations and Communications for Natural Resources Management*, Dubuque, Iowa: Kendall Hunt Publishing Co., 1981.

FISHER, FRANCIS D., "Teaching, Scholarship, and the Computer: Perspectives of a Generalist," *AAHE Bulletin*, November 1982, pp. 3–6.

KRAUS, RICHARD, *Therapeutic Recreation Service*, New York: Saunders College Publishing, 1983, p. 454.

MOORE, RICHARD L., *Computers and Continuing Education*, Manhattan, Kansas: Learning Resources Network, 1982.

NELSON, HAROLD AND RICH FRIEDMAN, "Seymour Papert: Spearheading the Computer Revolution," *On Computing*, Summer 1981, pp. 11–12.

PRATT, ED. "Ever Wonder What Recreation Will Be Like 50 Years From Now? . . ." *Dateline: NRPA*, May 1982, pp 6–7. Taken from Jay Young treatsie, "A Scenario . . . A Future View of Leisure," George Williams College.

SESSOMS, H. DOUGLAS, AND JACK L. STEVENSON, *Leadership and Group Dynamics in Recreation Services*, Boston: Allyn and Bacon, 1981.

STUYT, JEFF A., *Computer Update*, a quarterly publication dealing with computer uses in the Parks and Recreation field. H.P.E.R., Texas Tech University.

TINDELL, BEE, "Create a Computer Newsletter," *Educational Computer Magazine*, November/December 1982.

ADDITIONAL SPORTS/FITNESS RESOURCES

Rules

Aerial Tennis, Sells Aerial Tennis Co., Box 42, Kansas City, KS 66103.

Archery (Field), National Field Archery Assn., Rt. 2, Box 514, Redlands, CA 92373.

Archery (Target), National Archery Assn., 23 E. Jackson Blvd., Chicago, IL 60604.

Archery (Indoor), American Archery Council, 23 E. Jackson Blvd., Chicago, IL 60604.

Badminton, American Badminton Association, Donald Richardson 20 Wamesit Rd., Waban, MA 02168; Dayton Racquet Co., 302 S. Albright St., Arcanum, OH 43504.

Baseball (Nonprofessional) Guide, National Baseball Congress, Wichita, KS 67202.

Baseball (copyrighted Rules), National Baseball Congress, Wichita, KS 67202.

Baseball (American Legion), American Legion, Box 1055, Indianapolis, IN 46206.

Baseball, Babe Ruth League, Babe Ruth League, Inc., 524½ Hamilton Avenue, Trenton, NJ 08609.

Baseball, Little League, Little League Baseball, Inc., P.O. Box 925, Williamsport, PA 17704.

Baseball, Little League (Umpire's Handbook), Little League Baseball, Inc., P.O. Box 925, Williamsport, PA 17704.

Baseball, Bronco-Pony-Colt, Boys Baseball, Inc., P.O. Box 225, Washington, PA 15301.

Baseball (See NCAA listing).

Baseball Scorer's Handbook (does not include actual rules), American Amateur Baseball Congress, P.O. Box 44, Battle Creek, MI 49016.

Baseball, League Organization, American Baseball Congress, P.O. Box 44, Battle Creek, MI 49016.

Basketball (see AAU listing).

Basketball (Biddy), Jay Archer, 701 Brooks Bldg., Scranton, PA 18501.

Bicycling, Bicycle Institute of America, 122 E. 42nd St., New York, NY 10017.

Billiard (Rules and Records), Billiard Congress of America, 20 N. Wacker Drive, Chicago, IL 60606.

Bocce, General Sportcraft Company, Ltd., 33 New Bridge Road, Bergenfield, New Jersey/ Lignum-Vitae Products Corp., 96 Boyd Avenue, Jersey City, NJ 07303.

Bowling (Duck Pin), National Duck Pin Bowling Congress, 1420 New York Avenue NW, Washington, DC 20005.

Bowling (Ten Pin), American Bowling Congress, 1572 E. Capitol Drive, Milwaukee, WI 53211.

Darts, General Sportcraft Co., Ltd., 33 New Bridge Rd., Bergenfield, NJ 07621.

Deck Tennis, General Sportcraft Co., Ltd., 33 New Bridge Rd., Bergenfield, NJ 07621.

Fencing, Amateur Fencer's League of America, William Latzko, 33-62nd St., West New York, NJ 07093.

Football (Six-Man)(See High School listing).

Football (See NCAA listing).

Golf, U.S. Golf Assn., 40 E. 38th Street, New York, NY 10016.

Gymnastics (See AAU listing).

Gymnastics (See NCAA listing).

Handball, U.S. Handball Association, 4101 Dempster, Skokie, IL 60076.

Horseshoes, General Sportcraft Co. Ltd., 33 New Bridge Rd., Bergenfield, NJ 07621.

Ice Hockey (See NCAA listing).

Ice Skating, Amateur Skating Union, Edward J. Schmitzer, 4135 N. Troy St., Chicago, IL 60618.

Indoor Hockey, Cosom Corp., 6030 Wayzata Blvd., Minneapolis, MN 55416.

Marbles Shooting, National Marbles Tournament, Cleveland Press Bldg., Cleveland 14, OH 44101.

Paddle Tennis, General Sportcraft Co. Ltd., 33 New Bridge Rd., Bergenfield, NJ 07621.

Paddleball, Rodney J. Grambeau, Sports Bldg., University of Michigan, Ann Arbor, MI 48106.

Quoits, General Sportcraft Co., Ltd., 33 New Bridge Rd., Bergenfield, NJ 07621.

Scoopball (Rules for 26 different games), Cosom Industries, 6030 Wayzata Blvd., Minneapolis, MN 55416.

Shuffleboard (Deck), General Sportcraft Co. Ltd., 33 New Bridge Road, Bergenfield, NJ 07621.

Skating (Figure), U.S. Figure Skating Assn., 575 Boylston St., Boston, MA 02116.

Skating (Roller), U.S. Amateur Roller Skating Assn., 120 W. 42nd Street, New York, NY 10036.

Skating (Speed), Edward J. Schmitzer, Amateur Skating Union of the United States, 4135 N. Troy St., Chicago, IL 60618.

Skiing (Downhill Slalom, Giant Slalom, Jumping, and Cross-Country, FIS and USSA Rules), U.S. Ski Assn., Gloria C. Chadwick. Executive Sec'y., Broadmoore, Colorado Springs, CO 80906.

Soccer (See NCAA listing).

Softball (12"-fast and slow pitch), Amateur Softball Association, Suite 1300, Skirvin Tower, Oklahoma City, OK 73100.

Softball (16"), Edw. Weinstein, Chairman Rules Committee, Umpires Protective Assn. of Chicago, Apt. 710, 3550 Lake Shore Drive, Chicago, IL 60607.

Squash Racquets, U.S. Squash Racquets Assn., 200 E. 66th St., New York, NY 10021.

Swimming (See AAU listing).

Swimming (See NCAA listing).

Swimming (Synchronized—See AAU listing).

Table Tennis, General Sportcraft Co. Ltd., 33 New Bridge Rd., Bergenfield, NJ 07621.
Tennis, Dayton Racquet Co., 302 S. Albright St., Arcanum, OH 45304.
Tennis Umpire's Manual (includes rules), United States Lawn Tennis Assn., 51 E. 42nd St., New York, NY 10017.
Tether Ball (Inflated Ball), W. J. Voit Rubber Corporation, 3801 S. Harbor Blvd., Santa Ana, CA 92704.
Touch Football, The Athletic Institute 805, Merchandise Mart, Chicago, IL 60654.
Volleyball (includes rules), U.S. Volleyball Assn. USBVA Printer, P.O. Box 109, Berne, IN 46711.
Water Polo (See AAU listing).
Weight Lifting (See AAU listing).
Wrestling (See NCAA listing).
National Collegiate Athletic Association, P.O. Box 1906, Shawnee Mission, KS 66222.

Baseball	Skiing
Basketball	Soccer
Fencing	Swimming
Football	Track and field
Gymnastics	Water Polo
Ice hockey	Wrestling
Lacrosse	

National Federation of State High School Athletic Assns., 7 South Dearborn Street, Chicago, IL 60603.

Basketball Rules	Football Rules
Basketball Casebook	Football Casebook
Basketball Player Handbook	Football Player Handbook
Basketball Official's Manual	Football Official's Manual
Baseball Rules	Football, Touch Football
Baseball Casebook	Six Man Football and Soccer
Baseball, Umpire's Manual	Track and Field (Rules and Records)

Amateur Athletic Union of the United States, 231 W. 58th Street, New York, NY 10019.
AAU Handbooks

Basketball	Swimming, water polo, and diving
Boxing	Swimming (synchronized)
Gymnastics	Track and field
Handball	Weightlifting
Judo	Wrestling

TOURISM—COMMERCIAL RECREATION CAREERS

A PROFILE OF THE U.S. TRAVEL INDUSTRY

The common interests of the United States travel industry are represented by the Travel Industry Association of America. According to its research affiliate, the United States Travel Data Center, we note the following highlights on tourism and its importance in our society:

The travel and tourism industry is the nation's third-largest retail or service industry.

Some $210 billion was spent on travel and tourism in the United States during 1983, representing 6.4 percent of the U.S. gross national product.

Travel supports 6.8 million jobs directly and indirectly—one of every fifteen working Americans.

Travel and tourism generated $45.8 billion in U.S. wages and salaries in 1983.

At least $25.3 billion a year in local, state, and federal taxes were earned from U.S. travel and tourism in 1983.

Travel and tourism rank as the first-, second-, or third-largest employer in forty-one states; in fourteen states, they are the number-one employer.

States benefit substantially from travel and tourism and annual receipts range from a high of $24.6 billion in California to a low of $355 million in Rhode Island.

Business travelers account for 29 percent of all travel receipts in the United States, approximately $61 billion.

More than 145 million Americans travel for business or pleasure during the year—*each day* nearly 15 million Americans travel at least 100 miles from home on a trip requiring an overnight stay.

Some 21.7 million international travelers visited the United States in 1983, spending an average $525 each while in this country.

International travel services ranked as the second-largest services export in 1983.

STATE SOURCES OF TRAVEL AND TOURISM

Alabama:
Alabama Bureau of Tourism and Travel
532 S. Perry Street
Montgomery, AL 36104-4614
(205) 261-4169

Alaska:
Alaska Division of Tourism
Pouch E
Juneau, AK 99811
(907) 465-2010

Arizona:
Arizona Division of Tourism
1480 E. Bethany Home Road
Phoenix, AZ 85014
(602) 255-3618

Arkansas:
Arkansas Department of Parks and Tourism
One North Capitol Mall
Little Rock, AR 72201
(501) 371-1087

California:
California Office of Tourism
1121 L Street—Suite 103
Sacramento, CA 95814
(916) 322-1396

Colorado:
Colorado Tourism Board
5500 S. Syracuse Street, #267
Englewood, CO 80110
(303) 779-1067

Connecticut:
Connecticut Dept. of Economic Development
Tourism Division
210 Washington Street
Hartford, CT 06106
(203) 566-3336

Delaware:
Delaware State Travel Service
99 Kings Highway
P.O. Box 1401
Dover, DE 19903
(302) 736-4254

District of Columbia:
Washington, Convention and Visitors Assoc.
1575 Eye Street NW
Suite 250
Washington, DC 20036
(202) 789-7048

Florida:
Florida Division of Tourism
107 West Gains Street, Room 105
Collins Building
Tallahassee, FL 32301
(904) 488-5606

Georgia:
Georgia Department of Industry and Trade
Tourist Division
1400 N. Omni International
P.O. Box 1776
Atlanta, GA 30301
(404) 656-3545

Hawaii:
Hawaii Visitors Bureau
2270 Kalakaua Avenue
Suite 801
Honolulu, HI 96815
(808) 923-1811

Idaho:
Idaho Travel Council
Division of Economic and Community Affairs
Room 108, Capitol Building
Boise, ID 83720
(202) 334-2470

Illinois:
Illinois Office of Tourism
Department of Commerce and Community Affairs
310 South Michigan Avenue
Chicago, IL 60604
(312) 793-4732

Indiana:
Indiana Tourism Development Division
Indiana Commerce Center
One North Capitol, #700
Indianapolis, IN 46204
(317) 232-8860

Iowa:
Iowa Development Commission
Capitol Center
600 E. Court Avenue, Suite A
Des Moines, IA 50309
(515) 281-3100

Kansas:
Kansas Department of Economic Development
503 Kansas Avenue, 6th Floor
Topeka, KS 66603
(913) 296-2009

Kentucky:
Department of Travel Development
Capitol Plaza Tower
22nd Floor
Frankfort, KY 40601
(502) 564-4930

Louisiana:
Louisiana Office of Tourism
P.O. Box 44291
Baton Rouge, LA 70804
(504) 925-3850

Maine:
Maine Division of Tourism
189 State Street
Augusta, ME 04333
(207) 289-5710

Maryland:
Maryland Office of Tourist Development
45 Calvert Street
Annapolis, MD 21401
(301) 269-2686

Massachusetts:
Department of Commerce and Development
Division of Tourism
100 Cambridge Street
Boston, MA 02202
(617) 727-3201

Michigan:
Michigan Department of Commerce
P.O. Box 30226
Lansing, MI 48909
(517) 373-0670

Minnesota:
Department of Energy and Economic Development
Office of Tourism
419 N. Robert Street
240 Bremer Building
St. Paul, MN 55101
(612) 296-2755

Mississippi:
Department of Economic Development
Tourism Division
P.O. Box 849
Jackson, MS 39205
(601) 359-3418

Missouri:
Missouri Division of Tourism
P.O. Box 1055
Jefferson City, MO 65102
(314) 751-4133

Montana:
Montana Travel Promotion Bureau
Department of Commerce
1424 Ninth Avenue
Helena, MT 59620-0411
(406) 444-2654

Nebraska:
Division of Travel and Tourism
301 Centennial Mall South
P.O. Box 94666
Lincoln, NE 68509
(402) 471-3111

Nevada:
Nevada Commission on Tourism
Capital Complex
Carson City, NV 89710
(702) 885-4322

New Hampshire:
New Hampshire Office of Vacation Travel
Department of Resources and Economic Development
Prescott Park, Building #2
P.O. Box 856
Concord, NH 03301
(603) 271-2343

New Jersey:
Division of Travel and Tourism
CN 826
Trenton, NJ 08625
(609) 292-2470

New Mexico:
New Mexico Economic Development and Tourism Department
Battan Memorial Building
Santa Fe, NM 87503
(505) 827-6323

New York:
Division of Tourism
New York State Commerce Department

One Commerce Plaza
Albany, NY 12245
(518) 473-0715

North Carolina:
North Carolina Division of Travel and Tourism
Department of Commerce
430 N. Salisbury Street
Raleigh, NC 27611
(919) 733-4171

North Dakota:
North Dakota Tourism Promotion
Capital Grounds
Bismarck, ND 58505
(701) 224-2525

Ohio:
Office of Travel and Tourism
Ohio Department of Development
P.O. Box 1001
Columbus, OH 43216
(614) 466-8844

Oklahoma:
Oklahoma Tourism and Recreation Dept.
Division of Marketing Services
505 Will Rodgers Building
Oklahoma City, OK 73105
(405) 521-2406

Oregon:
Tourism Development Division
595 Cottage Street NE
Salem, OR 97310
(503) 378-6309

Pennsylvania:
Pennsylvania Bureau of Travel
Department of Commerce
416 Forum Building
Harrisburg, PA 17120
(717) 787-5453

Puerto Rico:
Puerto Rico Tourism Company
1290 Avenue of the Americas
New York, NY 10104
(800) 223-6530

Rhode Island:
Department of Economic Development
7 Jackson Walkway
Providence, RI 02903
(401) 277-2601

South Carolina:
South Carolina Department of Parks, Recreation
and Tourism
Division of Tourism
1205 Pendleton Street, #113
Columbia, SC 29201
(803) 758-2536

South Dakota:
South Dakota Division of Tourism
State Development
711 Wells Avenue, Box 600
Pierre, SD 57501
(605) 773-3301

Tennessee:
Tennessee Department of Tourist Development
601 Broadway
P.O. Box 23170
Nashville, TN 37202
(615) 741-1904

Texas:
Texas Tourist Development Agency
Box 12008 Capital Station
Austin, TX 78711
(512) 475-4326

Utah:
Utah Travel Council
Division of Travel Department
Council Hall/Capital Hill
Salt Lake City, UT 84114
(801) 533-5681

Vermont:
Vermont Travel Division
134 State Street
Montpelier, VT 05602
(802) 828-3236

Virginia:
Virginia Division of Tourism
202 North 9th Street
Suite 500
Richmond, VA 23219
(804) 786-2051

Washington:
Washington Department of Commerce and
    Economic Development
101 General Administration Building
Olympia, WA 98504
(206) 753-5600

West Virginia:
Governor's Office of Economic & Community
    Development
Travel Development Division
Room B-564, Capitol Building
Charleston, WV 25305
(304) 348-2286

Wisconsin:
Wisconsin Division of Tourism
123 W. Washington Avenue
Madison, WI 53702
(608) 266-2147

Wyoming:
Wyoming Travel Commission
Frank Norris Jr. Travel Center
Cheyenne, WY 82002
(307) 777-7777

U.S. CHAMBER OF COMMERCE DIRECTORY

For your convenience in obtaining up-to-date scenic information and accommodations, listed below is a Chamber of Commerce Directory showing the chambers of commerce for the capital cities of each state.

ALABAMA
41 Commerce St.
Montgomery, AL 36101
(205) 834-5200

ALASKA
310 2nd
Juneau, AK 99801
(907) 586-2323

ARIZONA
34 W. Monroe St.
Suite 900
Phoenix, AZ 85003
(602) 254-5521

ARKANSAS
One Spring St.
Little Rock, AR 72201
(501) 374-4871

CALIFORNIA
1027 10th St.
Sacramento, CA 95808
(916) 444-6670

COLORADO
1301 Welton St.
Denver, CO 80204
(303) 534-3211

CONNECTICUT
250 Constitution Plaza
Hartford, CT 06103
(203) 527-0258

DISTRICT OF COLUMBIA
1615 "H" Street NW
Washington, DC 20063
(202) 659-6000

FLORIDA
P.O. Box 1639
Tallahassee, FL 32302
(904) 224-8116

GEORGIA
1300 North-Omni
International
Atlanta, GA 30303
(404) 521-0845

HAWAII
735 Bishop St.
P.O. Box 3108
Honolulu, HA 96813
(808) 531-4111

IDAHO
711 W. Bannock
Boise, Id 83701
(201) 344-5515

ILLINOIS
3 S. Old State
Capitol Plaza
Springfield, IL 62701
(217) 525-1173

INDIANA
320 N. Meridian St.
Suite 928
Indianapolis, IN 46204
(317) 267-2900

IOWA
800 High St.
Des Moines, IA 50307
(515) 286-4950

KANSAS
722 Kansas
Topeka, KS 66603
(913) 234-2644

KENTUCKY
100 Capitol Ave.
P.O. Box 654
Frankfort, KY 40602
(502) 223-8261

LOUISIANA
P.O. Box 3217
Baton Rouge, LA 70821
(504) 381-7125

MAINE
28 Preble St.
Portland, ME 04101
(207) 774-9871

MARYLAND
60 West St., Suite 405
Annapolis, MD 21401
(301) 269-0642

MASSACHUSETTS
125 High St.
Boston, MA 02110
(617) 426-1250

MICHIGAN
P.O. Box 14030
Lansing, MI 48901
(517) 487-6340

MINNESOTA
701 N. Central Tower
St. Paul, MN 55101
(612) 222-5561

MISSISSIPPI
P.O. Box 22548
Jackson, MS 39225
(601) 948-7575

MISSOURI
P.O. Box 776
Jefferson City, MO 65102
(314) 634-3616

MONTANA
201 E. Lyndale
Helena, MT 59601
(406) 442-4120

NEBRASKA
1221 N. St., Suite 606
Lincoln, NE 68508
(402) 476-7511

NEVADA
1191 S. Carson St.
Carson City, NV 89701
(702) 882-1565

NEW HAMPSHIRE
244 N. Main St.
Concord, NH 03301
(603) 224-2508

NEW JERSEY
240 W. State St., Suite 1404
Trenton, NJ 08608
(609) 393-4143

NEW MEXICO
P.O. Box 1928
Santa Fe, NM 87501
(505) 983-7317

NEW YORK
Albany—Colony Reg. Comm.
14 Corporate Woods Blvd.
Albany, NY 12211
(518) 434-1214

NORTH CAROLINA
335 S. Salisbury St.
Raleigh, NC 27602
(919) 833-3005

NORTH DAKOTA
425 S. 7th St.
Bismarck, ND 58502
(701) 223-5660

OHIO
17 S. High St., 8th Floor
Columbus, OH 43215
(614) 288-4201

OKLAHOMA
701 S.W. 74th
Oklahoma City, OK 73139
(405) 634-1436

OREGON
220 Cottage St. NE
Salem, OR 97301
(503) 581-1466

PENNSYLVANIA
P.O. Box 969
Harrisburg, Pa 17108
(717) 232-4121

RHODE ISLAND
10 Dorrance
Providence, RI 02903
(401) 521-5000

SOUTH CAROLINA
P.O. Box 1360
Columbia, SC 29282
(803) 733-1110

SOUTH DAKOTA
300 S. Highland
Pierre, SD 57501
(605) 224-7361

TENNESSEE
161 Fourth Ave. N.
Nashville, TN 37219
(615) 259-3900

TEXAS
901 W. Riverside Dr.
Austin, TX 78767
(512) 478-9383

UTAH
19 East Second S.
Salt Lake City, UT 84111
(801) 364-3631

*VERMONT
P.O. Box 336
Barre, VT 05641
(802) 229-5711

VIRGINIA
201 E. Franklin St.
Richmond, VA 21324
(804) 648-1234

WASHINGTON
1000 Plum
Olympia, WA 98507
(206) 357-3362

WEST VIRGINA
818 Virginia St. E.
Charleston, WV 25301
(304) 345-0770

WISCONSIN
615 E. Washington Ave.
Madison, WI 53703
(608) 256-8348

WYOMING
301 W. 16th St.
Cheyenne, WY 82001
(307) 638-3388

*Statewide Chamber of Commerce Address

Appendix C

The Expanding Older Population: A Challenge to the Leisure Services Profession

RETIREES AND LEISURE-TIME PURSUITS

In a survey conducted by the Teachers Insurance and Annuity Association, retirees were queried as to their leisure-time pursuits.[1] The respondents' ages ranged from 60 to beyond 90.

On the whole, the respondents were healthy and active. Most had a wide array of interests and were involved in many pursuits. They report being healthy, happy, and getting by financially. Despite unprecedented inflation, changing retirement-age patterns, and increased longevity, the survey's findings were quite similar to those found in a similar survey conducted 10 years prior to this study. (See Figure C–1).

Admittedly, this earlier survey was conducted within a stratified group. However, its scope and unusually high percentage of response adds significantly to its importance. Another look at elderly quality of life is to be found in the April 1985 issue of *Leisure and Recreation*.[2]

---

1. Conducted in October 1982 based on a 17-page questionnaire sent to 2200 selected annuitants; 84 percent responded to this study.
2. *World Leisure and Recreation Association*, vol. 27, no. 2, pp. 49–51.

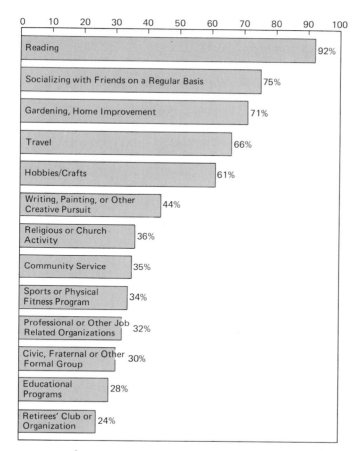

Scale: 0 10 20 30 40 50 60 70 80 90 100

Activity	Percentage
Reading	92%
Socializing with Friends on a Regular Basis	75%
Gardening, Home Improvement	71%
Travel	66%
Hobbies/Crafts	61%
Writing, Painting, or Other Creative Pursuit	44%
Religious or Church Activity	36%
Community Service	35%
Sports or Physical Fitness Program	34%
Professional or Other Job Related Organizations	32%
Civic, Fraternal or Other Formal Group	30%
Educational Programs	28%
Retirees' Club or Organization	24%

FIGURE C-1. [3]

REFERENCES IN GERONTOLOGY [4]

Acronyms formed from the first letter of words in a title are frequently used to abbreviate the names of laws, agencies, regulations, and programs. This guide is intended to identify acronyms commonly used in the field of aging.

AAA—AREA AGENCY ON AGING

AAHA—AMERICAN ASSOCIATION OF HOMES FOR THE AGING
  1050 17th Street NW
  Suite 770
  Washington, DC 20036

    3. Reproduced by permission of Teachers Insurance and Annuity Association, New York, NY.
    4. National Gerontology Resource Center, American Association of Retired Persons, 1909 K Street NW, Washington, DC 20049.

AHA—DIVISION OF AMBULATORY CARE

American Hospital Association
840 North Lake Shore Drive
Chicago, IL 60611

AARP—AMERICAN ASSOCIATION OF RETIRED PERSONS

1909 K Street NW
Washington, DC 20049

ACTION

806 Connecticut Avenue NW
Washington, DC 20525

AFAR—AMERICAN FEDERATION FOR AGING RESEARCH

335 Madison Avenue—4th Floor
New York, NY 10017

AGHE—ASSOCIATION FOR GERONTOLOGY IN HIGHER EDUCATION

600 Maryland Avenue SW
West Wing, Suite 204
Washington, DC 20024

AHCA—AMERICAN HEALTH CARE ASSOCIATION

1200 15th Street NW
Washington, DC 20005

ANPPM—ASOCIACION NACIONAL PRO PERSONAS MAYORES

Office of the Executive Director
1730 W. Olympic Boulevard—#401
Los Angeles, CA 90015

AOA—ADMINISTRATION ON AGING

Office of Human Development
Services
U.S. Department of Health and
Human Services
330 Independence Avenue SW
Washington, DC 20201

CHHS—COUNCIL OF COMMUNITY HEALTH SERVICES

National League of Nursing
10 Columbus Circle
New York, NY 10019

DI—DISABILITY INSURANCE

See Social Security Act, Title II.

ERISA—1974 EMPLOYEE RETIREMENT INCOME SECURITY ACT

FCA—FEDERAL COUNCIL ON THE AGING

330 Independence Avenue SW
Room 4260
Washington, DC 20201

FGP—FOSTER GRANDPARENT PROGRAM

806 Connecticut Avenue NW
Washington, DC 20525

GP—GRAY PANTHERS

3635 Chestnut Street
Philadelphia, PA 19104

GSA—GERONTOLOGICAL SOCIETY OF AMERICA

1411 K Street NW
Washington, DC 20005

HCFA—HEALTH CARE FINANCING ADMINISTRATION

330 C Street SW
Washington, DC 20201

HHS—DEPARTMENT OF HEALTH AND HUMAN SERVICES

200 Independence Avenue SW
Washington, DC 20201

HI—HOSPITAL INSURANCE

See Social Security Act, Title XVIII.

HUD—DEPARTMENT OF HOUSING AND URBAN DEVELOPMENT

451 Seventh Street SW
Washington, DC 20410

ICF—INTERMEDIATE CARE FACILITY

ICSG—INTERNATIONAL CENTER FOR SOCIAL GERONTOLOGY

600 Maryland Avenue SW
West Wing, Suite 147
Washington, DC 20024

IFA—INTERNATIONAL FEDERATION ON AGING

Publications Division:
1909 K Street NW
Washington, DC 20049
Headquarters:
Bernard Sunley House
60 Pitcairn Road
Mitchum, Surrey
England, CR4 3LL

I&R—INFORMATION AND REFERRAL

N4A—NATIONAL ASSOCIATION OF AREA AGENCIES ON AGING

600 Maryland Avenue SW
Suite 208
Washington, DC 20024

NAHC—NATIONAL ASSOCIATION FOR HOME CARE

519 C Street SE
Washington, DC 20002

NAMP—NATIONAL ASSOCIATION OF MATURE PEOPLE

Box 26792
Oklahoma City, OK 73126

NARFE—NATIONAL ASSOCIATION OF RETIRED FEDERAL EMPLOYEES

1533 New Hampshire Avenue NW
Washington, DC 20036

NASC—NATIONAL ALLIANCE OF SENIOR CITIZENS

101 Park Washington Court
Suite 125
Falls Church, VA 22046

NASSE—NATIONAL ASSOCIATION FOR SPANISH SPEAKING ELDERLY

See ANPPM

NASUA—NATIONAL ASSOCIATION OF STATE UNITS ON AGING

600 Maryland Avenue SW
Suite 208
Washington, DC 20024

NCBA—NATIONAL CAUCUS AND CENTER ON THE BLACK AGED, INC.

1424 K Street NW
Suite 500
Washington, DC 20005

NCCNHR—NATIONAL CITIZENS COALITION FOR NURSING HOME REFORM

1309 L Street NW
Washington, DC 20005

NCOA—NATIONAL COUNCIL ON THE AGING, INC.

600 Maryland Avenue SW
Washington, DC 20024

NCSC—NATIONAL COUNCIL OF SENIOR CITIZENS

925 15th Street NW
Washington, DC 20005

NHC—NATIONAL HOMECARING COUNCIL

235 Park Avenue South
New York, NY 10003

NHCOA—NATIONAL HISPANIC COUNCIL ON AGING

c/o Daniel T. Gallego
Dept. of Sociology, 1208
Weber State College
Ogden, UT 84408

NIA—NATIONAL INSTITUTE ON AGING

9000 Rockville Pike
Bethesda, MD 20205

NICA—NATIONAL INTERFAITH COALITION ON AGING, INC.

Executive Offices
P.O. Box 1924
298 S. Hull Street
Athens, GA 30603

NICOA—NATIONAL INDIAN COUNCIL ON AGING

P.O. Box 2088
Albuquerque, NM 87103

NIMH—NATIONAL INSTITUTE OF MENTAL HEALTH

Public Health Service
Alcohol, Drug Abuse and Mental
Health Administration
5600 Fishers Lane
Rockville, MD 20857

NP/ARCA—NATIONAL PACIFIC/ASIAN RESOURCE CENTER ON AGING

811 First Avenue
Colman Building, Suite 210
Seattle, WA 98104

NRTA—NATIONAL RETIRED TEACHERS ASSOCIATION

1909 K Street NW
Washington, DC 20049

NSCLC—NATIONAL SENIOR CITIZENS LAW CENTER

1302 18th Street NW
Suite 701
Washington, DC 20036

OAA—OLDER AMERICANS ACT OF 1965

OASI—OLD-AGE AND SURVIVORS INSURANCE

See Social Security Act, Title II.

OHDS—OFFICE OF HUMAN DEVELOPMENT SERVICE

U.S. Department of Health and
Human Services
Washington, DC 20201

OWL—OLDER WOMEN'S LEAGUE

1325 G Street NW
Lower Level B
Washington, DC 20005

PSA—PLANNING AND SERVICE AREAS

RFP—REQUEST FOR PROPOSALS

RSVP—RETIRED SENIOR VOLUNTEER PROGRAM

ACTION
806 Connecticut Avenue NW
Washington, DC 20525

SCORE—SERVICE CORPS OF RETIRED EXECUTIVES

Small Business Administration
Room 410
1129 20th Street NW
Washington, DC 20416

SCP—SENIOR COMPANION PROGRAM

ACTION
806 Connecticut Avenue NW
Washington, DC 20525

SMI—SUPPLEMENTAL MEDICAL INSURANCE

See Social Security Act, Title XVIII.

SNF—SKILLED NURSING FACILITY

SSA—SOCIAL SECURITY ADMINISTRATION

6401 Security Boulevard
Baltimore, MD 21235

SSA—SOCIAL SECURITY ACT

SSI—SUPPLEMENTARY SECURITY INCOME

SUA—STATE UNIT ON AGING

TROA—THE RETIRED OFFICERS ASSOCIATION

201 North Washington Street
Alexandria, VA 22314

VA—VETERANS ADMINISTRATION

810 Vermont Avenue NW
Washington, DC 20420

WGS—WESTERN GERONTOLOGICAL SOCIETY

833 Market Street
Suite 516
San Francisco, CA 94103

Index